Supermajorities in Constit Courts

Constitutional adjudication is a subject of fascinati annul the will of a democratically elected Parliar ian fashion. Although conceived as a remedy agai also decide cases by voting. Whether they do so tl supermajorities is not trivial.

The debate around supermajorities has awaken judicial limitation and new conceptions of judicial our knowledge of systems employing superm adjudication by performing a comparative analy twelve supermajority models. It introduces a typo institutional design, the reasons leading policyma the impact supermajorities have on courts. It explo supermajorities grant deference and foster co constitutional courts from exercising judicial revie practice, and effects of supermajority rules in cou an ongoing conversation on the democratic implic constitutional courts. It will be a valuable resourc and researchers working in the areas of compar constitutional politics.

Mauro Arturo Rivera León is Assistant Profess in Katowice, Poland. From 2023 to 2024 he "Qualified majorities in counter-majoritarian mec ory of supermajorities in judicial review" funded Mechanism 2014–2021. He obtained his PhD at in Madrid, Spain. Dr. Rivera has been visiting Institute for Comparative Public Law and Inter Germany, the Perelman Center for Philosophy of Brussels, Belgium. He is a member of the Researchers in Mexico (CONAHCYT-SNI), lev the author of six books, including four legal re than fifty scientific papers/book chapters in Spa has received seven national prizes for his researc

Supermajorities in Constitutional Courts

Mauro Arturo Rivera León

Routledge
Taylor & Francis Group
LONDON AND NEW YORK

First published 2024
by Routledge
4 Park Square, Milton Park, Abingdon, Oxon OX14 4RN

and by Routledge
605 Third Avenue, New York, NY 10158

Routledge is an imprint of the Taylor & Francis Group, an informa business

British Library Cataloguing-in-Publication Data
A catalogue record for this book is available from the British Library

Library of Congress Cataloging-in-Publication Data
Names: Rivera León, Mauro Arturo, author.
Title: Supermajorities in constitutional courts / Mauro Arturo Rivera León.
Description: Abingdon, Oxon [UK] ; New York, NY : Routledge, 2024. |
Includes bibliographical references and index. | Summary: -- Provided by publisher.
Identifiers: LCCN 2023049448 | ISBN 9781032599694 (hardback) | ISBN 9781032602462 (paperback) | ISBN 9781003458272 (ebook)
Subjects: LCSH: Constitutional courts. | Constitutional law.
Classification: LCC K3370 .R58 2024 | DDC 347/.035--dc23/eng/20231023
LC record available at https://lccn.loc.gov/2023049448

ISBN: 978-1-032-59969-4 (hbk)
ISBN: 978-1-032-60246-2 (pbk)
ISBN: 978-1-003-45827-2 (ebk)

DOI: 10.4324/9781003458272

Typeset in Galliard
by Deanta Global Publishing Services, Chennai, India

Publication co-financed by the University of Silesia in Katowice.

UNIVERSITY OF SILESIA
IN KATOWICE

The research leading to these results has received funding from the Norwegian Financial Mechanism 2014–2021, Research Project No. 2020/37/K/HS5/02758 titled "Qualified majorities in counter-majoritarian mechanisms: Towards a new theory of supermajorities in judicial review."

Badania naukowe prowadzące do osiągnięcia tych wyników zostały sfinansowane ze środków Norweskiego Mechanizmu Finansowego na lata 2014 – 2021, projekt nr 2020/37/K/HS5/02758.

For Barbara and Amelia, the supermajority of my family.

Contents

Acknowledgments

Many people have contributed to this book. In the first place, this research would not have been possible without the financial support of the Norwegian Financial Mechanism 2014–2021, through Research Project No. 2020/37/K/HS5/02758 entitled “Qualified majorities in counter-majoritarian mechanisms: Towards a new theory of supermajorities in judicial review.” The faculty at my institution (the University of Silesia in Katowice, Poland) has been incredibly supportive. I thank my Dean, Prof. Witold Kurowski, and the Director of the Institute of Legal Sciences, Prof. Piotr Pinior (¡gracias, Piotr!), for their constant guidance and encouragement. Regarding this project, I wish to acknowledge the enormous support of Prof. Łabno, Prof. Rott-Pietrzyk, Monika Łyczba, and Agnieszka Maroń.

Interviews were a significant aid to my research. I benefited from talking to multiple Constitutional Court and Supreme Court judges, justices, and magistrates who spoke candidly to me about their views and theories on their supermajorities. I want to thank Juan Luis González Alcántara (Mexico), César Landa and Eloy Andrés Espinosa-Saldaña (Peru), Hermógenes Acosta (Dominican Republic), Jiří Zemánek (the Czech Republic), Piotr Tuleja and Mirosław Granat (Poland), and Jerod Tufte (North Dakota).

I want to thank scholars and law clerks who kindly discussed with me numerous ideas and draft chapters of this book or provided me valuable insights into their legal systems. I thank Jonathan Entin, Evan Caminker, Katarína Šipulová, David Kosař, Tomáš Langášek, Steven Willborn, Anthony Schutz, Eduardo Jorge Prats, Vlastimil Göttinger, Hui-Wen Chen, Ming-Sung Kuo, Mariana Peguero, Yuri Aleksandrov Tornero, Juan Domingo Moreno Fernández, Fernando Sosa Pastrana, and Giorgi Chitidze.

The book also benefited from valuable comments at many academic conferences, such as the European Consortium for Political Research Annual Conference (2022), the International Association of Public Law Annual Conferences (2022 and 2023), the 11th Annual YCC Global Conference (2022), and the discussion group at the Judicial Studies Institute at the Masaryk University Faculty of Law in Brno (2022).

Many people assisted me in providing access to court documents, legislative reports, and bibliographic resources. Their help was invaluable in doing legislative and judicial research in many jurisdictions. I am grateful to Jully Vives, Elaine Settergren, Paula Amelsberg, Maureen Eck, Gustavo Jiménez, Petr Dvořáček, Jindřiška Syllová, and Ľubomír Majerčík. I am grateful to Dominika Krupa for her invaluable assistance in reviewing my quantitative analysis. All mistakes are my own.

Finally, I am indebted to my family, whose patience has been deeply tested in recent years.

PART I

THEORY OF SUPERMAJORITIES

1 Introduction

1.1 Why Supermajorities?

Constitutional adjudication is an intriguing topic. The fact that judicial review can annul the will of a democratically elected Parliament or Congress deeply reflects its counter-majoritarian nature.[1] Deciding whether constitutional or apex courts vote to do so through simple majorities or supermajorities goes beyond a decision of numerical thresholds: it is a debate of constitutionalism, democracy, and the role of judges and political branches in the separation of powers.

Supermajorities are almost as old as judicial review itself. The first supermajorities, which originated at the subnational level in the United States, appeared at the same time as the first constitutional court, which also functioned under a supermajority. Overlooked by scholars for some time, the debate seems to have awakened anew amidst theories of judicial limitation and new conceptions of judicial review.[2]

The discussion on supermajorities has not been confined to legal scholarship. Recent political events have brought the rule to the global stage. In 2015, the widely discussed Polish constitutional crisis featured a new supermajority employed by an illiberal regime as a weapon against an independent court.[3] A similar situation occurred in Georgia in 2016.[4] Furthermore, in 2022–2023, the so-called Israel Constitutional Crisis also saw its share of proposals requiring qualified voting to strike down legislation.[5] Finally, in the United States,

1 A concept coined by Alexander M. Bickel, The Least Dangerous Branch (1962).

2 For a literature review, *see* Chapter 2.

3 Wojciech Sadurski, Poland's Constitutional Breakdown 73 (2019).

4 Mauro Arturo Rivera León, *Judicial Review of Supermajority Rules Governing Courts' Own Decision-Making: A Comparative Analysis*, 1 Glob. Const. 9 (2023).

5 Joseph Weiler, *Israel: Cry, the Beloved Country*, Int'l J. Const. L. Blog (Dec. 28, 2022), http://www.iconnectblog.com/2023/01/red-lines-for-israels-constitutional-reforms/ (last visited Feb. 28, 2023); Glia Stopler, *The Israeli Government's Proposed Judicial Reforms: An Attack on Israeli Democracy*, ConstitutionNet (Feb. 16, 2023), https://constitutionnet.org/news/israeli-governments-proposed-judicial-reforms-attack-israeli-democracy (last visited Feb. 28, 2023).

DOI: 10.4324/9781003458272-2

the polarization of the Supreme Court reached unprecedented levels when a series of events, including maneuvers that prevented an Obama nominee from even having a floor hearing, allowed former President Trump to appoint one-third of the Supreme Court in only four years.[6] President Biden assembled a commission of jurists to analyze reform proposals for the Supreme Court. The Commission extensively examined supermajority rules, receiving testimonies from top scholars.[7] Even in the United States, the birthplace of supermajorities, the debate seems to be reopening.

From the Dominican Republic to Nebraska, Mexico to Poland, and South Korea to the Czech Republic, supermajorities have been tested in controversial circumstances such as favoring or limiting abortion,[8] fighting presidential reelection,[9] deciding on transgender rights,[10] and sovereignty disputes.[11] The discussion is relevant and timely.

1.2 Scope of the Book

This book analyzes the impact of supermajority rules to strike down legislation in constitutional courts. Certain methodological precisions are required in attempting the endeavor.

In the first place, focusing on supermajorities, the book will analyze jurisdictions instituting a rule surpassing the traditional majority threshold, defined and examined in Chapter 2. The book will analyze normative supermajority rules, that is, rules requiring a de jure supermajority vote. In several jurisdictions, a majority of the members of the entire court is required, not of those present and voting.[12] If a majority of the full court is required, in cases of absences, the majority rule becomes, de facto, a supermajority vis-à-vis the sitting judges through the threshold distortion.[13] As interesting as such cases may be, they exceed the scope of this book.

6 The story is compellingly narrated by Joan Biskupic, Nine Black Robes: Inside the Supreme Court's Drive to the Right and Its Historic Consequences 111–12 (2023).

7 Presidential Commission on the Supreme Court of the United States, *Final Report*, 288 167–82 (2021), https://www.whitehouse.gov/pcscotus/ (last visited May 25, 2022).

8 Favoring abortion in Mexico, *see* 2 Steven Gow Calabresi, The History and Growth of Judicial Review: The G-20 Civil Law Countries 239 (2021). Disfavoring abortion in North Dakota, *see* North Dakota Law Review Associate Editors, *North Dakota Supreme Court Review*, 90 N. D. L. Rev. 637, 639 (2014).

9 *See* Chapter 4.1.2.

10 Nikolas Sabján, *Critical Legal Perspective on the Recent Czech Transgender Case: (Pl. ÚS 2/20)*, 6 Bratisl. L. Rev. 125 (2022).

11 *See* Chapter 4.4.2.

12 Such requirements are analogous to what in legislative contexts are termed absolute majority rules. *See* Adrian Vermeule, *Absolute Majority Rules*, 37 Br. J. Polit. Sci. 643, 644 (2007).

13 When all members are present, both rules "perfectly converge." Adrian Vermeule, Mechanisms of Democracy: Institutional Design Writ Small 119 (2007).

Secondly, this book will center on supermajorities in constitutional adjudication when deciding on the constitutionality of statutes. Constitutional adjudication focuses on constitutions, highly political normative acts embodying popular sovereignty. The political nature of constitutions is well known, and decisions deriving from constitutional conflicts have significant implications for democracy, the political branches, and the lives of ordinary citizens.

This book argues that supermajorities in constitutional adjudication differ from those in other adjudicative procedures, as they consider in particular the democratic and political implications of invalidating legislation: imposing supermajorities to strike down statutes defends a unique set of goals, needs, and models. Supermajority rules applicable only to strike down legislation promote deference to the elected branches, while supermajority rules to issue any decision of a constitutional court aim at consensus and legitimacy. Those are different objectives than the ones embodied by other types of supermajorities.

This book does not delve into supermajority rules that ordinary, apex, and even constitutional courts might use with different aims. For example, several courts employ supermajority rules in approving their internal regulations.[14] This requirement ensures that internal norms enjoy enough consensus and are not unilaterally imposed by the weight of political dynamics. Some courts might employ supermajorities in electing the Chief Justice to grant legitimacy to the presiding judge[15] or require supermajorities for the court to impose sanctions leading to judicial removal.[16] Supermajorities might be employed in criminal procedures to protect the presumption of innocence[17] and, in some jurisdictions, political parties can only be banned through supermajorities[18] to safeguard the democratic debate. The book will also not delve into

14 However, the book briefly addresses that debate in the Dominican Republic and Peru cases, as it is strictly related to the court thresholds. *See* Chapter 4.

15 See Article 7 of the Organic Law on the Tribunal of Constitutional Guarantees (Peru).

16 In the Spanish Constitutional Court, a three-fourths supermajority is required to deprive a judge of his/her status as a sanction for infringing judicial duties. Scholarship deems that the supermajority "protects impartiality and independence surrounding Magistrates." Nieves Corte & Juan Moreno, *Artículo 90, in* Comentarios a la Ley Orgánica 2/1979, de 3 de octubre, del Tribunal Constitucional 1019, 1020 (Juan José González Rivas & Andrés Javier Gutiérrez Gil eds., 2020).

17 In the United States, there is a rich literature on supermajorities and the unanimity rule in criminal trials. *See* Edward Schwartz & Warren Schwartz, *Decisionmaking by Juries under Unanimity and Supermajority Voting Rules*, 80 Georgetown L.J. 775 (1992); Michael Glasser, *Letting the Supermajority Rule: Nonunanimous Jury Verdicts in Criminal Trials*, 24 Fla. State Univ. L. Rev. 659 (1997); Ethan Leib, *Supermajoritarianism and the American Criminal Jury*, 33 Hastings Const. L.Q. 141 (2006).

18 Germany exemplifies this case. However, as Kaiser argued, German scholarship considers this procedure to bear parallels to criminal law and have a punitive character. Roman Kaiser, Das Mehrheitsprinzip in der Judikative 165 (2020).

supermajorities to strike down higher normative acts such as constitutional amendments, although such proposals exist.[19]

By focusing on adjudication of the constitutionality of statutes, the quintessential function of constitutional courts, the book explores the democratic and political implications of the least studied decision-making mechanism of the counter-majoritarian branch.

Finally, the study analyzes supermajorities within formal constitutional courts[20] or adjudicating bodies that perform similar functions, such as apex courts either tasked mainly with constitutional adjudication functions or with general jurisdiction but also having a final word on the meaning and interpretation of the constitution and the constitutionality of statutes in their jurisdictions.

1.3 Overview of the Main Arguments and Approach

Since Shugerman's[21] and Caminker's[22] work, several scholars have attempted to defend supermajority rules as superior models to simple majorities or as part of alternative designs that could improve judicial review and its impact on the elected branches.[23] The discussion, nonetheless, has remained mainly theoretical, with very scarce empirical analysis of the rule's impact in those jurisdictions in which it functions.[24]

My argument is simple. I deem that comparative law can provide evidence to suggest that constitutional courts employing supermajority requirements

19 Some scholars have pointed out that supermajorities in judicial review of legislation and judicial review of constitutional amendments are of a different nature. Rubens Beçak & Jairo Lima, *When 5x4 Is Not a Winning Majority: Judicial Decision-Making on Unconstitutional Constitutional Amendments*, *in* VIOLENT CONFLICTS, CRISIS, STATE OF EMERGENCY, PEACEBUILDING: CONSTITUTIONAL PROBLEMS, AMENDMENTS AND INTERPRETATION 161, 178 (Oesten Baller ed., 2019).

20 I understand constitutional courts as "[a] constitutionally established independent organ of the state whose central purpose is to defend the normative superiority of the constitutionality law within the juridical order." Alec Stone Sweet, *Constitutional Courts*, *in* THE OXFORD HANDBOOK OF COMPARATIVE CONSTITUTIONAL L. 817, 817 (Michel Rosenfeld & András Sajó eds., 2012).

21 Jed Handelsman Shugerman, *A Six-Three Rule: Reviving Consensus and Deference on the Supreme Court*, 37 GA. L. REV. 893 (2003).

22 Evan H. Caminker, *Thayerian Deference to Congress and Supreme Court Supermajority Rules: Lessons from the Past*, 78 INDIANA L.J. 73 (2003).

23 Pablo Castillo-Ortiz, *The Dilemmas of Constitutional Courts and the Case for a New Design of Kelsenian Institutions*, 39 L. PHILOS. 617 (2020); Yaniv Roznai, *Introduction: Constitutional Courts in a 100-Years Perspective and a Proposal for a Hybrid Model of Judicial Review*, 14 ICL J. 355 (2021); Cristóbal Caviedes, *A Core Case for Supermajority Rules in Constitutional Adjudication*, 20 INT. J. CONST. L. 1162 (2022).

24 Caviedes claims that "more empirical research—or small-scale, context-sensitive experimentation—on constitutional courts using supermajority rules is needed." Caviedes, *supra* note 23, at 1187.

may prove functional by delivering their theoretical advantages while avoiding the drawbacks conventionally attributed to them. The empirical evidence indicates that this is true in many jurisdictions. In such cases, the rule might change the outcome of a handful of contested cases, privileging deference or consensus, depending on the rule's configuration. Rather than paralyzing the court and obstructing judicial review itself, supermajorities may shift the last word in closely contested cases from courts to the elected branches. I posit that, under specific configurations, *ceteris paribus*, supermajorities would produce constitutional courts that will place checks on the elected branches similar to those functioning under simple majorities.

Supermajorities nonetheless present significant challenges. In many jurisdictions, the way the rule is drafted results in the supermajority increasing when justices are absent, creating threshold distortion. There are instances in which supermajorities have been weaponized to obstruct, attack, or control independent courts. The book recognizes these problems and addresses the comparative practice to understand when and how supermajorities serve as valid deferential or consensus-privileging mechanisms and when they turn into a political straitjacket. Finding which institutional designs may contribute to the rule's success or failure is part of the intended contribution of this book.

To determine the rule's functionality, I delve into the empirical practice of supermajority rules in eight jurisdictions through twelve different models.[25] I analyze the subnational U.S. supermajorities of Ohio, North Dakota, and Nebraska, the former Czechoslovakia, Peru—through its four sets of supermajority rules—the Czech Republic, Mexico, the Dominican Republic, Poland, and Georgia. Despite the present or past existence of other noteworthy supermajority rules—Costa Rica, Taiwan, Lebanon, Chile, El Salvador, and subnational Mexican supermajorities, inter alia—the sample is arguably sufficient to provide representative results. In selecting these jurisdictions, I endeavored to explore supermajorities introduced through democratic debate and through authoritarian impulses, rules with high and low consensus thresholds, and models that have functioned through different periods. Finally, I deliberately attempted to present jurisdictions with different formulations of neutrality, which the book will later address as decisional and deferential supermajorities.

The analysis follows a consistent pattern: explaining the history and position of the court, the way the supermajority was introduced, the reasons that led policy makers to support such rules, their legal source, and the degree of consensus. Furthermore, the two empirical chapters offer insight into what

25 According to the definition explained in the previous subsection, the book analyzes formal constitutional courts, such as in the former Czechoslovakia, Peru, the Czech Republic, the Dominican Republic, Poland, and Georgia, apex courts primarily tasked with constitutional adjudication—such as the Mexican Supreme Court—or apex courts that, having general jurisdiction, are also entitled to have a final word within their legal order on constitutional issues, such as the Supreme Courts of Ohio, Nebraska, and North Dakota.

I deem "supermajority failure decisions"—the consequences of not meeting the qualified threshold, their precedent status, and the impact of absences and known episodes of rule evasion.

The study also strives to show how supermajority rules interact with other procedural rules and requirements in their constitutional systems. I subsequently discuss the most critical decisions in which the supermajority played a part and whether the rule has been subjected to judicial review, as well as the scholarly opinion and amendment proposals.

The book's methodology incorporates semi-structured interviews with constitutional and apex court judges from the relevant jurisdictions. Even though supermajorities tend to be formalized norms existing in constitutions, statutes, or regulations, their application is governed by a series of complementary informal institutions,[26] unwritten conventions, and non-formalized understandings developed through court practice. Informal rules are sometimes unknown to the audience[27] as such practices might not be reflected in judicial decisions or opinions.

Exploring such informal aspects through semi-structured interviews allows us to gather invaluable empirical data to understand better how supermajority rules work in a given jurisdiction. For example, although the court does not function in chambers in the Dominican Republic, an informal practice creates working groups to facilitate the supermajority threshold required for all decisions. In North Dakota, despite an appearance of broad discretion by the Chief Justice in appointing surrogate judges who might be prone to vote with his position, strong informal practices limit such a possibility. In Poland, even though the supermajority rule was a shock to the public in 2015, an informal practice had already introduced a largely unknown informal supermajority requirement for the tribunal's panels. In the Czech Republic, only through interviews could the author gather an approximate account of the times the supermajority has been applied. The insights provided by justices, magistrates, judges, and law clerks have been vital in understanding how supermajority rules operate in practice.

1.4 Plan of the Book

I attempt to bridge theoretical discussion with empirical comparative analysis to assess supermajority rules. To do so, Chapter 2 provides an overview of the literature discussion on supermajorities at a theoretical and empirical level.

Chapter 3 explores what I call the "historical supermajorities." Four supermajorities emerged in the decade from 1910 to 1920: three subnational

26 Gretchen Helmke & Steven Levitsky, *Informal Institutions and Comparative Politics: A Research Agenda*, 2 PERSPECT. POLIT. 725, 728 (2004).

27 Referring to the Supreme Court of the United States, *see* Lisa Schultz Bressman, *The Rise and Fall of the Self-Regulatory Court*, 101 TEX. L. REV. 1, 82 (2022).

supermajorities in the United States—Ohio, North Dakota, and Nebraska—and the Czechoslovak supermajority in 1920. I analyzed the empirical practice of all of them. Of the four historical supermajorities, two no longer exist. Ohio repealed its supermajority in 1968 after fifty-six years of court resistance, while Czechoslovakia's rule faded away soon after the Nazi aggression in 1938. Nonetheless, the supermajorities of North Dakota and Nebraska still remain active, and their characteristics and impact on their respective jurisdictions are analyzed up to this date.

Chapter 4 delves into contemporary supermajorities. Even if scarce, enough supermajorities exist in comparative law to make it impossible to scrutinize them all in a single study systematically. However, I endeavor to present those supermajorities whose practice could offer insights for a deeper assessment of supermajority rules showing a plurality of different institutional design features. For this reason, I analyze the following jurisdictions: Peru—which has experimented with up to four different versions of supermajority rules—the Czech Republic, Mexico, the Dominican Republic, Poland, and Georgia.[28]

Based on these jurisdictions, Chapter 5 proposes a new classification of supermajorities as deferential or decisional. It explains how the two models privilege different outcomes and goals, namely deference to the elected branches on the one hand and consensus and deliberation within decision-making on the other. The chapter also offers an overview of the reasons that led policy-makers to introduce supermajorities: caution, deference, consensus, and attack. The chapter finishes by analyzing the classification of supermajorities by legal source and its consequence for the rule's acceptance and judicial review.

Chapter 6 offers insight into the most significant non-philosophical objection to supermajorities: the court paralysis argument. I comparatively analyze the mechanics of multiplicands, the critical influence of absences on moving thresholds, and the thresholds' consensus requirements. Finally, I empirically overview the impact of supermajority rule on courts, attempting to assess whether they significantly hinder judicial review.

Chapter 7 provides conclusions and highlights the implications of the empirical evidence presented, shedding light on areas for future research. The book hopes to contribute to the fascinating ongoing conversation on voting in courts.

28 South Korea's supermajority is noteworthy, but Hong has already performed an extensive analysis. *See* Joon Seok Hong, *Signaling the Turn: The Supermajority Requirement and Judicial Power on the Constitutional Court of Korea*, 67 Am. J. Comp. L. 177 (2019).

2 Voting Protocols and Supermajorities: A Conceptual Introduction

2.1 Voting Protocols in Constitutional Adjudication

2.1.1 Introduction

Constitutional law scholars have studied constitutional courts extensively in their composition, jurisdiction, case law, and contribution to democratic consolidation.[1] However, paradoxically, significant areas related to their internal functioning remain largely unexplored: the voting protocols are one of them.[2]

Deliberation lies at the core of constitutional courts.[3] We assume that, as deliberative institutions, courts engage in careful argument confrontation and, through rational persuasion,[4] create a decision rather than arrive at it: decisions are deemed to be born of deliberation confronting different positions.[5]

1 The literature is too vast to cite. Among the most relevant studies, *see* Tom Ginsburg, Judicial Review in New Democracies: Constitutional Courts in Asian Cases (2003); Wojciech Sadurski, Rights before Courts: A Study of Constitutional Courts in Postcommunist States of Central and Eastern Europe (2005); Víctor Ferreres Comella, Constitutional Courts and Democratic Values: A European Perspective (2009); Allan R. Brewer-Carías, Constitutional Courts as Positive Legislators: A Comparative Law Study (2011); Consequential courts: judicial roles in global perspective (Diana Kapiszewski, Gordon Silverstein & Robert A. Kagan eds., 2013); Judicial Power: How Constitutional Courts Affect Political Transformations (Christine Landfried ed., 2018); Francesco Biagi, European Constitutional Courts and Transitions to Democracy (2019).

2 Particularly of courts employing supermajority rules. Mattias Kumm, *Constitutional Courts and Legislatures: Institutional Terms of Engagement*, I Católica L. Rev. 55, 62 (2017).

3 John Ferejohn & Pasquale Pasquino, *Constitutional Courts as Deliberative Institutions: Towards an Institutional Theory of Constitutional Justice*, *in* Constitutional Justice, East and West. Democratic Legitimacy and Constitutional Courts in Post-Communist Europe in a Comparative Perspective 21, 22 (Wojciech Sadurski ed., 2002). Rawls deemed the Supreme Court the "exemplar" of public reason in the United States. John Rawls, Political Liberalism 231 (1993). The notion is not uncontroversial. *See* Wojciech Sadurski, *Judicial Review and Public Reason*, *in* Comparative Judicial Review 337, 354–55 (Erin F. Delaney & Rosalind Dixon eds., 2018).

4 Ranieri Resende, Deliberation and Decision-Making Process in the Inter-American Court of Human Rights, 17 Northwestern L.J. Hum. Rts. 32 (2019).

5 However, as Hübner Mendes reminds us, even judicial deliberation remains a mystery. Conrado Hübner Mendes, Constitutional Courts and Deliberative Democracy 92 (2014).

DOI: 10.4324/9781003458272-3

Although deliberation may ensure that decisions attain greater consensus and broader internal legitimacy, it may not guarantee a unanimous decision. In "hard" or controversial cases, judges may have reasonable disagreements on what the Constitution means or whether a statute conforms with it.[6] Thus, even in a deliberative constitutional court, judges must still reach a decision when the court cannot speak unanimously: here, voting protocols come into play.

Voting protocols are the rules surrounding voting and the formula for converting the number of votes into a decision. They dictate how, when, and on what judges vote. Once judges have voted, a voting protocol translates such votes into the case's decision.[7]

In some jurisdictions, judges vote directly on the case at hand. In others, they vote on drafts whose preparation is tasked to a judge-rapporteur, thus only indirectly voting on the case's outcome. The distinction between case voting and draft voting[8] impacts the case's deliberation.[9] In the first model, voting is less structured regarding a free case discussion. In the second model, the judge-rapporteur has the opportunity to influence the court strongly, as inertia may lead judges into agreeing with the proposed draft.

Another element is what judges vote on. In general, courts tend to vote on either the outcome of cases (outcome voting) or the legal issues presented in a case (issue voting).[10] The topic has received attention, particularly in the United States.[11]

6 Jeremy Waldron, Law and Disagreement 91 (1999).

7 This is "The method by which several judges' opinions are fused in deciding the case at hand, and also in shaping the law of the land." Wolfgang Ernst, *The Fine-Mechanisms of Judicial Majoritarianism*, *in* Collective Judging in Comparative Perspective: Counting Votes and Weighing Opinions, 4 (Birke Häcker & Wolfgang Ernst eds., 2020).

8 See Mitchel De S.-O.-L'E. Lasser, Judicial Deliberations: A Comparative Analysis of Transparency and Legitimacy 38–39 (2009); Lena Hornkohl et al., *Judicial Deliberation: A Comparative Analysis of the Decision-Making Processes in the Highest Civil Courts, Constitutional Courts and International Courts*, Max Planck Inst. Luxemb. Proced. Law Res. Pap. Ser., 33–48 (2022).

9 See Mathilde Cohen, *Ex Ante Versus Ex Post Deliberations: Two Models of Judicial Deliberations in Courts of Last Resort*, 62 Am. J. Comp. L. 951 (2014) (arguing that courts deliberating upon the basis of drafts have an ex-ante deliberation, while courts deliberating in conference after the case has been orally argued have an ex-post deliberation model).

10 Ernst prefers the terminology "Integral or sequential voting." See Ernst, *supra* note 7, at 14–15.

11 David Post & Steven C. Salop, *Rowing Against the Tidewater: A Theory of Voting by Multijudge Panels*, 80 Georgetown L.J. 743 (1991); Lewis Kornhauser & Lawrence Sager, *The One and the Many: Adjudication in Collegial Courts*, 81 Calif. L. Rev. 1 (1993); John Rogers, *Issue Voting by Multimember Appellate Courts: A Response to Some Radical Proposals*, 49 Vanderbilt L. Rev. 997 (1996); David Post & Steven Salop, *Issues and Outcomes, Guidance, and Indeterminacy: A Reply to Professors John Rogers and Others*, 49 Vanderbilt L. Rev. 1069 (1996); Jonathan Nash, *A Context/Sensitive Voting Protocol Paradigm for Multimember Courts*, 56 Stanford L. Rev. 75 (2003); Saul Levmore, *Fractured Majorities and Their Reasons*, 127 Penn State L. Rev. 331 (2023). The debate has resurfaced in the Roberts Court based on

Suppose a nine-member constitutional court analyzes a challenge to a statute regarding the rights of disabled persons. The petitioner claims that the law was not subject to a proper public consultation as required by the national constitution, and infringed on the right to equality. Imagine the constitutional court divided into three equal groups. Group A believes the binding nature of consultations derives from the Constitution but that such consultations occurred, and that the law infringes no further right—therefore, their preferred outcome is to uphold the statute. Group B believes that the Constitution does not impose an obligation to make public consultations. They also deem that such consultations did not fully occur within the legislative procedure, and the statute infringes no right. They intend to uphold the law. Finally, Group C believes consultations are binding, were inadequately held, and the statute is unconstitutional as it disproportionally limits the right to equality. Under the outcome voting protocol, the statute would be upheld 6:3 since both Group A and Group B agree on its constitutionality, with only Group C intending to strike it down. However, under an issue voting protocol, the statute may fall. In the event of an initial vote on whether or not public consultations are binding, a 6:3 vote would settle the matter, and a second vote on whether or not public consultations occurred under the constitutional standards would again finish 6:3 with a negative answer. Thus, the voting protocol determines the case's outcome and may lead to voting paradoxes[12] considering judgment aggregation on judicial preferences. Outcome voting privileges the court's function as a judgment issuer, while issue voting promotes precedent stability on legal issues.

Finally, a third essential element concerns the number or percentage of votes that constitute a decision-making threshold and the multiplicand from which such a majority will be calculated. The following sections will focus on that element, introducing majority and supermajority thresholds and relative and absolute multiplicands.

2.1.2 Types of Decision-Making Thresholds

Voting protocols must provide a concrete number of votes to achieve specific results or a percentage to be converted into such a number. A case requires a certain number of judges in agreement to be considered resolved and awards a judicial outcome to it. We commonly refer to this set number as a "majority."

---

specific vote switching. See David Cohen, *A Tale of Two Vote Switches*, 100 Tex. L. Rev. 39 (2021). At the comparative level, *see* Gertrude Lübbe-Wolff, *Integrating or Polarising? How to Promote Integrative Decision-Making in Constitutional Courts*, *in* Constitutional Review in the Middle East and North Africa 189, 202–206 (Anja Schoeller-Schletter ed., 2021).

12 There is ample literature concerning voting paradoxes at an aggregative level regarding issue and outcome voting. Dimitri Landa & Jeffrey Lax, *Disagreements on Collegial Courts: A Case-Space Approach*, 10 Disagreements Coll. Courts Case-Space Approach 305 (2008); David Cohen, *The Precedent-Based Voting Paradox*, 90 Boston Univ. L. Rev. 183 (2010); Giovanni Tuzet, *More Votes, More Irrationality*, 64 Am. J. Jurisprud. 61 (2019).

However, the term is contingent on conversion rules, which are usually majoritarian but need not be.[13]

Suppose a constitutional court was deciding if a statute is constitutional. If there is a bare majority vote to strike down the legislation, applying the voting protocol of the United States, Italy, or France, the legislation would be declared unconstitutional. However, the legislation would be upheld under the Peruvian, Czech, or South Korean voting protocol. The same situation would lead to the court formally dismissing the case without upholding the legislation by the Mexican voting protocol. Simultaneously, under the rules of the Dominican Republic, the court would be unable to decide, and the case would remain pending. Finally, supposing different courts would vote on certiorari admissions, the differences would be striking. In certiorari decisions in individual constitutional complaints in Mexico or Spain, losing by a single vote implies the plaintiff's case is dismissed, while in the United States a four-vote minority suffices to require the Supreme Court to hear the case.[14]

Voting protocols may provide varying impasse rules to guarantee that the court will reach a decision in the event the decision-making threshold is unmet. A tie would lead to upholding the legislation in some courts, as in the case of Germany,[15] but striking it down in others, as in Italy[16] or Spain, given the President's possible casting vote.[17] In contrast, in the United States, under the "affirmance by an equally divided court" doctrine, a tie would confirm any decision the lower court took on the matter, be it the constitutionality or unconstitutionality of the statute.[18]

13 It is possible to set minority thresholds for affirmative decision-making. Vermeule refers to them as "submajority voting rules." He defines them as voting rules authorizing a predefined minority to change affirmatively the status quo regardless of the distribution of other votes. Adrian Vermeule, Mechanisms of Democracy: Institutional Design Writ Small 87 (2007). Some scholars employed the label "nonmajority rules." Richard Revesz & Pamela Karlan, *Nonmajority Rules and the Supreme Court*, 136 Univ. Pa. L. Rev. 1067 (1988). In the United States Supreme Court, a four-vote minority suffices to grant certiorari. The rule of four, a self-imposed voting mechanism, is arguably minoritarian (i.e., it does not grant certiorari out of an impasse rule). On the rule of four, *see* Joan Leiman, *The Rule of Four*, 5 Columbia L. Rev. 975 (1957). Given that the rule was self-adopted and not provided by a statute, it presents an interesting case of a self-imposed voting protocol that departs from majority vote. See Patrick Yingling, *Judicial Conventions: An Examination of the US Supreme Court's Rule of Four*, 38 Dublin Univ. L.J. 477 (2015) (considering whether the rule of four would qualify as a convention).

14 See *supra* note 13.

15 See § 15 of the *Gesetz über das Bundesverfassungsgericht* (BVerfGG).

16 Raffaele Bifulco & Davide Paris, *The Italian Constitutional Court*, *in* The Max Planck Handbooks in European Public Law: Volume III: Constitutional Adjudication. Institutions 447, 460 (2020).

17 For a classic analysis, *see* Fernando Santaolalla, *El Voto de Calidad Del Presidente Del Tribunal Constitucional*, Rev. Esp. Derecho Const. 201 (2009).

18 Much attention has been devoted to the practice of affirmance by an equally divided court in the United States. Inter alia, *see* Edward Hartnett, *Ties in the Supreme Court of the United*

Most voting protocols contain some form of majority or supermajority rule. For methodological clarity, we may divide judicial majority rules into two components. In the first place, the threshold—i.e., the number or percentage required—and in the second place, the multiplicand—i.e., the number over which that threshold is calculated. In the phrase "a simple majority of those voting and present," "a simple majority" is the threshold, while "those voting and present" is the multiplicand.

Seemingly, at least, we should distinguish between majority and supermajority voting protocols. I define a majority voting protocol as a rule allowing a bare majority to decide a case. In constitutional adjudication, and broadly, in judicial procedures, scholarship tends to use the terms "majority," "simple majority," or "bare majority"[19] interchangeably for a rule requiring 50 percent +1 of the court. In other words, when faced with a binary question of law, a simple judicial majority arises where more court members vote in favor of a given solution than against it.[20]

While the concept of simple majority may also be occasionally employed as referring to the largest plurality,[21] "simple majorities," understood as the "largest plurality,"[22] are not usually entitled to make decisions on the outcome of a case.[23] Perhaps the terminology arises from the fact that, since constitutional

---

States, 44 Wm. & Mary L. Rev. 643 (2002). At the appellate level, the rule exists in other jurisdictions. Ernst, *supra* note 7, at 11.

19 Jeremy Waldron, *Five to Four: Why Do Bare Majorities Rule on Courts*, 123 Yale L.J. 1692 (2014).

20 That is standard usage in English. Evan H. Caminker, *Thayerian Deference to Congress and Supreme Court Supermajority Rules: Lessons from the Past*, 78 Indiana L.J. 73, 94 (2003); Guha Krishnamurthi, *For Judicial Majoritarianism*, 22 Univ. Pa. J. Const. L. 1201, 1246 (2019). The same term is employed in Spanish (*mayoría simple*). Joaquín Brage, La acción abstracta de inconstitucionalidad 126 (2005). A similar approach is used in German (*einfache Mehrheit*). See Roman Kaiser, Das Mehrheitsprinzip in der Judikative 39 (2020). The Polish language employs the same terminology (*większość zwykła*). Andrzej Mączyński & Jan Podkowik, *Art. 190*, 2 *in* Konstytucja Rzeczypospolitej Polskiej 1125, 1181 (Marek Safjan & Leszek Bosekeds., 2016).

21 Several scholars have noted the double usage of the term "simple majority." For example, Fedeli posits that a simple majority "may refer to a voting requirement of half of either all ballots cast or those voting on the given alternative plus one and also to the highest number of votes cast for any one alternative, while not constituting a majority." Silvia Fedeli, *Simple Majority*, *in* Encyclopedia of Law and Economics 1918, 1918 (Alain Marciano & Giovanni Battista Ramello eds., 2019).

22 The concept is sometimes defined as "relative majority." However, the terms relative and simple majority are often used interchangeably. A relative majority implies that "whichever alternative receives more votes, relative to the other alternative, is declared the winner." Jac C. Heckelman, *A Note on Majority Rule and Neutrality with an Application to State Votes at the Constitutional Convention of 1787*, 167 Public Choice 245, 245 (2016).

23 Scholars such as Caminker have mentioned the possibility of voting protocols considering the largest plurality a possible decision-making rule, but in most jurisdictions it remains a largely theoretical discussion. Evan H. Caminker, *Playing with Voting Protocols on the Supreme Court [Unpublished Draft]*, 3 (2002).

cases are often thought of as narrowed down to binary choices,[24] a simple majority of the court often equals 50 percent plus one of the court.[25] However, judges may sometimes divide in non-binary[26] ways when a third option is present.[27] Constitutional and apex courts commonly employ several mechanisms to create majorities in case of plurality disagreements.[28]

Simple majorities have multiple advantages. They tend to be neutral and anonymous, treating equally all alternatives by favoring no outcome and granting analogous influence to all votes.[29] Majority rule is a natural and usual decision-making rule and effective in achieving decisions.[30] It is the most common voting protocol for courts and the standard rule while performing constitutional adjudication in countries such as the United States, Spain, Germany, Austria, Italy, India, Israel, Japan, and South Africa, among many others.

In the second place, supermajority voting protocols require constitutional or apex courts to achieve a qualified vote toward general or specific outcomes. Since judicial simple majorities force the court to have more members in favor than against a proposal, a supermajority is a decision-making rule that demands at least one further vote than a simple majority would.

24 Krishnamurthi, *supra* note 20, at 1209; Cristóbal Caviedes, *A Core Case for Supermajority Rules in Constitutional Adjudication*, 20 Int. J. Const. L. 1162, 1172 (2022).

25 Courts with an odd number of judges best serve to exemplify the concept. If a question of law may be narrowed to a binary choice and all judges vote in favour of one of the two available positions, the largest plurality will simultaneously be 50 percent plus one. Contrary to parliamentarians, judges are often banned from abstaining without proper legal cause. Even though recusals may be allowed in constitutional courts, a recused judge is excluded from the concrete case, and by not sitting on the bench, the court's membership is temporarily recomposed, with the recused judge not counting commonly in determining the applicable majority.

26 As Caruso explains, "a relative majority presupposes at least three positions ..." Corrado Caruso, *Majority*, Max Planck Encyclopedia of Comparative Constitutional Law, para. 6 (2022).

27 Suppose a nine-member constitutional court is analyzing if a statute infringes the Constitution. If four judges deem the statute unconstitutional, three constitutional, and three consider that the court lacks jurisdiction to hear the case, the four justices command a simple majority understood as the largest plurality, but not a "simple majority" or a "majority" in the judicial sense. Hartnett analyzes several cases where the U.S. Supreme Court faced situations where a three-way split prevented a judgment from being entered. Edward A. Hartnett, A Matter of Ju*dgment, Not a Matter of Opinion*, 74 N.Y. Univ. L. Rev. 123, 138–39 (1999).

28 This has been referred to as "redefining" the simple majority. Fedeli, *supra* note 21, at 1919. On vote-switching, *see* Ron Davidson, *The Mechanics of Judicial Vote Switching*, 38 Suffolk Univ. L. Rev. 17 (2004); Cohen, *supra* note 11. For example, some courts engage with what Ernst calls "forcing a judge to stay in play." Ernst, Wolfgang, *supra* note 7, at 15. The Mexican Supreme Court divides voting on admissibility and on the case's merits. If a justice believing that the court lacks jurisdiction maintains a 5:5:1 tie by preventing the Court from reaching a binary question, the court would vote first on the court's jurisdiction, and the "defeated" justice would be forced to give his/her opinion regarding the statute's constitutionality, creating a majority.

29 As stipulated by May's theorem. See Kenneth O. May, *A Set of Independent Necessary and Sufficient Conditions for Simple Majority Decision*, 20 Econometrica 680 (1952).

30 Krishnamurthi, *supra* note 20.

Supermajorities need not be neutral. Some jurisdictions establish a supermajority rule only to strike down a statute while preserving a simple majority requirement for other outcomes. That is the case in jurisdictions such as South Korea, the Czech Republic, or Mexico. Nonetheless, supermajorities may be established neutrally, requiring a qualified vote for any outcome, such as in the Dominican Republic or the former Peruvian Court of Constitutional Guarantees.

This book argues that establishing supermajorities privileges different aims contingent on their configuration. The institutional design of supermajority rules may serve to provide deference to the democratically elected branches, act as a taming mechanism of the counter-majoritarian difficulty, or, in Condorcetean fashion, as an epistemological bet on a more precise decision.

2.1.3 Quorums and Majorities

A crucial aspect concerning majorities is the choice of the multiplicand. Vermeule asserted that any majority rule is incomplete if it does not provide a multiplicand from which the majority will be calculated.[31] There are two main systems: relative and absolute multiplicands.[32]

A relative multiplicand is a system that computes majorities over a set quorum. As is well known in the judicial branch, several circumstances may prevent judges from taking part in a case. A judge may be recused on legal grounds or be absent due to sickness, an official commission, or vacation. The court may also lack members, given the failure of political branches to replace a retiring judge. Relative multiplicands consider those circumstances by setting a quorum that does not alter majority requirements. Quorums are a minimal number of judges required for the court to conduct business.[33] Even if the majority threshold remains unchanged, the number over which such a majority is to be calculated varies.[34]

Quorum and majorities are separate concepts. A quorum sets the required number of judges for a court to be validly constituted, and the majority sets the number or percentages of votes required to decide a case. A constitutional court may have a quorum but lack a majority to issue a decision. However,

31 Adrian Vermeule, *Absolute Majority Rules*, 37 Br. J. Polit. Sci. 643, 644 (2007).

32 I follow Vermeule's terminology. Vermeule, *supra* note 13, at 119. Caminker has employed the term "denominator." Caminker, *supra* note 20, at 117.

33 Jonathan Nash, *The Majority That Wasn't: Stare Decisis, Majority Rule, and the Mischief of Quorum Requirements*, 58 Emory L.J. 831, 840 (2009).

34 Take, for example, the American Supreme Court that resolved *Marbury v. Madison*. In 1803, the Supreme Court was composed of six members, and thus four justices (66%) were required to decide. However, since a quorum of four justices was set, upon enough absences, three justices could validly decide a case. Relative multiplicands may allow non-majoritarian factions to occasionally speak on behalf of the court without constituting a majority of the full court. Nash has referred to this situation as "minority majorities." Nash, *supra* note 33, at 835.

there can be no majority without a quorum. Absent quorum, there is no court. Even though the distinction appears simple, since majority and quorum are intrinsically linked concepts, they may be hard to distinguish in some cases.[35]

In turn, absolute multiplicands preserve the court's total number of members as a reference to compute the majority, regardless of the absences.[36] Even if the court is allowed to session with a quorum, the majority is computed over the total of court judges.[37] Absolute multiplicands attempt to prevent "minority majorities," the circumstance that a group inferior to the court's membership majority speaks on behalf of it. Calculating the majority over the court's total membership equals requiring a fixed number of votes and, therefore, produces variable percentages, deeming absences as negative votes[38] rather than eliminating them from the majority calculation.[39] Under absolute multiplicands, simple majorities may become supermajorities of the new voting group,[40] and supermajorities may become more aggravated.

2.2 A Brief History of the Discussion on Supermajorities in Constitutional Adjudication

2.2.1 The Birth of a Debate

The debate on supermajorities in constitutional adjudication began close to the inception of judicial review. Nonetheless, judicial review was born employing simple majorities. In *Marbury v. Madison*,[41] Chief Justice John Marshall

35 Several authors have employed the concepts interchangeably. For an English example, Thomas Bustamante, *The Ongoing Search for Legitimacy: Can a 'Pragmatic yet Principled' Deliberative Model Justify the Authority of Constitutional Courts?* 78 Mod. L. Rev. 372 (2015). In German, Jana Osterkamp, Verfassungsgerichtsbarkeit in der Tschechoslowakei (1920-1939): Verfassungsidee, Demokratieverständnis, Nationalitätenproblem 105 (2009). In Spanish, Nestor Sagües, *Los Poderes Implícitos e Inherentes Del Tribunal Constitucional Del Perú y El Quórum Para Sus Votaciones*, 3 *in* La Constitución de 1993. Análisis y comentarios (Francisco Fernández ed., 1996). José Ramón Cossío Díaz, *Artículo 105*, *in* Constitución Política Mexicana Comentada 1047 (1995).

36 Vermeule, *supra* note 31, at 646. Sometimes, scholarship also refers to absolute majority rules as a 50 percent plus one of the total possible votes. See Keith L. Dougherty & Julian Edward, *The Properties of Simple Vs. Absolute Majority Rule: Cases Where Absences and Abstentions Are Important*, 22 J. Theor. Polit. 85 (2010).

37 Let us turn back to the Marshall Court to exemplify the effects of absolute multiplicands. The absence of a justice would have rendered a five-member court. However, the same four votes (80% of the members present) and not three (60%) would have been required to resolve a case since absolute multiplicands require a majority of the entire judicial body to make a decision.

38 For a deeper theoretical insight into the feature, *see* Dougherty & Edward, *supra* note 36, at 110.

39 Vermeule, *supra* note 31, at 646.

40 This is the case in Puerto Rico. Puerto Rico's Constitution (Article V, Section 4) provides: "[N]o law shall be held unconstitutional except by a majority of the total number of Justices of which the Court is composed." Argentina is a similar case (*see* Law 26.183).

41 5 U.S. (1 Cranch) 137 (1803).

proclaimed the court's power to serve as the final arbiter of the constitutionality of laws. The United States Supreme Court did not have a statutorily prescribed majority to decide cases: both the Constitution and statutes left the matter unspecified.[42] However, the court functioned with a simple majority as a decision-making threshold and quorum rule "without even appearing to give the matter much thought."[43]

While the issue of the appropriated majority might have been evident for Marshall's Court, Congress had a different opinion.[44] Twenty years after the shocking *Marbury v. Madison* case, the first proposal deviating from majority rule appeared. In 1823, Senator Johnson proposed introducing a unanimity requirement to strike down legislation. Marshall was well aware of the proposal. In a private letter to Senator Clay in 1823, Marshall deemed that: "A majority of the court is according to . . . the common understanding of mankind as much as the court."[45] Marshall did not hide his discontent:

> When we consider the remoteness, the numbers, and the ages of the Judges, we cannot expect that the assemblage of all of them [a unanimous decision] . . . will be of frequent recurrence. The difficulty of the questions, and other considerations, may often divide those who do attend. To require almost unanimity is to require what cannot often happen, and consequently to disable the Court from deciding constitutional questions.[46]

Marshall would bear witness[47] that, from 1823 to 1827, every year in Congress at least one amendment proposal to establish supermajorities with different decision-making thresholds. While supermajority proposals kept appearing after 1827, their frequency declined. However, starting in 1911, triggered by the *Lochner* decision,[48] a new set of proposals emerged with renewed strength.

42 Akhil Reed Amar, America's Unwritten Constitution: The Precedents and Principles We Live By 357 (2012).

43 *Id.* at 360.

44 Particularly, Jeffersonians felt that the court had steered away from its assigned limits. At the time, Congress considered several supermajority rules proposals or bills to grant the Senate the power to decide constitutional questions. Walter Stahr, Salmon P. Chase: Lincoln's Vital Rival 130 (2021).

45 John Marshall, December 22, 1823, letter to Henry Clay. A digitalized copy is available at the Gilder Lehrman Institute of American History. gilderlehrman.org/collection/glc00141 (last visited June 9, 2023).

46 *Id.*

47 Nonetheless, even if Marshall disapproved of supermajority rules, he proclaimed that no decision on a constitutional question would be rendered unless four judges of the court concurred—a majority of the entire court membership, even if a majority of the justices sitting on a case would agree on an outcome. *See* Briscoe v. Commonwealth's Bank of Kentucky, 33 U.S. 118 (1834).

48 Lochner v. New York, 198 U.S. 45 (1905).

From 1911 to 1926, 30 supermajority proposals were introduced, including the famous bill sponsored by Senator Borah in 1923.[49]

While consensus to impose supermajorities was never achieved at the Federal level, during the same period, several states debated or approved supermajorities. Ohio, North Dakota, and Nebraska introduced supermajority rules in 1912, 1919, and 1920, while Minnesota (1913)[50] and Massachusetts (1917–1918)[51] discussed them, but they were not adopted. The decade of 1920 was a vibrant time for supermajority supporters and ideas associated with judicial limitation and deference to the elected branches.

Before the era of interest in supermajority rules, scholarship had largely ignored the topic. The new proposals and the recently created state supermajorities triggered a new wave of scholarship on the institutional design of federal proposals and empirical practice of the rules at the state level that would extend until 1940.[52]

In that era of interest, the debate emerged autonomously in Europe. After *Marbury v. Madison*, the second most crucial moment for judicial review was the emergence of contemporary constitutional courts. Inspired by the works of Jellinek[53] and Kelsen,[54] autonomous bodies outside the traditional separation of powers emerged: courts meant to engage only in constitutional adjudication, analyzing abstract challenges to legislation, with the ability to declare statutes invalid with an *erga omnes* effect. The American model had to wait 20 years before a supermajority proposal emerged. The European model did not wait for a single one.

In 1920, emerging from the ashes of World War I, Czechoslovakia established a seven-member constitutional court, which required a five-vote

49 Senator Borah, a known progressive, proposed in 1923 a 7:2 supermajority to overturn acts of Congress. Borah justified the proposal on the court's frequent divisions. For his defense of the idea, *see* Borah, William, *Five to Four Decisions as Menace to Respect for Supreme Court*, The New York Times, Feb. 18, 1923, at 21.

50 In the case of Minnesota, the amendment was approved by Congress on April 19, 1913, and submitted to the electorate (Chapter 585-H.F. no. 217). Even though it received a majority of votes favoring the amendment in 1914 (127,352 for the amendment, with only 68,886 against), it did not achieve the required majority of all voters in the election. Voters not voting on the amendment were counted as "no votes" by the amendment procedure.

51 Debates in the Massachusetts Constitutional Convention 1917-1918, 453–73 (1919).

52 Among the most relevant works, *see* Edward Selden, *Judicial Veto and the Ohio Plan*, 9 St. Louis L. Rev. 60 (1923); Edwin O. Stene, *Is There Minority Control of Court Decisions in Ohio?*, 9 Univ. Cincinnati L. Rev. 23 (1935); John W. Bricker, *Shall the Powers of the Supreme Court Be Abridged?*, 16 Proc. Acad. Polit. Sci. 40 (1936); Katherine B. Fite & Louis Baruch Rubinstein, *Curbing the Supreme Court: State Experiences and Federal Proposals*, 35 Mich. L. Rev. 762 (1937); William Redmond, *Requirement in State Constitution of More than a Majority of the Supreme Court to Invalidate Legislation*, 19 Neb. L. Bull. 32 (1940); Paul W. Madgett, *The Five-Judge Rule in Nebraska*, 2 Creighton L. Rev. 329 (1968).

53 Georg Jellinek, Ein Verfassungsgerichtshof für Österreich (1885).

54 Hans Kelsen, *La Garantie Juridictionnelle de la Constitution*, 45 Rev. Droit Public 185 (1928).

supermajority. The first constitutional court in the world[55] had been born under supermajority rule, one year after North Dakota's supermajority and in the same year that Nebraska adopted an identical 5:2 supermajority. The court's younger brother, the Austrian Constitutional Court, employed a simple majority rule.[56]

There is, however, no evidence that the Czechoslovak and American debates were interrelated. Unlike its American counterpart, the Czechoslovak supermajority triggered no specialized discussion.

In the United States, the clashes between the unelected Judiciary and the political branches over economic policy, starting in *Lochner*, peaked in 1937 with the Court Packing Plan proposed by President Roosevelt. Tired of struggling with a court that invalidated new economic policies, Roosevelt threatened to take control of the institution by expanding it and appointing new justices with closer ideological views to his own.[57] Supermajority proposals were introduced in the following weeks to Roosevelt's announcement.[58]

Radical as it was, Roosevelt's plan was never executed. In 1937, Justice Owen Roberts modified his views in the *West Coast Hotel* case,[59] upholding New Deal legislation. Whether a sincere switch or strategic behavior to deter Roosevelt's plan, the "switch in time that saved nine" probably spared the court from being packed. The *West Coast Hotel* case marked the end of the Lochner era.

The period from 1937 to 1938 saw a decline in supermajority debates. In 1938, Czechoslovakia's Constitutional Court disappeared under Nazi rule[60] and, with it, the supermajority. In the United States, debates on supermajority rule slowed down after Roosevelt's success. Scholarly analysis on supermajority

55 Czechoslovakia had the first constitutional court in the world with the ability to perform ex-post judicial review of statutes. However, it actually started functioning after the Austrian Constitutional Court, which was introduced later. David Kosař & Ladislav Vyhnánek, *The Constitutional Court of Czechia*, *in* THE MAX PLANCK HANDBOOKS IN EUROPEAN PUBLIC LAW: VOLUME III: CONSTITUTIONAL ADJUDICATION: INSTITUTIONS 119, 123 (Armin von Bogdandy, Peter Huber & Christoph Grabenwarter eds., 2020).

56 It is unclear if Kelsen preferred simple majorities to supermajorities for constitutional courts. In his seminal work, Kelsen only once refers to majorities as court decision-making mechanisms, and he does so in a more descriptive than normative way. Kelsen, *supra* note 54, at 245. While discussing his work at the *Institut International du Droit Public* Kelsen referred to simple majorities as the prevailing requirement in his jurisdiction only in passing. See the discussion at Domingo García Belaunde, *Apéndice: Instituto International de Derecho Público*, 2 *in* EL CONTROL DEL PODER 899 (Domingo García Belaunde & Peter Häberle eds., 2012).

57 Many progressives favored supermajorities at the time. Laura M. Weinrib, *From Left to Rights: Civil Liberties Lawyering Between the World Wars*, 15 L. CULT. HUMANIT. 622, 645 (2019).

58 As Cushman accounts, "No fewer than twelve such joint resolutions were offered in the wake of the President's February 5 announcement." Barry Cushman, *Court-Packing in Context*, 48 J. SUPREME COURT HIST. 174, 183 (2023). *See also* Cushman's compelling analysis of supermajority rules around the period. *Id.* at 183–87.

59 West Coast Hotel Co. v. Parrish, 300 U.S. 379 (1937).

60 Jaromír Tauchen, *The Supreme Courts in the Protectorate of Bohemia and Moravia*, *in* SUPREME COURTS UNDER NAZI OCCUPATION 227, 233–34 (Derk Venema ed., 2022).

rules became less common, and in 1968, Ohio repealed its rule.[61] While some proposals were still being submitted to Congress to establish a supermajority,[62] they became less frequent. By 1980, proposals had almost stopped completely.

Nonetheless, in the meantime, the world was changing. Inspired by the Kelsenian model, many countries began adopting constitutional courts or bodies performing judicial review.[63] Some of them adopted supermajority rules, such as the Philippines (1935), Costa Rica (1949), Taiwan (1958–2022), Peru (1982 and then 1995 and 2002), South Korea (1972, 1980, and 1987), India (1976), El Salvador (1984), the Czech Republic (1993), Mexico (1994), Lebanon (1993), the Dominican Republic (2010), among others. Even recently, transitorily, supermajorities were established in Poland (2015), and Georgia (2016). Supermajorities were no longer limited to two jurisdictions.

2.2.2 The Debate in the Scholarship

Even though many jurisdictions adopted supermajorities from 1940 to 2000, the scholarly debate remained scant apart from minimal discussion within the United States[64] and even less abroad.[65] Few works engaged in general considerations of models. No comparative work was published, and some even seemed to be unaware of the existence of other systems under supermajority rule.[66]

Supermajority rules had to wait until the 2000s to become part of a broader theoretical debate. Again, the trigger was a series of bare majority decisions in the United States. The Rehnquist Court, having a conservative majority of five, struck down several acts of Congress in a series of 5:4 decisions.[67] Against this backdrop, Professors Shugerman[68] and Caminker[69] published their widely

61 William W. Milligan & James E. Pohlman, *The 1968 Modern Courts Amendment to the Ohio Constitution*, 29 Ohio St. L.J. 811, 845–46 (1968).

62 See Caminker, *supra* note 20, at 121–22.

63 Alec Stone Sweet, *Constitutional Courts*, *in* The Oxford Handbook of Comparative Constitutional L. 817, 818–20 (Michel Rosenfeld & András Sajó eds., 2012). On the expansion of constitutional courts, *see also* Ferreres Comella, *supra* note 1, at 3–5.

64 Inter alia, Stewart T. Herrick, James J. Higgins & Nancy R. Tarlow, *Five-Four Decisions of the United States Supreme Court: Resurrection of the Extraordinary Majority*, 7 Suffolk Univ. L. Rev. 807 (1973).

65 For an exception, *see* Thomas von Danwitz, *Qualifizierte Mehrheiten Für Normverwerfende Entscheidungen Des BVerfG? Thesen Zur Gewährleistung Des Judicial Self-Restraint*, 51 JuristenZeitung 481 (1996). Sagües, *supra* note 35.

66 For an example of the tendency, *see* Brage, *supra* note 20.

67 Chemerinsky, analyzing the 1992–2002 period from the Rehnquist Court, asserts: "This era was marked by a dramatic lack of deference to Congress and the states." Erwin Chemerinsky, *Assessing Chief Justice William Rehnquist*, 154 Univ. Pa. L. Rev. 1331, 1388 (2006).

68 Jed Handelsman Shugerman, *A Six-Three Rule: Reviving Consensus and Deference on the Supreme Court*, 37 Ga. L. Rev. 893 (2003).

69 Caminker, *supra* note 20.

known proposals for adopting supermajority rules to ensure broader consensus and appropriate deference to Congress.

While it is true that supermajority proposals had been analyzed in scholarship previously, particularly in the United States, Shugerman's and Caminker's work had a distinctive quality. Instead of focusing on concrete normative formulations of a rule, they delved into the underlying theoretical framework of supermajority rules, providing a broader defense of their merits. While both scholars considered the experience of state supreme courts, such analysis comprised a minor part of their contribution with strong normative proposals.

Shugerman noted that the Supreme Court had granted the elected branches scarce deference. While it had claimed to employ a presumption of constitutionality of legislative acts,[70] this was primarily *in dicta*.[71] Hence, Shugerman posited that considering the unprecedented rate of invalidated federal legislation, a solution institutionalizing deference had to be implemented, such as a 6:3 supermajority. He claimed that such a rule could be defended from the perspective of deliberative democracy theory, epistemology, and constitutional values.[72]

Caminker argued that supermajorities could contribute to a more accurate guarantee of the Thayerian presumption of constitutionality. Caminker observed that the Thayerian presumption was an internalized rule, depending on the deference level granted by individual justices, a property he described as "atomistic."[73] A supermajority voting rule would turn the deference given by the presumption into an aggregative quality. Contrary to the number of votes required to strike down legislation, Caminker claimed, internal rules are not an objective measurement of deference. A supermajority, therefore, could either supplement or substitute the presumption of constitutionality.[74]

The works of Caminker and Shugerman triggered new debates and inspired others to explore new usages of the supermajority rules in courts. Since supermajorities were deemed deferential, Gersen and Vermeule[75] claimed that such rules could ensure Chevron deference to administrative agencies' interpretations. In turn, some scholars later suggested that supermajorities could be employed in other courts' more controversial doctrines, for example, when

70 The origin of the presumption of constitutionality is traced to Thayer's formulation. See James B. Thayer, *The Origin and Scope of the American Doctrine of Constitutional Law*, 7 HARV. L. REV. 129 (1893).

71 Shugerman, *supra* note 68, at 895.

72 *Id.* at 896.

73 Caminker, *supra* note 20, at 79–80.

74 *Id.* at 98.

75 Jacob E. Gersen & Adrian Vermeule, *Chevron as a Voting Rule*, 116 YALE L.J. 676 (2007). See subsequently ROBERT D. COOTER & MICHAEL D. GILBERT, PUBLIC LAW AND ECONOMICS 318–19 (2022).

deciding cases applying the unconstitutional constitutional amendments doctrine.[76]

The debate notably intensified in 2014 when Waldron published a provocative piece[77] questioning the legitimacy of a simple majority[78] as a decision-making rule. Waldron observed that judicial review has traditionally been perceived as a remedy against majoritarianism. Majoritarianism, often referred to as Tocqueville's "tyranny of the majority,"[79] is usually depicted by an image of representatives in parliament raising hands among superficial discussions and making controversial decisions by rash methods. Judicial review was a remedy against such majoritarianism by providing a principled forum of discussion[80] where cases were resolved through deliberation rather than by vote. Waldron questioned such a sublimated view of judicial review.

Waldron posited that courts also had profound disagreements about the meaning of the Constitution. In the case of court disagreements, judges vote in very much the same way as Parliaments do. There is something paradoxical, Waldron observed, about the fact that the remedy against majoritarianism employs the same methodology for deciding as the majoritarianism it tries to mitigate.[81] Why do bare majorities rule in court?—Waldron asked. Legal theory could consider using other rules, such as differently weighted voting

76 Rubens Beçak & Jairo Lima, *When 5x4 Is Not a Winning Majority: Judicial Decision-Making on Unconstitutional Constitutional Amendments*, *in* Violent Conflicts, Crisis, State of Emergency, Peacebuilding: Constitutional Problems, Amendments and Interpretation 161, 114 (Oesten Baller ed., 2019); Adem Kassie Abebe, *Taming Regressive Constitutional Amendments: The African Court as a Continental (Super) Constitutional Court*, 17 Int. J. Const. L. 89 (2019); Jairo Lima, *Decisão por Supermaioria nas Cortes Constitucionais: o caso das emendas constitucionais inconstitucionais*, 6 Rev. Estud. Inst. 1310 (2020). Most recently, Benítez-R. considered that supermajorities may guarantee a better standard for the Colombian Constitutional Court when reviewing constitutional amendments affecting the Court itself or the judiciary. Vicente F. Benítez-R., *Petrificando la Rama Judicial en Colombia: Auto-interés Judicial y Control de Constitucionalidad Inapropiado de Reformas Constitucionales a La Justicia*, 20 Int. J. Const. L. 1618, 1641 (2022). On the unconstitutional constitutional amendments doctrine, a contemporary reference is Yaniv Roznai, Unconstitutional Constitutional Amendments: The Limits of Amendment Powers (2017). On an empirical note, Article 149 of the Turkish Constitution requires a 2/3 supermajority out of its fifteen-member Constitutional Court to strike down constitutional amendments.

77 Waldron, *supra* note 19. In *Law and Disagreement*, Waldron had advanced some of the ideas that he developed at length in this piece. Waldron, *supra* note 6, at 90–91. He had also questioned simple majority voting in other works. Jeremy Waldron, *The Core of the Case against Judicial Review*, 115 Yale L.J. 1346, 1391–93 (2006).

78 In 2013, Mendes had already considered that some supermajority designs could more ideally balance the preference aggregation method. He questioned the notion of a most deliberative aggregation method, traditionally associated with simple majorities. Conrado Hübner Mendes, Constitutional Courts and Deliberative Democracy 184 (2013).

79 See Alexis de Tocqueville, Democracy in America: Translated, Edited, and with an Introduction by Harvey C. Mansfield and Delba Winthrop 204–208 (2000).

80 See Rawls' conception. Rawls, *supra* note 3, at 231.

81 Waldron, *supra* note 19, at 1726.

or supermajority rules.[82] Without directly endorsing supermajorities, Waldron shook the ground on which simple majorities have stood. A veil of inertia was unmasked.

Following Waldron's assertion, a broad debate ensued on different aspects of supermajorities. Some have taken up the challenge through philosophical debates of simple majority rule. For example, Krishnamurthi responded by attempting to prove that simple majorities had significant advantages over supermajority or unanimity rules.[83] He claimed that simple majorities had epistemic advantages, were efficient resource-wise, and were representationally fair, allowing collegial and party neutrality.[84] In response, Caviedes contended that majority rule was not grounded as a decision-making mechanism of constitutional adjudication.[85] Caviedes claimed that not only was it disputable that simple majorities had superior individual values to other decision-making methods, such as supermajorities,[86] but he further argued that there was no evidence to assert that the features of simple majorities inherently produce a better decision-making rule when considering their intersectional effect.[87]

Other scholars renewed their attention on existing supermajorities through empirical analysis. In the United States, Zellman and Miller examined the modern practice of the overlooked Nebraska supermajority,[88] while some scholars saw supermajorities or unanimity rules as a way to remedy the fractured U.S. Supreme Court.[89]

At a comparative level, Hong addressed the application of supermajority rules in the South Korean Constitutional Court, claiming that they had empowered the court and increased its prestige, signaling future shifts in constitutional doctrine.[90] Rivera undertook a similar contextual analysis of supermajorities regarding objections to court control by political branches and court paralysis on the basis of the Mexican example.[91] In the Polish case, Sadurski

82 *Id.* at 1730.

83 Krishnamurthi, *supra* note 20. *See also* Kaiser's work for an analysis of the majority principle within the judiciary in the German legal order. Kaiser, *supra* note 20.

84 Krishnamurthi, *supra* note 20, at 1269.

85 Cristóbal Caviedes, *Is Majority Rule Justified in Constitutional Adjudication?*, 41 Oxf. J. Leg. Stud. 376 (2021).

86 For example, although in an asymmetric manner, supermajorities may be more Condorcetianly accurate than majority rules in defending certain types of outcomes. *Id.* at 388–89.

87 *Id.* at 406.

88 Sandra Zellmer & Kathleen Miller, *The Fallacy of Judicial Supermajority Clauses in State Constitutions*, 47 Univ. Toledo L. Rev. 73 (2015).

89 Martin Wishnatsky, *Taming the Supreme Court*, 6 Lib. Univ. L. Rev. 597 (2012); Dwight Duncan, *A Modest Proposal on Supreme Court Unanimity to Constitutionally Invalidate Laws*, 33 Brigh. Young Univ. J. Public L. 1 (2018); Daniel Epps & Ganesh Sitaraman, *How to Save the Supreme Court*, 129 Yale L.J. 148 (2019).

90 Joon Seok Hong, *Signaling the Turn: The Supermajority Requirement and Judicial Power on the Constitutional Court of Korea*, 67 Am. J. Comp. L. 177 (2019).

91 Mauro Arturo Rivera León, *Control and Paralysis? A Context-Sensitive Analysis of Objections to Supermajorities in Constitutional Adjudication*, Int. J. Const. L. (2023), doi.org/10.1093/icon/moad074.

studied how supermajorities had been used to attack and tame a constitutional court by an illiberal regime.[92] Rivera analyzed episodes of judicial review of supermajority rules in the United States, Peru, Poland, and Georgia, noting that the legal source of the rules and the moment they were introduced could prompt adverse reactions or specific strategic court behavior in striking down the new thresholds.[93]

Another segment of the literature began advocating for supermajorities as a new decision-making model for constitutional courts. Contrary to previous literature, such as Shugerman and Caminker, primarily concerned about implementing the rule in a specific jurisdiction—even if broad in its scope—these latest scholars regarded supermajorities as a new, probably superior alternative to traditional simple majorities in courts. Their analyses had a predominant theoretical design, focusing on no jurisdiction.

Castillo-Ortiz considered several proposals to amend the institutional design of Kelsenian constitutional courts. He conceived that supermajorities could be introduced to ensure broader deference to the legislature.[94] Deeming that the option would entail significant shortcomings, Castillo-Ortiz then considered an intermediate solution. Constitutional provisions regarding human rights and democratic institutions would be protected through a simple majority threshold, while abstract provisions and principles would be subjected to a supermajority. In this way, he meant to avoid controversies of judicial activism and the politicization of courts stemming from the enforcement of unclear provisions prone to interpretative disputes, while preserving a strong rights enforcement model.[95]

Subsequently, Roznai proposed a hybrid model employing supermajorities. A supermajority would be required to strike down legislation. If a non-qualified majority deems the statute unconstitutional, the legislature must consider whether to amend the provision.[96] Roznai's idea had in mind fostering a judicial dialogue through a mixture of weak and strong forms of judicial review.

Most recently, Caviedes published a defense of supermajority rules as superior decision-making rules for constitutional adjudication.[97] In his work, Caviedes argued that supermajority rules boost group accuracy in Condorcetean fashion, foster judicial deliberation, increase the reputation of constitutional courts, and embody the Thayerian deference to legislation.

92 Wojciech Sadurski, Poland's Constitutional Breakdown 73, 81 (2019).

93 Mauro Arturo Rivera León, *Judicial Review of Supermajority Rules Governing Courts' Own Decision-Making: A Comparative Analysis*, Glob. Const. 1 (2023).

94 Pablo Castillo-Ortiz, *The Dilemmas of Constitutional Courts and the Case for a New Design of Kelsenian Institutions*, 39 L. Philos. 617, 639 (2020).

95 *Id.* at 642.

96 Yaniv Roznai, *Introduction: Constitutional Courts in a 100-Years Perspective and a Proposal for a Hybrid Model of Judicial Review*, 14 ICL J. 355, 374 (2021).

97 Caviedes, *supra* note 24.

Finally, in light of Biden's 2021 Presidential Commission on the Supreme Court, the debate has reignited in the United States. Not only did the Commission analyze supermajority rules, offering valuable insights,[98] but as a result of the report, more scholars began discussing supermajority[99] and unanimity proposals.[100]

While supporters of supermajorities claim they may enhance deliberation, grant institutionalized deference, and bring Condorcetean accuracy to decisions, numerous critics of supermajority rules exist. Some objections are principled, based on philosophic claims such as the theoretical superiority of majority rule.[101] Others argue that supermajorities infringe on some inherent majority principle[102] or create a disbalance between courts and the elected branches.[103]

Others have voiced concerns about the potential shortcomings of supermajority rules of a more practical nature, susceptible to empirical testing. For example, some have claimed that supermajorities increase the risk of court paralysis.[104] Others have posited that supermajorities may make courts more prone to control by political branches[105] through several methods, for example,

98 Presidential Commission on the Supreme Court of the United States, *Final Report*, 288 (2021), https://www.whitehouse.gov/pcscotus/ (last visited May 25, 2022).

99 Ryan D. Doerfler & Samuel Moyn, *Democratizing the Supreme Court*, 109 Calif. L. Rev. 1703 (2021); Amal Sethi, *Sub-Constitutionally Repairing the United States Supreme Court*, 52 Common Law World Rev. 128, 136–37 (2023). For an analysis of the prospected public acceptance of introducing a supermajority to the U.S. Supreme Court, *see* Lee Epstein, James L. Gibson & Michael L. Nelson, *Public Response to Proposals to Reform the Supreme Court (Report Prepared for the New York Times)* (2020), https://epstein.usc.edu/courtreformsurvey (last visited Sept. 6, 2023). On the constitutionality of imposing supermajority rules, *see* Stephen Gardbaum, *What the World Can Teach Us About Supreme Court Reform*, 70 UCLA L. Rev. Discourse 184, 197 (2023); Joanna Lampe, Congressional Control over the Supreme Court 1, 36–38 (2023).

100 David Orentlicher, *Judicial Consensus: Why the Supreme Court Should Decide Its Cases Unanimously*, 54 Conn. L. Rev. 303 (2022).

101 Krishnamurthi, *supra* note 20.

102 Robert A. Schapiro, *Contingency and Universalism in State Separation of Powers Discourse*, 4 Roger Williams Univ. L. Rev. 79, 103 (1998).

103 Maddox suggested that a supermajority entailed "legislative finality." W. Rolland Maddox, *Minority Control of Court Decisions in Ohio*, 24 Am. Polit. Sci. Rev. 638, 647 (1930). *See also* Zellmer and Miller, *supra* note 88, at 87.

104 Shugerman, *supra* note 68, at 985; Castillo-Ortiz, *supra* note 94, at 640; Roznai, *supra* note 96, at 371; Rosalind Dixon & David Landau, Abusive Constitutional Borrowing: Legal Globalization and the Subversion of Liberal Democracy 93 (2021). At the institutional level, *see also* Venice Commission, *Opinion No. 833/2015 On Amendments to the Act of 25 June 2015 on the Constitutional Tribunal (CDL-AD(2016)001*, 25 (2016); Venice Commission, *Preliminary Opinion 849/2016 on the Amendments to the Organic Law on the Constitutional Court and to the Law on Constitutional Legal Proceedings*, 10 (2016).

105 Sadurski, *supra* note 92, at 81; Roznai, *supra* note 96, at 371; Castillo-Ortiz, *supra* note 94, at 640. For a position claiming that the criticism may be refuted through context-sensitive analysis, *see* Rivera León, *supra* note 91.

court-packing of a minority sufficient to obstruct the supermajority.[106] Some scholars have pointed out that poor drafting of supermajority rules will lead to problems.[107] This set of empirically testable criticisms constitutes relevant objections to supermajorities worth addressing.

2.3 Looking Ahead

This chapter has attempted to provide a comprehensive conceptual analysis and literature review on supermajority rules understood as decision-making thresholds to invalidate legislation. Voting protocols remain one of the most understudied features of constitutional adjudication, and the complex, varying set of rules they embody may have a determinative effect on producing concrete outcomes.

Supermajorities emerged during the progressive era in the United States and the birth of formal constitutional courts in Czechoslovakia. The fact that two different systems arrived at similar proposals around the same period is an interesting feature.

Initially seen as a purely practical proposal, the concept of supermajorities has become a theoretically relevant debate. Throughout the scholarship, philosophical discussions have considered supermajorities as relevant substitutes or alternatives to majority rule.

However, much in this debate remains theoretical, and few empirical analyses have shed light on the practical consequences of supermajorities, their functioning, and how they affect the courts and legal systems they work within. Comparative law can contribute to this discussion through empirical analysis of the jurisdictions where such rules were implemented. Bridging the theoretical and comparative discussion is crucial. This book attempts to do so.

Chapter 3 will delve into the functioning of the four original historical supermajorities and how they shaped and molded their courts. In Chapter 4, our analysis will address examples of contemporarily introduced supermajorities. The study will provide a nuanced understanding of how supermajorities shape constitutional adjudication and impact constitutional courts and their relationship with the political branches.

106 Herrick, Higgins, and Tarlow, *supra* note 64, at 836–37; David Kosař & Katarína Šipulová, *Comparative Court-Packing*, 21 Int. J. Const. L. 80, 87 (2023).

107 See Jonathan L. Entin, *Judicial Supermajorities and the Validity of Statutes: How Mapp Became a Fourth Amendment Landmark Instead of a First Amendment Footnote*, 50 Case West. L. Rev. 441, 470 (2002) (particularly basing the analysis on Ohio's case).

PART II

SUPERMAJORITIES IN PRACTICE

3 Historical Supermajorities

3.1 The United States Subnational Supermajorities: The Birth of Supermajorities

The United States featured the first supermajorities applicable in constitutional adjudication: Ohio's 6:1 rule required to overturn decisions from the Court of Appeals upholding legislation, North Dakota (five members), and Nebraska (seven members), requiring respectively a 4:1 and a 5:2 supermajority to invalidate legislation.

After *Marbury v. Madison*,[1] intensive debates occurred on the role of the judiciary. As early as 1823, Senator Johnson proposed a supermajority rule to strike down legislation. The debate was beginning.

Discussions intensified in the period from 1896 to 1917, known as the Progressive Era. The United States had emerged as an economic and military power. Rapid industrialization brought pressing problems. Migration from rural areas produced overcrowded cities, unable to satisfy people's basic needs. Slums were spreading. Poverty and overexploitation of labor provoked social unrest. The Progressive Era aspired to a more egalitarian society, aiming at political and social reform.

While progressivism was winning followers, the judiciary leaned toward a conservative understanding of economic regulation. In 1905, the Supreme Court issued a pivotal decision in *Lochner v. New York*,[2] analyzing New York's 1895 Bakeshop Act. The regulation established a maximum working hours limit. The Court claimed the statute was an "unreasonable, unnecessary, and arbitrary interference with the right and liberty of the individual to contract in relation to labor." *Lochner* was decided by a 5:4 bare majority, with Justice Oliver Wendell Holmes Jr. issuing a prominent dissent.[3] The decision marked the beginning of the so-called "Lochner era," a time when the Supreme Court

1 5 U.S. (1 Cranch) 137 (1803).

2 Lochner v. New York, 198 U.S. 45 (1905).

3 Justice John Marshall Harlan the Elder issued a dissenting opinion joined by Justices White and Day. Harlan considered that the court should have deferred to the legislature's police power and its assessment that the forbidden intensive working regime endangered workers' health.

DOI: 10.4324/9781003458272-5

seemed to impose its beliefs on public policy over the elected branches.[4] The intertwining of the progressive movement and the Lochner era produced serious debates on limiting judicial review. In this context, three states successfully implemented supermajorities in judicial review. Two of them survive to this day.

3.1.1 The First Supermajority: From Rebellion to Extinction in Ohio's Supreme Court (1912–1968)

Ohio was not immune to the Progressive Era.[5] The so-called Ohio Civil Revival, led by politicians such as Samuel Jones, Brand Whitlock, and Tom L. Johnson,[6] aimed to uproot privilege and poverty in a progressive fashion.[7] Triggered by political and social reform demands, Ohio's progressive era resulted in a series of amendments to Ohio's 1851 Constitution through the 1912 Constitutional Convention. Prominent figures such as former Presidents William Taft and Theodore Roosevelt addressed the Convention, urging delegates to find solutions for pressing problems, such as adopting judicial recall.[8] Other figures, such as William Jennings Bryan, played a minor part in the Convention.[9]

While judicial review had existed in Ohio since the state Supreme Court recognized the doctrine in *Rutherford v. McFadden*,[10] the Court had arguably grown conservative. The Convention delegates saw the judiciary as a problem rather than an ally. Reformers and labor leaders accused state courts of striking down legislation in a manner that benefited employers and harmed

4 The Lochner era's influence went beyond American jurisprudence. It had considerable impact in comparative law regarding discussions of judicial activism, economic regulations, and judicial review. *See* Sujit Choudhry, *The Lochner Era and Comparative Constitutionalism*, 2 Intl J. Const. L. 1 (2004).

5 Warner's study is still considered the seminal work on Ohio's progressive movement. Hoyt Landon Warner, Progressivism in Ohio 1897-1917 (1964).

6 Robert H. Bremner, *The Civic Revival in Ohio*, 8 Am. J. Economics & Soc. 61, 61–63 (1948).

7 *Id.* at 64.

8 Roosevelt said: "If you don't like the word recall, say that the people will reserve for themselves the right to decide whether the legislature or the judiciary take the right view of the constitution if the two bodies clash." Ohio's 1912 Constitutional Convention, Twenty-Fourth Day (Legislative Day of Tuesday), 385.

9 Bryan even supported unanimity rules. Addressing the convention, the Great Commoner said: "Some advocate a constitutional provision limiting the power of the Court to declare a law unconstitutional to cases in which all the judges concur in the opinion. I am persuaded that the lawmakers are entitled to this presumption." Ohio's 1912 Constitutional Convention. Thirty-Sixth Day, Legislative Day of Mar. 11, Tuesday, Mar. 12, 1912, 669–70.

10 The Ohio State Constitution, 297 (2 ed. 2022). For the development of judicial review in Ohio, *see* William T. Utter, *Judicial Review in Early Ohio*, 14 The Mississippi Valley Hist. Rev. 3 (1927).

workers.[11] Ohio's Supreme Court was not neutral to progressive changes but was decisively anti-progressive.[12] The delegates reminded participants in the Convention debates that courts had struck down regulations on maximum working hours,[13] mechanics' liens,[14] miners' payment protection,[15] and disregarded safety law in child labor, declaring working children "assumed the risk."[16]

Delegates were also apprehensive about the judiciary's stance on minimum wages[17] and the deference courts granted to big corporations.[18] The Convention knew that many courts had also struck down workers' compensation and labor conditions laws in the United States.[19] Delegates proposed several amendments to counter conservative courts preventing the enforcement of rights granted by new statutes, such as recall of judicial decisions,[20] direct election of judges, and a unanimity rule to strike down legislation—proposal 184.

Even though Ohio's Convention ended up supporting a softer version of the unanimity rule, its introduction may be credited to the efforts of one man: Hiram D. Peck. A Harvard Law School graduate, Peck had served a six-year term in the Superior Court of Cincinnati and became a law professor at Cincinnati Law School.

11 Barbara A. Terzian, *Ohio's Constitutions: An Historical Perspective*, 51 Clev. St. L. Rev. 357, 387 (2004).

12 James L. Walker, *The Ohio Constitution: Normatively and Empirically Distinctive*, *in* The Constitutionalism of American States 447, 456 (George E. Connors & Christopher W. Hammons eds., 2008).

13 City of Cleveland v. Clements Bros. Const. Co., 7 Ohio St. 197, 65 N.E. 885 (1902).

14 Palmer v. Tingle, 55 Ohio St. 423, 45 N.E. 313 (1896).

15 Ohio's 1912 Constitutional Convention, Fiftieth Day (Legislative Day of April 2), 1029.

16 Jacobs v. Fuller & Hutsinpiller Co., 65 N.E. 617 (Phil. 1906). *See* the participation of Delegates Thomas and Peck. Ohio's 1912 Constitutional Convention, Fifty-First Day (Legislative Day of April 2), 1030. Early on, Peck declared: "There have been too many judgments made by the court which seem to the people not well grounded, in view of existing circumstances, and which operate as stumbling blocks to progress, upsetting statutes which were desirable in themselves."

17 Landon Warner, *Ohio's Constitutional Convention of 1912*, 61 Ohio St. Arch. and Hist. Q. 11, 25 (1952).

18 Delegate Anderson summarized it: "The corporations for so many years have been trying to escape liability through the avenue of the unconstitutionality of statutes that there is practically nothing left undecided." Ohio's 1912 Constitutional Convention, Fifty-Second Day (Legislative Day of April 2), 1089.

19 Edwin O. Stene, *Is There Minority Control of Court Decisions in Ohio?*, 9 U. Cin. L. Rev. 23, 25 (1935).

20 Direct democracy mechanisms were highly debated. Steven H. Steinglass, *Constitutional Revision: Ohio Style*, 77 Ohio St. L.J. 281, 307 (2016).

3.1.1.1 Constitutional Convention Deliberations: Unraveling the Supermajority Debate

At Ohio's Constitutional Convention, Peck served as the chairman of the Judiciary Committee. Peck's character was in itself the best defense of a supermajority. Having been a judge himself, Peck had a deep understanding of the judiciary.[21] His rank and knowledge commanded respect among progressive and conservative members alike, who called him "Judge Peck." With a measured manner of speaking, Peck was prone to compromise and reasonableness, thoughtful in his answers, and willing to concede that he could make mistakes.[22] He patiently rebutted objections to his proposal and clarified doubts.

Peck was not the only judge in the Convention. Judges King, Worthington, Taggart, Norris, and Dwyer were delegates. Other members were lawyers, such as Anderson. The Constitutional Convention had senior politicians and expert jurists who knew the judiciary and were familiar with the rules and case law of Ohio courts and other state and federal courts. Delegates were neither ignorant nor attempting to subdue the courts but wanted to lower working hours, raise salaries, prevent children from working, and, above all, stop the judiciary from sabotaging their efforts.[23]

After the Convention began debating the voting requirement, three distinct positions arose. The first position, led by Peck, proposed unanimity as a court requirement. A second intermediate position, led by Taggart,[24] counterproposed a supermajority rule,[25] an eclectic solution between unanimity and a majority rule. Finally, some conservatives, such as Worthington, opposed modifying the rule.[26]

Defending his proposal, Peck claimed it would prevent the Supreme Court from striking down legislation with little consensus, reminding participants that bare majority declarations of unconstitutionality were controversial.

21 Scholars have noted that Peck's expertise was so well recognized he was considered an excellent choice for the Committee. WARNER, *supra* note 5, at 328.

22 For example, Peck admitted: "[w]hen I was asked about it yesterday, I was surprised and answered before I thought. Your construction of that clause is absolutely correct according to my notion." In a different session, Peck acknowledged the merit of an objection, and admitted he would need more time to answer it. Ohio's 1912 Constitutional Convention, *supra* note 15, at 1036.

23 During the convention, many rights previously struck down as unconstitutional by courts were constitutionalized, such as mechanics' liens, comfort, health, safety, and general welfare of employees, workers' compensation, and an eight-hour day in public works. F. R. Aumann, *The Course of Judicial Review in the State of Ohio*, 25 AM. POLIT. SCI. REV. 367, 373 (1931).

24 Ohio's 1912 Constitutional Convention, *supra* note 16 at 1064–7. Constitutional Convention of Ohio, Fifty-First (Legislative Day of April 2), April 4, 1912, Morning Session, 1064, 1067.

25 Ohio's Supreme Court was formed by six members. Taggart, supporting Worthington's proposal of increasing the number to seven by adding a chief justice, argued that a five-vote supermajority should be required to strike down legislation.

26 Ohio's 1912 Constitutional Convention, *supra* note 15, at 1048.

Bowdle argued that the rule would soften the criticism of the courts, protecting them from the current dissatisfaction caused by their decisions. Delegates complained that judges were not deferring to legislative and popular will enough. For instance, Anderson claimed[27] that the opinion of the House of Representatives and the government deserved weight since they had also analyzed and interpreted the Constitution before issuing a given statute, a deferential argument.

Leading the opposition, Worthington claimed that modifying majority rule would violate fundamental legal principles. Worthington contended: "[F]rom the time of the beginning of judicial history, the judgments of courts are the judgments of a majority of the court, and you [Peck] are reversing the whole principle of jurisprudence when you introduce any such provision as that." Worthington also complained that Peck and other progressive delegates did not provide empirical analysis on the unconstitutionality rates of the state Supreme Court. How can we criticize the Court's conservative activism—thought Worthington—if we do not have a concrete numerical balance? For Worthington, an amendment to majority rule could not result "from discussion on the street or elsewhere, but from actual ascertainment, the results—how many statutes have been declared unconstitutional and how many of those decisions are wrong."[28] Peck had to recognize that he did not possess the information.[29]

Other objections voiced were weaker, such as the resistance of members of the legal profession and the opposition of the Hamilton County Bar Association. Delegate Anderson swiftly disregarded such opinions. He repeatedly claimed: "We are not legislating with an eye single for attorneys and the supreme court: we are trying to legislate for the whole people of the state of Ohio."

Taggart's counterproposal, an intermediate position, emerged triumphant in the debate: a six-vote supermajority. However, the rule's final drafting was the product of two perhaps incoherent aims. During the discussions, a sentiment emerged regarding making the Court of Appeals the final stage of judicial procedures to the detriment of the Supreme Court. Delegates decided to supplement such deference to the supermajority rule. To grant weight to a Court of Appeals' decision, delegates lowered the threshold if the Court of Appeals had considered a statute unconstitutional before appealing to the Supreme Court. The approved text of the relevant rule in section 2 of Article

27 Ohio's 1912 Constitutional Convention, *supra* note 18, at 1091.

28 Ohio's 1912 Constitutional Convention, *supra* note 15, at 1048.

29 In 1931, Aumann answered the question by stating that "the supreme court has declared acts of the legislature invalid in no less than 200 cases." Aumann, *supra* note 23, at 372. Aumann stated that the United States Supreme Court held 247 laws unconstitutional between 1850 and 1911. If we consider that this number comprehends both federal legislation and legislation of all the states, Ohio's Court was definitively not showing judicial restraint by those standards.

IV of the Ohio Constitution was that: "[N]o law shall be held unconstitutional and void by the Supreme Court without a concurrence of at least all but one of the judges, except in the affirmance of a judgment of the Court of Appeals declaring a law unconstitutional and void."

The rule had two components, namely a supermajority rule for striking down legislation but, exceptionally, a majority rule to uphold a Court of Appeals declaration of unconstitutionality.

3.1.1.2 The Supermajority and Ohio's Supreme Court: The Sabotage Campaign

The supermajority survived for over half a century, from 1912 to 1968. It took six years for the supermajority to influence any case,[30] which first occurred in *Barker v. City of Akron.*[31] The rule protected workers' rights in the first years, just as the Convention had foreseen. In *DeWitt v. State ex rel. Crabbe*,[32] by a 2:5 vote, the court was unable to strike down workers' compensation regulations, "vindicating the progressive reformers who believed that the supermajority requirement would make it more difficult for the supreme court to strike down worker-protection laws."[33]

Ohio's Supreme Court was not pleased with the approval of the supermajority rule. From the first day of the rule's reign, the Court openly started a sabotage campaign through three fronts: open complaint, evasion, and undermining the precedential status of minority decisions.

Regarding complaints, the Court did little to hide its discontent. Stene observed that the Court took an antagonistic attitude toward the rule and encouraged its evasion.[34] The Court said that its members "deplore such a constitutional provision" in *Jones v. Zangerle*[35] and that the fault of the decisions' consequences "lies, not in the court, but in the constitutional provision which produces such a result." In another case, the Court argued that the rule held the Court in "an unenviable, not to say ridiculous light before courts and lawyers of other states" and that the rule "is violative of the basic principle of popular government."[36] In *Board of Education v. Columbus* the Court also narrated cases in which the rule influenced the outcome to reflect "the extent of the evil which has grown out of the constitutional amendment of 1912."[37]

30 Katherine B. Fite & Louis Baruch Rubinstein, *Curbing the Supreme Court: State Experiences and Federal Proposals*, 35 Michigan L. Rev. 762, 775 (1937).

31 121 N.E. 646 (Ohio 1918).

32 151 N.E. 759 (Ohio 1926).

33 Jonathan L. Entin, *Judicial Supermajorities and the Validity of Statutes: How Mapp Became a Fourth Amendment Landmark Instead of a First Amendment Footnote*, 50 Case. Wes. L. Rev. 441, 455 (2002).

34 Stene, *supra* note 19, at 32.

35 159 N.E. 564 (Ohio 1927).

36 Board of Education v. Columbus, 60 N.E. 902 (Ohio 1928).

37 *Id.*

The Court did everything possible to avoid applying the rule, including insincere voting. In *Board of Education v. City of Columbus*[38] Chief Justice Carrington Marshall admitted two justices had voted to strike down a statute they believed to be constitutional in part.[39] It was open defiance.

Furthermore, the Court sometimes openly disregarded the requirement. In *Patten v. Aluminum Castings Co*[40] a bare majority of the Court held a provision null and void but refrained from using the wording "unconstitutional." The trick was so blatantly illegal that Chief Justice Carrington Marshall issued an opinion calling the decision a "distinct transgression upon the constitution."[41] In *Meyers v. Copeland*[42] the Court concluded that municipal ordinances, although commonly understood as laws enacted by local governments, were not laws in the meaning of the supermajority requirement. Thus, a simple majority sufficed to consider them unconstitutional. Other examples of evasion exist.[43]

In precedential terms, the Court deprived minority decisions under the supermajority rule of precedential status and encouraged the rest of the judiciary to follow suit. *In Board of Education v. Columbus*[44] the Court of Common Pleas and the Court of Appeals refused to follow a previous minority decision, arguing that a minority decision is "binding only in that particular case as an adjudication but is not binding in other cases under the rule of stare decisis." Visibly pleased, the Supreme Court added that courts were "justified in disregarding the former decision of this court rendered by two judges."[45]

The mixed messages sent by the Supreme Court created confusion. They often placed inferior courts in a dilemma, having decisions produced under a legal framework that the Supreme Court openly deemed lacking authority and precedence.[46]

Even Maddox, a critic of the rule, conceded that "the Ohio Supreme Court chafes under the restriction and demonstrates its impatience in no uncertain

38 160 N.E. 902 (Ohio 1928).

39 Chief Justice Carrington Marshall admitted that a 4:2 majority had formed, but judges "who even dissented therefrom, nevertheless concurred in declaring the statute unconstitutional ... This was a plain concession on the part of two of the judges in order to avoid a situation created by the amendment of Section 2 of Article IV."

40 Patten v. Aluminum Castings Co., 105 Ohio St. 1 (1921).

41 "The judgment of this court, agreed in by a bare majority, rendering the provisions of Section 12593, General Code, null and void, even though the decision does not in terms declare it to be unconstitutional, nevertheless constitutes a distinct transgression upon the constitution, because that section cannot be unenforceable upon any grounds other than its unconstitutionality." *Id.*

42 117 Ohio St. 622, 624 (Ohio 1927).

43 Entin, *supra* note 33, at 463. Fite & Rubinstein, *supra* note 30, at 777.

44 118 Ohio St. 295, 299 (Ohio 1928).

45 *Id.*

46 William A. Eggers, *Influence of the Non-Participating Judge*, 5 U. Cin. L. Rev. 375, 378 (1931).

terms, even going so far, seemingly, as to overstate the case at times."[47] Given that the Court openly sabotaged the rule, "overstating the case" seems to understate the Court's behavior.

Despite the Court's open rebellion, the U.S. Supreme Court refused to declare the rule unconstitutional when considering the question in 1930. In 1929, Ohio's Supreme Court decision *State, ex rel. v. Park District*[48] failed to muster a supermajority to strike down the Park District Act. The plaintiffs appealed to the U.S. Supreme Court, represented by Fredrick Henry, himself a former circuit court judge in Ohio until 1912. The Supreme Court unanimously upheld the supermajority in *Ohio v. Akron Park District.*[49] Never again did the U.S. Supreme Court analyze Ohio's supermajority.

3.1.1.3 Practice and Demise

Given that "all but one judge" was required, six of the seven justices of the Court had to concur to strike down legislation, an 85.7 percent supermajority. Originally, Ohio had no surrogate judges system, and thus, absences made it harder to achieve the supermajority.[50] In practice, absences played a minor part in Ohio's Supreme Court. However, there were some examples in which they influenced the case, as in *McBride v. White Motor Co.*[51] It was impossible to declare a law unconstitutional if more than one judge was absent.[52] The situation was repeated in *Pennsylvania Railroad Company v. Pottery Company,*[53]

47 W. Rolland Maddox, *Minority Control of Court Decisions in Ohio*, 24 AM. POLIT. SCI. REV. 638, 647 (1930).

48 120 Ohio St. 464 (Ohio 1929). *See* commentary on the case in Carl L. Meier, *Power of the Ohio Supreme Court to Declare Laws Unconstitutional*, 5 U. CIN. L. REV. 293 (1931).

49 281 U.S. 74 (1930).

50 In the Constitutional Convention, a debate arose on the possible impact of absences on the rule. Knight argued that, if so drafted, the rule could prohibit the Court from hearing constitutional questions if one or more judges were off the bench. Cunningham further argued that such absences were expected, given recusals. Peck replied that, in the case of an absence, the rule should require all sitting judges to concur. Ohio's 1912 Constitutional Convention, *supra* note 15, at 1028–29. After the absences debate occurred again, Peck agreed to require a supermajority of the judges "sitting in the case." Ohio's 1912 Constitutional Convention, Fifty-Fourth Day, 1145. Nonetheless, the quorum-related exception disappeared in the final draft.

51 106 Ohio St. 366, 138 N.E. 45 (1922). The decision was merely a couple of paragraphs. "Three of the members of this court as at present constituted, for personal reasons, declined to participate in the consideration or decision of this case … here being an insufficient number of judges concurring to reverse the judgment of the court of appeals same is hereby affirmed."

52 Wheeler was the first scholar to note that to prevent the court from striking down a law, "[i] t would only be necessary to secure the absence of two of these judges." Everett P. Wheeler, *The New Constitution of Ohio: Power of Courts to Review Acts of the Legislatures*, 75 CENTRAL L.J. 437, 440 (1912). *See also* Meier, *supra* note 48, at 301.

53 122 Ohio St. 503, 174 N.E.2 (1930).

with Justices Carrington Marshall and Robinson not participating, leading to criticism.[54]

After an absence influenced a case again in *State v. Chester*,[55] Ohio's Judicial Council proposed amending the Constitution to allow judges of the Court of Appeals to replace absent members of the Supreme Court. The amendment was approved in 1944, ending the problem.[56]

Supermajority failure decisions were concisely written. The Court issued short statements noting the vote count. Since *Barker v. City of Akron*, all failures to form a supermajority resulted in brief notes, merely a couple of paragraphs affirming or reversing the judgment. Soon, scholarship and courts began referring to these decisions as "minority decisions" or "minority-controlled" decisions.

The rule's biggest problem was not the supermajority but arguably the double threshold. A case required a supermajority only upon a previous upholding. If a court had previously declared a law unconstitutional, a simple majority sufficed to confirm such a decision. Why didn't the Constitutional Convention establish a supermajority for any decision holding a law to be unconstitutional? One theory is that it may have lacked electoral support. From the debates, it is unclear whether a supermajority rule would have attained approval without the double threshold.[57] One could even claim that Ohio's supermajority was the least intrusive design possible as it only functioned after a first instance upholding of a provision.[58]

Given the double threshold, the same statute could be constitutional and unconstitutional in different districts, and the likelihood to determine unconstitutionality might "[v]ary according as to how the Court of Appeals ruled."[59] Bricker, Ohio's Attorney General in 1931, summarized the double threshold problem, saying: "[t]he intermediate courts have greater power in some respects in constitutional questions than does the court of last resort."[60] Shugerman evaluated Ohio's rule negatively and claimed a supermajority should have been required "regardless of how lower courts resolved the matter

54 Eggers, *supra* note 46.

55 42 N.E.2d 993 (Ohio 1942).

56 Entin, *supra* note 33, at 461.

57 Delegate Anderson complained to Peck that the Supreme Court could uphold a previous decision striking down a law by a simple majority if the Court of Appeals held the same opinion. Anderson, considering the case, bitterly concluded: "That is not much of a reform." Peck replied: "That is all we can get." Ohio's 1912 Constitutional Convention, *supra* note 50, at 1142.

58 Michael L. Stokes, *Judicial Restraint and the Presumption of Constitutionality*, 35 U. Toledo L. Rev. 347, 360 (2003).

59 Robert L. Hausser, *Limiting the Voting Power of the Supreme Court: Procedure in the States*, 5 Ohio St. U. L.J. 54, 61 (1939).

60 John W. Bricker, *Shall the Powers of the Supreme Court Be Abridged?*, 16 Proceedings of the Academy of Political Science 40 (1936).

of the law's constitutionality."[61] However, some scholars subsequently disagreed and claimed that the lack of uniformity is not as problematic as it might seem at first glance.[62]

As a general balance, few scholars of the time approved of the rule,[63] most scholars disapproved of it,[64] and all contemporary scholars criticized it.[65] The criticism does not consider the vast impact of Ohio's Supreme Court on the rule's failure.[66] Stene claimed that "certainly the judges of the Supreme Court of Ohio have added to the confusion instead of attempting to do anything to avoid it."[67] The same can be said about the rest of the judiciary.[68] The few cases where the rule was applied were often cited as evidence of the rule's problems; hardly a convincing argument.

The *Mapp* case was probably the most influential supermajority failure decision in Ohio's history.[69] In *Mapp*, the supermajority prevented Ohio's Supreme Court from declaring Ohio's obscenity statute unconstitutional. Having lost in the state Supreme Court, the defendant appealed to the U.S. Supreme Court, which reversed the conviction in *Mapp v. Ohio*,[70] stating that evidence obtained in searches and seizures was inadmissible according to the Fourth Amendment if it had been obtained illegally.

Entin famously argued that *Mapp* would have become a First Amendment footnote without the supermajority requirement.[71] Indeed, had it not been for the supermajority, *Mapp v. Ohio* would not have become a landmark case since Ohio's Supreme Court would have been able to reverse the conviction.[72]

61 Jed Handelsman Shugerman, *A Six-Three Rule: Reviving Consensus and Deference on the Supreme Court*, 37 GA. L. REV. 893, 957 (2003).

62 Stewart T. Herrick, James J. Higgins & Nancy R. Tarlow, *Five-Four Decisions of the United States Supreme Court: Resurrection of the Extraordinary Majority*, 7 SUFFOLK U. L. REV. 807, 840 (1973).

63 For positive assessments, *see* Edward Selden, *Judicial Veto and the Ohio Plan*, 9 ST. LOUIS L. REV. 60 (1923); Aumann, *supra* note 23; Stene, *supra* note 19.

64 Wheeler, *supra* note 52; Maddox, *supra* note 47; Meier, *supra* note 48; Bricker, *supra* note 60.

65 Entin, *supra* note 33; Sandra Zellmer & Kathleen Miller, *The Fallacy of Judicial Supermajority Clauses in State Constitutions*, 47 U. TOL. L. REV. 73 (2015). Shugerman and Caminker are both skeptical of Ohio's design but solely on the double threshold problem. Shugerman, *supra* note 61, at 957; Evan H. Caminker, *Thayerian Deference to Congress and Supreme Court Supermajority Rules: Lessons from the Past*, 78 IND. L.J. 73, 91 (2003).

66 Aumann suggested that the Court's discontent aided the rule's unsatisfactory results. Aumann, *supra* note 23, at 374.

67 Stene, *supra* note 19, at 29.

68 For example, Hausser proposed an interpretation for trial judges and Courts of Appeals to produce consistent results under Ohio's supermajority. Hausser, *supra* note 59, at 84.

69 State v. Mapp, 166 N.E.2d 387 (1960).

70 367 U.S. 643 (1961).

71 Entin, *supra* note 33.

72 ALAN G. TARR & MARY CORNELLA PORTER, STATE SUPREME COURTS IN STATE AND NATION 125 (1988). On a general note, *see also* Entin, *supra* note 33.

In 1968, the supermajority was repealed amidst the so-called Modern Courts Amendment, the first major revision to Ohio's judiciary since its 1851 Constitution.[73] The amendments repealed the supermajority and granted the Supreme Court rule-making authority over its practice and procedure, superseding the authority of enacted statutes.[74] The paradigmatic shift seemed so strong that some called it a significant alteration in the relationship between the Court and the legislative branch.[75] If the supermajority came in with intensive debate in 1912, it went out silently in 1968.[76]

After the amendment to modify the supermajority was voted on, the Court rushed to change the outcome of one of the cases previously discussed in its internal conference. Impatient to get rid of the rule, in *Euclid v. Heaton*[77] the Court went to great lengths to argue that the new majority was applicable despite the date set for its entrance into force.[78] Justice Taft, dissenting, noted that the Court decided to ignore the "effective date and repeal provision," which set an entry into force on January 10, 1970 (after the Court's decision). Taft noted that the Court, in practice, "eliminates that part of the amendment."[79] Befitting its tradition, the Court decided to evade the rule one last time.

Ohio's initial experience had considerable influence in other states. Progressivism was highly influential in the United States, and other states experimented with restrictions on the judiciary during the period. Several proposals to establish supermajorities or a unanimity rule were put forward in Minnesota (1912),[80] Massachusetts (1917),[81] North Dakota (1919), and Nebraska (1920).

73 Maureen O'Connor, *The Ohio Modern Courts Amendment: 45 Years of Progress*, 76 Alb. L. Rev. 1963, 1964 (2012).

74 This particular feature also produced some problems. *See* Richard S. Walinski & Mark D. Wagoner Jr., *Ohio's Modern Courts Amendment Must Be Amended: Why and How*, 66 Clev. St. L. Rev. 69 (2017).

75 Jeffrey A. Parness & Christopher C. Manthey, *Public Process and Ohio Supreme Court Rulemaking*, 28 Clev. St. L. Rev. 249, 250 (1979).

76 Entin, *supra* note 33, at 466.

77 15 Ohio St. 2d 65, 83 (Ohio 1968).

78 Milligan and Pohlman noted at the time that the decision could generate some problems as legislatively the amendment was not intended to have immediate force. William W. Milligan & James E. Pohlman, *The 1968 Modern Courts Amendment to the Ohio Constitution*, 29 Ohio St. L.J. 811, 820 (1968).

79 *Euclid v. Heaton*, *supra* note 77, at 84.

80 Minnesota's amendment gained explicit approval from the electorate but failed under Minnesota's rules on adopting amendments. Minnesota Constitutional Amendments: History and Legal Principles, Research Department, Minnesota House of Representatives, 2013, 65. The amendment achieved 127,352 votes in favor and 68,886 votes against, with 160,668 blank ballots. Given that the rules required more than half of the votes, the measure fell short by around 50,000 votes.

81 The proposal failed to gain the support of Massachusetts' Constitutional Convention. Hausser, *supra* note 59, at 797.

3.1.2 North Dakota: A Nonpartisan Supermajority (1919-Present)

North Dakota's supermajority is intrinsically related to the Nonpartisan League (NPL). The NPL was a political organization founded by Arthur Townley that emerged in North Dakota in 1915. The League was created in response to farmers' concerns over exploitation by out-of-state companies and politicians. Since its founding, the NPL was controversial and associated with socialist ideas. As was typical of progressive movements in the period, the NPL mistrusted courts as defenders of corporations and elite economic interests. Leaguers believed they had been wronged through abusive bank loans and that ordinary politicians were doing nothing to improve their harsh conditions. NPL members were often stigmatized as socialists and anarchists but were primarily farmers searching for political equality.

3.1.2.1 The NPL and the Supermajority's Adoption

Even though the League rose to prominence in 1917, its incursion into the Supreme Court occurred a year earlier. In 1916, three of the five North Dakota Supreme Court justices were to be elected. The NPL, attempting to gain influence in the state, mobilized its supporters.

The NPL understood the importance of courts as enablers or blockers of social change. The North Dakota Supreme Court had limited the ability of the people to propose amendments to the Constitution through an initiative petition by interpreting that the legislature had to provide further legislation to place an amendment on the ballot.[82] The decision was controversial even among scholars at the time.[83] Perhaps, as one claims, the League was aware that the judiciary could stop future changes by determining they were unconstitutional.[84]

The League endorsed all three justices elected—Justices Grace, Birdzell, and the colorful Robinson.[85] With his unconventional manners and lack of respect for court protocol, Robinson clashed with then Chief Justice Bruce. After leaving the court, Bruce claimed that the newly elected justices behaved

82 State ex rel. Linde v. Hall, 35 N.D. 34, 159 N.W. 281 (1916).

83 *See* W.L.O., *Constitutional Amendments, Self-Executing and Otherwise, Providing for the Initiative and Referendum*, 15 Mich. L. Rev. 334, 338 (1917) (noting the Court's interpretation caused disappointment in the people who managed to attain support for proposing an amendment).

84 Andrew Alexander Bruce, Non-Partisan League 170 (1921).

85 Robert Vogel, *Justice Robinson and the Supreme Court of North Dakota*, 58 North Dakota L. Rev. 83, 84 (1982).

in an unprecedented partisan manner,[86] although some scholars challenged the claim.[87]

After its success in the Supreme Court elections, the NPL won the gubernatorial elections with Lynn Frazier in 1917 and soon had a majority in the House of Representatives. The legislative enactments of the NPL legislature included compensation for those who served jail time unjustly, a minimum wage for women, maximum working hours, and disability compensation for workers. Even Bruce, a fierce critic of the League, had to concede that the legislation "will appear to the casual reader unobjectionable."[88] Among many economic amendments, the NPL promoted a state-owned mill and elevator and a state-owned bank.

The legislation was not enough. There was a consensus that economic reform required constitutional change, partly because of the U.S. Supreme Court's Lochner doctrine. North Dakota's amendment procedure was particularly complicated. The NPL deemed a constitutional convention too time-consuming and decided to develop an alternative strategy for constitutional change.

Arguing that no procedure was foreseen to establish a new Constitution, the NPL contended that the legislature could frame a new Constitution and submit it directly to the people's vote.[89] While critics claimed the attempt would lead to anarchy and revolution, the League contended it was democratic and similar to a constitutional convention. The League moved forward with the proposal under House Bill 44.

House Bill 44 established the right to hold recall elections, imposed taxation for state hail insurance, raised the state debt limit, and provided a four-year term for state and county officers instead of the previous two-year period. Morlan's seminal work on the League considered the proposed changes "scarcely earth-shaking ... but in the minds of the anti-League press, the end of the American way of life was clearly at sight."[90] One proposed change was introducing a supermajority to strike down legislation, requiring a four-fifths vote in the Supreme Court. The House approved House Bill 44 with minor

86 Upon his exit from the Court, Bruce would write resentfully that the NPL conceived judges as elected representatives and narrated his personal clashes with Justice Robinson. Bruce, *supra* note 84, at 170.

87 Contemporary scholars have contended that the Court did not show a strong ideological shift. Vogel, *supra* note 85, at 89. Perhaps Vogel's view is more accurate. Had the three justices behaved in a partisan manner to the extent suggested by Bruce, the League would not have felt the need to support the majority required to strike down legislation, as Meschke and Smith claimed. Herbert L. Meschke & Ted Smith, *The North Dakota Supreme Court: A Century of Advances*, 76 North Dakota L. Rev. 217, 247 (2000).

88 Bruce, *supra* note 84, at 92.

89 Robert L. Morlan, Political Prairie Fire: The Nonpartisan League, 1915-1922 101 (1955).

90 *Id.* at 102.

changes by a wide margin.[91] Nonetheless, the NPL lacked a majority in the Senate at the time and, unsurprisingly, the Senate killed the bill a few days later.[92]

The NPL, however, kept gaining political strength and soon commenced bringing some of the failed "new constitution" proposals as individual amendments.[93] In view of this, in 1917, several non-League senators began introducing amendments "designed to take the wind out of the sails of House Bill 44."[94] Some opposition proposals even resembled those formerly endorsed by the NPL. The League became bitter towards the opposition because of "the efforts in the Senate to pirate league legislation."[95]

The supermajority seems to have been one of the aforementioned amendments, as it was proposed in HB 366, sponsored by Staale Hendrickson.[96] Hendrickson was not a leaguer. A core Republican himself, Hendrickson had openly spoken against the NPL. Furthermore, opposition Senator McBride chaired the Judiciary Committee in the Senate, which approved the amendment.[97]

The fact that a change in the majority required a constitutional amendment derived from the Constitution in force. Article IV of the Judicial Department of the 1889 Constitution provided for a majority threshold in section 89. In the 1889 Constitutional Convention, no debate occurred on why to establish a simple majority or to constitutionalize the rule. Had North Dakota followed the lead of other states that did not mention a majority in the Constitution, arguably an ordinary bill may have sufficed to raise the majority.

The supermajority found natural support in the NPL. Judicial limitation was entrenched in the NPL philosophy. North Dakota was among the states

91 Initially, the proposed language was "provided that no less than four of the five judges shall concur in any opinion declaring any law unconstitutional." The House Committee on State Affairs Report suggested the language "provided that no law shall be declared unconstitutional unless four of the five judges concur in the decision." *See* State of North Dakota. Journal of the House of the Fifteenth Session of the Legislative Assembly, Jan. 2–Mar. 2, 1917, Bismarck, North Dakota, Tribune State Printers and Binders, 1917, 241. I thank Paula Amelsberg from the North Dakota Supreme Court Library for her assistance in obtaining the historical records of HB 44 and HB 366.

92 Morlan, *supra* note 89, at 104.

93 Michael J. Lansing, Insurgent Democracy: The Nonpartisan League in North American Politics 144 (2015).

94 Morlan, *supra* note 89, at 105.

95 *Id.*

96 Hendrickson's proposal was briefly discussed in the newspaper *Jamestown Weekly Alert* on Mar. 8, 1917. Its approval in the Senate's Judiciary Committee was reported in the Grand Forks Herald on Mar. 1, 1917.

97 Furthermore, former Chief Justice Bruce, an open critic of the League and an expert on the judiciary, did not criticize the supermajority in his work on the League, even though he severely criticized the attitude of the League vis-à-vis the Supreme Court. Bruce's approach supports the theory that HB 366 was either a non-partisan compromise or a product of the phenomena described by Morlan.

that discussed supermajorities in the progressive era, based on a feeling that federal and state judges were rendering decisions that harmed the public interest.[98] The ethos of the supermajority seemed to guarantee higher deference to the elected branches. As Bosworth said: "[T]he founders did not want unelected officers overruling popular will."[99] The rule could also be interpreted in a broader context as complementing provisions that embraced popular democracy.[100]

Even though one could easily claim that the supermajority attempted to control the Court, that was hardly the case. By the time the supermajority was introduced, the NPL had already managed to get three of its candidates elected to the five-member North Dakota Supreme Court. In addition to not sponsoring the bill, the NPL did not need to defend itself against Supreme Court intrusion since it had a majority of justices ideologically aligned with it. As a matter of principle, the NPL felt that judicial review could be exercised as long as a clear consensus on what is unconstitutional had arisen in the Court.

HB 366 was approved in the House and the Senate[101] and put forward to the electorate. On May 11, 1918, the electorate considered ten constitutional amendments, including HB 366. The supermajority proposal received the most support of them all and soon entered into force.[102]

The supermajority is provided in Article VI, section 4 of the North Dakota Constitution, which states: "[T]he supreme court shall not declare a legislative enactment unconstitutional unless at least four of the members of the court so decide."

3.1.2.2 The Rule's Functioning

North Dakota's four-fifths supermajority is considerable. The rule means 80 percent of the court has to agree on a provision's unconstitutionality. Although slightly less than Ohio's counterpart (85.7 percent), in practical terms, the supermajority in both states implied that nothing more than a single dissent blocked an unconstitutionality decision. In a five-member Supreme Court, a 4:1 supermajority was the only possible alternative to a majority. It is unclear if North Dakota would have opted for a lighter version of the rule if the Supreme Court had had more members.

98 John J. Dinan, The American State Constitutional Tradition 126 (2006).

99 Matthew H. Bosworth, Courts as Catalysts: State Supreme Courts and Public School Finance Equity 169 (2001).

100 Theodore B. Pedelski, *A Constitution Implements Popular Democracy*, *in* The Constitutionalism of American States 549, 557 (George E. Connors & Christopher W. Hammons eds., 2008).

101 Unfortunately, it seems that in North Dakota, no legislative discussions are available predating 1957. I thank Paula Amelsberg from North Dakota's Supreme Court Library for her assistance in tracking down the historical records.

102 The amendment had a one-month *vacatio legis*.

Given the lack of referral to Ohio's amendment in the procedures and debates of the period, it is uncertain to what extent Ohio's supermajority influenced the North Dakota rule. Six years had passed since Ohio's experiment, already revealing some problems. The fact that North Dakota's rule covered them may indicate some reflection. For example, North Dakota had no double threshold. The court needs to muster a supermajority regardless of how inferior courts had ruled on the matter. Even if this meant disregarding the deference to first-instance decisions, as Ohio had attempted to ensure, it guaranteed stability and uniformity across the state.

Furthermore, contrary to Ohio—until 1944—absences did not increase the supermajority, which would otherwise result in a unanimity requirement. Conflicts of interest or incapacitation were addressed by appointing an acting or retired judge or justice to temporarily sit in the Court, as per Article VI, section 11 of the Constitution. The mechanism of surrogate judges was not new. It had existed since the 1889 Constitution before the supermajority was adopted.[103] Since 1916, in *State ex rel. Linde v. Robinson*,[104] the court confirmed that the votes of surrogate justices counted in determining the constitutionally required majority to decide. When adopting the supermajority, North Dakota lawmakers knew recusals or illnesses would not increase the required percentage. North Dakota may always decide a case with five justices on the bench.[105] Nonetheless, it seems that a surrogate justice need not always be called. For example, in *Daly* the court faced a situation in which two of the sitting members were already blocking a supermajority decision, and two surrogate justices had already disqualified themselves. The court felt no need to keep on calling a fifth judge and entered a four-justices decision[106] upon a 2:2 tie.

103 The substitution mechanism was briefly discussed. *See* R. M. Tuttle (Official Stenographer), Official Report of the Proceedings and Debates of the First Constitutional Convention of North Dakota (July 4th to August 17th, 1889) 274–76 (1889).

104 35 N.D. 417, 160 N.W. 514 (1916). The case, curiously, involved the ability of the NPL justices to sit in court immediately upon election.

105 Formally, the Chief Justice has the authority to appoint the surrogate justice. Theoretically, the Chief Justice could try to appoint a surrogate justice more likely to vote with his/her position. As Justice Tufte explained, a series of strong customary procedures limit the Chief Justice's discretion. In a nutshell, the Chief Justice traditionally delegates the task to the clerk of the court, which sends a mail to district court judges asking their availability to sit with the Supreme Court on a given session. As a matter of custom, the first judge to reply is conveyed, and the tight agenda of district court judges ensures diversity in the surrogates. Jerod Tufte, *Interview with a Justice of the North Dakota Supreme Court* (unpublished, 2023).

106 *See* Daly v. Beery, 45 N.D. 287, 178 N.W. Rep. 104. Christianson explained the situation swiftly: "Inasmuch as all members of the court were of the opinion that the act does not contravene the 14th Amendment; and inasmuch as two members of the court—Justices Grace and Robinson—declared themselves to be of the opinion that the act does not contravene any provision of the state Constitution, no other district judge was called ... for under our Constitution the vote of Justices Grance and Robinson is decisive on the constitutional question."

Finally, North Dakota fixed the covered scope of the supermajority. As discussed above, since Ohio's rule applied to "laws," its Supreme Court discussed whether it covered municipal ordinances, generating debate. North Dakota's version referred to the broader term "legislative enactments,"[107] thus settling the question.[108]

A vote failing to meet the supermajority blocks a declaration of unconstitutionality. North Dakota's Supreme Court has used the term "insufficient majority" to name the decisions. In a supermajority failure, it seems that the Court's majority still controls the case's disposition, issuing a decision joined by three votes.[109] Customarily, the Court may include a brief unsigned opinion explaining the holding.[110] In historical times, Justice Birdzell deemed that the rule forced justices in the majority to vote for the result that the minority preferred, a practice that was not followed.[111] Opinions issued by the majority and minority in such cases have led to debates on which is the controlling opinion.[112]

The supermajority did not produce significant problems, given the few occasions on which the Court applied the rule. Scarce analysis exists on any evasion mechanism. One prominent example is *Olson v. Maxwell*.[113] In the *Olson* case, the Court failed to gather a supermajority to strike down section 54-21-25 of the North Dakota Century Code, granting the Director of Institutions authority to transfer women and other prisoners outside the state.

107 The Supreme Court hinted in the *Materi* case that municipal ordinances were comprehended in the supermajority provision. *See* City of Bismarck v. Materi, 177 N.W.2d 530 (N.D. 1970). I thank Justice Tufte for pointing out this case.

108 However, this is not fully conclusive evidence that the problems of Ohio influenced North Dakota representatives. The municipality ordinances evasion cases occurred in 1927, a few years after North Dakota opted for the "legislative enactment" term. *See* Entin, *supra* note 33, at 457.

109 James E. Leahy, The North Dakota State Constitution 125 (2011). Accordingly, Chief Justice VandeWalle declared in 2003 that in supermajority failure decisions "[a] majority of three still controls the final disposition of the case [beyond the question of a law's constitutionality]." Shugerman, *supra* note 61. at 955.

110 Tufte, *supra* note 105.

111 In *Daly v. Beery*, Birdzell, having been on the insufficient majority, declared: "There is no way to give effect to this constitutional provision unless the members of this Court respect it as a part of the fundamental law by directing a judgment to be entered in individual cases which may not conform to their views as to what the judgment should be. Entertaining this opinion, I deem it my duty to vote for a reversal of the order." Despite Birdzell wanting to uphold the appealed decision, he voted for the reversal. This method differs from that which currently prevails, in which a 3:2 vote to strike down the outcome is considered as having equivalent effect to a vote to uphold the legislation.

112 In the *Mason* case, the Court issued an opinion explaining why the majority thought a statute unconstitutional, despite lacking the four votes required to strike it down. The opinion had no practical effect (other than conveying that a majority could not strike down legislation) and could even have confused lower courts about the relevant law. *See* State ex rel. Mason v. Baker, 288 N.W. 202 (N.D. 1939).

113 259 N.W.2d 621 (1977).

The three-justice majority expressly argued that the provision was unconstitutional[114] but recognized they lacked a supermajority to strike down the statute. The insufficient majority still claimed the prisoner's transfer was unconstitutional as it violated due process requirements. The effect of the decision on the petitioner was pretty much as if the statute would have been invalid.

Another example is *Bismarck Public School District 1 v. State*. The court analyzed an appeal against a district court decision that determined that a statute establishing the school financing scheme was unconstitutional. The court failed to secure the four votes. Nonetheless, the three-justice majority largely affirmed the district court's ruling.[115]

When interviewed by Shugerman in 2003, Chief Justice VandeWalle declared that the North Dakota Supreme Court had not had evasion attempts on the rule,[116] but this does not seem to be entirely the case. At least in a couple of instances, the insufficient majority has achieved the same result as striking down the statute without doing so, through interpretation and broad-reading techniques. However, the cases cited are insufficient to conclude that the rule is generally evaded.

The supermajority also seems to play a role when deciding whether or not the court will exercise its discretionary original jurisdiction. In the *Fighting Sioux* case[117] the court was asked in its original jurisdiction to decide if a statute complied with the Constitution by requiring the University of North Dakota to use "Fighting Sioux" as a nickname and logo.[118] Spirit Lake Sioux tribe members deemed the nickname offensive to Native Americans. Three justices believed the case to be ripe, while two believed the issue was improperly before the court. The court rejected the application because a supermajority to hear the case was not achieved, although the Constitution requires such a majority only for decisions involving the unconstitutionality of statutes. The court interpreted majority requirements for declaring a statute unconstitutional as homologated to majority requirements to exercise original jurisdiction. Some interesting debates might have ensued had the court taken the case.[119]

114 The majority claimed: "We therefore hold that Section 54-21-25, N.D.C.C., as written and as applied to female prisoners transferred to other States, is unconstitutional as violative of procedural due process and as an impermissible delegation to the Director of Institutions of legislative power."

115 511 N.W.2d 247 (N.D. 1994). Justice Sandstrom summarized the Court's path to avoid the rule in his dissenting opinion: "The majority purports to affirm the district court; yet it declares no statute unconstitutional but says the 'effect' of the education finance system is an unconstitutional result."

116 Shugerman, *supra* note 61, at 955.

117 North Dakota State Board of Higher Education v. Jaeger, 2012 N.D. 64 (N.D. 2012).

118 For an introduction to the case, *see* North Dakota Law Review Associate Editors, *North Dakota Supreme Court Review*, 88 North Dakota L. Rev. 516, 528 (2012).

119 In the *Akron* case, Ohio's supermajority had been deemed valid by the U.S. Supreme Court because the appellants had been able to test all issues thoroughly in the trial and Appellate Court. Hauser argued that the Supreme Court did not solve what would have occurred

The court has shown no signs of the discontent characterizing Ohio's Supreme Court. The supermajority even gained the approval of some justices early on, as some commentators noticed.[120] In *Daly v. Beery*[121] Justice Robinson made favorable comments regarding the supermajority, seconded by Birdzell's and Christianson's acceptance.[122] While Robinson could have been influenced by the fact that his criteria prevailed despite being in the minority, Birdzell was on the losing side of the insufficient majority. Both justices had been appointed with NPL support and could be deemed to share a similar philosophy of deference towards the elected branches. In no opinion has any justice criticized the rule. Acceptance seems to be universal.

Undoubtedly, the most well-known supermajority failure decision occurred in the 2014 abortion ban case: *MKB Management Corp. v. Burdick*.[123] In 2011 and 2013, North Dakota passed SB 2305 and HB 1456, also known as the "Heartbeat" abortion ban. The bill prohibited abortion after a detectable heartbeat in an unborn child, roughly a five-week period. Several clinics challenged the constitutionality of the provisions. A district court of Cass County enjoined the state from enforcing the provisions, considering the likelihood that the plaintiffs would prevail in the state constitutional challenge.[124] The Chief Administrator of the Department of Health appealed, and the Supreme Court of North Dakota had to decide the case. A curious paradox arose. The Plaintiffs seemed to have brought arguments on the provisions' unconstitutionality both vis-à-vis the state and federal constitutions.

Justice Kapsner and Surrogate Justice Maring considered the statute to infringe on the state Constitution, while Chief Justice VandeWalle and Justice Sandstrom considered that no right to abortion existed under the state Constitution. Justice Crothers believed it was unnecessary to decide the issue. However, Justices Crothers, Kesner, and Maring deemed the statute unconstitutional regarding the federal Constitution, as prescribed at the time by *Roe*

in *Akron* had Ohio's Supreme Court exercised its original and not appellate jurisdiction. Hausser, *supra* note 59, at 73. Hausser never had the chance to test the hypothesis. The *Fighting Sioux* case would have been an interesting opportunity, as the parties would only have been able to assert their claims once.

120 For Justice Robinson's approval, *see* Fite & Rubinstein, *supra* note 30, at 779. For Birdzell's, *see* Entin, *supra* note 33, at 168.

121 45 N.D. 287, 178 N.W. Rep. 104.

122 Robinson wrote: "A recent amendment to the Constitution indicates the people have come to learn that judges are not infallible, and it is well to limit the power to annul even an act of the legislative assembly … The power which courts have assumed, by a bare majority of one, to hold void acts of Congress and legislative enactments, may soon be a thing of the past." Birdzell said that, considering the supermajority rule, it was his duty to vote for reversing the order, although he disagreed with such an outcome. Christianson merely pointed out that he agreed that Justices Grace and Robinson's votes were decisive on the constitutional question.

123 2014 N.D. 197 (N.D. 2014).

124 North Dakota Law Review Associate Editors, *North Dakota Supreme Court Review*, 90 North Dakota L. Rev. 637, 639 (2014).

v. Wade.[125] Only the Chief Justice believed the provision to conform to the federal Constitution, while Sandstrom claimed the issue was improperly raised, and the court was constrained to analyzing only the provisions' conformity to the state constitution.

As a result, a 2:2:1 tie resulted in the conformity of the provision to the state constitution, and a 3:1:1 favored declaring it unconstitutional regarding the federal Constitution. No position commanded either the four votes to uphold the appealed decision or the three votes to reverse it.

Nonetheless, Kapsner and Maring deemed that the supermajority was only applicable to decisions employing the state Constitution as a parameter. Thus, they considered the three-vote bare majority sufficient to uphold the decision of unconstitutionality. The court voted on the supermajority's applicability. Crothers, who believed the abortion ban infringed the Federal Constitution, did not believe that the supermajority could be so evaded. Justice Crothers' opinion remarked that nothing in Article VI, section 4 allowed inferring that the supermajority applied only to state law, and thus, it also applied to legislation contrasted with the federal Constitution.

By a 3:2 vote, the Supreme Court held that no sufficient majority had been reached as to the provision's unconstitutionality. The vote is detailed in Table 3.1.

Table 3.1 MKB Management Corp. v. Burdick vote

Justice	*Unconstitutionality vis-à-vis the State Constitution*	*Unconstitutionality vis-à-vis the Federal Constitution*	*Was a supermajority reached?*
VandeWalle (CJ)	No	No	No
Sandstrom	No	Not properly raised	No
Crothers	Need not be decided	Yes	No
Kapsner	Yes	Yes	Yes
Maring (SJ)	Yes	Yes	Yes

CJ: Chief Justice
SJ: Surrogate Justice

In their dissenting opinion, Kapsner and Maring claimed that the supermajority could not dissolve an injunction correctly entered under federal law. Their opinion reasoned that the supermajority had to be read in light of Article I, section 23 of North Dakota's Constitution—the supremacy of the U.S. Constitution—and suggested that state judges disregard the supermajority clause when considering unconstitutionality claims under federal law.

125 410 U.S. 113 (1973).

Kapsner and Maring made an argumentative leap. By quoting Article VI of the federal Constitution, they suggested that a state judge may ignore state procedural regulations to protect federal law. Not only is the claim problematic, but it may also engage in a *petitio principii*. They claimed that since they understood the provision to be incompatible with the federal Constitution, they could disregard the method set forth by the state constitution to conclude so. The same argument could have been raised if the Court voted 3:2 to reverse the decision: majority voting should have been disregarded as a rule to protect federal law.

The supermajority is a decisional method. Absent a supermajority, even three votes are just the personal opinion of the Court's members and not a conclusion of the unconstitutionality of the challenged provision. Kapsner and Maring's objection is not a new one. In 1937, some scholars had already claimed that the *Akron* case—analyzing the constitutionality of Ohio's supermajority—left undecided "the question as to whether when a state statute is squarely challenged under the Federal Constitution, a state may constitutionally determine the vote required in its supreme court to hold the statute invalid under the Federal Constitution."[126] Nonetheless, supermajorities are similar to other internal procedural requirements in state law. The fact that federal law may be at stake does not deprive states of competence to determine their internal regulations for decision-making, and courts may only arrive at a decision through their valid procedures.[127]

The dispute did not end there. The United States District Court for the District of North Dakota, Southwestern Division, held that the bill was unconstitutional[128] based at that time on *Roe v. Wade*, a result the supermajority had prevented in North Dakota's Supreme Court.[129]

126 Fite & Rubinstein, *supra* note 30, at 778.

127 In 1970, Madgett considered such an argument under the supremacy clause. Madgett understood the paradox and conceded that "it requires reasoning from an ad hoc position. Its underlying premise is that there exists a federal right which demands recognition, but which the state court, solely because of the concurrence rule, refuses to recognize." Paul W. Madgett, *The Five-Judge Rule in Nebraska*, 2 Creighton L. Rev. 329, 336 (1968). Madgett elegantly argued that courts, not judges, make the law. Thus, under North Dakota's procedural regulations, the opinion of Crothers, Maring, and Kapsner is not law, as it is not the court's opinion—*i.e.*, it is insufficient to conclude the existence of an infringement of a federal right.

128 For a comment on the decision, *see* Annique M. Lockard, *Abortion and Birth Control: Constitutional Law: Constitutionality of North Dakota's Legislative Ban on Abortions before Viability*, 90 N. D. L. Rev. 212 (2014).

129 A few years later, *Roe v. Wade* was overturned in *Dobbs v. Jackson Women's Health Organization*, 142 S. Ct. 2228, 2240 (2022).

3.1.2.3 Assessing the Rule's Success

Scholars are not divided in the functioning of the rule. Most scholars who have analyzed the practical functioning of North Dakota's supermajority conclude that it works positively and unproblematically.[130] Others are neutral towards the rule,[131] and critics have disagreed with it mainly on principle[132] or atypical grounds.[133]

Justice Tufte considers a series of factors relevant as to why the rule has not been a burden to the court. First, North Dakota does not have an intermediate Court of Appeals[134] nor docket control through certiorari, solving its cases primarily through mandatory jurisdiction.[135] This feature results in plenty of ordinary cases, not as politically charged as those usually selected through certiorari in the U.S. Supreme Court, in which the Court can unanimously agree on outcomes. Justice Tufte considers that those cases perhaps foster collegiality, as justices are accustomed to agreeing in plenty of cases and contribute to an environment of consensus perceived throughout the Court.[136]

Furthermore, justices seem to place additional work in seeking common grounds even before deliberation formally commences. The North Dakota Supreme Court assigns opinions before oral arguments and conference deliberations. As such, a justice knows, sometimes six weeks in advance, that he/she will draft an opinion in a case involving the constitutionality of a statute where the supermajority is applicable. Justice Tufte reveals that he notices the unique nature of these cases and, as part of his working methodology, he pays particular attention to them, studying the briefs and the case many weeks in advance to be able actively to place the most relevant questions during oral

130 Fite & Rubinstein, *supra* note 30, at 779; Entin, *supra* note 33, at 468; Shugerman, *supra* note 61, at 955–56; Caminker, *supra* note 65, at 92–93; David Orentlicher, *Judicial Consensus: Why the Supreme Court Should Decide Its Cases Unanimously*, 54 Conn. L. Rev. 303, 423 (2022).

131 Meschke & Smith, *supra* note 87, at 247–48. Notably, Meschke was a Supreme Court justice for almost fifteen years, and thus had ample chance to have personal experience on whether the rule could cause problems.

132 Schapiro deemed the supermajority was "aberrational" on the grounds that it had saved a single statute in the Bismarck Public School District Case. Robert A. Schapiro, *Contingency and Universalism in State Separation of Powers Discourse*, 4 Roger Williams U. L. Rev. 79, 103 (1998). Without further study, Schapiro's argument is hardly more than personal preference.

133 Redmond disagreed with the supermajority in that it had saved too few provisions from being struck down and that the Court had still managed to find unanimity to declare laws unconstitutional on several occasions. William Redmond, *Requirement in State Constitution of More than a Majority of the Supreme Court to Invalidate Legislation*, 19 Nebraska L. Bull. 32, 34 (1940).

134 Gerald W. VandeWalle, *North Dakota Distinctives*, 76 Alb. L. Rev. 2019, 2023 (2012).

135 *Id.* at 2019.

136 Tufte, *supra* note 105.

arguments[137] and provide persuasive opinions during conference deliberations, which occur both in the same day.[138] Although we cannot generalize individual judicial methodologies, other justices may take a similar approach.

Other features of the court's working methodology contribute to the quest for consensus. Aside from conference deliberation, the court employs *Teams* as collaboration software. Each case is assigned a thread, and justices can express their doubts and suggestions on cases, with the remaining court membership bearing witness to the contentious issues.[139] This informal working mechanism may de facto extend direct deliberation among justices.[140] The fact that the court typically sees fewer than ten cases yearly involving the constitutionality of statutes grants additional time for deliberation and compromise, although the court has a numerically challenging remaining workload.

Individual judicial philosophies impact the degree of deference granted by the supermajority. In 2003, Caminker considered the supermajority operated in addition to the Thayerian presumption of constitutionality.[141] Nonetheless, justices may have different approaches. For example, Justice Jerod Tufte, an originalist who vigorously advocates for robust constitutional interpretation,[142] approaches cases by searching for the consistently best interpretation of the Constitution through his originalist methodology, not by deferring by principle to the legislature. Justice Tufte disagrees with a strong presumption of constitutionality but considers the supermajority rule helps the Court achieve the strong conviction required to invalidate a statute.[143]

137 The scholarship has debated the deliberative contribution of oral arguments. *See* Mathilde Cohen, *Ex Ante Versus Ex Post Deliberations: Two Models of Judicial Deliberations in Courts of Last Resort*, 62 AM. J. COMP. L. 951, 938 (2014). Others have highlighted that justices may use oral arguments to convey to their colleagues their current preferred positions. BRIAN M. BARRY, HOW JUDGES JUDGE: EMPIRICAL INSIGHTS INTO JUDICIAL DECISION-MAKING 194 (2021).

138 Tufte, *supra* note 105.

139 *Id.*

140 Scholarship has previously analyzed informal dynamics of inter-chambers deliberation. See Cohen, *supra* note 137, at 991. North Dakota's Supreme Court seems to benefit from broader informal dynamics of post-conference deliberation, allowed by contemporary technological advancements.

141 Caminker, *supra* note 65, at 92. *See also* State v. Miller, 129 N.W.2d 356, 361 (N.D. 1964). The Court even invoked the presumption relatively recently in Denault v. State, 2017 ND 167, § 16, 898 N.W.2d 452, 457–58 (2017).

142 For example, in his concurring opinion in *Ekstrom*, Justice Tufte rejected the notion that the North Dakota Constitution should be necessarily interpreted similarly to analogous provisions of the Federal Constitution. "When interpreting the North Dakota Constitution, we are not bound to follow in lockstep federal doctrine implementing similar federal provisions." City of W. Fargo v. Le Ekstrom, 2020 N.D. 37 (N.D. 2020).

143 Justice Tufte explained his view at length: "The Court must impartially seek the correct meaning of the Constitution without regard to the statute in question. For example, if a statute has more than one plausible meaning and only one of them is constitutional, we should apply that meaning. That's called constitutional avoidance. But if a statute has only one plausible meaning and the arguably conflicting constitutional provision has more than one plausible meaning, we should not presume the correct meaning of the constitution is the

North Dakota's supermajority keeps functioning to this date. The fact that the rule has worked swiftly resulted in no significant proposals to alter or modify it. Since its introduction in 1920, the rule has functioned for over a hundred years, producing less than ten instances of supermajority failures. It is the oldest supermajority in constitutional adjudication still functioning in the world.

3.1.3 Nebraska (1920–Present)

Progressivism also influenced Nebraska's Constitutional Convention. A desire to limit potential conservative court decisions roamed through the debates.[144] Starting in 1903, Nebraska enacted social legislation supported by progressive Governors Mickey and Sheldon.[145]

3.1.3.1 Constitutional Convention Discussion in Nebraska

In 1920, Nebraska convened a Constitutional Convention. The Lochner phantom was present in the discussions. Much like in Ohio, the presence of prominent political figures and their speeches left an imprint on the Convention. If Roosevelt was the dominant figure in Ohio's Convention, Nebraska's influencer was undoubtedly William Jennings Bryan.

Known as "The Great Commoner" due to his faith in ordinary people, Bryan had run for President three times and had been a Secretary of State under President Wilson. A powerful orator, Bryan urged the Convention to limit the judiciary's power to declare statutes unconstitutional. His political influence in Nebraska and former positions certainly made his opinion significant. Unlike Ohio's Convention, in which Roosevelt's speech, or his own, did little in favor of a supermajority, Bryan's address seems to have had a powerful effect in Nebraska.[146]

---

one that permits the statute to stand. I think courts err when they use the presumption of constitutionality to interpret a constitutional provision to avoid conflict with a statute. The Court should reach a clear, strong conviction of a conflict before declaring a statute invalid. The supermajority rule helps ensure that the court as a whole has that strong conviction." Tufte, *supra* note 105.

144 Some scholars hold a contrary view and deem that the delegates elected were rather conservative. Addison E. Sheldon, *The Nebraska Constitutional Convention, 1919-1920*, 15 The American Political Science Review 391, 393 (1921). Winter disagrees and evaluates the constitutional outcome as very liberal, for the Convention's position on women's suffrage, binding public utilities, and labor dispute solutions. A.B. Winter, *Constitutional Revision in Nebraska: A Brief History and Commentary*, 40 Nebraska L. Rev. 580, 589 (1961).

145 John R. Wunder & Mark R. Scherer, Echo of Its Time: The History of the Federal District Court of Nebraska, 1867-1933 183 (2019).

146 Maddox held the view that, even though Roosevelt failed to convince Ohio's Convention to adopt judicial recall, his speech was so influential that he "[s]ucceeded in creating a feeling that something must be done; and an amendment to the judiciary article was adopted, read-

This time, in his address, Bryan said that the Supreme Court:

> [o]nly should have power to declare a law unconstitutional, and it only by a three-fourths vote of the Court. It is not fair to the legislators or to those who elect them—especially when we have the referendum—to allow what they have declared to be the people's will to be overthrown by one Judge. When a majority decision is permitted, a majority of one can nullify a law. If more than one-fourth of a court stands for the constitutionality of a law, they give support to the action of those who passed it. It is not fair to give to one Judge the power to make his opinion supreme, not only over a minority of his associates, but over the entire legislature.[147]

Since 1912, Bryan had clearly refined his views and decided to favor a supermajority to conciliate consensus, legitimacy, and the practical nature of the mechanism. His words resounded on Nebraska's delegate, Isaiah David Evans.

Evans put forward proposal 313 on the supermajority. Evans was not a member of the Judiciary Committee. He listed "farmer" as his main occupation in the Convention's debates. Although the law was not Evans' primary expertise, he had been a representative before. Being a firm believer in popular democracy, he had been a candidate of his party for house speaker. As a politician, Evans' interests had been workers' compensation, liability, and telephone monopolies.[148]

Unlike Peck in Ohio, to whom unanimity was another piece in a coherent theory of jurisprudence, for Evans, the supermajority rule did not form part of his legal vision. Bryan, a reputed politician with whom Evans shared progressive ideas, certainly was a significant influence.

Evans' proposal was discussed in the Judiciary Committee and the Plenary. Andrew Robert Oleson, a lawyer and Swedish émigré who had been a district court judge, attempted to prevent the supermajority from being adopted and moved to suppress the rule. Oleson claimed that citizens depended on courts to defend their rights, thus hindering the Court's ability to do so struck at the heart of judicial function. Oleson even suggested that, if anything, it would be better to create a rule that requires "more than a majority" in order to declare

ing as follows [supermajority]." Maddox's interpretation seems unlikely. Judicial recall and supermajorities were radically different forms of limiting the judiciary. Furthermore, Peck had proposed the supermajority before Roosevelt's speech to the Convention. Peck is to be credited for vigorously defending the rule in the discussions. Considering that Bryan had urged Ohio's Convention to take up unanimity requirements, if any speech is to be considered influential, it is Bryan's, although still minorly.

147 Journal of the Nebraska Constitutional Convention 319 (Clyde H. Barnard ed., 1921).

148 Evans' biography is available in 3 Albert Watkins, Illustrated History of Nebraska: A History of Nebraska 490 (Julius Sterlin Morton, Albert Watkins & George Miller eds., 2005).

a law constitutional.[149] He claimed that the Judiciary Committee had been "led astray" and was making a "direct attack upon" constitutional rights.[150] Mockingly, he said that if requiring a supermajority was possible, unanimity was only a step further.

The last remark infuriated Wilbur Bryant, a lawyer with judicial experience and a former Supreme Court reporter who believed in the unanimity rule. Bryant objected, in general, to judicial review as a non-express power of the judiciary. Taking Oleson's remarks personally, he stressed the experience of the Judiciary Committee, primarily lawyers, that approved the notion. Evans finally spoke and even cited Ohio's supermajority as a similar experience. After quoting the income tax, Lochner, and child labor cases, he noted that bare majorities created reasonable doubt on a statute's constitutionality. Elegantly, he concluded: "It is no injustice and no reflection on the courts to say that they should have more than a mere majority behind their decisions."[151]

Votava, the son of Czechoslovak immigrants, clarified that delegates directed most arguments for judicial limitations to the United States Supreme Court, but Nebraska's Court had shown considerable restraint.[152] Flansburg concurred in subsequent interventions and even said the rule would create a "subservient court."[153] Adler argued that there was a growing theory "among intelligent people" favoring the establishment of a supermajority, perhaps a reference to Bryan's speech and the increasing debate in other states. Beeler, a lawyer, put forward a precedent argument. He claimed that precedents set by bare majorities on constitutional questions were often overturned "because those decisions were not considered by the courts themselves of any very great binding effect by the fact that they were rendered by a bare majority."[154] The supermajority would add stability without diminishing the independence of Nebraska's Supreme Court, Beeler claimed. Last in the discussion was Petrus Peterson, a reputed lawyer, who contended that the rule prevented bare majorities from creating instability and that supermajorities generally "attempt to leave matters in the status quo."

After a few hours, the debate ended, and the supermajority survived, endorsed by a largely bipartisan agreement.[155] The rule was submitted to the electorate as Amendment 16 and gained approval by a significant margin.[156]

149 Journal of the Nebraska Constitutional Convention, *supra* note 147, at 1135.

150 *Id.*

151 *Id.* at 1140.

152 Little did Votava know that in Czechoslovakia, his parents' home country, a supermajority was being debated in the same historical period.

153 Journal of the Nebraska Constitutional Convention, *supra* note 147, at 1146.

154 *Id.* at 1147.

155 Ronald C. Naugle, History of Nebraska 317 (4 ed. 2014).

156 Sheldon, *supra* note 144, at 398–99.

3.1.3.2 The Rule's Practice

Ohio's double threshold had been analyzed by 1919, and some studies pointed out that the duality of majorities might lead to problematic outcomes. Unsurprisingly, Nebraska adopted a supermajority that fixed the seemingly problematic double threshold. A supermajority was required to strike down legislation, regardless of whether the statute had been considered constitutional or unconstitutional in the first instance.[157]

Nebraska's seven-member Court implemented a 5:2 supermajority, which required a 71.4 percent consensus. Delegates of the 1920 Convention were aware of the problems created by absences, not only regarding supermajority rule but also in majority rule, for example, affirmances by an equal division. The 1920 Convention established a system for replacements. When a justice is recused from a case, a district court or Court of Appeals judge is asked to sit in the Supreme Court.[158] Nebraska has always had a full bench in this way, and absences did not influence the supermajority.[159]

Many years later, the Court further implemented rules to ensure a full bench. Rule § 2-109(E) of the Nebraska Court Rules of Appellate Practice requires that, in cases involving the constitutionality of a statute, the party "must file and serve notice thereof with the Clerk by a separate notice or by notice in a Petition to Bypass at the time of filing such party's brief." Additionally, it requires a copy of the brief for the Attorney General if he is not a party to the action. The Court has linked the requirement to the supermajority.[160] Failure to comply with the requirement results in the Court not addressing the constitutional challenge.[161]

157 In Nebraska, the issue of absences related to the supermajority received attention in the debates. Flansburg, opposing the supermajority, argued: "Suppose a district judge should hold a law unconstitutional. Suppose there is an appeal. How many judges would it take to affirm the unconstitutionality ... under your provision, it would take five [a supermajority]." Comparing Ohio's rule to Evans' proposal, Riley claimed that the lack of a double threshold made the rule "in one respect more oppressive and in another much less confusing." *See* William Jay Riley, *To Require That a Majority of the Supreme Court Determine the Outcome of Any Case Before It*, 50 Neb. L. Rev. 622, 629 (1970).

158 Article V, s. 2 of Nebraska's Constitution provides that district court judges may be called when the court sits on two five-judge divisions, when analyzing a statute's constitutionality, when hearing a capital case, and when reviewing a decision from a division of the Supreme Court. Robert D. Miewald & Peter Joseph Longo, The Nebraska State Constitution 24 (2011).

159 The Court claimed that this mechanism was an "elastic system which would enable the court to clear its docket, keep it so, and ultimately allow matters to be determined by a full court of seven judges." *See* ConAgra, Inc. v. Cargill, Inc., 388 N.W.2d 458 (1986).

160 The Court held the opinion that: "The rule 9E notice to the Supreme Court Clerk assists the clerk and this court in ensuring that an appeal involving the constitutionality of a statute is heard by the full court." State v. Johnson, 269 Neb. 507, 513, 695 N.W.2d 165, 170–71 (2005).

161 *See* State v. Boche, 294 Neb. 912, 916, 885 N.W.2d 523, 528 (2016); Smith v. Wedekind, 302 Neb. 387, 394, 923 N.W.2d 392, 398 (2019); State v. Catlin, 308 Neb. 294, 300, 953 N.W.2d 563, 568 (2021).

Nebraska's Supreme Court has held that the supermajority requirement applies both in facial and as-applied constitutional challenges.[162] Supermajority failure decisions lead to a decision taken in accordance with the statute being upheld. The opinions of the minority have been termed "controlling minority opinions."[163]

Nebraska's Supreme Court has also shown no significant signs of evasion attempts.[164] In general, it has been considered a collegiate court.[165] Nonetheless, the issue of the precedential value of controlling minority opinions has not been easy. An analysis of the sale of school lands saga illustrates the above.

A statute passed in 1967 obliged the Board of Educational Lands and Funds to sell school lands whenever a buyer would offer to pay the price of the land as previously appraised, even if the board could reasonably attempt selling at a higher price.[166]

The constitutionality of the bid rejection prohibition was questioned in the *Belker* case.[167] Justice Carter was ill and failed to participate in the discussion, being replaced by District Judge Coldwell. A four-vote majority considered that the statute encroached on the board's powers provided by the Constitution. Furthermore, it conflicted with the trustees' obligations to guarantee the trust's best interest. A three-judge minority dissented. The controlling opinion claimed that an omission of the statute to provide for bid rejection could not equal a binding sale obligation. Since the board was acting within the broader responsibilities of a trust, it could set aside or confirm sales, while the courts had jurisdiction to enforce this rule. The majority claimed the statute's language was clear, and Justice Newton filed a dissenting opinion accusing the minority of seeking to avoid the law.

The Court's decision to uphold the district court's dismissal of the action is a paradox. In fact, Nebraska's Supreme Court unanimously considered that

162 "[A] supermajority is required to declare any statute unconstitutional, without regard to whether the challenge is facial or as-applied." State v. Boche, *supra* note 161.

163 *See* the terminology in State Ex Rel. Belker v. Board of Educational L&F, 185 Neb. 270, (Neb. 1970) and Bessey v. Board of Educational Lands and Funds, 185 Neb. 801, 802 (Neb. 1970).

164 Shugerman interviewed Nebraska Justice Wright, who claimed that "the Nebraska Supreme Court has not considered evading the rule, and willingly abides by it." Shugerman, *supra* note 61, at 956.

165 Fino analyzed the 1980 period and claimed that Nebraska's Supreme Court statistically showed little dissent, and the few dissenting opinions were attributable to a single justice. Susan P. Fino, The Role of State Supreme Courts in the New Judicial Federalism 101 (1987).

166 Since some senators supporting the bill were ranchers, some deemed the provisions were a cattleman's relief act, hinting at a possible conflict of interests. Miewald & Longo, *supra* note 158, at 75.

167 State ex rel. Belker v. Board of Educational Lands & Funds, 185 Neb. 270, 175 N.W.2d 63 (1970).

no land could be sold under a non-competitive scheme either because such a scheme is unconstitutional—as held by the majority—or because rejecting bids is within the power of a trustee, and land sales could be reviewed through the judicial procedure, as claimed by the controlling minority.

A year later, the Court agreed to rehear the case with Justice Carter on the bench. Carter agreed with the previous majority, and a 3:4 vote again upheld the statute. In his dissenting opinion, Carter even hinted at criticizing the supermajority rule by saying that "three members of the court under the provisions of Article V, section 2, of the Constitution [supermajority], are authorized to sustain the constitutionality of a legislative act without citing a single case or text authority." The criticism was unfair. The same can be said inversely of majority rules: a majority is authorized to strike down a law without citing a single applicable precedent. Carter disagreed more with the minority's reasoning than with the supermajority itself.

Belker would soon allow the Court to decide on the precedent value of controlling minority opinions. The challenge arose in the *Bessey*[168] case when the land trust regulation was questioned once again. In *Bessey*, the court majority "followed" the precedent by rejecting the claim to the statute's unconstitutionality based on *Belker*. However, the majority refused to follow the minority's interpretation of the statute.

Bessey showed that the majority was willing to attribute selective precedent status to controlling minority decisions. The majority applied the statute as formerly interpreted by the insufficient majority in *Belker* but confirmed the statute to be constitutional despite the former *Belker* controlling minority's clear hint that it would be unconstitutional as interpreted. *Belker* was granted a paradoxical half-precedent weight.

All the justices filed separate opinions. Justice McCown, from the former controlling minority, bitterly remarked that the opinion was "[a]n obvious desire to decide the *Belker* case once more." McCown was right. A substantial portion of the opinion was a refutation of the controlling minority's statutory interpretation rather than a dialogue with the parties' arguments. *Bessey* seems to confirm that controlling minority opinions are only binding regarding a law's constitutionality decision, but not other issues present in a case, such as statutory interpretation.

No further precedent debates occurred until 2015 in *Thompson v. Heineman*.[169] In *Thompson*, the Court upheld a statute for failing to muster a supermajority. The controlling minority contended that the plaintiff lacked standing. As Kauffman points out, the status of the majority's basing precedential value on standing is unclear.[170] Kauffman further claimed that the

168 Bessey v. Board of Educational Lands and Funds, 178 N.W.2d 794 (1970).

169 289 Neb. 798, 857 N.W.2d 731 (2015).

170 Adam W. Kauffman, *You Can't Take My Land: Is Thompson v. Heineman, 289 Neb. 798, 857 N.W.2d 731 (2015), Transformative Law or a Political Anomaly*, 95 Nebraska L. Rev. 548, 570 (2016).

supermajority prevented the majority from setting a precedent on standing issues, even if those are separate issues from the constitutionality of the statute.

It is currently debatable whether the supermajority applies to the case's decision or merely to decide the issue of the unconstitutionality of a law. In the *Thompson* case, a four-justice majority of the Court claimed that the rule should only apply to determine a statute's constitutionality. Therefore, if previous procedural issues arise, a simple majority would suffice to bind the Court to rule on the statute's constitutionality, only then requiring a supermajority. Effectively, this interpretation attempts to force issue voting, although it seems to be consistent with what the Court had previously decided in *Bessey*. The majority also claimed that the minority's opinion of the statute was not controlling in future constitutional challenges. The statement seems correct, as the minority in *Thompson* did not assert that the law was constitutional but merely that the plaintiffs lacked standing to raise a challenge. The minority responded that the supermajority rule should be interpreted as an outcome rule—five justices must concur in believing the statute is unconstitutional. The minority also criticized the majority's stance that the opinion contained an analysis of the constitutional issue at hand since, lacking the five votes, it was merely an advisory statement. The problem still seems to be under discussion.[171]

Nebraska's rule has not faced constitutional scrutiny like Ohio's supermajority. Langdale reported that there had been no challenge to the rule's constitutionality by 1968.[172] In 1970, a plaintiff—aware the rule had decided a prior case—raised its unconstitutionality.[173] The plaintiff claimed that the supermajority was unconstitutional as it "hampers the assertion of a federal right and unreasonably discriminates against litigants asserting the constitutional invalidity of legislation." The Court did not address the issue.[174] However, it did not restrain Justice Spencer from hinting that the rule might infringe the federal Constitution. Justice Spencer claimed that: "Any dilution of the judicial power ... shatters the fundamental principle of a republican form of Government. It goes without saying that if it is possible to require more than

171 In a recent 2020 case, parties claimed before the Court that *Thompson*'s majority opinion on standing was a controlling precedent. *See* Egan v. County of Lancaster, 308 Neb. 48 (Neb. 2020). The Court refused to address the claim since it had no impact on the case's outcome under the arguments provided by the parties. Other cases have indeed cited *Thompson* as a precedent by January 2021, although, to the best of my understanding, not on the new standing exception created by the majority.

172 Larry L. Langdale, *Constitutional Law: The Sterilization of the Mentally Deficient: A Reasonable Exercise of the Police Power*, 47 Nebraska L. Rev. 784, 785 (1968).

173 DeBacker v. Sigler, 185 Neb. 352, 175 N.W.2d 912 (1970).

174 Justice Spencer, dissenting, noted that even though the unconstitutionality of the supermajority requirement was raised, the opinion did not discuss the issue. *See* DeBacker v. Sigler, *supra* note 173, 914.

a majority vote, it is also possible to require a unanimous vote." Subsequently, no further challenges to the rule's constitutionality have occurred.[175]

Nebraska had so few supermajority failures that it is easy to select the most prominent cases: *Cavitt*, the school land sales saga, and *Thompson*. Let us address them briefly.

Since the rule's introduction in 1920, the Court functioned for forty-eight years without the rule preserving a single statute. A collegiate environment had characterized Nebraska's Supreme Court. It was only in 1968 that the rule influenced a case for the first time. In *State v. Cavitt*,[176] the Court faced a case in which a woman committed to a mental facility was ordered to undergo forced sterilization. A statute gave authority to the Board of Examiners of the Mentally Deficient to decide whether the state could impose sterilization as a release precondition. The woman appealed to the district court, which considered the statute unconstitutional. Influenced by a previous U.S. Supreme Court decision greenlighting forced sterilizations,[177] Nebraska's Supreme Court could not muster the five votes, and a three-justice minority sufficed to reverse the district court's decision. The plaintiff's guardian appealed to the U.S. Supreme Court. The Supreme Court granted certiorari, and the legislature amended the law, rendering the case moot.[178]

The second set of controversial decisions was the *Belker* and *Bessey* cases mentioned above. The school land saga proved to be a very divisive issue in the legislature, which fostered significant political disagreement. The political conflict in the House was so marked that it even played a role in a failed attempt to repeal the supermajority in 1970.

Finally, a recent broader debate arose in *Thompson v. Heineman*,[179] where the supermajority prevented striking down LB 1161. The *Thompson* case featured a conflict on Nebraska's legislative bill 1161, which allowed major oil pipeline carriers to avoid requesting approval from the Public Service Commission and obtain it directly from the governor. The law was seen as a specially tailored bill to allow TransCanada to build a pipeline route (Keystone XL) from Alberta to the heart of the United States, passing through Nebraska. A group of litigants lacking direct harm challenged the statute's constitutionality. The litigants claimed they should be allowed to sue since they were taxpayers in Nebraska, constituting a standing exception. Four justices favored granting the exception and ruling the statute unconstitutional, while three thought the

175 Miewald & Longo, *supra* note 158, at 106. The authors quote as the only example *State ex rel. Belker v. Board of Educational Lands and Funds*, *supra* note 163. However, the only challenge to the rule's constitutionality from the bench occurred in Spencer's dissenting opinion in *DeBacker v. Sigler*, *supra* note 173, which they probably intended to refer to.

176 182 Neb. 712, 157 N.W.2d 171 (1968).

177 Buck v. Bell, 274 U.S. 200 (1927).

178 James W. Hewitt, Slipping Backward: A History of the Nebraska Supreme Court 77 (2007).

179 289 Neb. 798, 857 N.W.2d 731 (2015).

litigants lacked standing. The Court was unable to strike down the law. While Zellmer and Miller argued that the supermajority forced an absurd decision, Kauffman claimed that it prevented the Court from issuing an incorrect one.[180]

3.1.3.3 Surviving Reform: An Assessment of the Supermajority

The rule enjoyed political support for most of its existence, although it survived an amendment attempt in 1970. Legislative bill 244 created a Constitutional Revision Commission to propose potential amendments to Nebraska's Constitution. The Commission was formed by members of the legislature, members proposed by the governor, and members submitted by the Supreme Court. The governor proposed, among other members, reputed law professor David Dow. Dow's wife was the daughter of Petrus Peterson, who had contributed to the adoption of the supermajority as a delegate of the 1920 Convention. Dow, contrary to his father-in-law, favored simple majorities.

In its two-paragraph defense of suppressing the supermajority, the Commission stated that "there is no good reason to make the exception" of requiring a supermajority vote in constitutional adjudication. The report noted that such a rule did not exist in other states[181] and that it "perpetuated minority rule, a concept repugnant to the Commission."[182] During the Commission debates, monopolized by Syas and Whitney, frequent allusions were made to the school lands cases. Syas suggested the amendment was due to a personal grudge in the *Belker* case. Members of the Commission seemingly wanted to delete or support the rule, depending on which side they had been on with the bill.[183] The discussion indeed centered more on the *Belker* case than on the supermajority. The proposal passed by a 9:2 vote and was presented as Legislative Bill 304 for consideration by the 1972 Legislature Session.[184]

The Constitutional Revision Committee public hearing featured a much more profound debate, with Syas defending the amendment and Whitney arguing for preserving the rule. Since both Syas and Whitney had formed part of the Constitutional Revision Commission, the public hearing was a continuation of their debate. Prof. Dow attended the public hearing to defend the proposed amendment.

180 Zellmer & Miller, *supra* note 65; Kauffman, *supra* note 170.

181 North Dakota required a supermajority at that time and Ohio had just barely repealed the rule a few years before in 1968.

182 Nebraska Constitutional Revision Commission, *Report of the Nebraska Constitutional Revision Commission: Submitted to the People, the Governor, and the Legislature of the State of Nebraska*, 64 (1970).

183 Nebraska Legislature, *Minutes of the Nebraska Constitutional Revision Commission*, 1056 (1970).

184 Stanley M. Talcott, *Amending the Nebraska Constitution in the 1971 Legislature*, 50 Nebraska L. Rev. 676, 683 (1971).

Syas was loyal to his former opinion. He deemed the supermajority problematic, given Court absences,[185] and suggested that the rule was unconstitutional.[186] Conversely, Whitney made a long speech on the 1920 debate of the Constitutional Convention and even reminded Dow that his father-in-law had supported the rule. Upon further discussion indirectly mentioning the *Belker* case, Senator Whitney furiously complained that the Committee should not decide which voting rule was appropriate "on the basis of the school land problem."[187] Senator Syas accused Whitney of defending the rule to keep the *Belker* decision alive. The debate proceeded in a heated exchange with the land sales case at its center and an active discussion about land values and leasing. During their interactions in both debates, Syas and Whitney had reciprocally tried to change or defend the rule based on their position in *Belker* rather than on constitutional adjudication principles. The bill was bracketed[188] and never passed. Peterson prevailed.

Given that the rule influenced the outcome of six cases before Nebraska's Supreme Court[189] in more than 100 years, scholarship has not paid much

185 Since Nebraska's Constitution had a surrogate system, Syas' argument was merely rhetorical. Absences had never produced any problems regarding the supermajority.

186 Nebraska Legislature, *Minutes of the Constitutional Revision Committee: Public Hearing on LB 301, 302, 304 and 305*, 19 (1971). However, Syas contended that the doctrine of the Supreme Court in electoral matters (one man, one vote) applied to courts generally, which it certainly did not.

187 *Id.* at 24.

188 Legislative Journal of the State of Nebraska. Volume I. Eighty-Second Legislature First Session, 712 (Vincent Brown ed., 1971). In Nebraska's legislative procedure, bracketing a bill means delaying its consideration, often indefinitely. It is one way to "kill a bill" without a formal vote.

189 I account for six supermajority failure decisions (SFDs) from 1921 to 2022. I consider *State v. Cavitt*, *DeBacker v. Brainard*, *State ex rel. Belker v. Bd. of Educ. Lands & Funds*, and *State ex rel. Spire v. Beerman*, *State v. Johnson*, and *Thompson v. Heineman* (all cited above). My account of SFDs in Nebraska is mostly consistent until 2015 with Zellmer & Miller, *supra* note 65; *see also* Kauffman, *supra* note 170. After *Thompson*, I did not account for any further SFD. I disagree with the list provided by Zellmer, Miller, and Kauffman in two instances, although reaching the same number of decisions. First, I differ with classifying as SFD *DeBacker v. Sigler*, *supra* note 173, as Kauffman did. In that case, the plaintiff was the same as in *DeBacker v. Brainard*. The Court did not fail to muster a supermajority but merely recalled that the issues were similar to the previous case. Secondly, I consider *State v. Johnson* to be an example of a supermajority failure. In such a decision, the Court provided: "We note that the separate opinion concluding that § 28–703 is unconstitutionally vague sets forth the opinion of four of the seven members of this Court. Despite the fact that this number is a majority of the Court, which would normally control the outcome of a case, article V, § 2, of the Nebraska Constitution provides that '[n]o legislative act shall be held unconstitutional except by the concurrence of five judges.' Therefore, our opinion that the constitutionality of the statute cannot be considered in this appeal controls the outcome of this case." Subsequently, in the *Archie* case, the Court admitted as much by describing Johnson's holding in the following manner: "Because '[n]o legislative act shall be held unconstitutional except by the concurrence of five judges,' the opinion of those three justices was the opinion of the Court." State v. Archie, 273 Neb. 612, 628, 733 N.W.2d 513, 528 (2007).

attention to it.[190] Nonetheless, those scholars who analyzed it offered divided opinions. Against the rule are Madgett[191] (for whom the supermajority proved to be a failure because it was never applied), Riley,[192] and Zellmer and Miller[193]—for whom the rule failed because it prevented striking down statutes in a handful of cases. However, favoring the rule or admitting its proper functioning are Redmond,[194] Fite and Rubinstein,[195] and Shugerman.[196] Opposition to the rule is based on principle rather than on its operative problems.

3.2 The Supermajority in the World's First Constitutional Court: Czechoslovakia (1920–1938)

From the beginning, the seven-member Czechoslovak Constitutional Court functioned with a 5:2 supermajority requirement to strike down legislation and ordinances, although its path differed from the United States' subnational supermajorities.

Czechoslovakia was a country that emerged as a consequence of World War I in 1918. Tomáš Masaryk, born to a Czech mother and a Slovak father on the border between the two countries, embodied the new state in which he was destined to play a decisive role. The Czechoslovak National Council declared Czechoslovakia an independent state on October 28, 1918.[197] The National Council would appoint itself as the government, temporarily accumulating executive and legislative power.[198] After the provisional 1918 Constitution, a non-elected assembly adopted the 1920 Constitution.[199] Even though the scholarship is not of one mind, the predominant opinion described Czechoslovakia as a democratic example and a unique enclave of Western values.[200]

The 1920 Constitution devoted its first three provisions to establishing a constitutional court similar to the one the Austrian Constitution would establish

190 For example, the most comprehensive study of Nebraska's Constitution takes no stand on the rule. Miewald & Longo, *supra* note 158, at 106. Kauffman, who involuntarily undertook one of the most extensive studies of the rule's functioning, takes no position on the debate. Kauffman, *supra* note 170.

191 Madgett, *supra* note 127.

192 *See* Riley, *supra* note 157.

193 Zellmer & Miller, *supra* note 65.

194 Redmond, *supra* note 133.

195 Fite & Rubinstein, *supra* note 30, at 780.

196 Shugerman, *supra* note 61, at 955.

197 Jiří Jirásek, *From Monarchy to the Independent Czechoslovakia*, *in* Legal Studies on Central Europe 57, 59 (Lóránt Csink & László Trócsányi eds., 2022).

198 Vilém Knoll & Tomáš Pezl, *Continuity and Discontinuity of Czechoslovak Interwar Law: Basic Introduction of the Topic with an Example of Criminal Law*, 15 Krakowskie Studia z Historii Państwa i Prawa 179, 181 (2022).

199 Jirásek, *supra* note 197, at 63.

200 For a critical view of the predominant opinion, *see* Andrea Orzoff, The Battle for the Castle 215–20 (2009).

under Kelsen's influence.[201] Czechoslovakia had the first constitutional court in the world, at least on paper, since the Austrian *Verfassungsgerichthof*, vested with judicial review powers a few months later, started functioning earlier than the Czechoslovak Constitutional Court.

The Czechoslovak Constitutional Court was a unique design and was far from being an imitation of its Austrian counterpart.[202] The designer of the newly created constitutional court is still debatable, although Hoetzel[203] and Weyr[204] are often credited as fathers of the institution.

The constitutional design of the court was peculiar. The court was vested with the competence to solve solely two types of cases: whether laws contradicted the Constitution and whether ordinances issued by the Permanent Committee of the National Assembly[205] complied with the Constitution. The court consisted of seven members. The President appointed three members among candidates provided by the Chamber of Deputies, the Senate, and the Diet of Carpathian Ruthenia. Two members were delegated from the Supreme Administrative Court, and two from the Supreme Court. The President could also appoint the Constitutional Court's President.

The Constitution did not regulate legal standing; nor did the majority require to strike down ordinances and legislation. Article II laconically provided that a statute would regulate the details, "delegation" of the Court members, proceedings, and term of office of the judges.

As some authors have pointed out, the Czechoslovak legislature may have presupposed that, given the constitutional referral to law, matters not regulated in the Constitution could be freely addressed in any manner the legislature

201 Osterkamp delves on the common characteristics of constitutional review in both countries as a heritage of the discussions under the Habsburg monarchy. Jana Osterkamp, *Verfassungshüter ohne politischen Rückhalt. Das tschechoslowakische Verfassungsgericht nach 1920 im Vergleich mit Österreich*, BRGOE 275, 276 (2011).

202 However, Jellinek's *Ein Verfassungsgerichtshof für Österreich* considerably influenced the Czechoslovak Constitutional Court and was even quoted in the opinion of the Constitutional Committee of February 24, 1920, while adopting the Act on the Constitutional Court. Georg Jellinek, Ein Verfassungsgerichstshof Für Österreich (1885).

203 Jiří Hoetzel claimed to be responsible for introducing the Constitutional Court to the Constitution. Several scholars agree with the claim. Jana Osterkamp, Verfassungsgerichtsbarkeit in der Tschechoslowakei (1920-1939): Verfassungsidee, Demokratieverständnis, Nationalitätenproblem 10 (2009).

204 Dimitrios Parashu, *Die Entwicklung der Verfassungsgerichtsbarkeit in Tschechien und der Slowakei*, 57 OER Osteuropa Recht 47, 47 (2011). *See also* Jan Kysela & Jakub Stádník, *Kam Ústavní Soud Nechodí (a Nejen o Tom)*, Pravnik 899, 901 (2021).

205 The Permanent Committee comprised twenty-three members elected by Members of Parliament from their own ranks. The body could issue ordinances that would otherwise require a law and even exercise supervision over the executive. *See* Tomáš Langášek, Ústavní Soud Československé Republiky a Jeho Osudy v Letech 1920-1948 27 (2011). For an historical analysis, *see* František Weyr, Das Verfassungsrecht Der Tschechoislowakischen Republik 17 (1920).

deemed fit.[206] While Hoetzel was involved in the constitutional design, he had no intervention in drafting the secondary legislation.[207]

3.2.1 Introducing a Supermajority

The law on the Constitutional Court of March 9, 1920 (No. 162/1920 Coll) introduced crucial nuances. First, legal standing to challenge the constitutionality of laws was severely restricted. Only the Chamber of Deputies, the Senate, the Diet of Carpathian Ruthenia, the Supreme Court, the Supreme Administrative Court, and the Electoral Court could initiate proceedings. Parliamentary minorities had no right to challenge legislation, and the majority had little incentive to challenge its own laws. The Diet of Carpathian Ruthenia was never created. The Electoral Court behaved passively,[208] and the Supreme Court and Supreme Administrative Court had little incentive to challenge laws.[209] Furthermore, judicial bodies needed to present a challenge abstractly *en banc* and could not refer to an ongoing case. In turn, it was obligatory to review ordinances following promulgation. The review was automatic, without the need for a challenge.

The Constitutional Court was not a permanent body. There was no incompatibility between being a standing lawyer, prosecutor, mayor of a city, or even Minister of Justice and a constitutional court judge simultaneously. The judges from the Supreme Court and Supreme Administrative Court retained their functions while serving as constitutional judges. A three-year limitation was established to review the legislation. After three years passed, laws were de jure exempted from constitutional review.

Finally, Article 8 of the Law on the Constitutional Court introduced a supermajority. The Czechoslovak Constitutional Court was the first constitutional court in the world to employ supermajority rules. Five votes were required to strike down legislation or provisional ordinances. A majority

206 Villalón raises a similar argument concerning legal standing. *See* Pedro Cruz Villalón, *Dos Modos de Regulación Del Control de Constitucionalidad: Checoslovaquia (1920-1938) y España (1931-1936)*, Rev. Esp. Derecho Const. 115, 138 (1982).

207 In an article in 1928, Hoetzel himself claimed: "Thus, as it is already clear from the text, I did not work on law 161/1920 ... nor law 162/1920 on the Constitutional Court". Jiří Hoetzel, *Ku Vzniku Ústavní Listiny*, LXVII Právník 558, 562 (1928). Nonetheless, Hoetzel's opinion seems to have been heard by the drafters.

208 Osterkamp, *supra* note 203, at 17.

209 *Id.* at 19–24. Furthermore, one must also account for power struggles. Both courts "had little incentive to create another strong judicial institution." *See* David Kosař & Ladislav Vyhnánek, *The Constitutional Court of Czechia*, *in* The Max Planck Handbooks in European Public Law: Volume III: Constitutional Adjudication: Institutions 119, 123 (Armin von Bogdandy, Peter Huber & Christoph Grabenwarter eds., 2020). Furthermore, the Supreme Court and Supreme Administrative Court engaged in power games attempting to control the vice-presidency of the Constitutional Court as a matter of power and prestige.

sufficed to uphold legislation, analyze procedural formalities, or issue statutory interpretation.

The Committee's opinion on the draft discussed the supermajority requirement. Deputy Meissner chaired the Constitutional Committee. Weyr himself drafted the Committee's opinion. The report stated that Article 8 "does not require further justification ... it is such an important matter that it was recommended to require a supermajority for it."[210]

The National Assembly discussed the Law on the Constitutional Court in 1920, with Weyr sponsoring and defending the proposal. Weyr declared that the Court had to be independent, composed of experts who were profoundly independent of political parties.[211] While the supermajority did provoke discussion in the Committee's deliberation and report, no discussions arose in the parliamentary debate.

The supermajority in the Czechoslovak case was introduced as a cautious measure toward a new powerful institution. As Langášek narrates, Hoetzel even suggested requiring unanimity for the Court to strike legislation in the Constitutional Committee, although the Committee rejected the notion.[212] The supermajority guaranteed that the members of judicial bodies alone could not declare the unconstitutionality of a law or an ordinance: one vote of the "nonprofessional judges members" was required.[213]

The situation contrasted strongly with the Austrian regulation. In the Austrian Constitutional Court, political members elected from the legislative bodies could be appointed judges. The Czechoslovak system did not allow legislators[214] but did not prohibit government members or acting politicians from belonging to the court. However, as Kelsen remarked, most judges were elected "particularly from Public Law Professors. Thus, non-parliamentary members constitute a majority and take the decisions."[215] The Austrian Court, composed of 30–70 percent of politicians versus legal experts, allowed strictly legal judges to overcome opposition from non-legal judges requiring a simple majority. The Czechoslovak Court, with a similar composition of 42–58 percent of politicians versus professional judges, provided for a supermajority requiring consensus between members of both groups.

210 Report of the Constitutional Committee to the Bill on the Act on the Constitutional Court, Prague (Feb. 24, 1920). Cruz Villalón offers an alternative explanation deeming that the supermajority was related to the fact that judges appointed by the political branches were a minority. PEDRO CRUZ VILLALÓN, LA FORMACIÓN DEL SISTEMA EUROPEO DE CONTROL DE CONSTITUCIONALIDAD (1918-1939) 411 (1987).

211 *See* the National Assembly Session of Mar. 9, 1920, Item no. 5 of the agenda.

212 LANGÁŠEK, *supra* note 205, at 32.

213 OSTERKAMP, *supra* note 203.

214 FRANTIŠEK ADLER, DIE GRUNDGEDANKEN DER TSCHECHOSLOWAKISCHEN VERFASSUNGSURKUNDE IN DER ENTWICKLUNGSGESCHICHTE DES VERFASSUNGSRECHTS 116 (1927).

215 Domingo García Belaunde, *Apéndice: Instituto Internationl de Derecho Público*, 2 *in* EL CONTROL DEL PODER 899, 904 (Domingo García Belaunde & Peter Häberle eds., 2012).

Decisions on the unconstitutionality of normative provisions were seen as potentially disruptive of the political process and democratic procedures. At first glance, the supermajority might have appeared to be purely political insurance. However, the protection was twofold. The Czechoslovak model understood constitutional law as a highly political realm. Professional judges and politicians had to agree on striking legislation, guaranteeing both that the decision would have at least some political perspective and that politicians could not employ the Constitutional Court on raw political intent.[216] Caution was at the heart of the rule.

3.2.2 The Rule's Functioning

Since Article 8 of the Law on the Constitutional Court required "five votes," absences could have severely hindered the court. However, the Czechoslovak Constitutional Court had a system of substitutes to replace absences.[217] Substitute judges were pre-appointed and could only replace the specific judge they were meant to substitute.

In the Constitutional Committee, Karel Kramář argued in favor of substitutes to guarantee that "the substitute would always come to represent the same interests."[218] It is unclear if substitutes were a remedy for increasing the supermajority in the event of absences, part of a defective understanding of constitutional judges conceiving them as representatives of the appointing bodies rather than impartial constitutional interpreters, or both.

The qualified voting requirement was not an authoritarian imposition. Laws were a product of vibrant and deep discussions. The supermajority was a genuine bargain to produce a coherent model. It is interesting to note that no discussion ensued on approving the Constitutional Court's law.

The court was granted the power to issue its internal regulation and did so in August 1922 by issuing the procedural rules of the Constitutional Court (*Jednací řád ústavního soudu*). The internal rules devoted considerable space to regulating quorum, majorities, and decisional procedures. The original judges deeply understood judicial proceedings and wanted to formalize practices adopted in ordinary courts.

Articles 22 and 32 established a five-member quorum. Even if the court could theoretically uphold laws or ordinances with only four members, the supermajority was considered a natural functional quorum.[219] The regulations

216 However, the restricted legal standing already restricted the second feature. If more entities had access to the Constitutional Court, such as parliamentary minorities, a concern for the politicization of judicial review would have been more grounded.

217 Substitutes would be incorporated into the Act on the Constitutional Court only in 1938. However, they were present from the beginning as the Constitutional Court introduced them in its internal regulations.

218 Langášek, *supra* note 205, at 32.

219 *Id.* at 33.

foresaw a detailed procedure for the plenary sessions,[220] sessions in which the court attended administrative or organizational internal matters, such as financial decisions or electing the Vice-President. The Czechoslovak Constitutional Court decided that the vote was to be done by age (Article 12), with the youngest member voting first and the President of the Court voting last, attributing him special seniority. Voting and deliberations were secret (Article 42). The crown jewel was Article 13, which established a complex procedure to reach a majority of votes. Article 13 provided that if the court failed to reach a majority, the President shall "divide the questions" and submit the proposal for a vote "point by point," thus effectively stating that the Constitutional Court switched from outcome voting to issue voting to break an impasse. Article 43, which regulated the rules of the court while adjudicating cases, provided explicitly that Articles 11 to 14 were only applicable regarding the voting procedure. Quorum and the prescribed majority varied in cases that required a supermajority.

The rules forbade abstentions even in the case of someone who "remained in the minority during an early voting," thus guaranteeing that a majority could be coerced out of the court in cases where the legal matters were not binary. It is paradoxical that the internal rules so meticulously established majoritarian decision procedures but failed to address the results of a potential supermajority failure. Was the court to issue a ruling upholding the legislation, or was the court to refrain from resolving it?

During the first term of the judges (1921–1931), the Constitutional Court only decided on ordinances, issuing eighteen decisions. Not a single law was challenged. The court upheld the ordinances in all cases. The first of the ordinance decisions—Judgment of November 7, 1922—came to be the best-known and most controversial decision of the period, also being the only supermajority failure decision. On July 23, 1920, the Permanent Committee issued ordinance No. 450/1920 on the incorporation of the territories of Vitorazsko and Valčicko.

The government named Hoetzel to defend the constitutionality of the ordinance. As several scholars noted, delegation legislation was common in Germany. Osterkamp discovered that several judges of the Constitutional Court knew the German doctrine on delegation legislation but disregarded it. As was recorded in the court's protocol, several judges deemed that German constitutional doctrine was "under the influence of a monarchist point of view."[221]

The court was deeply divided on the issue. A 4:3 vote favored the unconstitutionality of the ordinance, but the five-vote supermajority requirement

220 I thank Tomáš Langášek for bringing to my attention the distinction between adjudicating sessions and plenary sessions in the Constitutional Court's rules.

221 Osterkamp, *supra* note 203, at 102.

prevented the outcome.[222] The historical research of Osterkampf[223] and Langášek[224] on the court's internal protocols revealed the judges' positions. President Baxa, the case's Judge-Rapporteur Bobek, Vlasák, and Bílý wanted to strike down the ordinance. In turn, Vážný, Bohuslav, and Mačík deemed the ordinance to be constitutional. The group favoring unconstitutionality was formed equally of politicians and judges. Baxa was the mayor of Prague, and Bobek was a high official from the Ministry of the Interior. While the other two members were indeed judges, they did not even belong to the same judicial body—Vlasàk to the Supreme Administrative Court, while Bílý was a Supreme Court judge. In turn, the minority that prevented the statute from being declared unconstitutional was formed entirely of judges. If the ordinance was in danger, this happened mainly due to the opposition of the government's appointees occupying a high political office. Weyr's speech before the National Assembly stating that judges should be independent of political ideology proved prescient, perhaps to the great displeasure of Hoetzel.

Since Article 8 of the Law on the Constitutional Court required five votes, but did not explicitly say what the consequence was of a majority that failed to attain the necessary five votes, the Constitutional Court had to interpret the rule. The court concluded that the statute had to be upheld. Seventy-two years later, the Czech Constitutional Court would face the same dilemma in Pl. ÚS 36/93. An upheld decision was by no means a foregone conclusion.

In the only supermajority failure decision, the court took separate votes on the case's disposition and the argumentation. The majority wrote the court's opinion. The court enabled the group that wanted to strike down the ordinance to explain why it was to be deemed constitutional.

The chosen system created a coherence problem. One might argue that judges in the majority, having lost on the case's outcome, would try through the court's opinion to circumvent the supermajority or read the ordinance as narrowly as possible to bring the decision closer to their preferred outcome. The first case would prove it so. Under the influence of Baxa, Bobek, Vlasák, and Bílý, the court's opinion stated at length the unconstitutionality of delegation laws. Reading the court's opinion, the upholding of the ordinance seemed paradoxical. The court claimed that Ordinance 450/1920 had not crossed the delegation limits of the doctrine in that specific case. Given how the court narrowly interpreted the ordinance, authors such as Osterkamp called it a true example of a constitutionally conforming interpretation.[225]

222 Kysela & Stádník, *supra* note 204, at 903.

223 Osterkamp, *supra* note 203, at 105.

224 Langášek, *supra* note 205, at 74–90.

225 Osterkamp, *supra* note 203, at 106. A modern view from American law may deem it constitutional avoidance. *See* Brian Slocum, *Rethinking the Canon of Constitutional Avoidance*, 23 U. Pa. J. Const. L. 593 (2021).

The Constitutional Court faced tremendous criticism for its decision. In the heated debates that ensued, the court commissioned Kelsen and Hauriou to issue opinions on the judgment. Both of them held that the court's decision was correct.[226] A furious Hoetzel published a fierce article in *Právník*, defiantly accusing Kelsen and Hauriou of being fundamentally wrong and ignoring the Czechoslovak constitutional debate.[227] The only good thing about their opinions, said Hoetzel, "is that they are short."[228]

The remaining ordinances scrutinized under the first period were deemed constitutional. No other supermajority failures arose, and the Judge-Rapporteurs found no problems getting their proposals approved by the Constitutional Court.[229]

However, the decision on the delegation was not to be forgotten so quickly. Retaliation was to come. The 1930s were known as the "golden age of delegation laws."[230] In 1933, the Parliament further approved Law 95/1933 on the extraordinary power of ordinances, disregarding the Constitutional Court's interpretation. Knowing the Constitutional Court was an inconvenience, the government purposely prevented the court from functioning by refraining from appointing new judges,[231] effectively making the Court disappear. Even though the first judges decided to remain in office until new judges were appointed, by the middle of the 1930s the court's composition had been so decimated that even if the court wanted to sit, it would have been unable to do so. In the middle of this de facto disappearance of the Constitutional Court, the Supreme Court, for the first time, challenged the constitutionality of a statute (Law No. 147/1933).

Did the supermajority cause this political struggle or did it reduce it? The government actively attempted to obstruct the court, and several scholars, led by Hoetzel, denounced it, even though it upheld the ordinance.[232] What clash would have unfolded had the court struck it down instead? Did the supermajority precipitate or slow down the fall of the Constitutional Court?

226 Cruz Villalón narrates the episode. *See* Cruz Villalón, *supra* note 210, at 294–95

227 Jiří Hoetzel, *Ke Sporu o Meze Moci Nařizovací*, LXII Právník 390 (1923).

228 *Id.* at 390.

229 Osterkamp, *supra* note 203, at 109.

230 Jaromír Tauchen, *Ermächtigungsgesetzgebung in der Tschechoslowakei*, 1 BRGOE 428, 434 (2018).

231 Osterkamp, *supra* note 203, at 84. Regarding the probable intention of the government to disable the court, we should also consider the lack of consensus among political parties to appoint new judges.

232 Jaroslav Krejčí, the Court's general secretary, published a vigorous defense of the Court's decision. *See* Jaroslav Krejčí, Delegace zákonodárné moci v moderní demokracii 111–18 (1924).

3.2.3 Demise and Assessment of the Rule

In 1938, the Constitutional Court was finally reinstated. Jaroslav Krejčí, a prominent constitutional scholar[233] who would become a controversial figure, was chosen to replace former President Baxa, who had been re-elected to preside over the court but did not live to take the oath. A few months after the appointment of the new judges in May 1938, the Munich agreement was signed in September 1938, granting Germany the territory of Sudetenland. The second Czechoslovak Republic was established on the remaining territory. As Tauchen argues, 1938 signals the end of parliamentary democracy and the beginning of signs of a totalitarian regime.[234] During the brief second republic, the court would scrutinize twenty-eight ordinances, upholding them all. The life of the fragile republic would be short.

Germany invaded Czechoslovakia in 1939, establishing the Protectorate of Bohemia and Moravia. After the German invasion and the effective occupation of Czechoslovakia, the Constitutional Court's status was unclear since the German decrees did not explicitly ban it. Curiously, the court continued to function briefly, although severely hindered in its membership given the declaration on the Protectorate of Bohemia and Moravia. In 1939, the court issued several resolutions. The situation could not be more paradoxical. The court "was evaluating the compliance of laws with the 1920 Constitution, which had not been officially abolished, but in practice was no longer valid."[235] The Court's functioning under occupation even produced judgments striking down an ordinance and a law.[236] In the case of Law 147/1933, the Constitutional Court declared the unconstitutionality of a law that would allow disciplinary motions against judges for "antistate activity" by civil servants. Missing two members, the court issued a 5:0 unanimous decision.[237]

However, the Court was living on borrowed time. A few months later, the court closed as there was no place for a constitutional court under Nazi rule.[238] Benák claims that there is no better evidence of how irrelevant the

233 It is interesting to note that, prior to his appointment, Krejčí published an influential book on the principle of legality. In his book, Krejčí claimed that as a principle of constitutional law, the judiciary should disregard ordinary statutes contradicting the Constitution, thus concluding that the Law on the Constitutional Court was unconstitutional insofar as it granted the Constitutional Court a monopoly on judicial review. Michal Šejvl, *Fundamental Rights in Czechoslovakia between 1920 and 1938: Their Doctrinal Theorizing and Judicial Application*, 15 Krakowskie Studia z Historii Państwa i Prawa 413, 424 (2022).

234 Tauchen, *supra* note 230, at 437.

235 Jaromír Tauchen, *The Supreme Courts in the Protectorate of Bohemia and Moravia*, *in* Supreme Courts Under Nazi Occupation 227, 234 (Derk Venema ed., 2022). For example, in 1939 the court issued two resolutions upholding the conformity of two laws challenged.

236 The court partially struck down Ordinance 291/1938 and Law 147/1933.

237 I take the voting from Langášek, *supra* note 205, at 233.

238 Jaromír Tauchen, *Tschechoslowakei/Tschechien*, 4 *in* Konfliktlösung im 19. und 20. Jahrhundert 417, 423 (Peter Collin ed., 2021). Schelle & Bílý trace the last activity of the court in 1941, when Krejčí, still the court's President and Minister of Justice of the Protectorate,

constitutional court had grown to be than the fact that the German occupation did not even bother to abolish it formally, arrest the judges, or replace its members.[239] The President of the Constitutional Court, Jaroslav Krejčí, would serve as a minister of justice and even as prime minister of the Protectorate from 1941 to 1945. After liberation, Krejčí was charged with being a collaborator and, after a trial, he died in prison.

The supermajority prevented striking down only one ordinance, although it was the first and arguably most important case that the court would have the opportunity to resolve. In turn, the only ruling in which the court addressed a law's constitutionality occurred in 1939, and the court did strike down the statute, despite having two absences. Nonetheless, some commentators have characterized the supermajority as one factor contributing to the failure of the 1920 Constitutional Court.[240] One might wonder whether the critique is reasonable if the supermajority influenced less than 1 percent of the cases of the court.

However, experts on the Czechoslovak Constitutional Court deemed early on that its demise resulted from its limited legal standing and the rule allowing only three years to challenge laws.[241] Other reasons for its failure were the lack of jurisdiction over federalism conflicts or the lack of individual constitutional complaints and the political environment.[242] The supermajority has not been considered a factor by top experts on the Czechoslovak Constitutional Court.

The fact that the court published decisions without dissenting opinions or vote counts prevented commentators from knowing that the supermajority modified the outcome. Nonetheless, the criticism of delegation legislation alone was enough to result in public and academic disapproval of the court. It is very likely that a frontal clash, preventing Czechoslovakia from declaring Vitorazsko and Valčicko immediately part of its territory, would have had even more significant consequences for the nascent court.

The supermajority was established in a system saturated with institutional safeguards against a powerful court. In the only case in which it blocked a declaration of unconstitutionality, judges were divided by honest and reasonable constitutional disagreements and not along political or institutional lines.

---

granted Julia Holána (Secretary General of the Court) retirement. Karel Schelle & Jiří Bílý, Dějiny Českého Soudnictví 290 (2018).

239 Jaroslav Benák, *Historický Vývoj Ústavního Soudnictví a Přístupu Jednotlivce k Ústavnímu Soudu*, 26 Časopis pro právní vědu a praxi 397, 409 (2018).

240 Bernd Wieser, *Prag Und Wien*, Austrian L.J. 39, 45 (2022). Néstor Pedro Sagüés, *Tras Las Huellas de Hans Kelsen. A Cien Años de La Primera Corte Constitucional y Ochenta de La Primera Sala Constitucional*, Parlamento y Constitución 179, 183 (2020). There is a moderate criticism in Villalón, *supra* note 206, at 136. The complaint is unfounded. Other reasons are much more important. *See* further below.

241 František Adler, Grundriss Des Tschechoslowakischen Verfassungsrechtes 66–68 (1930); Osterkamp, *supra* note 203, at 12; Kosař & Vyhnánek, *supra* note 209, at 123–24.

242 Kosař & Vyhnánek, *supra* note 209, at 124.

3.3 What Does History Teach Us?

The first four supermajorities specifically concerned with constitutional adjudication were introduced in a short period, from 1912 to 1920. The distance between the subnational supermajorities debate in the United States and Czechoslovakia's constitutionalism makes it unlikely that one influenced the other. The first supermajority, Ohio, was not entirely a model privileging deference to the legislature, as it only required a supermajority when a court of appeals had already upheld a statute.

The failure of Ohio's experiment may be credited to factors other than the pure supermajority requirement, such as the Supreme Court's open sabotage of the rule and the problems deriving from the institutional design chosen—mainly the double threshold. The subsequent subnational supermajorities in North Dakota and Nebraska adopted improved versions of supermajority rules, and they remain functioning to this date, producing hardly any operative problems.

In turn, Czechoslovakia's Constitutional Court had a turbulent history. While Ohio, North Dakota, and Nebraska already had judicial review in place when introducing the supermajority, Czechoslovakia, as a new country, created *ex novo* a constitutional court and employed a supermajority mechanism as a cautionary tool. Although it played a significant role in the Vitorazsko and Valčicko case, it only influenced one case in the court's history, and it is unlikely to have contributed to the court's demise, which resulted from a significant struggle with the political branches and, subsequently, the Nazi invasion.

4 Contemporary Supermajorities

4.1 Peru: A Jurisdiction of Many Supermajorities (1963, 1982, 1995, and 2002)

Peru is a country rich in judicial review history which has had no less than four supermajorities in constitutional adjudication throughout multiple stages, as reflected in Table 4.1. The most prominent ones are the 1982 6:3 supermajority required for the Tribunal of Constitutional Guarantees, and the subsequent 6:1 and 5:2 supermajorities of the Constitutional Court arising from Fujimori's influence and subsequent demise.

Table 4.1 Supermajorities in Constitutional Adjudication in Peruvian History (1963–Present)

Year	*Supermajority*	*Supermajority type*	*Judicial body*	*Democratic regime*
1963–1979	4:1 (80%)	Decisional	Supreme Court	No
1982–1993	6:3 (66.6%)	Deferential	Tribunal of Constitutional Guarantees	Yes
1995–2000	6:1 (85.7%)	Deferential	Constitutional Court	No
2002–present	5:2 (71.4%)	Deferential	Constitutional Court	Yes

Until 1979, Peru went through multiple constitutions. Like many Latin American countries, the Peruvian story is marked by a series of constitutions that reflected a struggle of *caudillos*, failed limitations on executive powers, and dictatorships employing the Constitution as a legitimizing tool.

Peru has known judicial review since 1939. The Civil Code provided that the Constitution should be preferred when the Constitution and the ordinary law conflicted. Diffuse judicial review had a minor influence.[1]

1 Francisco Fernández Segado, *El Control Normativo de La Constitucionalidad En El Perú: Crónica de Un Fracaso Anunciado*, 11 Rev. Esp. Derecho Const. 409 (1999).

DOI: 10.4324/9781003458272-6

In 1963, the Organic Law of the Judiciary—Decree-Law 14605—provided a brief procedure for judicial review foreseen in the Civil Code. Every ruling in which the ordinary judiciary performed judicial review was submitted for revision to the First Chamber of the Supreme Court. It can be argued that it is actually here, in 1963, that the Peruvian supermajority experiment started. Article 116 of the Organic Law established two chambers, each with five magistrates. Article 119 required four votes to issue a decision.

A supermajority was established for both chambers. The rule applied to ordinary cases and constitutional adjudication alike. The mechanism was ineffective, and the judiciary was criticized as passive. The first 1963 supermajority required four out of five possible votes to issue any decision, whether to confirm a law's unconstitutionality, or to reverse such a decision. A lack of effective judicial review characterizes this period, although the supermajority played no role.

October 1968 saw a *coup d'état* that opened the door to twelve years of dictatorships, destroying all remains of democratic institutions. However, the winds began to change by 1978. The deep political and economic crisis forced the government to make democratic concessions. A democratic Constitutional Assembly was formed, and a new Constitution was enacted in 1979.

4.1.1 The Supermajority in the Tribunal of Constitutional Guarantees (1982–1992)

The 1979 Constitution was intended to help the country transition to democracy after a decade of military rule. It was a very extensive Constitution with more than 300 articles. One of its main innovations was the introduction of formal procedures for judicial review. Delegates wanted new institutions of judicial review. The Constitutional Assembly debates reveal that mistrust of the ordinary courts, particularly skepticism of the Supreme Court's ability to perform independent judicial review, was one of the main reasons why Peru opted for a separate Constitutional Court.[2]

Inspired by the Spanish Court of Constitutional Guarantees, the Peruvian 1979 Constitution created a nine-member body in charge of performing constitutional review. Three magistrates each were chosen by the Executive, Congress, and the Supreme Court. The *Tribunal de Garantías Constitucionales* (TGC) was granted the resolution of individual complaints (Amparo), habeas corpus, and abstract normative review under a Kelsenian model. The court, however, could not directly strike down legislation and had to order Congress to issue a law repealing the statute (Article 302).

The 1979 Constitution did not regulate voting protocols. The only mention of a majority was Article 304, which provided that the court would hold

2 Eduardo Dargent, *Determinants of Judicial Independence: Lessons from Three "Cases" of Constitutional Courts in Peru (1982–2007)*, 41 J. Lat. Am. Stud. 251, 259–60 (2009).

sessions in the city of Arequipa unless "an agreement by a majority of its members" decided to hold a session in a different place. Article 303 of the Constitution delegated the regulation of the functioning of the TGC to an organic law.

It took several years for the legislature to issue a statute pertaining to the court and start the court's functioning. The government's draft proposed a simple majority for most court decisions, with a two-thirds supermajority required only to reject a claim on formal grounds. The Senate proposed to raise the quorum to seven members and require five votes to prevent a minority from deciding.[3] The supermajority for constitutional adjudication originated in the Constitutional Commission of the Chamber of Deputies, which modified the majority to six votes. The Commission justified this change by stating: "The importance and significance of the resolutions that the Court makes in this matter, such as striking down legislation or declaring a plea inadmissible, demand at least a two-thirds vote of its members." Although no official records exist of the Commission's discussion, Enrique Chirinos Soto, who was destined to play a decisive role in the Fujimorist supermajority, was among the report's signing members.

In 1982, the Organic Law on the Court of Constitutional Guarantees (Law 23385) was finally published. The quorum was set at six members (Article 6). Article 5 of the statute provided for a five-vote majority to take ordinary decisions "except to resolve the unconstitutionality or inadmissibility of an action, in which six votes are required."

Contrary to the 1963 supermajority, only certain cases required qualified voting. Thus, a supermajority was needed on formal dismissals and to resolve constitutional challenges on legislation. Scholarship has not addressed whether the previous supermajority influenced the new one, but there is a strong possibility that it did. If the contemporary history of constitutional review in Peru starts with the Court of Constitutional Guarantees, as some suggested,[4] then it began with supermajorities.

In November 1982, the Court formally began functioning after Magistrates Vázquez, Silva, Euguren, Corso, Vargas, Peláez, Rodríguez Mantilla, Rodríguez Domínguez, and Aguirre Roca were appointed. The last name "Aguirre Roca," would be relevant for the nascent court and the story of the unfolding Peruvian supermajority.

The court's interpretation of the supermajority requirement heavily restricted its decision-making capabilities. Even though the statute's language was ambiguous, the court interpreted that the supermajority was required to

3 Peruvian Senate, 2a Sesión-Martes, 4 de agosto de 1981, 95 (1981).

4 Maria Bertel, *El Test de Proporcionalidad en la Jurisprudencia del Tribunal Constitucional Peruano*, 15 Int'l J. Const. L. 541, 541 (2017).

strike down and uphold legislation alike,[5] as shown by Judgment 003-84-I/TGC. Some scholars criticized this interpretation as erroneous.[6]

Furthermore, the court interpreted that the statute required a supermajority not only in the outcome but also in the reasoning. Suppose three magistrates considered that a statute infringed Article X of the Constitution, while three considered that it infringed Article Y. In such a scenario, the statute would survive as the supermajority would not have been reached. Votes could only be added up when outcome and reasoning matched, making it difficult to achieve any consensus.[7] Curiously, magistrates agreed on such a restrictive interpretation. In a court riddled with dissent, the interpretation of the supermajority was the only unanimous criterion.

The court's judgment comprised the individual opinions of the magistrates with a conclusion summarizing their decision. Court decisions were short, while the magistrates' opinions were very long, explaining their reasoning and votes.

The law did not guide the effects of supermajority failure decisions. However, the court interpreted that the claim was to be formally dismissed, and the plaintiff retained the right to bring an action on another occasion,[8] presumably allowing the plaintiff to seek a future supermajority. The case was not decided, and the court did not issue a formal "judgment" but rather a "pronouncement" (*pronunciamiento*) briefly stating the dismissal of the case. The *pronunciamiento* itself asserted such right explicitly. Nonetheless, no case was filed anew. However, since concrete and abstract judicial review coexisted, even if the supermajority failed, individual plaintiffs could still challenge a statute before the ordinary judiciary, as proven by the 25022 Union Job Placement Act.[9] Regardless of whether the doctrine was sound in the cases of

5 The court's point of view could have been fostered by the previous supermajority established in the 1963 Organic Law of the Judiciary, which required a supermajority regardless of the outcome of the case. However, the 1963 statute was clear in requiring a supermajority for a decision itself to exist and additionally provided mechanisms to replace absences, which the Organic Law of the TGC did not contemplate.

6 In 1986, Quiroga posited that the supermajority could be interpreted to require a simple majority in case of upholding legislation since the statute's language alluded to "inadmissibility" and "unconstitutionality" when referring to the voting protocol. Aníbal Quiroga, *El Tribunal de Garantías Constitucionales: Ante el Dilema de Ser o No Ser*, THEMIS: REVISTA DE DERECHO 40, 43 (1986).

7 CÉSAR LANDA, TRIBUNAL CONSTITUCIONAL Y ESTADO DEMOCRÁTICO 394 (1999).

8 César Landa, *Del Tribunal de Garantías al Tribunal Constitucional: El Caso Peruano*, 2 PENSAMIENTO CONSTITUCIONAL 73, 80 (1995).

9 The government created a law reserving 25 percent of positions needed in civil construction to workers belonging to the Union. The law was controversial, and many considered it unconstitutional. The TGC upheld the law in Judgment 003-90-I/TGC. According to the court's law (art. 39), the ordinary judiciary could not refrain from applying the statute in diffuse judicial review once the court upheld the law. Nonetheless, the Supreme Court of Lima claimed that Article 39 of the Organic Law of the TGC was unconstitutional and refrained from applying Law 25022. *See id.* at 102.

statutes upheld, it is clear that a supermajority failure did not preclude further constitutional litigation.

Magistrate Aguirre Roca complained about the six-vote requirement[10] and the difficulty of achieving even a simple majority. Aguirre Roca would show himself to be the biggest enemy of the supermajority model. As a magistrate, he certainly was not moderate. He used to respond vehemently, even to academic criticism, in a scornful tone that would have made Scalia blush.[11] He mocked critics and fellow magistrates alike.[12] Aguirre took pride in remarking that he dissented in more than 95 percent of the Constitutional Guarantee Court's decisions: not exactly a model of consensus and collegiality.[13] He sometimes refused to sign resolutions with which he disagreed.[14] Aguirre, who was a trained journalist, understood the media's importance and used both dissenting opinions and academic writing to propagate his ideas.

The supermajority was not very high compared to that in other jurisdictions, standing at 66.6 percent.[15] Nonetheless, it dramatically hindered the court, mainly given the constant absences of magistrates for health reasons or appointment delays.[16] A six-vote majority was proving a tough challenge when only eight magistrates sat on the bench. According to historical records, the court never functioned with all nine magistrates. In Judgment 002-84-I/TGC, it even had to work under a minimum six-judge quorum. According to the records, sixty percent of the time, the Court functioned with eight magistrates and more than thirty percent of the time with seven magistrates.

The mobile threshold did not stem from deficient institutional design. Peruvian legislators purposely adopted such a system. The Constitutional

10 Yuri Tornero, *Estudio Liminar*, *in* Jurisprudencia Relevante del Tribunal de Garantías Constitucionales. Procesos de Inconstitucionalidad 13, 39 (Constitutional Court of Peru ed., 2018).

11 For example, he claimed that the court's critics were "short-sighted," "disrespectful," and "superficial." He also said that if critics had done a better job, other magistrates of the court—whom he called "less capable magistrates"—would have ended up doing theirs. Aguirre also enjoyed using the expression "specialized critic" in quotation marks, as if the text itself was not already mocking enough. Manuel Aguirre Roca, *La Razón Principal del Fracaso del TGC*, Themis: Revista de Derecho 7, 9, 11 (1991).

12 Upon his exit from the court, Aguirre Roca summarized the reasons for the court's failure. He considered magistrates themselves were a primary cause since (1) many magistrates should have never been appointed, (2) the magistrates were so incompetent that even when he explained things to them, they were incapable of understanding, and (3) his fellow magistrates were lazy and incapable of doing their jobs. *Id.* at 7, 9.

13 Manuel Aguirre Roca, *El Tribunal de Garantías Constitucionales ante la Crítica*, Derecho PUCP 187, 191 (1988).

14 For example, *see* Judgment 003-84-I/TGC.

15 *See* Chapter 6, Table 6.1. From twelve supermajority models, the Peruvian TGC stands as the second mildest supermajority.

16 Tornero, *supra* note 10, at 39.

Commission expressly analyzed the problem and considered it preferable to ask directly for votes rather than for percentages.[17]

Since 33 percent of the court's decisions were supermajority failure decisions, one could theorize that the supermajority played a key role in the court's most important cases, but it was not so. The lack of consensus affected both politically charged cases[18] and ordinary ones alike. For example, the court could not resolve non-political controversies such as routine expropriations but was able to strike down legislation of great importance, such as the law regulating the much-needed urban mass transportation (004-005-91-I/TGC).

The most prominent cases in which the supermajority played a controversial role were the invalid ballot and the preferential vote cases related to electoral matters, a sensitive area in the nascent democratic republic.

Article 203 of the 1979 Constitution stated: "The President of the Republic shall be elected by direct vote and by more than half of the validly issued ballots." If none of the candidates achieved the required majority, a second vote was to be held between the top two candidates. Law 23903 regulated presidential elections. Article 6 provided a controversial definition of valid votes, including void ballots and blank votes. As a result, the required majority increased substantially in the first round despite the Constitution hinting at a narrower definition of "valid votes."[19] Even though Article 6 was a single provision, it had two clearly differentiated rules: void ballots as valid votes and blank votes. A Congressional minority challenged the law, and the court divided in Judgment 003-84-I/TGC. Functioning with eight magistrates, the court had to gather six votes to strike down legislation and could not form a consensus, being forced to issue a *pronunciamiento*. A 5:3 vote resulted in a non-qualified majority upholding the requirement on blank votes, whereas a 5:3 majority failed to strike down the void votes requirement. A furious Aguirre Roca refused to sign the ruling as registered by the court's general secretary.

The second case was equally controversial. A senatorial minority questioned Articles 10, 11, 12, and 20 of the Electoral Law 23903. The provisions challenged established a "preferential vote," an open list system within a proportional representation that allowed voters to modify the list's order. The plaintiffs argued that the system was complex and thus discriminated against illiterates. The court again split in a 5:3 vote, with Aguirre Roca in the non-qualified majority.

17 *See* Dictamen de la Comisión de Constitución en los Proyectos de Ley Referente a la Ley Orgánica del Tribunal de Garantías Constitucionales, Chamber of Deputies, Proy. Sen-Just. 10 y Proy. No. 669, 1ra Legislatura ordinaria de 1981, para. 4.

18 The court was unable to muster a supermajority in an expropriation case in Judgment 062-90-I/TGC.

19 It could be argued that under a strict definition of "valid votes," white votes should be deemed valid, but void votes should be excluded.

The court had initially proved to be of minimal relevance, but that changed after Alberto Fujimori's election in 1990. Prone to authoritarian policies and questionable pacification views, Fujimori was averse to checks and balances. Under Fujimori's regime, the court began to show its teeth. As Landa documents, the court declared several decrees and a law unconstitutional between August 1991 and March 1992.[20] Other laws and decrees from Fujimori awaited resolution.

Alberto Fujimori undertook the so-called *Fujimorazo*, a self-coup in 1992. Menaced by tanks, Congress was forced to shut down, and hundreds of opposition members were detained. The National Council of the Judiciary and the TGC were dissolved.[21] Tanks, not the supermajority, permanently paralyzed the court.

It is hard to assess the impact of the supermajority in the TGC definitively. Several factors, such as highly restricted access to the court and the constant absences of court members, took a significant toll on the institution. The profile of the magistrates did not contribute significantly to a collegial environment. Magistrates were more accustomed to individual opinions rather than consensus-seeking agreements.[22] Furthermore, the court interpreted the supermajority more restrictively than it could have. The TGC coexisted with diffuse judicial review. Individual plaintiffs could argue the unconstitutionality of statutes before ordinary judges and courts with inter partes effects.

4.1.2 The Fujimorists' Supermajority

The Fujimori *coup* received international criticism. The Organization of American States dispatched a special mission to Peru.[23] Fujimori was soon forced into democratic concessions. As a result, a new Constitution was born. Contrary to the 1979 Constitution, which was constructed with full participation, the 1993 Constitution was hastily drafted. Fujimorian forces saw the Constitution as a legitimizing façade rather than a proper normative foundation of democracy. Unsurprisingly, the new Constitution fostered the concentration of powers in the executive. Fujimori's faction pushed hard to allow immediate presidential reelection for at least one period, contrary to the former 1979 Constitution that forbade immediate reelection.

However, the 1993 Constitution had some concessions and contained certain provisions that Fujimori would have preferred not to include. Fujimori certainly would have eliminated the "single reelection" rule, and his forces

20 Landa, *supra* note 8.

21 Camila Gianella Malca & Ursula Baertl Espinoza, *Peru*, *in* The Oxford Handbook of Constitutional Law in Latin America 239, 243 (Conrado Hübner Mendes, Roberto Gargarella & Sebastián Guidi eds., 2022).

22 Quiroga remarked that magistrates were to blame in certain cases for the TGC's inability to decide. Quiroga, *supra* note 6, at 44.

23 Gianella Malca & Baertl Espinoza, *supra* note 21, at 243.

were against including a Constitutional Court. The former TGC had shown Fujimori that judicial review in the hands of an independent body was dangerous to his power. Judicial review in the hands of the ordinary jurisdiction, which Fujimori controlled, was preferable.

Initially, the Constituent Assembly did not provide for a Constitutional Court. Enrique Chirinos openly spoke against it.[24] Nevertheless, international pressure, the pressure of the legal profession—through the Lima Bar Association—and the need to prove a credible commitment to democratic institutions[25] forced Fujimorians to concede to the inclusion of a constitutional court.

Fujimori's opposition continued even after the court was included in the Constitution. His parliamentary majority avoided its implementation as long as possible, the court's law was delayed, and magistrates were not appointed. It took three years for the court to function.

The constitutional regulation of the court was brief. Articles 201–205 stated the court's competence and the number of magistrates. In the same way as its predecessor, the Constitution did not provide a concrete majority for the court to decide. The supermajority would come back with a vengeance in the court's legislation.

As Landa recalls, even if the Fujimorian majority dominated the Justice Commission in the Constituent Assembly, its President was César Fernández.[26] César Fernández Arce was part of the Fujimorian majority but was considered to have inklings of independence.[27] The first draft of the court's organic law provided for a simple majority.

A vigorous constitutional court was not in Fujimori's plans. Enrique Chirinos Soto exerted intense pressure to raise the threshold first to require unanimity[28] and then to require at least six votes out of seven (85 percent), much higher than the former 66 percent in the TGC. Independent parliamentary groups, accustomed to supermajority rules in the 1963 and 1982 experiences, leaned towards a 5:2 supermajority.

Even though a few independent representatives outside of Fujimori's party approved of the proposal,[29] most not loyal to Fujimori were skeptical of the high consensus required. Deputy Flores Nano, a supporter of supermajorities,

24 Congreso Constituyente Democrático, Debate Constitucional. Pleno: 1993 1970 (1998).

25 Dargent, *supra* note 2, at 267.

26 Landa, *supra* note 7, at 393.

27 For example, Fernández Arce voted against the Amnesty Law. *See* Democratic Constituent Assembly, *Sesiones de La Comisión de Constitución y Reglamento* (1993), http://www.congreso.gob.pe/index.php?Kfn=enlaces%2Fhistorico%2FCCD%2Fsesiones-comision-constitucion&K=27208&File=%2FDocs%2Fspa%2Ffiles%2Fccd%2F20-1.htm (last visited Feb. 6, 2023).

28 *See* Parliamentary Debates, 13th Session, Wednesday, Oct. 5, 1994, at 978.

29 For example, Roger Cáceres Velásquez from the National Front of Workers and Peasants openly spoke in favor of the supermajority. *See id.* at 955.

considered that the importance and nature of the functions of the Constitutional Court indeed deserved a supermajority. However, he argued that "if the Court's members are seven, it is excessive that six votes are required. I deem . . . that five would be a reasonable number." Deputy Marcenaro and Ferrero Costa[30] agreed with that view.[31] Deputy Olivera was the most vigorous critic: "To impose six votes out of seven members for the Constitutional Court to decide is a requirement not established in the Constitution, and I believe it is an excess of Parliament to handcuff the Constitutional Court."[32]

Deeply angered by the criticism of his proposal, Chirinos Soto intervened and claimed that a 6:1 supermajority was not impossible to achieve. Chirinos argued that if fewer than six magistrates believed a law to be unconstitutional, it was a good thing that they could not declare the statute unconstitutional, since otherwise "that second chamber would exert an excessive power of reverting the laws given by the Congress, representing the full country."[33] Chirinos, the Fujimorist, had used the word "chamber" as he probably saw the court as another political body.

Contrary to the 1982 supermajority, a product of institutional design and careful debate, the 1995 supermajority seemed like a frontal attempt to paralyze the court. The discussion continued in several sessions. Fujimorists made clear that the six-vote supermajority was not negotiable.[34] Deputy Olivera had the arguments, but Chirino had the votes. The supermajority was approved.

While the 1982 supermajority resulted from a democratic debate and a legitimate desire to impose constraints on a counter-majoritarian body, the 1995 supermajority had profoundly authoritarian roots.

Contrary to the 1982 supermajority, Fujimori's forces did not leave much room for interpretation. The TGC had assumed the position that supermajority failure decisions lack precedential status and plaintiffs could sue anew. The Fujimorist supermajority did not allow such possibilities.

Article 4 of the Organic Law on the Constitutional Court not only set a high supermajority but also provided that if the court failed to reach the qualified majority, the court should issue an opinion declaring the action of unconstitutionality groundless [*declarando infundada la demanda*]."[35] The

30 *See* Parliamentary Debates, 13th Session, Wednesday, Oct. 5, 1994, 974.

31 *Id.* at 963.

32 *Id.* at 966.

33 *Id.* at 967.

34 In a subsequent session, Deputy Ferrero complained about the majority's position: "it seems that currently either we approve the law with the six votes [supermajority] or there won't be a law at all." Olivera insisted, "With this proposal, there won't be any real possibility of exercising judicial review in practice." *See* Parliamentary Debates, 22nd Session, Wednesday, Nov. 30, 1994, at 2091, 2102.

35 The drafting was clear, but nonetheless Aguirre Roca complained about its application. In his dissenting opinion to Decision 001-96-I/TC, he claimed the judgment should not have declared the claim groundless, nor should the court have upheld the statute.

drafting can be seen as a reaction to the previous interpretation of the TGC. Fujimorists wanted not only to paralyze the Court but to convert it into a vehicle to legitimize statutes, even if they lacked the support of a majority of magistrates. Furthermore, they wanted to preclude the judiciary from any intervention, as in the previously described Union Job Placement Act case.

Contrary to the former TGC's interpretation, the new Constitutional Court understood the statute as requiring only a consensus on the outcome. Plurality decisions were permitted, and as long as six magistrates considered a statute unconstitutional, an agreement in their reasoning was not required. This feature persists in the contemporary Constitutional Court.

The first appointment of magistrates was complicated. The majority wanted to push loyal magistrates onto the court.[36] Fujimorists knew that the Constitutional Court might prove problematic even with the supermajority. After years of delay, the court finally began functioning in 1996 with Magistrate Nugent as President and Magistrates Acosta Sánchez, Díaz Valverde, Rey Terry, Revoredo Marsano, García Marcelo, and Aguirre Roca. A survivor of regime change, Aguirre Roca was the only magistrate of the TGC that made it to the newly created Constitutional Court, probably thanks to his friendship with Chirinos.[37] Fujimori's regime was confident since two loyal magistrates were appointed,[38] Magistrates García Marcelo and Acosta Sánchez.

The supermajority was to be put to the test quickly. In 1996, several Congressmen challenged the constitutionality of the supermajority requirement. The court decided by a 4:3 margin to uphold the supermajority.[39] Aguirre Roca, Rey Terry, and Revoredo Marsano filed a dissenting opinion. The supermajority played no role in the ruling, as a majority sufficed to uphold the legislation.

Aguirre Roca was clearly furious. In his dissenting vote alongside two magistrates,[40] he went on at length claiming that the supermajority infringed the Constitution and that the court could even disregard it. For nine years, Aguirre Roca had belonged to the TGC, which had a statutory supermajority itself. This was the first time he had hinted that legislative modulations of the court's voting protocol were unconstitutional.[41]

36 Dargent, *supra* note 2, at 268.

37 Chirinos and Aguirre Roca were longtime friends. Catherine M. Conaghan, Fujimori's Peru: Deception in the Public Sphere 130 (2005).

38 Dargent, *supra* note 2, at 268.

39 Judgment Exp. No 005-96-I/TC. For an analysis, *see* Chapter 5.2.4.2.

40 It is reasonable to assume that Aguirre Roca himself drafted the dissent, since some paragraphs take the redaction he previously employed in his dissenting opinion to Judgment 001-96-I/TC.

41 Among the Peruvian scholarship, only Landa has pointed out Aguirre Roca's sudden change of opinion. Landa, *supra* note 7, at 395. Had Aguirre Roca maintained the same opinion he had in his dissenting votes and academic articles, the supermajority would have been upheld by a 5:2 vote.

The first case in which the supermajority played a decisive role would come at the end of 1996 in the so-called referendum case. The Fujimorian majority issued the Referendum Law 26592, making a sham of the institution. The requirements for a referendum were high, and Congress was given powers to decide if it was binding or not. The minoritarian parties challenged the law, and the supermajority yielded fruit. A 5:2 majority was achieved to strike down the statute. Magistrates Acosta and García Marcelo, loyal to the government, managed to save the statute. In Judgment 003-96-I/TC, the court noted, almost regretfully, that "the Court is forced, against the express will of the majority of its members, to uphold the law."

Fujimori's forces were undoubtedly pleased with both rulings as they prepared to push Fujimori's reelection forward. The 1979 Constitution did not provide the possibility of immediate reelection. The 1993 Constitution, *au contraire*, allowed a single immediate reelection. The parliamentary majority, employing a legalistic argument, issued Law 26657, interpreting Article 112 of the Constitution. According to the parliamentary majority, Fujimori had never been elected President under the 1993 Constitution and thus could run for office again. The law tried to circumvent the fact that Fujimori had two previous terms. The Lima Bar Association challenged the law before the Constitutional Court, and all hell broke loose.

The two magistrates loyal to Fujimori ensured that no law could be declared unconstitutional. However, the court's majority had been working on a draft to refrain from applying the supermajority. Under Justice Rey Terry, the court was preparing to declare the law "inapplicable," albeit not unconstitutional. Circumventing the mechanism by changing the wording was dubious. A 5:2 majority favored such a solution. However, Fujimori had placed allies on the court. Magistrate García Marcelo handed the internal draft to the police, arguing that "the document was proof of a scheme designed to thwart the President's reelection."[42]

The draft leaking led to massive pressure from the government on the rest of the magistrates. Nugent and Díaz Valverde cracked and requested a further vote. Magistrates Nungent, Velarde, Acosta, and García Marcelo abstained in the new vote, arguing that they had given an opinion on the law's constitutionality beforehand. Only Aguirre Roca, Rey Terry, and Revoredo voted to sustain the court's original criteria. There was no quorum. There was no court.[43]

Nonetheless, Aguirre Roca was not having it this time and, alongside Rey Terry and Revoredo, issued a 3:0 "Judgment" declaring the law inapplicable. Aguirre, Rey, and Revoredo violated the court's regulations by issuing a

42 Inter-American Court of Human Rights, Case of the Constitutional Court v. Peru, Judgment of Jan. 31, 2001 (Merits, Reparations, and Costs).

43 Article 4 of the Organic Law (Law 26435) provided that six members were required to make decisions validly. Three votes were as good as none.

decision when a quorum was not present and evaded a clear rule. The other magistrates infringed the law by abstaining without valid cause, and García had been an informer and a traitor, stealing court documents. Amidst this political struggle, it is hard to find lawful conduct.

Aguirre, Rey, and Revoredo's "decision" seemed to have been a strategic mistake.[44] The rest is history. The Peruvian Congress impeached Rey Terry, Revoredo, and Aguirre Roca for breaking the court's quorum regulation in issuing a judicial decision.[45] Again, almost poetically, Aguirre Roca's friend was in charge of accusing him.[46] Being the supermajority's creator, Enrique Chirinos was tasked with accusing those who had evaded the rule.[47]

After impeachment, Congress passed Law 26954, temporarily establishing a four-member quorum and majority to resolve all constitutional procedures except the action of unconstitutionality. Four members meant unanimity. The court continued to function with four magistrates entering a period of servility.[48] The supermajority was no longer required. History would side with the minority. In 2001, the Inter-American Court of Human Rights ruled in favor of the impeached magistrates and condemned Peru.[49]

Toward the end of the conflict, corruption scandals unmasked Fujimori's regime. Several videos leaked in September 2000 revealed the true extent of Fujimorist corruption. Political unrest flourished more than ever before. Fujimori's "attempt for a second reelection was the demise of his political project."[50] Fujimori tried to resign by fax from Japan in 2000. Congress rejected the resignation and removed him from office through an impeachment procedure.

44 Citing Dixon and Issacharoff: "Lessons abound of courts that misplayed their hands, sought to thwart a too-powerful executive and were quickly relegated to irrelevance . . . the results were simply the shuttering of the courts and institutions and the increasing consolidation of autocratic power." Rosalind Dixon & Samuel Issacharoff, *Living to Fight Another Day: Judicial Deferral in Defense of Democracy*, 2016 Wis. L. Rev. 683, 689 (2016). Even though Dixon and Issacharoff do not analyze this precise judgment, they consider the Peruvian case in relationship with the Peruvian Supreme Court's efforts to discipline President Fujimori.

45 Alfredo Schulte-Bockholt, Corruption as Power 121 (2013).

46 Conaghan, *supra* note 37, at 130.

47 It would not be the last time Aguirre Roca would evade the rule. Upon his return to the Court (*see infra*), he purposely voted insincerely in 006-2000-AI/TC. Believing that a statute was constitutional, he voted to invalidate it. In his dissenting opinion, he confessed he had switched votes: "in light of the absurd rule [the supermajority] . . . which would produce the inadmissible, illogical and unconstitutional effect of allowing the vote of a Magistrate to prevail over those remaining."

48 Luis López Zamora, *Constitutional Court of Peru*, 11 *in* The Max Planck Encyclopedia of Public International Law, 6 (Rüdiger Wolfrum, Frauke Lachenmann & Ana Harvey eds., 2021).

49 Tom Ginsburg, *International Courts and Democratic Backsliding*, 37 Berkeley J. Int'l L. 265, 282 (2019).

50 López Zamora *supra* note 48, at 6.

4.1.3 The Supermajority in Peru's Contemporary History

The end of Fujimori's regime led to the death of the third supermajority. After Fujimori's regime fell, the Constitutional Court was restored to its seven-member composition. Upon the return of the impeached magistrates in 2000, the court began functioning relatively normally. Several statutes were struck down, and the supermajority did not produce any perceivable influence.[51] Nonetheless, the supermajority had played a part in the political crisis, and Congress deemed it was time to change it.

4.1.3.1 The Birth of a New Supermajority

In 2002, Congress, already enjoying political pluralism,[52] issued Law 27780 to modify only one article of the Organic Law on the Constitutional Court: the majority threshold. External observers may have thought the court would be switched to a simple majority, but this was not to be.

During Fujimori's regime, parliamentary groups had supported a supermajority, albeit of a lesser degree than Chirino's proposal. After Fujimori, the idea returned. Article 4 of the Act on the Constitutional Court was amended to require a 5:2 supermajority to dismiss an action of unconstitutionality or to strike down legislation. A plural Congress decided to diminish the Fujimorist supermajority but maintain it.[53]

Paese García, President of the legislative committee that analyzed the proposal, stated that during "several years, there has been a petition in several bills to lower the threshold to five votes."[54] Various parliamentary groups intervened, but not one proposed adopting a simple majority. There was even some opposition to lowering the threshold.[55] The amendment opened the era of the fourth supermajority in Peruvian constitutional adjudication.

In 2004, Congress issued a new Organic Law on the Constitutional Court (Law 28301), maintaining a five-vote supermajority in Article 5.

Supermajorities seem to be at the heart of Peruvian design. Not only do some ordinary judicial bodies function under supermajority requirements,[56] but the Peruvian Constitutional Court's ability to work in subdivisions,

51 Luis Huerta Guerrero, *El Proceso de Inconstitucionalidad en el Perú*, II *in* El Derecho Procesal Constitucional Peruano 839, 883 (José Palomino ed., 2 ed. 2015).

52 Dargent, *supra* note 2, at 254.

53 In a further amendment, Congress also reduced the quorum set for the court. Deputy Pease referred to the former supermajority, underscoring it was too high: "[W]ith it, the Fujimori regime sought somehow to prevent the Court from functioning." *See* Parliamentary Debates, 13th Session, Thursday, Sept. 2002, at 752.

54 *See* the Parliamentary Debates, 13th Session, Thursday, Sept. 6, 2001, at 813.

55 *Id.* at 816.

56 Article 141 of the Organic Law on the Judiciary requires four votes in chambers in the Supreme Court to issue a resolution. The chambers operate with the exact "magistrado dirimente" [tie-breaking magistrate] mechanism, explained below.

chambers formed by three magistrates, is not exempt from supermajorities either. Chambers adjudicate constitutional questions, mainly related to rights infringements, such as individual constitutional complaints or habeas corpus. Article 117 of the Constitutional Procedural Code and Article 4 of the Organic Law on the Constitutional Court require three votes in agreement to issue any decision. The rule is not new, as it was established when the first legislation of the constitutional court was issued.

The three-vote rule has an impasse mechanism. If the chamber fails to summon three votes, the chamber may call magistrates from the other chambers until three votes are met. The same mechanism functions in the case of absences or recusals. Thus, ordinarily, chambers may resolve cases only unanimously. In practice, one disagreement turns the chamber into a larger body.[57]

4.1.3.2 Practice of the Contemporary Supermajority

From 2004 onwards, the court has been considered relatively independent. It has been able to rule against the interests of political branches,[58] and has consolidated as a significant actor in the Peruvian institutional background.[59] Under a more independent court, the supermajority has not faded away but has thrived.

Five votes still present challenges. Magistrates are known to act carefully on propositions in seeking consensus. Former Magistrate Espinosa-Saldaña remembers tailoring his drafts in a more minimalistic way when proposing to strike down a law, hoping to discourage dissent from blocking a supermajority: "A judgment is a consensus on the minimums,"[60] he is known to say. A supermajority failure leads to upholding the statute and yields control to the minority to write the opinion.[61] The majority, in turn, files a dissenting opinion.

Even though the voting protocol is nominal, and magistrates should vote by raising hands, the excessive workload generated a dynamic in which every

57 Enough disagreements would make the court solve the challenge *en banc*. While it is true that the unanimity requirement may turn to a simple majority when disagreement arises in the first instance, it is a mechanism that may sacrifice effectiveness and rapid solutions in favor of seeking high consensus. In most cases, decisions appear unanimous to the parties, and the fact that magistrates are added "on demand" makes it likely to obtain supermajority results.

58 Dargent, *supra* note 2, at 271.

59 López Zamora, *supra* note 48, at 4.

60 Eloy Espinosa-Saldaña, *Interview with a Former Magistrate of the Peruvian Constitutional Court* (2023).

61 Some exceptions exist. For example, in 00018- 2013-PI/TC, the court seemed to have turned to a seriatim-style opinion by formally communicating the court's result and attaching the individual opinions as an addendum.

magistrate may vote simply in his own office, and deliberation is severely diminished.[62]

Supermajority failure decisions lack precedential status. However, they do have some binding status from the way the system is designed. Ordinary judges in Peru may find a statute unconstitutional through diffuse review even if it has not been challenged before the Peruvian Constitutional Court. Historically, the Constitutional Procedural Code has provided that judges may not perform a diffuse judicial review on statutes upheld by the Peruvian Constitutional Court,[63] currently in accordance with Article VII of the Constitutional Procedural Code.[64] Thus, even if lacking a formal precedent status, the decision still binds all branches and judges to consider the statute constitutional.[65] The binding effect on the outcome extends to the Peruvian Constitutional Court itself,[66] which may not analyze the unconstitutionality of the same provision on the same grounds in future cases.[67]

62 César Landa, *La Jurisdicción Constitucional En El Perú: Parte I*, IV Revista do Curso de Direito 27, 43 (2014).

63 This provision existed already in the Organic Law on the TGC. Nonetheless, its consequences were different. Given that the TGC interpreted that a supermajority was required to uphold and strike down legislation, failing to gather a six-vote supermajority, the Court would issue a *pronunciamiento*, not a decision. Ordinary judges could perform judicial review of the law. Currently, as explained, failing to muster the five-vote supermajority results in immunizing the statute from judicial review by the ordinary judiciary.

64 The provision does not distinguish the different ways a statute may be upheld. A statute may be upheld in three different ways: (1) by a supermajority, creating a formal binding precedent; (2) by a simple majority, not creating a formal binding precedent; and (3) by a minority preventing reaching a supermajority to strike down the law. Only the first method may create a binding precedent, but all three methods equally bind ordinary courts to apply the provision. By settling the dispute and binding all judicial bodies, the supermajority has some of the effects usually credited to binding precedents. Nonetheless, the decision is only binding regarding the upheld provision.

65 Early on, García Belaunde justified this provision to guarantee the Constitutional Court's central role and ensure coherence and unity on the criteria on which statutes are valid within the legal system. Domingo García Belaunde, El Derecho Procesal Constitucional en Perspectiva 242 (2 ed. 2009).

66 The reasoning set forth by the minority's opinion does not bind ordinary judicial bodies or the Constitutional Court. Indeed, the Constitutional Court may quote this decision in future opinions. All decisions lacking binding precedent status may be invoked, but it is unlikely. Former Magistrate Espinosa-Saldaña states that "the Court rarely quotes minority opinions, although sometimes such opinions are quoted either in their dictum or when the former minority becomes a majority." Espinosa-Saldaña, *supra* note 60.

67 The Court should declare an individual complaint "*improcedente*" (inadmissible) if it were to question the same provision protected by previous supermajority failure decisions. Evasion of this rule is uncommon but has occurred. In the Amparo 03338-2019-PA/TC, the Court claimed that despite the questioned provision failing to gather a supermajority in 00015-2018-PI/TC and 00024-2018-PI/TC, in the present case, "its application to a concrete case is unconstitutional." Magistrates Ledesma and Miranda issued dissenting opinions, accusing the majority of evading the rule since the provision failed to attain a supermajority previously.

By institutional design, absences should rarely impact the Peruvian Constitutional Court. Justices are appointed for five years, but the court functions with a prorogation system. Unless new magistrates are appointed, the outgoing magistrates continue to serve their tenure.[68] Short absences have not been problematic. Former President Landa deemed that during his term, no case arose in which an absence hindered the court's functioning by raising the supermajority.[69]

Nonetheless, some problems may occur due to unforeseeable circumstances, such as death or health-related resignations. As former Magistrate Espinosa-Saldaña conveyed, political negotiations to appoint magistrates are very complicated in Peru. For example, upon the unfortunate death of Magistrate Ramos in September 2021, Congress could not appoint a new magistrate for an extended period, and Ramos's place was vacant up to May 2022. The problem left the court with the challenge of having to muster five votes on a court effectively composed of six members. Magistrate Saldaña deems the Peruvian supermajority's main shortcoming stems from the lack of substitute magistrates.[70]

The Peruvian Constitutional Court has not always abided by the rule, and some evasion attempts have existed through two different mechanisms: interpretative decisions and the so-called "clarification of judgment" (*aclaración de sentencia*). Regarding the first one, the former President of the Peruvian Constitutional Court, César Landa, stated that the supermajority did not obstruct the court considerably since the majority keeps the possibility of interpreting statutes narrowly in a constitutional conforming interpretation.[71] For example, struggling to find the supermajority to strike down some controversial provisions of the Free Trade Agreement between Peru and Chile, the court resorted to an aggressive interpretative decision. In the second place, some analysts claim that magistrates interpret the power to clarify previous judgments or opinions too widely, sometimes introducing variations in the decision itself.[72]

68 For example, up to the 2021 new appointments, several Magistrates served up to three extra years beyond their original term.

69 César Landa, *Interview with a Former President of the Peruvian Constitutional Court*, (unpublished, 2023).

70 Espinosa-Saldaña, *supra* note 60.

71 Landa, *supra* note 69.

72 *El Frontón* is perhaps the most visible case, although not associated with a supermajority. The Constitutional Court issued an opinion in 2013 (01969-2011-PHC/TC) which practically forbade prosecuting a group of marines allegedly implicated in a massacre, while repressing a mutiny in El Frontón Prison in San Juan Bautista. A four-magistrate majority (Justices Vergara, Mesía, Calle, and Álvarez), seemingly considering that since it was not a crime against humanity, the statute of limitations had expired. In 2016, the court (with new magistrates) issued a new resolution clarifying the previous ruling. The court contended that Justice Vergara's vote was contradictory to the arguments in his opinion (*i.e.*, he had voted in favor of the decision while, in fact, disagreeing that the crime's statute of limitations had expired). The new court "changed" Vergara's vote (he was no longer a magistrate) and clarified the previous ruling, modifying the case's outcome and allowing the marines to be prosecuted. The case

The impact of the supermajority has varied across periods. Following the return to democracy, the court began working rather effectively, particularly after the original four magistrates that had remained after impeachment left the court. Even though some supermajority failure decisions arose—such as 0032-2005-PI/TC regarding vehicle traffic regulations—the court was prone to consensus. In 2014, a 3:4 vote saved the Act on Military Service. The decision upheld the lottery recruitment system for filling vacancies and the temporary suspension of civil rights to those failing to attend the call although it struck down fines imposed by the act on non-compliant individuals. In 2020, the court was forced by a 3:4 vote to uphold a statute prohibiting persons with prior corruption charge convictions from running for public office.[73]

In 2020, the court would face a particularly tough debate in the bullfighting case.[74] A large number of citizens challenged the constitutionality of the 2016 Animal Protection and Welfare Act (Law 30407). The statute prohibited animal cruelty and forbade harming animals. However, in its transitory provisions, the statute created an exception allowing bullfighting, bull wrestling, cockfighting, and "other spectacles declared to be cultural by the competent authority."

The plaintiffs claimed that the exception contradicted the very purpose of the statute, allowing what they deemed a barbaric spectacle. The nation was divided. Many sided with the petitioners, but an important part of the country considered those spectacles embedded in the local culture. Spaniards might have brought the spectacle under the colony, but they deemed it Peruvian at its core. The court would prove to be as equally divided as the population.

The case had two further particularities which contributed to the heat. The case's Judge-Rapporteur, prominent Magistrate Carlos Ramos, made his draft public before the deliberation, a newly introduced but relatively uncommon practice in the Peruvian Constitutional Court.[75] Furthermore, since the 2020 Covid-19 pandemic, it was one of the first cases in which the court would hold

---

led to Congress attempting to impeach the magistrates who had changed the judgment. *See* Erika García Cobián, *Límites Del Control Parlamentario Frente a las Decisiones de la Jurisdicción Constitucional: Reflexiones a Propósito de la Acusación Constitucional contra Magistrados del Tribunal Constitucional por el Caso el Frontón*, *in* Libro Homenaje del Área de Derecho Constitucional por los 100 Años de la Facultad de Derecho de la Pontificia Universidad Católica del Perú 15 (2019). Former Magistrate Espinosa-Saldaña contends that the decision resulted from a stratagem by former magistrates, which purportedly manufactured a majority where there was none since Magistrate Vergara's vote contradicted the decision it supposedly supported. Espinosa-Saldaña, *supra* note 60.

73 *Expediente* 0015-2018-PI/TC and 0024-2018-PI/TC.

74 *Expediente* 00022-2018-PI/TC.

75 The Mexican Supreme Court is another constitutional court that has the same practice. The Judge-Rapporteur may discretionally publish the draft before the discussion. In Peru, this possibility was introduced by the court's administrative resolution 058-2020-P/TC. After the amendment, Article 43-A of the internal regulations provides that public deliberations may be held and "a draft or a draft's summary shall be published previous to the discussion."

a public deliberation in the style of courts such as the Mexican or Brazilian Supreme Courts.[76] Thousands of Peruvians would watch the debate live.

While upholding most of the statute, Ramos' draft proposed a broad interpretation of the Constitution, which stated that animal welfare and protection was an implicit constitutional principle. Furthermore, the ruling proposed a set of criteria to be filled for allowing such spectacles, which was relatively narrow. Ramos also suggested considering a State obligation to restrict children's attendance to them. The draft seemed to want to strike down the statute rather than uphold it. However, it concluded that such spectacles were exceptionally permitted in the areas where they constituted a cultural heritage. Given the contradictory nature of the arguments and conclusion, one could wonder whether it was an instance of strategic deferral.[77] However, the ruling proposed to strike down cockfighting with gaffs (blades).

The court was divided, as reflected by the magistrate's interventions. For example, Magistrate Ferrero resorted to poetry in defending the beauty of bullfighting, while Magistrate Ledesma, the court's president, in a semi-theatrical display, took out two sharp bullfighting banderillas in the middle of the deliberations. A majority of the court upheld bullfighting and bullwrestling. However, a 3:4 minority upheld the constitutionality of cockfighting. As Hong argued in the South Korean case, the arguments of the decision and the supermajority failure may have signaled a turn[78] in the Peruvian debate. It is not unlikely that a future court will finally strike down such exceptions, and political branches know there is a growing consensus within the court of their unconstitutionality.

A year later, in 2021, the tragic death of Magistrate Carlos Ramos led to a temporary six-member court and a couple of contentious supermajority failure decisions. In Judgment 922/2021, the court failed to achieve the supermajority against a controversial law allowing the Peruvian tax administration to break bank secrecy. Afterward, in Judgment 954/2021, the court faced a challenge against the new Constitutional Procedural Code (regulating the

76 Several authors have analyzed public deliberation in those jurisdictions. Inter alia, *see* Francisca Pou Giménez, *Changing the Channel: Broadcasting Deliberations in the Mexican Supreme Court*, *in* Justices and Journalists 209 (Richard Davis & David Taras eds., 2017); Virgílio da Silva, *Deciding without Deliberating*, 11 Int'l J. Const. L. 557 (2013); Virgilio da Silva, *Big Brother Is Watching the Court*, 51 Verfassung und Recht in Übersee/Law and Politics in Africa, Asia and Latin America 437 (2018).

77 Dixon and Issacharoff, *supra* note 44, at 731 (discussing the concept). Taking Dixon's and Issacharoff's argument, similarly, in Marbury vs. Madison, the Court expanded its power, introduced a more robust standard, but "maintained that assertion of power ensconced in dictum, with a holding that left intact the challenged refusal…" *Id.* at 686. Magistrate Ramos was proposing reading into the Constitution an implicit right to animal welfare and establishing standards that in the future would make it hard to allow the events the ruling was not prohibiting this time.

78 Joon Seok Hong, *Signaling the Turn: The Supermajority Requirement and Judicial Power on the Constitutional Court of Korea*, 67 Am. J. Comp. L. 177 (2019).

court's procedures). Even though the new law also established the supermajority, the applicant's challenge was on formal grounds and did not question the rule. There was a tie, and by a 3:3 vote, the court had to uphold the law's constitutionality.

Since 2004, the court has functioned with normality and achieved some prestige. Nonetheless, a sector of the Peruvian scholarship agrees on amending the supermajority. Even if most scholars are neutral towards the rule and accepted it without much reflection,[79] classical constitutional scholars such as César Landa[80] or Abad Yupanqui, heavily influenced by the 6:1 Fujimorist supermajority, believe the institution should be changed, even if empirically it is not blocking the court.[81] However, other scholars consider that the supermajority should be maintained[82] or that modifying the supermajority is not particularly important to the court's functioning, as are other rules.[83]

4.1.3.3 Expansion of Supermajority Rules by the Constitutional Court

An already established independent court has even expanded the scope of the supermajority several times. Between 2010 and 2015, up to five supermajority rules governed the court's procedures. Two of them were provided by law: the supermajority to strike down legislation and the supermajority for the chambers. Three were self-imposed: the transitory *Sangüesa* impasse rule doctrine, the precedent supermajority, and the manipulative judgments supermajority.

In 2006, the court faced a challenge against the Law on Political Parties (Law 28617) on the constitutionality of the electoral threshold. The law

79 This is the opinion of Landa. Landa, *supra* note 69.

80 However, Landa would later go on to defend introducing a supermajority to approve binding precedents on the Constitutional Court. César Landa, Derecho Procesal Constitucional 81 (2018).

81 Joaquín Brage, an influential Spanish scholar, has criticized the supermajority. Brage's criticism of the Peruvian case is solely based on normative provisions and ignores Peru's constitutional history or the empirical functioning of the supermajority. Brage even claims that the supermajority in the Peruvian case is solely linked to Fujimorism. Joaquín Brage, *La acción peruana de inconstitucionalidad*, 2 *in* El Derecho Procesal Constitucional Peruano 801, 829 (José Palomino ed., 2 ed. 2015). The claim is false. The supermajority emerged as a coherent institutional design in the 1979–1982 democratic momentum. Contrary to the Mexican case (*see* Chapter 4.3.3), Brage's criticism does not seem to have influenced the Peruvian debate.

82 Francisco Morales Saravia, El Tribunal Constitucional del Perú: Organización y Funcionamiento. Estado de la Cuestión y Propuestas de Mejora 90 (2014). Years later, Morales Saravia would be appointed as a magistrate to the Constitutional Court and currently (2023) presides over the institution. Huerta deems the supermajority as "plainly justified." Huerta Guerrero, *supra* note 51, at 883. Quispe and Chilo deem as "ideal" that important decisions on the unconstitutionality of statutes require supermajorities. Víctorhugo Montoya, Evelyn Chilo & Carlos Quispe, El Proceso de Inconstitucionalidad en la Jurisprudencia (1996-2014) 306 (2015).

83 Gorki González Mantilla, *La Reforma de La Justicia En El Perú: Entre La Constitución y Las Demandas de La Realidad*, 2004 Parlamento y Constitución 239, 257 (2004).

required a party to attain 5 percent of the valid votes or secure more than six seats distributed in more than one electoral circumscription to qualify for representation. The petitioners deemed the requirement to infringe on political rights, as the Constitution did not establish threshold conditions for the right to be elected. The court had previously employed the technique of so-called "manipulative" or "additive" judgments, *i.e.*, judgments that interpret the text of a law introducing new normative content.[84] In the electoral threshold case (Exp. N° 00030-2005-PI/TC), the court reasoned that such rulings were legitimate only if the court made convincing constitutional arguments justifying them. However, it concluded by creating a supermajority rule stating that "issuing such rulings requires a supermajority of this Constitutional Court."[85]

Manipulative rulings are a valuable tool in circumventing the supermajority's application. Without declaring the statute's unconstitutionality, they allowed the court to make the law say what, arguably, it does not. The self-imposed supermajority doctrine on manipulative rulings would end in 2015 when the court modified its internal rules to eliminate such supermajority. Interestingly, a simple 4:3 majority had to pass the amendment as Magistrates Oscar Urviola, José Luis Sardón, and Marianella Ledesma opposed lowering the threshold. The paradox was noted by the minority, which filed a dissenting opinion on the changes. The minority claimed that, given the importance of the internal regulations of the court, they should also have been modified by a supermajority and not a simple majority. This debate would also take place in the Dominican Republic. The minority noted that all previous reforms to the court's internal rules had been adopted either by a supermajority or unanimously. Furthermore, a simple majority was a poor criterion to abandon binding case law adopted by a supermajority in Exp. N° 00030-2005-PI/TC.

After 2006, the court proceeded with other supermajority rule incursions. For example, in 2009, in the well-known *Sangüesa* case,[86] the court faced gridlock while resolving an individual constitutional complaint (*recurso de agravio constitucional*). Since one magistrate could not participate in the deliberations due to a conflict of interest, the court faced an impasse in a 3:3 tie. Unlike the United States, the Peruvian Constitutional Court does not have the doctrine of affirmance by an equally divided court. The tie did not allow the court to confirm or reverse the ruling. The court similarly applied the impasse

84 *See* Nausica Palazzo, *Law-Making Power of the Constitutional Court of Italy*, *in* Judicial Law-Making in European Constitutional Courts 46 (Monika Florczak-Wątor ed., 2020); Irene Spigno, *"Additive Judgments": A Way to Make the Invisible Content of the Italian Constitution Visible*, *in* The Invisible Constitution in Comparative Perspective 457 (Rosalind Dixon & Adrienne Stone eds., 2018).

85 Scholars reacted positively to this doctrine. Hakansson-Nieto deemed that the supermajority was natural in this case since it was inspired by the principle of judicial collegiality. Carlos Hakansson-Nieto, *Los Principios de Interpretación y Precedentes Vinculantes en la Jurisprudencia del Tribunal Constitucional Peruano*, 23 Díkaion 57, 72 (2009).

86 Case 04664-2007-PA/TC.

mechanism of the supermajority rule to break the deadlock. Since a supermajority was required to strike down legislation and its failure led to upholding the law, the court reasoned that individual complaints involving infringement of rights should follow the same logic. Thus, failure to achieve a majority had to be interpreted as leading to a dismissal of the claim. A year later, the court abandoned the *Sanguesa* criteria by amending its internal rules on March 15, 2011, to establish the casting vote in individual complaints.[87] Nonetheless, the modification met with harsh criticism, internally and externally.[88] Scholars pointed out that neither the Constitution nor any statute allowed a casting vote.

Finally, the court also adopted a five-vote supermajority to issue precedents. The 2004 Constitutional Procedural Code only required the court to identify which decisions constituted a precedent. Nonetheless, an internal practice of the court required a five-vote supermajority to establish a precedent, which even the court admitted to in the *Huatulco* case.[89]

On October 7, 2015, an amendment to the internal rules of the court supported by a bare majority of the magistrates lowered the threshold to four votes. All magistrates published separate opinions justifying or disapproving of the change, which revealed a fracture within the court.[90]

However, Peruvian legislators disliked the change of the informal rule. Supermajorities had been at the heart of Peru's constitutional structure, and simple majorities were deemed too unstable. In 2021, Congress issued a new Constitutional Procedural Code regulating the creation of binding precedents. Article VI of the 2021 statute provided that binding precedents could only be issued, altered, or abandoned by a five-vote supermajority.

87 In Judgment 00228-2009-PA/TC the Court would end up claiming that the casting vote rule created was "not only legitimate, but absolutely necessary towards fulfilling the constitutional obligation" of deciding cases.

88 Landa, *supra* note 62, at 44.

89 *See* Exp. N. 05057-2013-PA/TC. The Court stated that "even if currently there is no provision that expressly establishes the number of votes required to set a binding precedent of the Constitutional Court, it has been a reasonable and longstanding practice that precedents are set with at least five votes."

90 Given that, at the time, two distinct groups seemingly clashed in constant 4:3 decisions, the binding precedent/interpretative decisions supermajorities may have related to the supermajority to strike down legislation. Previous to the amendment, the three-Magistrate minority held considerable veto power. After the amendment, the bare four-magistrates majority was able to evade the supermajority in cases of unconstitutionality of legislation by setting binding precedents reading statutes narrowly or by issuing interpretative decisions adding in practice new normative content to the provisions, thus avoiding handing the opinion to the minority upon failing to gather the five votes required to strike down a provision. Magistrate Ramos revealed as much. In his concurring opinion to the amendments, he accused the minority of opposing on concrete interest grounds (*asuntos de coyuntura*) rather than for institutional policy reasons.

4.2 The Supermajority in the Contemporary Czech Constitutional Court (1993–Present)

After 1945,[91] many of the constitutional institutions of the Czechoslovak 1920 Constitution were reactivated. That was not the case for the Czechoslovak Constitutional Court, which continued existing merely on paper for a few years.[92] The 1948 communist *coup d'état* would seal the court's death sentence. Communists did not establish a constitutional court in the new 1960 Constitution.

After the Prague Spring suppression, a constitutional court would resurface in 1968 in the Constitutional Act on the Czechoslovak Federation.[93] The court was set to function with eight members (eight justices and four alternates), which could function in chambers, contrary to the 1920 Constitutional Court. As with the previous 1920 Constitution, the 1968 Constitutional Act did not define the type of majority required to strike down legislation and delegated to ordinary legislation of the Federal Assembly the "details on jurisdiction and organization of the Constitutional Court." Whether or not the legislature would have established a statutory supermajority is a purely theoretical line of inquiry. Secondary legislation was never established, nor did the court function in practice.[94] It is interesting to guess whether or not a supermajority would have been included. The act even envisaged two separate constitutional courts for the Czech and Slovak nations, which were never established.

In 1989, the Velvet Revolution took place. Soon after, a new court was established by the Constitutional Act 91/1991 Coll, from February 27, 1991. The Constitutional Court of the Czech and Slovak Federal Republic was now organized with twelve justices (Article 10) and a wide array of competences. Article 18 of the 91/1991 Act delegated the power to issue secondary legislation to the Federal Assembly.[95] In the secondary legislation, the Federal Assembly established a simple majority to decide (Article 9.3) but a 9 out of 12 supermajority for the court *en banc* to deviate from precedent (Article 9.5).[96]

The Czech and Slovak Federal Republic would collapse in less than two years. However, that time was sufficient for the court to leave its imprint. In

91 For an introduction to the legal and political context, *see* Chapter 3.2 on Czechoslovakia.

92 David Kosař & Ladislav Vyhnánek, *The Constitutional Court of Czechia*, *in* The Max Planck Handbooks in European Public Law: Volume III: Constitutional Adjudication: Institutions 119, 125 (Armin von Bogdandy, Peter Huber & Christoph Grabenwarter eds., 2020).

93 *Id.* at 126.

94 Stanislav Zdobinský, Československá Ústava : Komentář 38 (1988).

95 Act 491/1991 Coll. *Zákon o Organizaci Ústavního Soudu České a Slovenské Federativní Republiky a o řízení před ním* (Act on the organization of the Constitutional Court of the Czech and Slovak Federal Republic).

96 *See id.*

the well-known *Lustration* case,[97] the court declared the unconstitutionality of several provisions forbidding former communists from taking public office. The court produced more than a thousand decisions and achieved considerable prestige. Its prominence was so notable that most of the Czech justices who served under the 1992 Constitutional Court were reappointed in the first period of the Czech Constitutional Court.[98]

The fall of the Federal Republic led to the adoption of the 1993 Czech Constitution. Slovakia adopted a Constitution of its own, but its constitutional court was not placed under a supermajority.[99] The Czech Republic designed a modern constitutional court vested with powers to decide competence conflicts, individual complaints, abstract normative review, and other ancillary powers.

The court is composed of fifteen justices. Although the Czech Republic has a parliamentary system, the appointment mechanism resembles the American model. The President nominates, and the Senate confirms. Since only the President may nominate candidates, de facto, presidents can create their own court.[100] In the Czech Republic, constitutional courts are known by the president, who nominates the justices—Havel's Court, Klaus' Court, Zeman's Court.

Even though appointment delays, resignations, and deaths have created small gaps, the court is still mostly renewed in bulk.[101] To the above, we must add that justices serve non-staggered ten-year renewable terms. The possibility of reelection also existed in the 1920 Constitution. Reelection creates an unpleasant system of incentives for justices at the end of their term to behave to please political majorities.[102]

97 Pl. ÚS 1/92.

98 Kosař & Vyhnánek, *supra* note 92, at 127.

99 The Slovak Constitutional Court is regulated by law 314/2018. The quorum and majority are prescribed in Article 8 of the law (curiously, the same Article used to provide a supermajority in the 1920 Act on the Constitutional Court of Czechoslovakia). The court employs a simple majority.

100 Kosař & Vyhnánek, *supra* note 92. Nonetheless, *see infra* note 102 on the new practice.

101 Zdeněk Kühn, *The Constitutional Court of the Czech Republic*, *in* COMPARATIVE CONSTITUTIONAL REASONING 199, 209 (András Jakab, Arthur Dyevre & Giulio Itzcovich eds., 2017). Kosař & Vyhnánek, *supra* note 92, at 130–31. Appointment delays have currently dispersed the appointments into two groups with a two-year separation. For example, in 2023, seven justices were appointed, while eight will be appointed in 2025. Nonetheless, so far, the Senate has been a sufficient counterweight and has actively rejected extremely partisan designations, rendering a plural court.

102 In 2013–2015, four justices at the Constitutional Court appointed by President Klaus sought reappointment from President Zeman. Semkal *et al.* narrate that judges who had previously voted in favor of the Senate's position in key cases were reappointed, while those who had adopted decisions hostile to senatorial policy got rejected, clearly signaling that reappointment may depend on docility. Hubert Smekal, Jaroslav Benák & Ladislav Vyhnánek, *Through Selective Activism towards Greater Resilience: The Czech Constitutional Court's Interventions into High Politics in the Age of Populism*, 26 THE INT'L J. HUM. RTS. 1230, 1242 (2022).

One could presume that ideological alignment would be natural since the President dominates the appointment procedure. However, two robust features coexist in creating a court independent from the political branches. In the first place, the Senate has shown itself willing and able to control Presidential nominations. Since the Senate's electoral system of single-seat constituencies differs from the party-list proportional representation of the Chamber of Deputies, there is a potential check on majoritarianism. In the second place, Czechia introduced a direct election of the President in 2012.[103] Thus, Presidents have strong incentives to staff the court as they could appeal to it to resolve political conflicts and exert governmental influence. In contrast, the Prime Minister and Chamber of Deputies have no say in who becomes a justice in the constitutional court.

4.2.1 Czechoslovakia's Heritage: The Resurrection of the Supermajority

The Constitution did not specify which majority is required as a decisional threshold. The decision was understood to belong to the legislature. As Czech scholarship has noted, the law on the Constitutional Court is "technically a mere ordinary Act of Parliament lacking constitutional rank—which means that, in principle, its rules can be flexibly amended."[104] The government's sponsored bill originally proposed a supermajority of a more limited scope. The supermajority did not concern the invalidation of laws, but only decisions concerning the President of the Republic, such as impeachment or vacancy-related matters. Thus, the supermajority was not discussed at length in the explanatory memorandum. The only consideration was about the supermajority's size. The memorandum deemed such a majority "not so small that

---

Nonetheless, Petr Pavel, the new President, established a new procedure for appointing judges. Petr Pavel created an "Advisory Board" of six jurists to screen candidates and relied on different professional institutions to suggest names. *See* Andrea Procházková, *How to Form the Czech Constitutional Court?*, VERFASSUNGSBLOG: ON MATTERS CONSTITUTIONAL (2023), https://intr2dok.vifa-recht.de/receive/mir_mods_00016003 (last visited Sept. 9, 2023). Of the recent five appointments, none of them were reelections.

103 By making the President independent of parliamentary majorities, the amendment intensified the debates on whether Czechia should be considered a semi-presidential system. Lubomír Kopeček & Jan Petrov, *From Parliament to Courtroom: Judicial Review of Legislation as a Political Tool in the Czech Republic*, 30 EAST EUROPEAN POLITICS AND SOCIETIES 120, 124 (2016).

104 Jan Malíř & Jana Ondřejková, *Law-Making Activity of the Czech Constitutional Court*, *in* JUDICIAL LAW-MAKING IN EUROPEAN CONSTITUTIONAL COURTS 111, 112 (Monika Florczak-Wątor ed., 2020). Furthermore, in the Czech Republic, it is not entirely clear whether the Court can strike down the Act on the Constitutional Court, since it is constitutionally bound by it. Additionally, the Court has hinted at some doubts on the matter since the judgment PL. ÚS 23/12. Nonetheless, Semekal *et al.* argue that if an amendment were to truly encroach on its powers, the Constitutional Court would strike it down. Smekal, Benák & Vyhnánek, *supra* note 102, at 1250.

a change in the Court's opinion does not require a substantial majority of judges, but not so big to block the development of the Constitutional Court's case law."[105]

The supermajority was added during the parliamentary proceedings[106] in the Chamber of Deputies, presumably to ensure the court would grant proper deference to Parliament. The supermajority was not viewed as controversial, having been a part of the Constitutional Court in Czechoslovakia, itself considered a golden era of Czech Constitutionalism.[107] Lengthy discussions arose during the parliamentary deliberations regarding dissenting opinions. Interestingly, Deputy Dobal claimed that rulings that did not indicate the number of votes against the court's proposal attained a higher legitimacy, quoting German scholarship. As we will see, the vote secrecy model adopted affects the supermajority.

The statute was approved as Law 182/1993 Coll on the Czech Constitutional Court. Article 13 provides that the court can issue a decision with a simple majority of justices present. Since the Plenum's quorum is ten justices, as few as six justices may decide under certain circumstances. However, a nine votes supermajority is required to strike down legislation, resolve accusations against the President (or resolutions on the presidency's vacancy), and review international treaties. The same supermajority applies when overruling a precedent set forth by the court.[108] The supermajority had resurfaced.

4.2.2 The Supermajority in Practice

The Czech Constitutional Court decisions do not reveal a specific count of votes. It is impossible to determine what the voting was in a given case without separate opinions or an acknowledgment of the decision. Dissenting and separate opinions are optional, not mandatory. It is not uncommon for justices who voted against a decision not to issue a dissenting opinion. Furthermore, deliberation and voting are secret. Revealing the vote count of a session may be a cause for administrative liability. Czech justices are disciplined, so even though leaks have been known to happen, general information on the internal

105 *See* the explanatory memorandum (*Důvodová zpráva*) to Law 182/1993, https://bit.ly/43vieNz (last visited Jun. 16, 2023).

106 I wish to thank Jindřiška Syllová from the Parliamentary Institute of the Chamber of Deputies for her help in tracking down the parliamentary origin of the Czech supermajority.

107 David Kosař & Ladislav Vyhnánek, *The Evolution and Gestalt of the Czech Constitution*, *in* The Max Planck Handbooks in European Public Law 56, 58 (Armin von Bogdandy, Peter M. Huber & Christoph Grabenwarter eds., 2023).

108 On the ability of a relevant minority to avoid a change of precedent and the precedential supermajority, *see* Jan Filip, Pavel Holländer & Vojtěch Šimíček, Zákon o Ústavním Soudu 68–69 (2 ed. 2007).

deliberations (and, thus, the way in which each justice has voted) is kept out of the public eye.[109]

In view of the system, there are two different ways[110] in which a supermajority failure decision may come to light. First, a decision can frontally admit to it[111] or allow inferring it.[112] In the second place, if the number of dissenting opinions constitutes a majority of justices that took part in a decision, the supermajority rule must have influenced the case.[113] Even if votes are secret within the court, a supermajority failure would often reveal the voting result.[114] For example, if 15 justices took part in the decision, and eight justices filed dissenting opinions claiming a statute was unconstitutional, it is possible to guess that Article 13 protected the law from being invalidated. A variation of this possibility would be a dissenting opinion indicating that a supermajority was not achieved (while the decision omits such information).

If a decision refrains from quoting the supermajority rule and not all justices file dissenting opinions, there would be no possibility of knowing if the supermajority rule was applied. There are decisions in which neither scholars nor politicians can know whether a law was upheld because a majority of justices considered so or because the supermajority blocked an invalidation.

Recently, it seems more often that decisions openly admit to being a consequence of Article 13 of the Act on the Constitutional Court, but this is far from an obligation imposed either by statute or by internal regulations. Some debates have arisen. For example, in the famous transgender case Pl. ÚS 2/20 (see comments below), Justice Kateřina Šimáčková issued a dissenting opinion

109 Jiří Zemánek, *Interview with a Justice of the Czech Constitutional Court* (unpublished, 2022).

110 Not considering, of course, the possibility of informal leaking of information.

111 *See* decision ÚS 2/20, paragraph 20. The decision revealed: "Kateřina Šimáčková was originally appointed as Judge-Rapporteur and submitted in a closed session a draft which proposed repealing Article 29.1 . . . The draft . . . did not obtain the necessary majority of votes, which is considered to lead to a rejection under the case law of the Constitutional Court."

112 For example, ÚS 12/94. The judgment does not admit to being a supermajority failure decision. There is no counting of votes, and even the dissenting opinions do not allow making such an assumption as only five judges signed dissenting opinions. Nonetheless, since one of the dissenting votes argues that the interpretation of Article 13 of the Act on the Constitutional Court should be a qualified threshold for both outcomes, it is almost certain that the supermajority played a role. This decision comes from the period in which Article 13 was still disputed. Had the dissenting opinions merely centered on the substantive law disagreement, we would be unable to know that the supermajority was applied.

113 Filip *et al.* offer a similar account, analyzing several judgments in which the supermajority failure was acknowledged explicitly and provide examples where only other mechanisms allow inferring the vote count of the supermajority failure. They argue that the Court is not obliged to disclose the vote count to the parties, as "For them it is decisive whether or not the proposal was granted and what is the legal opinion of the Constitutional Court in the matter." Filip, Holländer & Šimíček, *supra* note 108, at 66. Furthermore, *Filipt et al.* noted that, by 2007, the proportion of votes had only been mentioned in two judgments.

114 Venice Commission, *Opinion No. 932/2018 On Separate Opinions on Constitutional Courts*, 32 16 (2016).

complaining that the ruling failed to emphasize that it was a decision taken as a consequence of a supermajority failure. Justice Šimáčková admitted to having been originally a Judge-Rapporteur of the case and declared her proposal attained a non-qualified majority of the court. The court's decision did briefly indicate (paragraph 21) that the ruling was taken in conformity with Article 13, but Justice Šimáčková considered that such information should take a more prominent place.

The supermajority shared some characteristics with the old 1920 supermajority. Both were established by statute, not in the Constitution, and required a concrete number of votes, not a percentage. Both provided one single vote more than a simple majority would. However, significant differences also exist. In the seven-member Czechoslovak Constitutional Court, the supermajority was 71 percent. The contemporary fifteen-member Czech Constitutional Court has a reduced 60 percent. This difference seems to favor the new legal configuration, but other differences might favor the 1920 regulation. For example, the contemporary Czech Constitutional Court avoided substitutes. An absent justice may not be replaced. Absences due to sickness, leave, or, more commonly, appointment delays substantially impact the court. This problem was partially solved by the 1920 and 1938 regulations providing substitutes, thereby preventing the lack of appointments from increasing the majority.

Appointment delays are an important contextual feature of the Czech system. The Czech Constitutional Court de facto often operates under a higher majority than the statutorily established 9/15. When a justice is absent, the supermajority grows. Since the quorum is 10, the supermajority might rise theoretically to 90 percent, but in practice, 75 percent is the maximum threshold increase, as explained below.

In 1993, President Havel's staffing of the court was relatively smooth, aside from two rejections and one candidate resignation. Havel proposed anticommunists and dissidents to the court. It took Havel only a few months[115] to produce a full court. His task was eased by the lack of a Senate and, thus, the Chamber of Deputies performed the confirmation. Things began changing with President (formerly Prime Minister) Klaus. Klaus did not enjoy total support in the Senate and mistrusted the Czech Constitutional Court. For example, Klaus criticized his predecessor for filing too many constitutional challenges.[116] After a couple of successful nominations in 2003, the situation rapidly deteriorated. In July 2003, the Senate rejected Aleš Pejchal, Klaus' closest legal advisor. After four new nominations, the Senate rejected three candidates. Klaus became reluctant to make further nominations after losing four of his last five appointments. A desperate Klaus "even nominated Aleš

115 Kühn, *supra* note 101, at 2018.

116 Zdeněk Kühn & Jan Kysela, *Nomination of Constitutional Justices in Post-Communist Countries: Trial, Error, Conflict in the Czech Republic*, 2 European Const. L. Rev. 183, 195 (2006).

Pejchal, already rejected by the Senate, again."[117] His second attempt was as unsuccessful as the first one. Since many of the justices' terms had expired, the court was now barely functioning with eleven members.

Chief Justice Pavel Rychetský declared that the court would not resolve any abstract challenges unless a twelfth justice were appointed (which did not happen until 2004!). It seems that under Rychetský's presidency of the court, such usage has been firmly established. The appointments were completed in late 2005 when the last two justices were appointed. Between July 2005 and December 2005, the supermajority oscillated between 73 percent and 86 percent, giving the missing justices. President Zeman had less troublesome renewals, but the court had an extensive set of appointments that occurred in a vast space between May 2013 and December 2015, causing some absences. In 2023, several vacancies are set to appear, marking the beginning of a new cycle.

When the court began functioning in 1993, it soon faced the question of the consequence of supermajority failure decisions. The opportunity presented itself in Pl. ÚS 36/93 regarding termination of fixed-termed contracts of university teachers, which allegedly infringed the non-discrimination clause. The court had to address two questions the previous Czechoslovak Constitutional Court had faced more than seventy years before: how the supermajority worked regarding the potential outcomes of the case and who would author the court's opinion.

The court reached the same answer as the Czechoslovak Constitutional Court in 1920 in the first matter. However, some judges dissented from that way of interpreting the supermajority. Justices Holländer, Jurka, and Ševčík filed a separate opinion claiming that since striking down legislation and upholding it both have the strength of *res iudicata*, a supermajority was necessary for both outcomes. Thus, they implied that a seven-justice minority did not have a decisional majority to uphold the legislation. However, they did not suggest what should have been the case's outcome then.[118] That opinion remained under debate for a few years[119] but faded away.

117 Kosař & Vyhnánek, *supra* note 92, at 132.

118 Varvařovský also filed a dissenting opinion. However, he merely claimed that the provisions should have been declared unconstitutional but did not disagree with how the supermajority was to be interpreted.

119 Even in 2008, in the face of the Lisbon Treaty case, some commentaries pointed out that it was debatable whether a qualified majority was required to uphold the treaty and not only to consider it unconstitutional. Thus, the commentary suggested that "the ratification of the Lisbon Treaty could be blocked by two votes if the quorum is 10 judges or by 7 votes if the quorum is 15 judges." Jan Filip, *Procedure of Preventive Review of the Lisbon Treaty in the Czech Republic*, 16 Časopis pro právní vědu a praxi 206, 211 (2008).

The solution preferred by the court to the first problem generated some debate among scholars, with Šimíček in an intermediate position,[120] Sládeček[121] in the opposition, and Wagnerová fully defending the outcome.[122]

Opinion assignment in decisions failing to meet the threshold was a complicated topic. Even though initially some doubts arose about the structure of judgment Pl. ÚS 36/93,[123] the court settled in a practice that allows minorities to author the opinion. In contrast, the majority of the court is allowed to write a separate opinion dissenting.[124]

Subsequent rulings of the court would consolidate this judicial doctrine in Pl. ÚS 3/96 and Pl. ÚS 14/02, where the court employed for the first time a specific term to describe the paradox: "relevant minority" (*relevantní menšina*). A relevant minority was the term that the court (and soon the scholarship) employed to refer to the minority that blocked the invalidation. In turn, the losing majority is named "non-relevant majority" (*nei relevantní menšina*).

Ševčík's position did not achieve consensus, and the court formulated a doctrine allowing the minority to develop the grounds and doctrine in supermajority failure rejections. The court even devoted express attention to the matter. Reasoning on whether a minority should be entitled to speak on behalf of the body, the Czech Constitutional Court said in Pl. ÚS 17/97 that "the fact that it [the legal reasoning to uphold a provision] could have been adopted by a minority of judges is not relevant for the substantive justification of the rejection." The court further emphasized that the law provided a procedure

120 Vojtěch Šimíček, *Poznámky k Proceduře Rozhodování Pléna Ústavního Soudu*, 5 Časopis pro právní vědu a praxi 458, 462–3 (1997). Simíček admitted being aware that a grammatical interpretation of the statute might lead to a supermajority being required by any outcome, although saw equally undesirable the lack of a decision, and deemed reasonable that the petition should be rejected if it failed attaining the supermajority.

121 Vladimír Sládeček, *Ještě k Otázce Rozhodování Pléna Ústavního Soudu o Návrhu Na Zrušení Zákona*, 6 Časopis pro právní vědu a praxi 99 (1998). Sládeček deemed that the Court (and other scholars) had misread not only the statute but the intention of the legislature.

122 Curiously, all three participants of the debate were eventually appointed Justices of the Constitutional Court. Sládeček even had the opportunity to repeat his scholarly position from the bench. *See infra.*

123 In Pl. ÚS 36/93, the Court summarily announced that it could not strike down one provision as no qualified majority voted to strike down the provision or uphold it. The opinion contained no justification for this. Subsequent rulings would lean toward allowing the minority to present the Court's opinion. Filip *et al.* argued that this case implied that initially, the Court considered that failing to achieve a supermajority meant that the case "would be dismissed without the Constitutional Court addressing the question of whether or not the provision was in accordance with the constitutional order." Filip, Holländer & Šimíček, *supra* note 108, at 71.

124 In Pl. ÚS 3/96, Vlastimil Ševčík (who had formerly dissented in Pl. ÚS 36/ 93) argued that it was a contradiction to have the minority writing legal reasoning as to why the challenge was rejected. Ševčík concluded that "it was not those reasons [the relevant minority's arguments], but the failure to meet the formal conditions as to the number of votes required ... that was decisive for the fate of the motion."

for public authorities to decide, and thus, it was tasked to provide its reasoning, namely, to "explain the legal (and possibly factual) arguments justifying the judgment, irrespective of the manner of its adoption."

The Czech Constitutional Court concluded that a minority opinion is "[a] justification of the decision of the public authority and not a justification of the opinion of the part of the members of the decision-making body whose opinion led to the adoption of the decision in question." In the Czech Republic, the court conceived decisions issued by a minority not as failures of the court but simply as a result assigned by the legal framework to concrete voting. After this opinion, subsequent rulings, such as Pl. ÚS 14/02 did not produce much controversy, although new appointments guarantee that from time to time, a new opinion resurfaces.[125]

The court has not delved intensively into the rationale of the supermajority, but it has indeed provided some justifications. For example, in Pl. ÚS 17/97, the court directly related the supermajority with the "principle of sovereignty of the people . . . which is linked to the presumption of constitutionality of laws." Wagnerová has been critical of this justification, claiming sovereignty may only be invoked in pre-state stages (such as revolution or exercise of constituent power). Even so, Wagnerová's dissent seems to be merely nominal.[126]

The precedential status of rulings issued by relevant minorities seems to be weak, if any.[127] Supermajority failure decisions are rarely quoted as authoritative. When done so, dissenting opinions often indicate that relevant minorities adopted those decisions to undermine their strength.[128] In other cases, the court has even quoted dissenting opinions by non-relevant majorities as

125 For example, in judgment Pl. ÚS 49/10 (decided in 2014), the newly appointed Justice Vladimír Sládeček faced for the first time a supermajority failure decision. Having previously, as a scholar, debated the issue with Wagnerová and Simíček, he was eager to repeat his position now from the bench. In his dissenting opinion, he disagreed with how the Court interpreted the rule. In his opinion, a supermajority should be required regardless of the outcome. Sládeček deemed that the Court's interpretation of upholding the legislation in the event of a non-qualified majority was far from forced and that there was a need to clarify the law. Sládeček hinted that if the Act on the Constitutional Court would expressly force the Court to uphold the law with a minority vote (as currently interpretated by the Court), "to legalize such a procedure would be blatantly unconstitutional." Sládeček's opinion did not gain further support, and the Court continued applying the rule as it had done for more than twenty years.

126 Eliška Wagnerová, *§ 13*, *in* Zákon o Ústavním soudu s komentářem 56, 60 (Eliška Wagnerová et al. eds., 2007). I deem Wagnerová's dissent semantical. Her alternative justification of the rule is the presumption of legality of all statutory and non-statutory acts, leading to judicial self-restraint. The Court did not claim that parliamentary sovereignty was the only justification of the supermajority but rather the presumption of constitutionality to which the principle is linked. At the core, the Court and Wagnerová agree.

127 "The problem still remains, however, whether a default judgment adopted by a 'qualified minority' constitutes *res iudicata* and whether it even has some precedential binding power." Kosař & Vyhnánek, *supra* note 92, at 156.

128 For example, *see* Pl. ÚS 11/17 and the arguments raised in the joint dissenting opinion.

precedents. In Pl. ÚS 42/2000, the Czech Constitutional Court considered the dissenting opinions filed in Pl. ÚS 3/96 as relevant precedent. The precedential nature of the rulings appears to depend on whether the relevant minority or non-relevant minority is consistent with the new criteria of the court. The fact that a supermajority is required to deviate from the established case law of the court could be seen as a protection to the doctrine settled by a relevant minority. If a supermajority was not required to change doctrine, simple majorities might easily switch legal criteria in cases in which the constitutionality of a statute is not in play.[129]

4.2.3 Assessing the "Silent" Supermajority

The Czech Constitutional Court has amassed significant public trust[130] and acceptance of its decisions, and has contributed significantly to preserving the rule of law[131] in a region characterized recently by democratic backsliding.[132]

As some scholars have argued, the court has notably asserted its position towards cases of so-called mega-politics,[133] intervening in politically relevant cases on electoral law and transitional justice.[134] The court cemented its role as a strong actor within the Czech political landscape through firm decisions in core political areas.[135]

129 Nonetheless, the supermajority for departing from previous case law is entirely a different topic and has provoked numerous discussions, even in how it interacts with the supermajority to strike down legislation, being able in some cases to supersede it. Wagnerová, *supra* note 126, at 59. Multiple fascinating concerns arise. For example, Wagnerová discussed what could be considered a departure from doctrine and whether the Court *en banc* and its chambers were both subject to the rule. Furthermore, Wagnerová analyzed cases where a statute was invalidated despite not reaching the required supermajority if a previous supermajority had struck down a similar law on similar grounds. The supermajority that protects the Court's doctrine was interpreted as lex specialis vis-à-vis the supermajority to strike down legislation.

130 The Court ranks consistently well in public opinion surveys. Malíř & Ondřejková, *supra* note 104, at 114.

131 For a very favorable view of the Court's contribution *see* Francesco Biagi, European Constitutional Courts and Transitions to Democracy 176–77 (2019).

132 Smekal, Benák & Vyhnánek, *supra* note 102.

133 Hirschl coined the term. *See* Ran Hirschl, *The Judicialization of Mega-Politics and the Rise of Political Courts*, 11 Annu. Rev. Polit. Sci. 93 (2008).

134 Katarína Šipulová, *The Czech Constitutional Court: Far Away from Political Influence*, *in* Constitutional Politics and the Judiciary 32, 56 (Kálmán Pócza ed., 2018).

135 The Court does not shy away from polemics, such as in the Slovak pensions saga. In the famous *Landovà* case, the court decided that the Court of Justice judgment in Case C-399/09 was an ultra vires exercise of jurisdiction. Zdeněk Kühn, *The Czech Republic: From a Euro-Friendly Approach of the Constitutional Court to Proclaiming a Court of Justice Judgment Ultra Vires*, *in* National Constitutions in European and Global Governance: Democracy, Rights, the Rule of Law 795 (Anneli Albi & Samo Bardutzky eds., 2019). Jan Komárek, *Czech Constitutional Court Playing with Matches: The Czech Constitutional Court Declares a Judgment of the Court of Justice of the EU* Ultra Vires; *Judgment of 31 January 2012, Pl. ÚS 5/12,* Slovak Pensions XVII, 8 European Const. L. Review 323 (2012).

Simultaneously, the court is somewhat reluctant to engage with what Smekal, Benák, and Vyhnánek deem "cultural wars," steering away from sensitive social issues.[136] In its few interventions on these topics, the court has sometimes been criticized for not taking a more active stance.[137] Smekal *et al.* seem to credit this distinction with some of the resilience of the court.[138]

Since several supermajority failures occurred in rights-related cases, it is interesting to ponder if the supermajority has not played a role in steering the court to struggles concerning the division of power and elections rather than controversial human rights issues. In this sense, the supermajority may have helped the court attain further resilience.

The supermajority seems not to have hindered the court's function. Justice Zémanek believes that the rule is unproblematic in the current composition and has influenced very few cases.[139] In his view, consensus, seeking common ground, and a desire to increase the legitimacy of decisions may explain why the supermajority does not influence the court. Justice Zémanek considers that the rule may have impacted previous court compositions differently, as it depends highly on the predisposition to consensus of individual judges. The first court consisted of political dissidents and academics who went abroad. They had little possibility of sharing a bench on the judiciary or knowing each other in academia. Being dissidents and opposers, they were undoubtedly accustomed to independent thinking and tenacity in defending their positions and ideals.

The law on the Czech Constitutional Court has been amended twenty times,[140] but the supermajority remained. Policymakers and political branches, majority and opposition, have grown accustomed to it.

Even if supermajority failure decisions have not been abundant, they have played a role in important cases. In the free health care case (Pl. ÚS 14/02), the supermajority forced the court to uphold the constitutionality of a statute forbidding doctors and health workers from receiving payments for any treatments related to, although not covered by, general health insurance. In Pl. ÚS 9/07, the supermajority led to rejecting a petition to declare unconstitutional the Act of Lands due to a legislative omission in adopting a regulation settling

136 Smekal, Benák & Vyhnánek, *supra* note 102, at 1239.

137 In the transgender case (Pl. ÚS 2/20), scholarly commentary deemed the Court's decision as "insensitive" and "ignorant." Zuzana Vikarská, *Evasive, Insensitive, Ignorant, and Political*, VERFASSUNGSBLOG: ON MATTERS CONSTITUTIONAL (Apr. 6, 2022), https://intr2dok.vifa-recht.de/receive/mir_mods_00012411 (last visited Mar. 17, 2023).

138 Smekal, Benák & Vyhnánek, *supra* note 102, at 1246.

139 "We have no problem with the rule. It occurred [supermajority failure decisions] perhaps ten times during my full period. It is a matter of true discussion and making an effort to find common ground." Zemánek, *supra* note 109.

140 *See* the acts Nos. 331/1993 Sb., 236/1995 Sb., 77/1998 Sb., 18/2000 Sb., 132/2000 Sb., 48/2002 Sb., 202/2002 Sb., 320/2002 Sb., 114/2003 Sb., 83/2004 Sb., 120/2004 Sb., 234/2006 Sb., 342/2006 Sb., 227/2009 Sb. 404/2012 Sb., 275/2012 Sb., 303/2013 Sb., 90/2017 Sb., 173/2018 and Sb. 111/2019.

historical property of churches and religious communities after communist rule.[141] In Pl. ÚS 16/2000, the supermajority led to upholding a statute lowering judges' salaries, withdrawing some amounts of the so-called "additional salary" in light of extraordinary circumstances. Most recently, in the transgender case (Pl. ÚS 2/20), the court could not strike down a provision of the Act on Population Record. The provision stated the requirements for changing gender and conditioned such change on performing a gender reassignment surgery "while simultaneously disabling the reproductive function and transforming the genitalia."[142] The court upheld the provision conveniently evading the sterilization issue.[143]

Czech scholars have not paid much attention to the rule after the original Sládeček-Simíček-Wagnerová discussion. Wagnerová subsequently viewed the supermajority as theoretically sound, although under a rationale of the presumption of legality of statutory acts, but made no assessment of its behavior in practice. In turn, Kosař and Vyhnánek considered the supermajority problematic because of the initial doubts on whether a non-qualified majority should lead to the dismissal of the petition. As they admit, the court early on settled the matter.[144] The second argument is concerned with practical aspects. Kosař and Vyhnánek note that when several justices are missing, there is a point at which two justices could theoretically block an invalidation. However, as shown, not only are absences not exactly a feature of the supermajority, but also, they have not proven insurmountable obstacles for the court to place checks on the legislative branch, except in specific cases.

141 Andrea Procházková, *Ústavní Soud ČR Mezi Právem a Politikou*, 161 PRÁVNÍK 1084, 1092 (2022). Procházková further argues that these decisions are in line with other judgments granting the elected branches broad deference in dealing with the communist past. A brief commentary to the decision in Soňa Matochová, *The Role of Constitutional Courts, Particularly of the Constitutional Court of the Czech Republic, While Introducing Human Rights*, *in* FROM EASTERN PARTNERSHIP TO THE ASSOCIATION: A LEGAL AND POLITICAL ANALYSIS 206, 230–1 (Naděžda Šišková ed., 2014). Nonetheless, the Court managed to declare that while the challenged statute was not unconstitutional, the legislative omission in itself was. Šipulová, *supra* note 134, at 45.

142 I take Doubek's translation. Pavel Doubek, *Sterilization of Transgender People: A Worrying Judgement of the Czech Constitutional Court*, ECHR BLOG, https://www.echrblog.com/2022/04/sterilization-of-transgender-people.html. Therefore, the ruling confirmed a legal status quo in which only women can give birth in the Czech Republic, as any gender reassignment only is possible "if the reproductive function is rendered impossible." Anna P. Durnová & Eva M. Hejzlarová, *Navigating the Role of Emotions in Expertise: Public Framing of Expertise in the Czech Public Controversy on Birth Care*, POLICY SCI 549 (2023).

143 Nikolas Sabján, *Critical Legal Perspective on the Recent Czech Transgender Case: (Pl. ÚS 2/20)*, 6 BRAT. L. REV. 125, 133 (2022).

144 Kosař & Vyhnánek, *supra* note 92, at 156.

4.3. Bargain and Transition: The Mexican Supermajority (1995–Present)

Mexico is one of the most stable supermajorities in the world. In recent years, particularly under López Obrador's Presidency (2018-2024), the 8:3 supermajority to invalidate legislation has played a crucial role in defending governmental policy but also arguably avoiding an even bigger clash between the government and the judicial branch.

4.3.1 From Otero to the Supermajority

Mexico has a long history of judicial review. However, supermajorities were not present until 1994. The 1836 Constitution created a supreme conservative power through the ideas of Sánchez de Tagle. The body resembled a constitutional court and was able to strike down legislation and even review constitutional amendments.[145] With its seven members, the short-lived *Supremo Poder Conservador* employed a simple majority. In 1841, Manuel Crescencio Rejón created the Amparo writ, an individual constitutional complaint that allowed constitutional review of legislation. Nonetheless, only in 1849 would Amparo acquire an actual constitutional status through the "Acta de Reformas," a document restoring the 1824 Federal Constitution with some fundamental changes.[146] Since 1849, Amparo became the only mechanism of judicial review in Mexico.

Amparo rulings traditionally have only inter partes effect. If an Amparo judge rules that a given statute is unconstitutional, the decision solely benefits the plaintiff.[147] The statute remains applicable and valid to everyone else. Amparo was a competence of the federal judicial branch, resolved through a tier of district court judges, circuit courts, and the Supreme Court. In multimember courts, a simple majority sufficed to find a statute unconstitutional, but the benefit was limited to that single case.

From 1849 to 1994, Amparo undoubtedly was the jewel of the crown of Mexico's constitutionalism. Amparo would influence most Latin American countries and even the universal declaration of human rights.[148] However, under the 1917 Constitution, Amparo started losing relevance. From 1929, the same political party (*Partido de la Revolución Institutional* or PRI)

145 *See* Frida Osorio Gonsen, *Seeking a Balance of Power through a Neutral Third Party Mechanism*, 33 Mexican Studies/Estudios Mexicanos 125 (2017).

146 Mauro Arturo Rivera León, *An Introduction to "Amparo" Theory: A Complex Mexican Constitutional Control Mechanism*, 12 KP 190, 196 (2020).

147 Mauro Arturo Rivera León, Las Partes En El Juicio de Amparo 126 (2023).

148 *See* UNESCO'S collection ID: 2014-100, Judicial files concerning the birth of a right: the effective remedy as a contribution of the Mexican writ of amparo to the Universal Declaration of Human Rights (UDHR) of 1948.

dominated elections. Nobel Prize-winning author Vargas Llosa depicted the PRI as "the perfect dictatorship."[149]

Through corporatism and fraud, PRI maintained uninterrupted control of the Presidency, the federal and state Congresses, and every governorship.[150] Since the president nominated justices and the Senate appointed them, PRI controlled the Supreme Court,[151] which, in turn, freely appointed and removed federal judges. Division of powers and judicial review was just one more piece of the façade. There was no democracy, competitive elections, or adequate checks on power. Vargas Llosa was right.

Things began to change in 1990. People were growing tired of the PRI. The opposition increased its numbers, and fabricating electoral results was getting more complicated. Pluralism grew faster than the PRI could circumvent it, and the government was increasingly forced to make concessions. Soon, it became clear that the old party's grip was crumbling. In this context of fading single-party rule, President Zedillo, a pragmatist, decided to reform the Supreme Court.

Since 1936, the court barely showed its teeth. Justices were figures often related to the party through previous political positions,[152] and de facto judicial independence was minimal. Zedillo understood that the PRI could not afford to lose power without the structures to be a powerful opposition.[153] President Zedillo proposed a constitutional amendment to transform the Supreme Court into a constitutional court. The court returned to eleven members after having achieved a membership of twenty-six justices. The court was granted the power to perform abstract review and the authority to resolve conflicts of competences between branches and bodies.[154] For the first time in Mexican history, the Supreme Court was vested with the power to invalidate statutes with *erga omnes* effect in full Kelsenian fashion.

149 In a televised debate with several academics in Mexico, the Nobel prize winner said, "Mexico it's a perfect dictatorship. The perfect dictatorship is neither communism, the Soviet Union, nor Fidel Castro. It is Mexico because it is a camouflaged dictatorship which PRI uses." The phrase left a deep imprint on Mexico's social debate.

150 Andrea Pozas-Loyo, *Assessing Constitutional Efficacy: Lessons from Mexico's Hegemonic Party Era*, *in* Morality, Governance, and Social Institutions 233, 233 (Thomas Christiano, Ingrid Creppell & Jack Knight eds., 2018).

151 Julio Ríos-Figueroa, *Fragmentation of Power and the Emergence of an Effective Judiciary in Mexico, 1994–2002*, 49 Lat. Am. polit. soc. 31, 26 (2007).

152 Pilar Domingo, *Judicial independence: the politics of the Supreme Court in Mexico*, 32 J. Lat. Am. Stud. 705, 722 (2000).

153 One of the main theories on the 1994 amendment is that it constituted an "insurance policy", as defended by Finkle. Jodi Finkel, *Judicial Reform as Insurance Policy: Mexico in the 1990s*, 47 Lat. Am. Politics Soc. 87 (2005). The theory was widely followed. Stephen Zamora & José Ramón Cossío, *Mexican Constitutionalism after Presidencialismo*, 4 International Journal of Const. L. 411, 421 (2006).

154 Susana Berruecos García Travesí & Laurence Whitehead, *Constitutional Controversies in the Subnational Democratization of Mexico, 1994–2021*, 12 Lat Am Policy 405, 406 (2021).

Although dominated by the PRI, the appointment procedure was reasonably pluralistic, and competent jurists were appointed justices. However, the ruling party did take some safeguards. Under the excuse of creating staggered terms, some PRI-appointed justices went on serving much longer terms than the constitutionally established number of years. Legal standing for the newly created action of unconstitutionality and constitutional controversies was limited.[155] Finally, Amparo still preserved inter partes effects. Only actions of unconstitutionality and constitutional controversies could produce *erga omnes* effects, provided an 8:3 supermajority was reached.

President Zedillo proposed an even higher 9:2 majority. The proposal was reduced during the parliamentary procedures in the Senate without further explanation.[156] The supermajority was a compromise between creating an effective judicial review capable of placing constraints on political branches and a too-powerful court.[157] It was a balance between granting power and ensuring deference.[158]

The rule was not alien to Mexican institutional design. Since the days of Rejón, Otero, and the birth of Amparo, Mexican constitutionalism was wary of the disruptive potential of an unchecked judiciary in political life. The fact that an Amparo decision proclaiming a statute unconstitutional (even from the Supreme Court) could only benefit the plaintiff was part of a conscious design to avoid politicizing justice. Furthermore, supermajorities existed in Mexican judicial review for precedential purposes. Historically, in Amparo, for a decision to attain precedent status and become binding (*jurisprudencia*) a criterion had to be reiterated five times and voted by a supermajority.[159] Since 1936, the law required a supermajority of at least 52 percent in the Plenary (the degree increased throughout the years) for a ruling to be counted as one of the five required cases. In the case of the Chambers, the supermajority was at least 80 percent.

The Mexican rule may have originated from a rule for precedent purposes. Since the amendment proposal and discussions referred to the "general effects" (terminology that was also used in the debate on precedents), it might have been natural to require a supermajority that was already in force for the so-called "jurisprudencia." The explanatory memorandum made no comment on

155 For a full critique of the limited legal standing, *see* Mauro Arturo Rivera León, Las puertas de la Corte: la legitimación en la controversia constitucional y acción de inconstitucionalidad en México (2016).

156 *See* the Legislative Opinion of the Joint Constitutional and Legislative Studies Commission, Mexican Senate, December 16, 1994.

157 José María Serna, The Constitution of Mexico: A Contextual Analysis 127 (2013).

158 *Id.*

159 José María Serna, *The Concept of Jurisprudencia in Mexican Law*, I Mexican L. Review 131, 135 (2009).

the matter. Early scholarship from the period justified the rule on the grounds of the importance of the decision.[160]

4.3.2 The Mexican Supermajority at Work

Article 105 of the Mexican Constitution requires eight votes to strike down a law either in actions of unconstitutionality or constitutional controversies. A simple majority suffices to uphold legislation. Curiously, the Mexican Constitution, of a remarkable regulatory nature,[161] said nothing about the consequences of a supermajority failure decision. This point was also absent in the parliamentary proceedings and debates. The secondary legislation clarified the consequences in Articles 42 and 72 of the *Ley Reglamentaria de las fracciones I y II del artículo 105 constitutional.* Article 72 provides that the court "shall dismiss [*desestimará*] the claim and close the case if the supermajority fails to be met in actions of unconstitutionality."

Article 42 provided the effects of supermajority failure on constitutional controversies (federalism and competence conflicts). The statute offered similar mechanics. However, the law stipulates that the decision would only benefit the parties to the controversy in specific cases.[162] Naturally, disputes arose. The supermajority was a requirement associated with the power of invalidating legislation *erga omnes.* Why was the supermajority required when such an effect was off the table? The opportunity to address the issue would arise in Case CC 66/2002 ten years later. Broadly reading the statute, the court concluded that striking down legislation required a supermajority in the new procedures regardless of the *erga omnes* or inter partes effects. In a strong dissenting opinion, Justices Gudiño and Aguirre accused the majority of ignoring that the statute contravened the Constitution in requiring a supermajority for cases with no *erga omnes* effects. Gudiño and Aguirre deemed the extension of the supermajority provided by the statute unconstitutional, at least in this configuration. Table 4.2 outlines the thresholds required in different procedures.

160 Jorge Carpizo, *Reformas constitucionales al Poder Judicial Federal y a la jurisdicción constitucional*, 1995 Boletín Mexicano de Derecho Comparado 807, 834 (1995).

161 Scholarship has been critical of Mexico's hyper-reformism and very detailed Constitution. *See* Mauro Arturo Rivera León, *Understanding Constitutional Amendments in Mexico: Perpetuum Mobile Constitution*, 1 Mex. L. Rev. 3 (2016); Mariana Velasco-Rivera, *Constitutional Rigidity: The Mexican Experiment*, 19 Intl J. Const. L. 1043 (2021); Francisca Pou Giménez & Andrea Pozas-Loyo, *The Paradox of Mexico's Constitutional Hyper-Reformism: Enabling Peaceful Transition While Blocking Democratic Consolidation*, *in* Constitutional Change and Transformation in Latin America 221 (Richard Albert, Carlos Bernal & Juliano Zaiden Benvindo eds., 2019).

162 Namely, federalist conflicts where a lower-level entity brings the challenge (Municipality v. State, Municipality v. Federation and State v. Federation). Inter alia, Herrera has criticized the rule. Alfonso Herrera García, *Algunas Propuestas de Reforma a La Controversia Constitucional En El Contexto de La Función de Jurisdicción Constitucional En México*, *in* Derecho Procesal: Estudios en homenaje a don Jorge Fernández Ruiz 273, 286 (David Cienfuegos & Miguel López Olvera eds., 2005).

Table 4.2 Majorities to decide and set precedents in the Mexican legal system

Procedure	*Majority to strike down legislation*	*Majority to set a precedent*	*Effects of unconstitutionality*
AI	8/11 in the outcome	8/11 in the reasoning	*Erga omnes*
CC	8/11 in the outcome	8/11 in the reasoning	*Erga omnes*
CCFC*	8/11 in the outcome	8/11 in the outcome	*Inter partes*
Amparo	6/11 in the outcome	6/11 in the reasoning	*Inter partes*
DGI	8/11 in the outcome	Not applicable	*Erga omnes*

AI: Action of unconstitutionality; CC: Constitutional Controversies
*In cases where a lower-level entity brings the challenge.

Failing to meet a supermajority leads to dismissing the challenge. Grammatically, the word "*desestimar*" may mean either formally to reject a case/argument or to find an argument ungrounded. The Supreme Court chose from early on to follow the first approach. Supermajority failures lead to the Court issuing rulings that contain no legal reasoning. No doctrine is set forth; nor is the minority able to uphold the law's constitutionality. The Court, in a way, ***decides not to decide***. The statute is not struck down, but neither does the Court uphold it. Supermajority failure decisions lack any precedential status and are never cited as an authoritative source of law by the Court.

The lack of an upholding might be a weakness of the Mexican supermajority. The challenge is not resolved in a dismissal decision. Even though another applicant may not bring the same claim, individual plaintiffs may still challenge the law's constitutionality through Amparo. Amparo requires only a simple majority when resolved by multi-member courts (either circuit courts or the Supreme Court). Consequently, the effects of such a declaration of unconstitutionality would vary. Even if a provision fails to attain a supermajority in the Supreme Court, individual applicants may still obtain a declaration of unconstitutionality, only applicable to their concrete case, in district courts or even in the Supreme Court through Amparo (which would produce inter partes and not *erga omnes* effects).[163]

163 Theoretically, although highly complicated, there is a way in which the court could again consider the *erga omnes* invalidation of a provision that failed to achieve a supermajority. If the Supreme Court in chambers or the circuit courts would issue binding precedents in individual complaints, the General Declaration of Unconstitutionality could allow the court to reopen the discussion. Even though the previous voting is likely to repeat, some factors may cause a surprise, such as vote-switching or the philosophy of some justices, which consider that the general declaration of unconstitutionality is not a judicial review of a provision, but merely a formal verification about whether or not a binding precedent on such provision's unconstitutionality was settled (a position championed by Justice Aguilar in DGI 6/2017).

The same situation occurs even if a simple majority upholds a statute in actions of unconstitutionality or constitutional controversies. If the ruling only attains a simple majority, it will lack precedential value.[164] Other judges will not be legally bound by it (for example, in Amparo). Such a decision will likely be followed if the statute is further challenged in Amparo, which stems from respect for the court's prestige, not the decision's binding legal nature.

Even though the Mexican model formally requires a supermajority to strike down legislation, in a certain sense, it also requires a supermajority to uphold it conclusively. Lacking a supermajority, an upholding means that further challenges in individual complaints (Amparo) may still persuade district court judges that the very same provision infringes the Constitution. Absent a Supreme Court supermajority, district courts would be free to depart from the court's prior decision.

Early on, the Supreme Court coined the expression non-qualified majority (*mayoría no calificada*) to refer to a majority that failed to muster eight votes. Curiously, since a dismissal in a supermajority failure neither upholds nor strikes down legislation, both groups file dissenting opinions. The majority files a "non-qualified majority vote," while the minority issues a "minority vote." Both groups opposed the decision, proposing an alternative outcome that should have taken place. When the supermajority fails, the court's minority achieves only a temporary victory. Political branches are aware that consensus is growing on a provision's constitutionality and might be declared unconstitutional in future individual cases. The supermajority is Mexico's institutionalized deferral.

Since the supermajority requires a fixed number of eight votes out of eleven justices, every absence favors the statute. In full composition, striking down legislation requires 72 percent of the court. However, every missing justice increases such percentage. The court's quorum is eight justices in procedures functioning under supermajority rule. Theoretically, unanimity may be required with three absences. Temporary absences are typical (vacations, sick leaves, official commissions) but hardly impact the court for two reasons. In the first place, the Supreme Court does not hold oral hearings and decides based on written documents submitted by the parties. Since the Court has agenda-setting capabilities, it may postpone the full deliberation of the case

164 This feature requires unpacking. In abstract normative review and constitutional controversies, a supermajority was always required to grant precedential value to the reasoning of the Court, even upholding legislation. That is, if the Court interprets Article X of the Constitution to mean Y, it requires eight votes for this interpretation to be binding on all lower courts. Otherwise, lower courts are free to provide alternative interpretations. This feature refers to the status of a precedent and not to the *erga omnes* or inter partes nature of the remedy. In Amparo, the Court may set a binding precedent claiming that a statute is unconstitutional in a single case by an eight-vote supermajority. The remedy will be inter partes (but other judges, in future cases, will be bound by the settled precedent and will declare the unconstitutionality of the provision, if challenged).

or the voting. It has not been uncommon for the Court, when a single vote was necessary to strike down legislation or decide a matter, to await the return of a missing justice. In AI 6/2022, the Court postponed voting on several provisions until Justices Aguilar and Pérez Dayán returned from official commissions and joined deliberations. In the second place, since the 2020 Covid-19 pandemic, which forced the Court to switch to online sessions, several instances occurred in which justices on official commissions were allowed to take part and vote on cases remotely while the Court was physically deliberating (such as CC 44/2021 and AI 171/2022). The flexible management of the agenda and the possibility of allowing participation via Zoom seems to take the sting out of short absences.

However, appointment delays may prove more challenging. Article 96 of the Mexican Constitution provides that, once a vacancy arises, the President shall submit three proposals to the Senate, and the Senate shall appoint a justice within thirty days. If the Senate were to reject the shortlist, a new shortlist with three candidates would be submitted. The procedure may constitutionally last sixty days even if the President submits the proposal on time. However, as Astudillo and Estrada have noted, the President and the Senate enjoy broad discretion in the procedure.[165] Several instances exist where delays exceed more than 100 days.[166] Even though significant appointment delays are uncommon, the court might occasionally be short a court member for some months, which would either recalibrate the supermajority's weight or force the court to delay a case several months until a new justice is appointed.

A few features of the Supreme Court voting protocol influence the supermajority. First, the Court functions under an outcome voting, not an issue voting model.[167] Thus, it is enough that eight justices consider a statute unconstitutional even if they disagree on the reasons to do so. In the second place, Mexico holds public court deliberations, broadcast live on television and social media.[168]

Public deliberations may discourage evasion of the rule through other mechanisms such as narrow interpretation, interpretive decisions, or vote bargains. Judges may be reluctant to show compromise and bargain in public and thus be concerned about openly being seen as maneuvering towards achieving the closest desired policy outcome. Nonetheless, there are several examples

165 César Astudillo & José Estrada, Nombramiento de Ministros de la Suprema Corte de Justicia de la Nación en el Contexto de los Modelos de Designación en el Derecho Comparado 253 (2019).

166 *Id.* at 253–56.

167 Regarding the difference between an outcome voting model and an issue voting model, *see* David Post & Steven C. Salop, *Rowing Against the Tidewater: A Theory of Voting by Multi-judge Panels*, 80 Geo. L.J. 743 (1991). More recently, *see* Wolfgang Ernst, *The Fine-Mechanisms of Judicial Majoritarianism*, *in* Collective Judging in Comparative Perspective: Counting Votes and Weighing Opinions, 14 (Birke Häcker & Wolfgang Ernst eds., 2020).

168 Pou Giménez, *supra* note 76.

where this has occurred. Justices have occasionally switched their votes and voted to strike down legislation they have argued is constitutional.[169] Such vote-switching depends solely on the justices, and it seems to arise only in non-controversial cases. In most cases, justices stick to their views.

Apart from vote-switching, other instances of strategic judicial behavior have been known. For example, in 2022, Chief Justice Zaldívar (widely perceived as ideologically close to President López Obrador)[170] seemingly changed the Supreme Court's voting protocol from outcome voting to issue voting in one case and managed to save an essential provision of the Federal Electric Industry Act.[171] Another instance occurred during the deliberation on AI 95/2021. The Court analyzed the constitutionality of a transitory provision that extended Chief Justice Zaldívar's term as Court President. The statute was openly unconstitutional, violating the Chief Justice's constitutionally provided fixed four-year term. In an interview, Chief Justice Zaldívar declared that he would recuse himself from the discussion, as he would benefit directly if the statute were declared constitutional. Constitutional experts deemed this could be a strategic maneuver hoping to preserve the statute if a tight division were to arise.[172] Not only was there a view that recusals were genuinely exceptional in actions of unconstitutionality,[173] but recusing himself would only contribute to defending the statute. The Court would have been forced to achieve an 8 out of 10 supermajority. Concerning the outcome, a recusal was no different than directly voting to uphold the law. Nonetheless, after

169 Clear examples of the above occurred in AI 15/2018 (Justice Pardo), AI 54/2018 (Justice Gutiérrez), AI 125/2022 (Justice Zaldívar), or AI 125/2022 (Justices Pérez and Aguilar).

170 Mariana Velasco-Rivera, *When Judges Threaten Constitutional Governance: Evidence from Mexico*, Int'l J. Const. L. Blog (2022), http://www.iconnectblog.com/2022/06/when-judges-threaten-constitutional-governance-evidence-from-mexico/ (last visited May 9, 2022).

171 The incident was debated in the ICON Blog. *See id.*; Roberto Niembro Ortega, *Seeing the Whole Picture of the Debate in the Mexican Supreme Court: A Response to "When Judges Threaten Constitutional Governance: Evidence from Mexico,"* Int'l J. Const. L. Blog (2022), http://www.iconnectblog.com/2022/06/seeing-the-whole-picture-of-the-debate-in-the-mexican-supreme-court-a-response-to-when-judges-threaten-constitutional-governance-evidence-from-mexico/ (last visited May 9, 2022).

172 Zaldívar's original intention of not participating may be deemed as "strategic nonparticipation" in Vermeule's theoretical account of absolute majority rules (understood as fixed-majority requirements). Adrian Vermeule, Mechanisms of Democracy: Institutional Design Writ Small 137 (2007).

173 In a first interpretation, the Court even considered that recusals could not be raised in actions of unconstitutionality since it would conflict with the qualified majority required to strike down legislation (CC 51/2004). A few years later, in Impedimento 16/2011-CC, the Court changed its doctrine to state that exceptional recusals were possible when a situation could conflict with a justice's impartiality. Nonetheless, the Court was emphatic in saying that recusals depended on pondering "the seriousness of the reasons argued by a Justice which deems he/she should be recused, to protect the effective functioning of judicial review mechanisms regarding the qualified majority required by the Constitution." *See also* the binding case law P. XX/2013 (10a.) from the Court's Plenary.

enormous media pressure, the Chief Justice did not recuse himself and, visibly displeased, voted to strike down the statute.

Court decisions provide detailed information on voting. Therefore, from the Court's decision, it is clear whether the supermajority influenced a case, which provision was protected, and which justices constituted the blocking non-qualified majority. In turn, the video records and transcripts of deliberations reveal the arguments and reasons behind each group's positions.

4.3.3 Scholarship and Politics: The Controversies on the Supermajority Rule

Scholarship has opposed the Mexican supermajority. The supermajority went relatively unnoticed during the early years (1994–2004). It was not until 2005 that the scholarship began shifting under Brage.[174] A Spanish scholar, Professor Brage published an influential book on the Mexican action of unconstitutionality.

Brage was unfamiliar with the Mexican legal system[175] and primarily analyzed the normative provisions of the newly created mechanism. However, Brage was an expert in the Spanish abstract normative review *recurso de inconstitucionalidad* and knew similar mechanisms functioning in comparative law. Hungry for legal analysis on a procedure alien to the Mexican system (introduced just in 1994), Mexican scholarship avidly devoured Brage's monograph, which possessed a solid theoretical background. Brage devoted one section of the book to analyzing the supermajority, being very critical of it. Brage went as far as to claim that the supermajority implied that Mexican judicial review was "born condemned to death."[176]

Even though Brage's book is a good account of abstract normative review, the supermajority played a minor role in it. Brage was unaware of the leading scholarship on supermajorities and examples in comparative law. His analysis also failed to mention how the supermajority functioned in practice despite the available relevant experience.

Early on, Brage set the tone of the main arguments against the supermajority. Namely, he claimed that the supermajority was non-existent in comparative law and that it obstructed the court.[177] The criticism has continued

174 Joaquín Brage, La acción abstracta de inconstitucionalidad 341 (2005).

175 For example, Brage makes mistakes on several occasions due to a lack of knowledge of the Mexican legal system. For instance, he claims that the supermajority lacks consistency since a simple majority suffices to strike down a law *erga omnes* in constitutional controversies. That is not the case. *Id*. at 343. He makes the same argument in Amparo, but as mentioned, the effects differ radically.

176 *Id*. at 350.

177 *Id*. at 345–50.

in a similar tone.[178] Subsequent scholars such as Fix-Zamudio,[179] Carpizo,[180] and Ferrer Mac-Gregor & Sánchez Gil have often followed Brage's analysis.[181] Herrera claimed that Mexican scholarship is "generally uncritical of the qualified majority requirement."[182] Perhaps, in general, constitutional scholars pay little attention to the rule, but those who do usually are opponents of the requirement,[183] although some have accepted it.[184]

Contrary to the academic debate, at the political level, there is no controversy on the rule. Despite Mexico's hyper-reformism, there has been no serious proposal to suppress the supermajority, and new supermajorities have even been introduced to the legal system since 1994. In 2011, a procedure called "general declaration of unconstitutionality" (DGI) was introduced. DGI allowed the court to analyze *ex officio* the constitutionality of a statute and strike it with *erga omnes* effect if binding case law about its unconstitutionality had previously been issued in Amparo. The procedure bridges the inter partes and *erga omnes* effect. Unsurprisingly, the new procedure requires a supermajority.[185]

178 On March 26, 2022, Professor Ana Laura Magaloni, an influential Mexican scholar, published a widely known newspaper article titled "Eight votes," analyzing the challenges ahead of a future Supreme Court case. She claimed that "No relevant Constitutional Court in the world has such a straitjacket" despite several examples of supermajorities in comparative law. Ana Magaloni, *Ocho Votos*, REFORMA, Mar. 26, 2022, https://bit.ly/3lJrhXH (last visited May 25, 2022).

179 HÉCTOR FIX-ZAMUDIO, INTRODUCCIÓN AL ESTUDIO DE LA DEFENSA DE LA CONSTITUCIÓN EN EL ORDENAMIENTO MEXICANO 82–84 (1998).

180 Jorge Carpizo, *Propuestas de modificaciones constitucionales en el marco de la denominada reforma del Estado*, *in* EL PROCESO CONSTITUYENTE MEXICANO 183, 82–84 (Diego Valadés & Miguel Carbonell eds., 2007). Carpizo initially defended the supermajority. Carpizo, *supra* note 160, at 834. Less than ten years later, Carpizo changed his opinion without providing further arguments as to why he did so.

181 EDUARDO FERRER MAC-GREGOR & RUBÉN SÁNCHEZ, EFECTOS Y CONTENIDOS DE LAS SENTENCIAS EN ACCIÓN DE INCONSTITUCIONALIAD 19 (2009). Ferrer Mac-Gregor and Sánchez Gil seem to base their opinion on Brage's analysis of comparative law and scholarship.

182 Alfonso Herrera, *¿4 es más que 7? Por qué debe eliminarse la mayoría calificada en acciones de inconstitucionalidad*, NEXOS: EL JUEGO DE LA SUPREMA CORTE (Feb. 10, 2022), https://bit.ly/3Gqe4wz (last visited May 25, 2022).

183 Gómez recently argued that most Mexican scholarship disapproves of the supermajority requirement. Carlos Gómez, *La Ley Federal de Revocación de Mandato y la mayoría calificada en la Suprema Corte de Justicia Mexicana*, HECHOS Y DERECHOS (2022), https://revistas.juridicas.unam.mx/index.php/hechos-y-derechos/article/view/16705/17299 (last visited May 25, 2022).

184 Such as Figueroa, Serna, or Rivera. Giovanni Figueroa, *La presunción de constitucionalidad de la ley como criterio jurisprudencial: Especial análisis del caso mexicano*, *in* CONSTITUCIONALISMO: DOS SIGLOS DE SU NACIMIENTO EN AMÉRICA LATINA 237, 246 (César Astudillo & Jorge Carpizo eds., 2013); SERNA, *supra* note 157, at 127.

185 Mauro Arturo Rivera León, *¿La tumba de Otero? Naturaleza, funcionamiento y problemáticas de la declaratoria general de inconstitucionalidad en México*, 26 ANUARIO IBEROAMERICANO DE JUSTICIA CONSTITUCIONAL 57, 69 (2022).

In 2020, the Court was allowed to set binding precedents in all proceedings provided a supermajority vote was reached. Previously, precedents issued in actions of unconstitutionality and constitutional controversies required an eight-vote supermajority, ensuring that a non-qualified majority could not avoid the rule by setting binding precedents reading the statute narrowly or binding ordinary judges to a conforming interpretation of the Constitution.

The supermajority has influenced several significant cases. After the rule was established in 1994, it took seven years to be applied. The first case in which the rule prevented an unconstitutionality decision was in 2002 in AI 10/2000, while analyzing the so-called "Robles Law."[186] The Court failed by a 6:5 vote to strike down a regulation allowing abortion in cases of rape. The decision showed a seriously divided court. All justices filed separate opinions, some even more than one.[187] Justices Aguinaco, Aguirre, Azuela, Díaz, and Ortiz remarked bitterly in their opinion that it was the first time in the history of the Court that a majority had not decided a case. The justices, furious at the survival of the abortion permission, concluded:

> Paradoxically, the six Justices that deem the provision to be unconstitutional and the five that have the conviction that it respects the Constitution both had simultaneously satisfactions and dissatisfactions, although contrary to each other. The first ones were discontent at not having struck down the law . . . but also had the satisfaction of not allowing the Court to uphold the provision through arguments in the decision. The second ones were dissatisfied with not having achieved an upholding . . . and the satisfaction of blocking the Court from striking down the law . . . and allowing the provision to remain valid, as the last Justice in the session claimed to be 'for the good of women.' We should reflect on whether the good of someone may come out of harm and the destruction of others.

The supermajority failure in the *Robles Law* case was an essential step toward protecting reproductive rights. In what Calabresi deemed a foundational case,[188] the supermajority prevented a conservative Supreme Court from striking down liberal abortion legislation. Using Hong's terminology also signaled a turn[189] in the Court's conservative case law. In the coming years, the Court would become one of the most liberal tribunals regarding abortion

186 A brief analysis of the case in Alejandro Madrazo & Estefanía Vela, *The Mexican Supreme Court's (Sexual) Revolution*, 89 Texas L. Rev. 1863, 1870–72 (2010).

187 For example, Justices Aguirre, Aguinaco, and Ortiz filed separate dissenting opinions regarding different topics of the decision.

188 2 Steven Gow Calabresi, The History and Growth of Judicial Review: The G-20 Civil Law Countries 239 (2021).

189 Hong, *supra* note 78.

regulations.[190] The decision also showed that the supermajority could not only prevent striking down harmful laws but could defend rights established by a liberal legislature from a conservative court. The situation arose again in AI 12/2002, where the Court failed to strike down legislation forcing banks to take security measures against robberies (such as installing security footage).

From 2010 onwards, the rule became standard in the Court's activity. It also began arising in cases lacking political controversy or merely technical, such as administrative fines. Between 2014 and 2015, a dispute on the competence of states to regulate electoral coalitions resulted in a series of almost twenty supermajority failure decisions on the same type of provisions issued by different state congresses.

The rule has faced harsher criticism of late, linked to recent political developments. In 2018, López Obrador won the presidential election. Commonly portrayed as a populist,[191] President López depicts himself as the people's champion against the corrupt political elite. True to his style, Lopez Obrador has severely criticized the federal judiciary, backed up by his unusually strong congressional majority.[192] He views judges, magistrates, and justices as an overpaid and privileged group more interested in keeping their privileges than doing justice and helping the poor. The criticism has placed the federal judiciary under enormous pressure.[193]

In classic populist fashion, he divides the *demos* into two groups: "*fifis*" (the corrupt rich elite), also referred to as "*la mafia del poder*" (the power mafia), and "*el pueblo bueno*," the good people who support him.[194] As a result, Mexico has never been so polarized in its history. President López Obrador devotes considerable time to criticizing the opposition and journalists in his daily press conferences. In turn, the opposition criticizes every executive policy

190 In 2021, the Supreme Court unanimously ruled that it was unconstitutional to criminalize abortion and sent out a binding precedent to the Federal and State Governments on the obligation to establish regulations allowing abortion. Risa Kaufman et al., *Global Impacts of Dobbs v. Jackson Women's Health Organization and Abortion Regression in the United States*, 30 Sexual and Reproductive Health Matters 2135574, 25 (2022); Julie C. Suk, *A World Without Roe: The Constitutional Future of Unwanted Pregnancy*, 64 Wm. & Mary L. Rev. 43, 468 (2022).

191 Mauricio I. Dussauge-Laguna, *The Promises and Perils of Populism for Democratic Policymaking: The Case of Mexico*, 55 Policy Sci. 777, 778 (2022).

192 Pozas-Loyo *et al.* consider that, during a long period, "political fragmentation has shielded the Court against political attack." Andrea Pozas-Loyo, Camilo Saavedra Herrera & Francisca Pou Giménez, *When More Leads to More: Constitutional Amendments and Interpretation in Mexico 1917-2020*, L. Soc. Inq. 1, 25 (2022).

193 Jaime Olaiz-González, *Mexican Supreme Court at Crossroads: Three Acts of Constitutional Politics*, 14 ICL J. 447 (2021).

194 Mauricio I. Dussauge-Laguna, *"Doublespeak Populism" and Public Administration: The Case of Mexico*, *in* Democratic Backsliding and Public Administration 178, 181 (Michael W. Bauer et al. eds., 2021).

and challenges it before the Supreme Court if possible.[195] In these challenges, the supermajority has played a crucial role.

The Supreme Court's staggered terms allow for periodic renovation. During his six-year term, a president will be able to nominate an average of four justices,[196] having a say in roughly one-third of the court's composition. Lopez Obrador's nominations so far have been criticized. He nominated González Alcantara and Ríos, a senior state magistrate and the Chief of the federal Tax Administration, respectively. Both have behaved independently and voted against the President in controversial cases. However, the remaining two nominees have been more questionable. Justice Ortiz Ahlf, an academic, was formerly a senator within the ranks of the President's party. In turn, Justice Esquivel is the wife of José María Riobóo, the President's most trusted contractor. Justice Esquivel made headlines for months after it was discovered that she plagiarized her law degree thesis and substantial parts of her Ph.D. thesis.[197] Esquivel is known to vote in favor of presidential politics regardless of the case.

Some scholars have expressed concerns that López Obrador's four appointments allow him to "block" the Court.[198] Nonetheless, the appointment mechanism, combined with the supermajority, does not allow Court control. A collaborative procedure is employed to appoint Supreme Court justices in Mexico. The President proposes three candidates, and the Senate confirms the justice through a two-thirds supermajority. Even though a default mechanism allows the President to select a justice if the Senate rejects a set of proposals twice, considerable political pressure encourages compromise and bargaining. Furthermore, even though there is an average of four nominations per president[199] during their six-year term, frequently, those nominations occur at the very end of the presidential term. Some of the appointed justices' terms start

195 The opposition files every challenge they can. In 2020, the government merged two bodies in charge of organizing charity lotteries. In AI 110/2020, a group of opposition senators claimed it was unconstitutional to join the bodies, as alternative regulation could be more suitable. Needless to say, the Court unanimously upheld the law stating that it lacked the power to determine what the ideal regulation for a matter is and could merely rule on infringements to the Constitution.

196 Villanueva deems at least three appointments are guaranteed. Rebecka Villanueva Ulfgard, *Separation of Powers in Distress: AMLO's Charismatic Populism and Mexico's Return to Hyper-Presidentialism*, 6 Populism 55, 65 (2023). Four appointments have been the norm.

197 *Id.* at 76.

198 Pedro Salazar, *Cuatro votos judiciales*, Hechos y Derechos (2022), https://revistas.juridicas.unam.mx/index.php/hechos-y-derechos/article/view/16642/17256 (last visited May 20, 2022). Villanueva Ulfgard, *supra* note 196, at 66.

199 President Fox appointed four Justices, President Calderón appointed five Justices, with Presidents Peña Nieto and López Obrador appointing three and four respectively. For further details on these features and the relationship between the appointment procedure and the court control claim, *see* Mauro Arturo Rivera León, *Control and Paralysis? A Context-Sensitive Analysis of Objections to Supermajorities in Constitutional Adjudication*, Int. J. Const. L. (2023), doi.org/10.1093/icon/moad074.

after the appointing President's term finishes, diminishing their impact and guaranteeing that a forthcoming president will coexist with a renewed court.

During López Obrador's term, the supermajority helped defend some key governmental policies. It played a minor role in protecting some provisions of the Federal Remunerations Act (AI 105/2018).[200] It also helped preserve more substantive governmental policies, the Federal Electric Industry Act (AI 64/2021) and the Federal Recall Act (AI 151/2021).

Nonetheless, even though the current government has lost key battles before the Supreme Court,[201] the polarized environment has led the opposition to mistrust the rule in a way that did not exist when they were in government. Current critics might be motivated more by a desire of the Court to serve as an opposition weapon against populist politics rather than by genuine considerations of the Court's institutional design.

The rule has potentially contributed to avoiding an even bigger clash between the executive and judicial branches, while still allowing the Court to signal the potential unconstitutionality of a provision and allowing the opposition to use the Court's opinion as further arguments in the political debate.

200 This Act was at the heart of López Obrador's ideology: lowering what he deemed to be unjustified high salaries of public officials was one of his central campaign promises. Judge-Rapporteur Pérez Dayán initially proposed striking down the entire law for infringing legislative procedure. The proposal failed to gather the required supermajority. In the merits, the Court struck down the act's core provisions achieving the supermajority with the decisive vote of Justice González Alcántara (appointed under President López Obrador), while Piña and Zaldívar (proposed by Presidents Peña and Calderón) defended the statute. In the most political case of López Obrador's Presidency, Justice González Alcántara put the nail in the statute's coffin. To understand President López Obrador's austerity policy, *see* Rebecka Villanueva Ulfgard & César Villanueva, *The Power to Transform? Mexico's 'Fourth Transformation' under President Andrés Manuel López Obrador*, 17 Globalizations 1027, 1036–39 (2020).

201 As said, the Court struck down key provisions of the Federal Remunerations act. In AI 137/2011, the Court declared the transfer of the National Guard to military control within the Ministry of Defense unconstitutional. The Court further invalidated a significant package of electoral amendments favored by MORENA in AI 29/2023. In AR 541/2021 and AR 540/2021, the Supreme Court ruled in favor of two people prosecuted allegedly by direct pressure of the MORENA-proposed Attorney General in an open political scandal. In April 2022, the Court unanimously struck down a provision from the Federal Republican Austerity Act, which established a ten-year prohibition on governmental officials from working in companies with whom they had had a relationship or supervised while working for the government (AI 139/2019). In another highly contentious case, when reviewing the constitutionality of a controversial referendum called to prosecute alleged former Presidential crimes, the Court indeed confirmed its constitutionality (favoring the majority and reaping massive criticism). However, the ruling dramatically altered the referendum question to such a degree that little of the original political intent remained (RCPR 1/2020). A critique of the last case in Alfonso Herrera García, *Jurisprudencia Constitucional de La Suprema Corte de Justicia de México En El 2020*, 25 Anu. Iberoam. Justicia Consti. 607, 618 (2021). Some of the cases mentioned here were analyzed in the 2020 ICON report. *See* Irene Spigno, Mauro Arturo Rivera León & Alfonso Herrera, *Mexico*, *in* 2019 Global Review of Constitutional Law 192, 194–195 (Richard Albert et al. eds., 2020).

Had the Court, severely antagonized by President López Obrador, managed to strike down relevant policies by bare majorities in controversial 6:5 decisions, rhetoric might have turned to frontal intervention faster. In the last year of his term, President López Obrador announced his intention to pursue an ambitious judicial reform program, which would possibly undermine judicial independence by making justices elected by the people. Future studies are necessary to assess the impact of the rule.

Supermajority failure decisions were relatively uncommon through the first period of the Court (1994–2010). Years went by initially without the rule saving a single statute. The Court's growing caseload may partially account for the increase. More cases mean less discussion time and less ability to compromise.

Although political consensus on the rule exists, some amendment proposals have emerged. In 2007, Senator Sansores sponsored a constitutional amendment proposal to introduce a system of mobile supermajorities. The proposal noted that absences could play a role in the weight of the supermajority and thus suggested constitutionally establishing different majorities depending on the number of justices present.[202] The proposal did not attain political support and was not approved.

Recently, two proposals to amend the supermajority were put forward by opposition Senators. The first one, sponsored by Senator Rojas, proposes maintaining a reduced seven-vote supermajority.[203] The second one, sponsored by Senator Téllez,[204] would have the court solve all issues by a simple majority. Both proposals seem to be a reaction to the cases in which the supermajority prevented the opposition from striking down governmental policy. The opposition lacks the votes to pass the required constitutional amendment to modify or suppress the supermajority, and the majority lacks any incentive towards diminishing the court's deference to legislation, which they endured while being in the opposition. The amendment proposal will surely fail.

4.4 The Dominican Republic: A Consensus Supermajority (2010–Present)

The Dominican Republic is a fascinating example of a functional supermajority. After volatile episodes of foreign intervention,[205] in 1844, the Dominican Republic gained independence and adopted its first Constitution. Dominican constitutional history is characterized by constitutional change. The 1844 Constitution has been revised thirty-eight times as of 2023. The country has

202 *See* the proposal published in the Parliamentary Gazette, LX/1SPR-12-347/12636, May 30, 2007, https://bit.ly/3FEIfko. The proposal reduced one vote for every absence, therefore requiring the following majorities: 7/10, 6/9, 5/8, and 4/6.

203 *See* the proposal at https://bit.ly/3M5R4rj (Sept. 8, 2022).

204 *See* the proposal at https://bit.ly/3LI92OV (Dec. 14, 2020).

205 Zachary Elkins, Tom Ginsburg & James Melton, The Endurance of National Constitutions loc. 4100 (2009).

gone through multiple *coups d'état*, dictatorships (particularly under Presidents Santana, Heureaux, and Trujillo), and democratic transitions. Traditionally, Dominican Republic scholars call each amendment a new Constitution. Amendments are voted on separately, but the full document as amended is discussed and approved, formally promulgating a new Constitution after every revision.

Several Constitutions lacking normative force occurred between 1844 and 1994. In 1994, amidst allegations of fraud, President Balaguer was forced to concede significant democratizing electoral reforms, establishing mechanisms of European judicial review in the hands of the Supreme Court[206] and creating a National Council of the Magistrature tasked with judicial appointment and administrative functions.

The reform trend continued with the 2010 constitutional amendment (also known as the 2010 Constitution), which considerably changed the Dominican judiciary. As some scholars have pointed out, the 2010 constitutional amendment procedure "is the most democratic and inclusive constitutional reform in the country's history to date."[207] The amendment process started in 2006 with a Commission of Constitutional Experts appointed by the President in Decree 323-06. The Commission organized extensive public consultations and drafted the amendments.

4.4.1 A Consensus Rule: Adoption and Objectives of the Supermajority of the Dominican Republic

The 2010 amendment modified the judicial review system by introducing a constitutional court in full Kelsenian fashion. The 1978 Spanish Constitutional Court influenced Dominican constitutionalism. Magistrates are appointed to staggered nine-year terms, with new magistrates replacing outgoing ones every three years.[208]

The court was granted the power to solve abstract normative review, preventive control of international treaties, and jurisdiction over conflicts between public branches. The Constitution opted for a supermajority, providing in Article 186: "The Constitutional Court shall be integrated by thirteen members, and its decisions shall be adopted with a qualified majority of nine or more of its members." The Organic Law of the Constitutional Court set a

206 The Supreme Court was vested with abstract constitutional review. Law 156-97 modified the Court's organic law, increasing the size of the Court to 16 justices (subsequently increased to 17 justices in 2011). The law vested the Court *en banc* with the authority to perform abstract judicial review. Decisions were taken by a simple majority (Article 1).

207 Leiv Marsteintredet, *Change and Continuity in Dominican Constitutions: The 2010 Reform Compared*, *in* New Constitutionalism in Latin America 223, 224 (Almut Schilling-Vacaflor & Detlef Nolte eds., 2016).

208 Leiv Marsteintredet, Eduardo Jorge Prats & Emmanuel Cedeño-Brea, *Dominican Republic*, *in* 2019 Global review of constitutional law 97, 97 (Richard Albert et al. eds., 2020).

quorum at nine members (Article 27). Contrary to other countries, the contemporary Dominican supermajority had no precedent in Dominican constitutionalism. The rule has no authoritarian origins either. It came through a procedure described as open, participatory, and inclusive across party lines.[209]

A former member of the Presidential Commission, renowned Dominican Constitutional Scholar Prof. Jorge Prats, recalled that unanimity and other higher supermajorities were considered in the Commission discussions of the 2010 Constitution.[210] The Commission viewed unfavorably the controversial 5:4 decisions of the American Supreme Court, and consensus-seeking was deemed as highly relevant.[211] However, such considerations occurred in the shadows in the debate of constitutional experts. The records of the constitutional debates in the National Assembly offer no insight into the rule's purpose, as legislators most likely trusted by and large the agreed draft.

The Constitutional Court was debated in the National Assembly on October 19, 2009. Originally, the Assembly considered creating a Constitutional Chamber within the Supreme Court. One of the legislative commissions had suggested returning to an autonomous Constitutional Court, having twelve members and deciding by a simple majority, which would have meant a minimum two-vote difference required for every decision.

Julio César Valentín was tasked with defending his party's position. The *Partido de la Liberación Dominicana* (PLD) proposed a Constitutional Court with thirteen members and a nine-vote supermajority requirement. The proposal triumphed on a non-partisan basis. Both majoritarian parties, PLD and PRD (*Partido Revolucionario Dominicano*), supported the supermajority, which the National Assembly approved by a strong 88:9 vote in the House of Representatives and an overwhelming 20:1 in the Senate. It was the product of an unprecedented political agreement, the so-called *Pacto Político por la Democracia*, signed by the leaders of the two dominant parties.

4.4.2 The Consensus Supermajority in Practice

The Constitution requires a symmetrical supermajority. Nine members must agree to take any decision at the Court.[212] Proposals attaining less than nine votes result in the Court not acting, and the case remains undecided. No default rule was established by Congress or interpreted by the Court (*i.e.*, a rule assigning a default Court outcome to decisions not attaining the required

209 Marsteintredet, *supra* note 207, at 242.

210 Eduardo Jorge Prats, *Interview with a Former Member of the Presidential Constitutional Commission for the 2010 Constitutional Amendment* (unpublished, 2022).

211 *Id.*

212 The system is not entirely undisputed. Prof. Eduardo Jorge Prats has noted that the law took a "restrictive" interpretation of the Constitution. He has advocated for possibly interpreting the supermajority requirement solely to invalidate legislation. I Eduardo Jorge Prats, Derecho Constitucional 515 (3 ed. 2015).

threshold). As of this writing, the precedents of the Constitutional Court are stable, and the Court abandons its established doctrine rarely, much less suddenly.

The supermajority precludes the possibility of the Constitutional Court working in Senates or Chambers. However, the practice of the Court created "commissions" (*comisiones operativas*) in which four magistrates work together on decision drafts and generate a first proposal to be put forward to the Plenum for consideration.[213] Commissions function as consensus-building committees. Through informal practice, the Court has considerably protected decision-making efficiency.[214]

After the Constitution's promulgation, Congress issued Law 137-11 regulating constitutional procedures in June 2011 (*Ley Orgánica del Tribunal Constitutional y de los Procedimientos Constitucionales*). The legislature introduced a new regulation on Amparo procedures (individual complaints). Even though traditionally the ordinary Dominican jurisdiction has heard Amparos, the Law introduced a new type of appeal (*recurso de revisión*), allowing the Constitutional Court to review all Amparo rulings. The new appeal substantially increased the Constitutional Court's workload and was not foreseen when introducing the supermajority.[215]

Since the Constitution requires a supermajority for the court's decisions, a debate arose among the court members in 2017 when approving the court's internal regulations, centered on whether the court rules were "decisions" within the meaning of Article 186 of the Constitution or whether the Constitution solely imposed a qualified majority for judicial cases. Upon a divided court, a simple majority approved the rules. Several magistrates disagreed and filed dissenting opinions. Magistrate Piña Medrano claimed that a supermajority was the only constitutionally acceptable decision-making method for the court. Magistrate Bonilla contended that the spirit of the Constitution privileges a qualified majority. Magistrates Jiménez and Cury, in a joint dissenting opinion, argued that the Constitution forbids modifying the majority in jurisdictional and administrative court decisions. The same debate occurred in Peru, although the Dominican Republic has normative provisions

213 Constitutional Court of the Dominican Republic, *Questionnaire of the Seminary (Dominican Republic)*, 25 4 (2019).

214 Former Magistrate Acosta points out that a problem of the "operative commissions" is that magistrates may switch their previous votes on the Commission in the deliberations. "I understand that commissions aid little in solving the problem since nothing prevents Magistrates from voting in the deliberations in a different way than they did on the Commission." Hermógenes Acosta de los Santos, *Interview with a Former Magistrate of the Dominican Constitutional Court* (unpublished, 2023).

215 Hermógenes Acosta, *El Proceso de Amparo En El Nuevo Modelo de Justicia Constitucional Dominicano*, *in* Treinta años de jurisdicción constitucional en el Perú 145, 185 (Gerardo Eto ed., 2014).

that strengthen the case for a supermajority approval of the court's internal rules.

The supermajority has also impacted the candidates supported by the political branches. Magistrates' personality, consensus capacity, and collegiality are highly valued. Former Magistrate Acosta sheds light on how non-collegiate magistrates may be seen as a liability if they have shown a tendency to issue multiple dissenting opinions.[216] Collegiality is critical to function in the Dominican Constitutional Court.

Political actors have grown accustomed to the rule. In the early years, most scholars accepted the supermajority as natural, although some paid attention to the requirement. Prof. Eduardo Jorge Prats was one of the earliest scholars to provide a theoretical framework for the rule by arguing that it resulted from the presumption of constitutionality. He further claimed that the rule guaranteed robust precedential status for the court's decisions since decisions require strong "consensus in the Constitutional Court and decisions are not taken by a passing or circumstantial majority."[217]

It is not uncommon for the court to postpone voting and repeat debates in search of consensus when it is clear that no position commands the nine votes required.[218] However, impasses rarely occur since "it is politically reprehensible for the Court not to rule. Magistrates are forced to build consensus as political pressure mounts to issue a resolution."[219] Nevertheless, former magistrate of the Dominican Constitutional Court, Prof. Acosta, deems that, in his experience, it was relatively common for a proposal not to achieve a supermajority. Magistrates would then go to further negotiation rounds to introduce changes to build the required consensus. Very often, magistrates would switch positions, but it also happened that some cases could not achieve the necessary supermajority even after changes and new rounds of debate.

In some cases, the triennial renovations help the court reach the supermajority, as new members of the court may side with already majoritarian views. Based on his own experience, Magistrate Acosta deems that cases in which an impasse occurred were numerically insignificant. Nonetheless, he claims those cases tend to be politically sensitive and important to the court.

As some have noticed, the Dominican Constitutional Court exercises broad powers. Even though most of them are theoretically related to constitutional adjudication, its jurisdiction on Amparo strongly resembles an ordinary

216 Acosta de los Santos, *supra* note 214. Delving into the profile of Constitutional Court magistrates, Prof. Acosta explained: "In our background, there is no culture of dissenting opinions. A judge filing dissenting opinions is considered a person with no aptitude to be part of a collegiate body."

217 I Jorge Prats, *supra* note 212, at 453.

218 Discursos del Presidente del Tribunal Constitucional: Milton Ray Guevara, 599 (Adriano Miguel Tejada ed., 2018).

219 Jorge Prats, *supra* note 210.

jurisdiction and constitutes an important portion of the court's total cases. Magistrate Acosta even proposed an interpretation of the Constitution that would allow the court to bypass the supermajority in individual constitutional complaints, although it failed to gain support.[220] In further analyses, Acosta insisted that the supermajority is too high, at least in respect of individual constitutional complaints.[221]

Given the supermajority rule, it would be reasonable to expect the court's decisions to be politically moderate. However, that has not always been the case. For example, in September 2013, the court issued the highly controversial decision TC/0168/13.[222] Complainant Juliana Deguis Pierre was born in the Dominican Republic to undocumented Haitian parents. Accordingly, she received a Dominican birth certificate from the Central Electoral Board. Upon requesting her Dominican national identity card (*Cédula de Identidad y Electoral*), the board refused the request and, presumably based on her Haitian last name, withheld her birth certificate, claiming that her registration had been fraudulent. Upon filing an Amparo suit, the Dominican Constitutional Court had to analyze whether Deguis was entitled to her identity document. In a ruling applicable in *erga omnes* fashion, the court revoked the nationality of thousands of Dominicans of Haitian origin. The court interpreted the provisions of the 1966 Constitution, which provided birthright citizenship to any person born in the Dominican Republic, except for those born "in transit." The court interpreted that people without a legal migration status were in transit (a rule that Congress introduced only in the 2010 Constitution).

Thousands of descendants of Haitian immigrants were deprived of nationality. Furthermore, refraining from applying the *ius soli* model was a direct contravention of the 2005 Yean and Bosico ruling of the Inter-American Court.[223]

220 Magistrate Acosta remarked that while Article 186 established a supermajority for all decisions of the Constitutional Court, Article 72 established the principles concerning individual complaints, among them simplicity and briefness. For Acosta, a supermajority would contradict such principles, and thus the Court could refrain from applying the Constitution itself and part with the supermajority, at least in individual complaints. Since the supermajority is established in the Constitution, Magistrate Acosta considers this to be a contradiction between constitutional provisions.

221 Hermógenes Acosta, *El Impacto de la Vigencia y Funcionamiento del Tribunal Constitucional Dominicano en la Protección de los Derechos Fundamentales*, Revista de la Sala Constitucional 36, 43 (2019).

222 For a brief introduction to the context and the decision, *see* Christina M. Cerna, *Judgment TC/0168/13 (Const. Ct. Dom. Rep.) & Statement of the Inter-American Commission on Human Rights on Judgment TC/0168/13*, 53 Int. Leg. Mater. 662 (2014).

223 Case of the Girls Yean and Bosico v. Dominican Republic. Judgment of Sept. 8, 2005 (Preliminary Objections, Merits, Reparations and Costs).

The decision received massive international[224] and academic criticism,[225] although it was well-received inside the country. However, the judgment seems to have been a product of true internal court consensus, not only achieving the supermajority but comfortably surpassing it.[226]

A year later, the court would again issue a controversial decision. TC/0256/14 concluded that accepting the Inter-American Court of Human Rights jurisdiction was unconstitutional as it was not subjected to congressional approval. The decision was criticized not only for ignoring relevant principles of international law[227] but also for the problematic outcomes in terms of human rights it may produce in the already backsliding region of Latin America.[228] Some claimed it was "shameful" and "without effect on the international plane."[229] The supermajority was again surpassed as a 10:3 majority approved the judgment.[230]

The supermajority has played a significant role in several cases by delaying court rulings. The most famous example is the so-called "preclearance case," still undecided as of January 2023. In 2016, then President Danilo Medina and United States Ambassador James Brew signed an international agreement regarding air preclearance at the Punta Cana airport. The preclearance program practically intends to extend the United States' borders to the most

224 Kristymarie Shipley, *Stateless: Dominican-Born Grandchildren of Haitian Undocumented Immigrants in the Dominican Republic*, 24 TRANSNAT'L L. & CONTEMP. PROBS. 459, 466–7 (2014).

225 Nicia C. Mejia, *Dominican Apartheid: Inside the Flawed Migration System of the Dominican Republic*, HARV. LATINO L. REV. 201 (2015); Ernesto Sagas & Ediberto Roman, *Who Belongs: Citizenship and Statelessness in the Dominican Republic*, 9 GEO. JL & MOD. CRITICAL RACE PERSP. 35 (2017).

226 An 11:2 majority adopted the judgment. Only Magistrates Isabel Bonilla and Katia Miguelina Jiménez dissented.

227 For example, regardless of the debate on whether or not the acceptance of jurisdiction constitutes an international treaty within the meaning of the Dominican Constitution, it has been argued that the Constitutional Court infringed the principle stated in the Vienna Convention on the Law of Treaties, whereby a State may not invoke domestic law as an excuse to refrain from complying with international obligations. This argument seems strengthened by the fact that the State provided other signs of acceptance of the ICHR's jurisdiction. Alexandra Huneeus & René Urueña, *Treaty Exit and Latin America's Constitutional Courts*, 111 AJIL UNBOUND 456, 459 (2017).

228 Dinah Shelton & Alexandra Huneeus, *In Re Direct Action of Unconstitutionality Initiated Against the Declaration of Acceptance of the Jurisdiction of the Inter-American Court of Human Rights*, 109 AM. J. INT. L. 866, 872 (2015). Raffaela Kunz, *Judging International Judgments Anew? The Human Rights Courts before Domestic Courts*, 30 EUROPEAN J. INT'L L. 1129, 1156 (2019).

229 Jorge Contesse, *Resisting the Inter-American Human Rights System*, 44 YALE J. INT'L L. 179, 203 (2019).

230 Magistrates Ana Bonilla, Hermógenes Acosta, and Katia Miguelina Jiménez filed dissenting opinions. This case may evidence a fracture in the Court's composition. Magistrates Jiménez and Acosta accused the majority of publishing the judgment without dissenting opinions, against constitutional regulations, the internal rules of the Courts, and the Court's practice.

remote point of departure. The agreement grants the United States power to place and perform customs and migration revisions, access control, and baggage screening on Dominican soil. Although a preclearance facility reduces the waiting at arrival and allows passengers to skip inspection lines, it might be considered controversial as it would grant a foreign nation considerable power on Dominican soil.

A prior attempt to sign a preclearance agreement had already been unanimously declared unconstitutional in TC/0315/15, where it was deemed to violate the principle of reciprocity and equality in international relations. However, in its judgment, the court acknowledged that political branches could renegotiate and restructure the treaty to sign a new agreement in terms that might be compatible with the Constitution.

A new preclearance agreement was signed in 2016 and immediately challenged through the mechanism for preventive review. Since 2016, no proposed position for the preclearance case has been able to command the required nine votes.[231] In 2021, four magistrates of the Constitutional Court were newly appointed. A media scandal proved that the preclearance case had deeply fractured the court.

Former Dominican Constitutional Court Magistrates Leyda Margarita Piña, Jottin Cury, Wilson Gómez, and Katia Jiménez publicly broke the silence and proclaimed that the agreement is unconstitutional, warning citizens against relinquishing sovereignty and possibly infringing international asylum regulations. Their media appearances provided some details from the closed-door internal deliberations. The curtain had lifted, and people gained insights into the internal factions that had prevented the court from ruling on the case. Since then, several former magistrates have been active media opposers of the treaty.

The appointment of four new magistrates to the court in 2021 renewed the hope of a resolution as the preclearance played a clear role in the appointment procedure. In the Dominican Republic, constitutional court magistrates are selected by the National Council of the judiciary, a body chaired by the President. In the hearings pertaining to the 2021 appointments, the President asked several questions to the candidates to scout their position on the preclearance agreement, much like in the United States, where a candidate's stance on the *Roe v. Wade* decision has been a line of questioning that dominates the hearings to fill court vacancies. In a televised interview,

231 In a public interview, former magistrate Katina Miguelina confirmed that there was still no majority of nine votes to approve the amendment: "The Court has not decided as no majority has emerged on Constitutional terms, that is, nine votes, to approve the agreement." "And to not approve it?" the journalist replied. "Not either, there is a deadlock." Katia Miguelina Jiménez, *Acento Dominicano* (2021), https://bit.ly/3JE46LJ (last visited Mar. 2, 2023). In a further interview, Magistrate Miguelina Jiménez revealed that the internal court simple majority had leaned towards the constitutionality of the preclearance agreement. Katia Miguelina Jiménez, *D'Agenda* (2021), https://bit.ly/3JD41I0 (last visited Mar. 2, 2023).

former Magistrate Katia Miguelina Jiménez expressed outrage at the ideological screening.[232] Despite the new appointments, the court has been unable to decide up to January 2023.

Another controversial case—openly known for the lack of a supermajority—was the 2015 abortion case. The 2010 Dominican Constitution seemingly protects life from the moment of conception: a reflection of the relatively conservative society in the Dominican Republic. In 2014, Congress passed a law prohibiting abortion in all cases, making it one of Latin America's most restrictive legislations regarding reproductive rights, penalizing both women and doctors. President Danilo Medina vetoed the law and argued that failure to provide an exception for cases of rape or incest, malformation, and life-endangering pregnancies (as provided for in the original bill) would violate women's rights. Congress approved the President's revisions and preserved the so-called "*tres causales*" into law (Law 550-14). The church actively resisted the law and called for public opposition. The circumstances created a polarized conflict between liberals and conservatives in the Dominican Republic.

Several civil associations challenged the law, arguing that it infringed on the right to life protected upon conception as established by the Constitution. It is well known that the court was divided on the issue. Abortion in the Dominican Republic is a sensitive topic, and the court struggled to issue a resolution. Finally, in December 2015, the court managed a supermajority to strike down the legislation but on formal grounds (namely, arguing that after the President's veto, the changes to the legislation were not discussed and approved in both chambers). The court could not muster a supermajority to substantively uphold or repeal the law. Since the court has a mandatory jurisdiction, faced with unsurmountable fractures, it strategically attempted to avoid a decision on the merits through formal means.

Is the supermajority a source of significant delays? The answer is not simple. Although the preclearance case is an extreme example of delays, sovereignty is a particularly sensitive topic in the Dominican Republic, as proven by the cases involving Haitian nationals, the jurisdiction of the Inter-American Court, and the preclearance itself. However, it is complicated to base a critique of the supermajority on isolated instances. Cases may be complex, and delays often occur in constitutional courts, even on simple majorities. The Spanish Constitutional Court, employing majority rule, barely solved in 2023 a 2011 challenge to an abortion law. It might be incorrect to attribute all delays to the supermajority. Furthermore, delays may result from strategic behavior by

232 Jiménez, *supra* note 231.

the court (strategic judicial avoidance)[233] or individual magistrates.[234] The fact that the court resolves most cases within a calendar year further strengthens this point of view.

4.4.3 Scholarly and Political Debate

The Dominican scholarship seems to have two different positions characterized by the Jorge Prats–Acosta debate. The first position, led by Professor Acosta, considers that the supermajority should be preserved for the most consequential court procedures. A simple majority would be preferable in individual complaints where the court's functions resemble ordinary justice since the supermajority hinders decision-making within the constitutional court, allowing five magistrates to block the court's decisions.[235] Prof. Acosta believes this opinion might be the majoritarian position in the scholarship.[236]

A second position by Prof. Jorge Prats considers the supermajority an ideal model.[237] Several scholars who have also served on the court adhere to this opinion. Current Chief Justice and influential scholar Ray Guevara argues that the supermajority "fosters solid and consensual majorities which privilege quality . . . over quantity of resolutions."[238]

A significant debate on the supermajority recently occurred in 2022. President Abinader proposed a constitutional amendment modifying several constitutional provisions. Regarding the judiciary, it mainly proposed forbidding former politicians from being eligible for the Supreme Court and constitutional court, establishing a rotative court presidency, and allowing ordinary legislation to modify the supermajority in specific procedures. Concretely, the proposal intended to maintain the supermajority regarding actions of unconstitutionality, preventive control of international treaties, and competence conflicts. However, it would delegate to Congress the power to establish a different majority (most likely a simple majority) in other procedures that are the competence of the constitutional court.

233 Delany understood avoidance as "postponing decision of contentious issues that might threaten a court's institutional viability [as] a way of engaging various external actors to create and secure institutional support." Erin F. Delaney, *Analyzing Avoidance: Judicial Strategy in Comparative Perspective*, 66 DUKE L. JOURNAL 1, 4 (2016). The concept of avoidance was comprehended within Bickel's passive virtues of a Court. ALEXANDER M. BICKEL, THE LEAST DANGEROUS BRANCH 69 (1962).

234 As analyzed by Diego Werneck Arguelhes & Ivar A. Hartmann, *Timing Control without Docket Control: How Individual Justices Shape the Brazilian Supreme Court's Agenda*, 5 J. L. COURTS 105, 110 (2017).

235 Acosta, *supra* note 215, at 183.

236 Acosta, *supra* note 214.

237 I JORGE PRATS, *supra* note 212, at 453.

238 Diario Listin, *Ray Guevara opuesto a división TC en salas mayoría*, LISTINDIARIO.COM (2019), https://listindiario.com/la-republica/2019/01/26/550978/ray-guevara-opuesto-a-division-tc-en-salas-mayoria (last visited Feb. 8, 2023).

The proposal appears to mainly be aimed at allowing the Organic Law of the Constitutional Court to employ a simple majority in Amparo procedures, which are not within the original jurisdiction of the constitutional court. President Abinader's government seems to have been persuaded by Acosta's position.[239] Nevertheless, there have been no proposals or suggestions to eliminate the supermajority from the central powers of the court. The intention seems only to accelerate individual constitutional complaints.

Even this limited restriction of the supermajority rule has encountered opposition. For example, Professor Jorge Prats claimed that a simple majority rule would weaken the court's legitimacy and would interrupt the court's dynamic of consensus.[240] Former magistrates, such as Katia Jiménez[241] and even the current court's President, Magistrate Milton Rey Guevara, have openly spoken against the reform.[242] As of now, the momentum toward the reform seems lost, and the constitutional amendment is unlikely to succeed. The supermajority is likely to remain intact.

4.5 The Illiberal Supermajorities: Transitory Supermajority Rules in Poland and Georgia (2015–2016)

Recently, scholars have employed the term "abusive constitutional borrowing" to label a transplant of institutions that may function under liberal democratic regimes but may lead to the erosion of democracy or justify anti-democratic turns.[243] Even though supermajorities in constitutional adjudication exist in countries classified as liberal, backsliding regimes in Poland (2015) and Georgia (2016) attempted to use them as tools to erode judicial review.

The Polish and Georgian cases share similar characteristics, featuring supermajority rules, increased quorums, and other court-curbing measures. In both cases, the Venice Commission rendered an opinion questioning the amendments, even though both Governments presented arguments from comparative law supporting the supermajority. In the end, the supermajority never became functional in either case, the constitutional courts ultimately striking down the requirement.

239 Acosta, *supra* note 215, at 145.

240 Eduardo Jorge Prats, Luis Sousa Duvergé & Roberto Medina Reyes, *Informe Sobre El Anteproyecto de Ley Que Declara la Necesidad de Reforma Constitucional*, 32 22 (2022).

241 Jiménez, *supra* note 231.

242 President Ray Guevera spoke at a conference commemorating ten years of the Constitutional Court. In his remarks, he strongly stated, "Let us reflect on the consequences for stability and legal security of the relevant decisions of the Court, which by the way are binding precedents for all public authorities, if suddenly such decisions could be taken by 7, 5 or 3 votes . . . Why should we change a system which has proven to work so well?"

243 Rosalind Dixon & David Landau, Abusive Constitutional Borrowing: Legal Globalization and the Subversion of Liberal Democracy 36 (2021).

4.5.1 Poland: The Threat of Court Paralysis (2015–2016)

After World War II, the Polish state, a vibrant promise during the interwar period (*dwudziestolecie międzywojenne*), fell under communist rule. Following a prolonged economic crisis starting in the 1970s, countless strikes and opposition to the regime ensued. The movement *Solidarność* took a prominent role in the protests, championing workers' rights and social reform. On the verge of collapse, in 1981, the communist regime announced the beginning of martial law, which would prolong its rule until 1983. Nonetheless, martial law did foster some concessions by the communist regime to partial democratization.[244] The Constitution was amended to provide referenda, a Commissioner for Citizen's Rights, and a Constitutional Tribunal. Born in an authoritarian regime, the Tribunal had a positive impact considering the circumstances[245] and survived the transition. In 1989, *Solidarność* won a convincing victory in the ballots, signaling the communist fall.

In 1992, the transitory *Mała Konstytucja* was adopted until Poland enacted the current Constitution in 1997. The 1997 Constitution featured a complete transition into a modern Western democracy. The Constitution foresaw a constitutional tribunal competent to resolve individual complaints, abstract normative challenges, and conflicts between public bodies. According to Article 194, the tribunal's membership is fifteen judges elected for a non-renewable nine-year term. The Constitution granted the low chamber (*Sejm*) the power to elect all judges through a majority vote. From 1997 onwards, the constitutional tribunal placed checks on the elected branches and was considered a prestigious institution within the Polish legal order.

As to the tribunal's decisional procedures, Article 197 delegated to ordinary law the organization of the tribunal "as well as the mode of proceedings before it." Article 190.5, in turn, provided that judgments of the constitutional tribunal "shall be made by a majority of votes." The meaning of "majority" (*większość*) would soon become a matter of dispute. The original Law of the Constitutional Tribunal specified that decisions are taken by a "simple majority" (*zwykła większość*).

Even if the Constitution referred to a "majority" and the Act on the Constitutional Tribunal reinforced that a simple majority was required to decide, the tribunal had some experience with internal supermajorities. The Polish Constitutional Tribunal could work in plenary (*en banc*) or subdivisions. The most common subdivision was a five-judge chamber (*pięcioosobowe składy*). An informal rule within the constitutional tribunal established a 4:1 supermajority to strike down legislation when the tribunal ruled in such a composition. Members of the tribunal felt that bare majorities (3:2 decisions)

244 Piotr Tuleja, *The Polish Constitutional Tribunal*, *in* The Max Planck Handbooks in European Public Law 619, 621 (Armin von Bogdandy, Peter M. Huber & Christoph Grabenwarter eds., 2020).

245 *Id.* at 623.

would not be perceived sufficiently legitimate to defeat the presumption of constitutionality. If the supermajority was not met, the case would be referred to the tribunal *en banc*, where a simple majority sufficed.[246] Prof. Granat, a former judge of the constitutional tribunal considers that the 4:1 supermajority for the tribunal in chambers came into being in approximately the year 2000 and was consistently applied during his term.[247]

In the recent political landscape, two parties have held power in contested elections, namely *Platforma Obywatelska* (PO), a centrist party built upon factions of the Solidarity movement, and *Prawo i Sprawiedliwość* (PiS), a right-wing populist party, of conservative and nationalist ideals. PiS first held power for a brief period from 2005 to 2007. Several reforms introduced by PiS were declared unconstitutional by the Polish Constitutional Tribunal, and thus, the tribunal was seen by that party as an obstacle to exercising power.[248]

A clash between PO and PiS for the control of appointments of judges of the constitutional tribunal would lead to the introduction of a supermajority amidst the so-called Polish constitutional crisis. Five judges of the Polish Constitutional Tribunal were to be renewed in 2015. Three judges were to finish their term during the seventh *Sejm*, while two would finish their terms afterward. Knowing the likely upcoming electoral results favoring PiS, the *Sejm*, still controlled by PO, passed a law attempting to appoint all five judges, even those whose term in office had not yet finished.[249] PO's maneuver proved to be a fatal mistake. PiS retaliated in full force. Newly elected President Andrzej Duda refused to swear in any of the elected judges and, upon the renewal of Parliament, the now PiS-dominated *Sejm* claimed all appointments were illegal and appointed five judges of its own.[250]

Court-packing was just the beginning for the new ruling party. Immediately, the parliament adopted a series of statutes attempting to gain further control of the Constitutional Court, the common courts, the National Council of the Judiciary, and the prosecutors. Regarding the Constitutional Tribunal, the PiS-dominated *Sejm* approved a new Act on the Constitutional Tribunal, which contained a series of provisions threatening to paralyze the tribunal, such as a high thirteen-judge quorum for the tribunal to convene *en banc*, a two-thirds supermajority to make decisions and the requirement to resolve cases in

246 Piotr Tuleja, *Interview with a Former Judge of the Polish Constitutional Tribunal* (unpublished, 2023).

247 Mirosław Granat, *Interview with a Former Judge of the Polish Constitutional Tribunal* (unpublished, 2023).

248 Adam Ploszka, *It Never Rains but It Pours. The Polish Constitutional Tribunal Declares the European Convention on Human Rights Unconstitutional*, 15 Hague J. Rule L. 51, 53 (2023).

249 Kosař and Šipulová catalogued the situation as "premature appointment". David Kosař & Katarína Šipulová, *Comparative Court-Packing*, 21 Int'l J. Const. L. 80, 94 (2023).

250 Wojciech Sadurski, Poland's Constitutional Breakdown 63 (2019).

sequence.[251] The Venice Commission issued an opinion reflecting negatively on most of the changes and particularly urged them to modify both the quorum and high majority provisions that threatened to disable the tribunal.[252]

The Polish Constitutional Tribunal itself had to review the constitutionality of the amendments. Most of the changes were deemed unconstitutional by the tribunal in Case K 47/15. The government refused to publish the decisions, alleging that the tribunal engaged in procedural irregularities.[253] Even though the supermajority was never applied, it triggered a reaction among scholars claiming that the Polish example deserves careful consideration on how supermajority rules may be employed to erode democratic institutions.[254]

The supermajority did not last for long. By 2016, PiS seemed to have gained sufficient control of the Polish Constitutional Tribunal to forego further constraints. The ruling party began to conceive the tribunal as an enabler rather than an obstacle,[255] weaponizing its usage as a tool.[256] The government has used the tribunal to confirm the constitutionality of its introduced measures or invalidate ideologically distant legislation previously enacted. In Case K 12/18, the National Council of the Judiciary (captured by the majority as well) challenged the constitutionality of the legislation introduced by PiS, obtaining the seal of approval of the Tribunal. In K 1/20, the right-wing majority successfully challenged abortion regulation in force since 1993.[257]

251 *Id.* at 73–74.

252 Venice Commission, *Opinion No. 833/2015 On Amendments to the Act of 25 June 2015 on the Constitutional Tribunal* CDL-AD(2016)001, 25 (2016).

253 The Constitutional Tribunal decided it could not apply the same provisions it was tasked to review (mainly quorum and majorities). *See* Mauro Arturo Rivera León, *Judicial Review of Supermajority Rules Governing Courts' Own Decision-Making: A Comparative Analysis*, Glob. Con. 1, 21–22 (2023). The government claimed that the decision had been rendered without a quorum, as only twelve and not thirteen judges were present, as required by the new law. Marcin Wiącek, *Constitutional Crisis in Poland 2015–2016 in the Light of the Rule of Law Principle*, 298 *in* Defending Checks and Balances in EU Member States 15, 28 (Armin von Bogdandy et al. eds., 2021).

254 Pablo Castillo-Ortiz, *The Dilemmas of Constitutional Courts and the Case for a New Design of Kelsenian Institutions*, 39 L. and Phil. 617, 639 (2020); Yaniv Roznai, *Introduction: Constitutional Courts in a 100-Years Perspective and a Proposal for a Hybrid Model of Judicial Review*, 14 ICL J. 355, 371 (2021). For a skeptical view, Cristóbal Caviedes, *A Core Case for Supermajority Rules in Constitutional Adjudication*, 20 Int'l J. Const. L. 1162, 1185 (2022).

255 Sadurski, *supra* note 250, at 75.

256 Pablo Castillo-Ortiz, *The Illiberal Abuse of Constitutional Courts in Europe*, 15 European Constitutional L. Rev. 48, 69 (2019).

257 Aleksandra Kustra-Rogatka, *The Hypocrisy of Authoritarian Populism in Poland: Between the Facade Rhetoric of Political Constitutionalism and the Actual Abuse of Apex Courts*, 19 European Const. L. Rev. 25, 37–39 (2023). Critics argued that PiS managed, without going through a debate within Parliament, to get rid of abortion regulations claiming that it was a decision rendered by an impartial Tribunal and not a political decision. Kovalčík deems this a "delegation technique." Michal Kovalčík, *The Instrumental Abuse of Constitutional Courts: How Populists Can Use Constitutional Courts against the Opposition*, 26 The Int'l J. Hum. Rts. 1160, 1169 (2022).

The supermajority seems to have played a minor temporary role in Polish constitutional review.

4.5.2 Georgia: A Six-Three Supermajority (2016)

Georgia declared its independence from the Soviet Union shortly before the latter's dissolution. Until 2012, Georgia faced considerable economic problems and acute conflicts between political factions. In a contested election, the Georgian Dream–Democratic Georgia party (GD), founded by the billionaire Bidzina Ivanishvili, challenged the incumbent United National Movement (UNM). The 2012 election and subsequent ones until 2016 were considered a significant breakthrough in democratization.[258]

During the 2012–2016 term, GD managed to amass considerable power through electoral victories and policies that eroded human rights, media institutions, and other institutional checks on power.[259] Several institutions complained about the judiciary's encroachment through irregular appointments of judges.[260]

In 2016, the Georgian Constitutional Court was set to decide on a number of cases[261] relevant to the parliamentary majority.[262] Amidst accusations of pressure,[263] the government moved forward with a law proposal amending the Organic Law on the Constitutional Court and the Law on Constitutional Legal Proceedings.

The law contained several provisions arguably destined to dismantle the court's ability to place checks on the elected branches. Among others, it modified the procedure to suspend a law pending abstract review, increased the

258 Lucan Ahmad Way, *Georgia, Moldova, and Ukraine: Democratic Moments in the Former Soviet Union*, *in* Democracy in Hard Places 128, 147 (Scott Mainwaring & Tarek Masoud eds., 2022); David Aprasidze, *Consolidation in Georgia: Democracy or Power?*, 2015 Yearbook on the Organization for Security and Co-operation in Europe (OSCE) 107, 108 (2016).

259 David Zedelashvili, *2017 Constitutional Reform in Georgia: Another Misguided Quest or Genuine Opportunity?*, ConstitutionNet (Jan. 31, 2017), https://constitutionnet.org/news/2017-constitutional-reform-georgia-another-misguided-quest-or-genuine-opportunity.

260 Tamar Avaliani, *Annual Report: State of Human Rights in Georgia*, 38 7–8 (2017).

261 For a list of cases, *see The State of the Judicial System 2016-2020*, *in* Transparency International: Georgia (Oct. 10, 2020).

262 Interestingly, Tsereteli points out that, initially, GD attempted to reform the judiciary in a positive way, breaking patterns of judicial oligarchy. Nonetheless, Tsereteli posits that once judges began ruling against the interest of the GD government, both the government and the parliamentary majority began cooperating with the previous judicial network. Nino Tsereteli, *Backsliding into Judicial Oligarchy? The Cautionary Tale of Georgia's Failed Judicial Reforms, Informal Judicial Networks and Limited Access to Leadership Positions*, 47 Rev. Cent. East Eur. L. 167, 187–88 (2022).

263 The President of the Constitutional Court, Giorgi Papuashvilly, claimed on February 29, 2016 that the Minister of Justice had directly offered to prolong his term of service in the Venice Commission in exchange for cooperating with governmental policies. Avaliani, *supra* note 260, at 9.

competencies of the Plenary, raised quorum requirements, and introduced a six-three supermajority to strike down legislation. The parliamentary procedure was particularly hasty,[264] being discussed and approved in two months.

The President of Georgia, Giorgi Margvelashvili, requested an opinion from the Venice Commission, which subsequently criticized the amendments.[265] President Margvelashvili vetoed the law on May 31, 2016. A few days later, Parliament made several changes and sent the bill back to the President, who signed it. The new version of the law did not alter the supermajority rule or the elevated quorum. The explanatory note of the Law justified raising the majority due to the "high importance of the matter."[266]

A group of opposition MPs and citizens challenged the amendments. In September 2016, four judges of the Georgian Constitutional Court ended their term. The new appointees were more deferential to the ruling party. The Georgian Constitutional Court subsequently struck down several provisions of the law, including the aggravated quorum and the supermajority.[267] The court membership that struck down the law was not the one potentially targeted by the original provisions.[268]

After the supermajority faded, the ruling party consolidated power and cemented itself through strong electoral support. The courts remained polarized and politically biased,[269] and even some reforms that theoretically appeared intended to ensure judicial independence in 2017 and 2018 consolidated the ruling party's influence over the judiciary.[270] In early 2021, the regime arrested the main opposition leader, a move that commentators assessed as an authoritarian drift.[271] Subsequent appointments to the Constitutional Court were widely criticized as being partisan, including the appointment of a former chairman of the ruling party.[272]

264 Eirik Holmøyvik & Anne Sanders, *A Stress Test for Europe's Judiciaries*, 1 European YB. Const. L. 2019 289, 296 (2020).

265 Venice Commission, *Preliminary Opinion 849/2016 on the Amendments to the Organic Law on the Constitutional Court and to the Law on Constitutional Legal Proceedings*, 10 (2016).

266 *See* the explanatory note to *Id*.

267 N3/5/768,769,790,792, Dec. 2016. *See* Chapter 5 for an analysis of the Georgian Constitutional Court's decision.

268 Rivera León, *supra* note 253, at 9.

269 According to Freedom House: "The judiciary has long been the Achilles' heel of Georgia's democratic transformation. Despite ongoing reforms, the judicial framework still suffers from public distrust and a high degree of politicization." Freedom House, *Georgia, 2018*, Freedom House (2018), https://freedomhouse.org/country/georgia/nations-transit/2018 (last visited Jun. 13, 2023).

270 Martin Russell, *Georgia's Bumpy Road to Democracy. On Track for a European Future?*, 12 7 (2021).

271 Way, *supra* note 258, at 132.

272 Malkhaz Nakashidze, *Georgia*, *in* 2016 Global Rev. Const. L. 102, 105 (Richard Albert et al. eds., 2018).

PART III

A COMPARATIVE ANALYSIS OF SUPERMAJORITIES IN CONSTITUTIONAL COURTS

5 An Empirical Theory of Supermajority Rules: Exploring the Why and How of Their Institutional Design

5.1 The Aims of Institutional Design: Deferential and Decisional Supermajorities

Supermajority rules may have different aims and values contingent on their institutional design. Based on the comparative examples, two main models exist within the spectrum: decisional and deferential supermajorities. This subsection further analyzes their characteristics and the different institutional objectives they promote.

5.1.1 Deferential Supermajorities

Deferential supermajorities are nonneutral voting rules which favor the constitutionality of legislation. Deferential supermajorities guarantee that a court grants aggregative deference to legislation, while performing judicial review by establishing a particular threshold to invalidate legislation. Other judicial outcomes require an ordinary majority. Such rules may function in parallel or as a substitute for the presumption of constitutionality.[1]

Deferential supermajorities are by far the most popular models appearing in comparative law. From the jurisdictions analyzed, Nebraska, North Dakota, the former Czechoslovakia, the Czech Republic, Mexico, the Fujimorist supermajority, the contemporary Peruvian supermajority, and Georgia exemplify current and former deferential supermajorities.

5.1.1.1 Breaking Collegial Neutrality: The Shadow Court and Decisional Power Redistribution

The creation of separate voting thresholds characterizes deferential supermajorities. One threshold is required to strike down legislation—a supermajority—while a different voting rule is in place to uphold legislation or dismiss a case on formal grounds, usually a majority rule. If we reasonably assume

1 Evan H. Caminker, *Thayerian Deference to Congress and Supreme Court Supermajority Rules: Lessons from the Past*, 78 IND. L.J. 73 (2003).

DOI: 10.4324/9781003458272-8

that constitutional courts tend to uphold legislation in many cases, deferential supermajorities often operate within majority thresholds. The court needs only to muster a majority to declare it lacks jurisdiction or to uphold the contested provision, while a supermajority vote is required for one specific outcome.

Different thresholds imply that justices will be awarded varying voting values depending on their stance on the provision's constitutionality—unequal voting power.[2] Deferential supermajorities break the equal value of votes,[3] which is sometimes called *collegial neutrality*.[4]

Let us exemplify the concept. The Mexican Supreme Court functions with an 8:3 (72.7 percent) supermajority. Under a simple majority, six justices are required to decide, representing 54.5 percent of the Court. Each justice in the majority would exercise roughly 9 percent of the Court's decisional power. Majority rule entails party neutrality.[5] Declaring a statute constitutional or unconstitutional would require 54.5 percent of the Court, and the influence that justices exert on those decisions would not vary according to their preferred position. However, Mexico functions under a deferential supermajority rule. While a majority threshold is applicable in declaring a statute constitutional, a different one applies to striking down legislation, namely 72.7 percent. A 36.3 percent threshold (4/11) is required to block an invalidation decision, and a 54.5 percent threshold to declare a statute constitutional. The variation of the threshold supplements deference to the legislation.

A four-justice minority constitutes enough of a voting threshold to decide through impasse rules. Under a simple majority, preserving a statute would have required 54.5 percent of the Court, but now it requires 36.3 percent. Jointly, the blocking majority exercises the same power as a simple majority in cases in which the Court upholds legislation. Each justice voting against striking down a law, when conforming to a blocking minority, holds 13.62 percent of decisional power. In cases in which the Court upholds legislation by a majority of votes, the power balance returns to the ordinary 9 percent. Justices voting to uphold legislation are supplemented with a 4.62 percent decisional value. The difference of influence exerted by justices depending on their positions amounts to the mathematical value granted to deference supplemented to the elected branches. The bigger the threshold, the more considerable the deference.

2 MELISSA SCHWARTZBERG, COUNTING THE MANY: THE ORIGINS AND LIMITS OF SUPERMAJORITY RULE 158 (2013).

3 Waldron refers to the "condition of equality." Jeremy Waldron, *Five to Four: Why Do Bare Majorities Rule on Courts*, 123 YALE L.J. 1692 (2014). Vermeule describes the quality as 'neutrality' adopting the social theory framework. Adrian Vermeule, *The Force of Majority Rule*, *in* MAJORITY DECISIONS 132, 141 (Stéphanie Novak & Jon Elster eds., 2014). *See also* SCHWARTZBERG, *supra* note 2, at 121.

4 Guha Krishnamurthi, *For Judicial Majoritarianism*, 22 U. PA. J. CONST. L. 1201, 1219 (2019).

5 *Id.*

Supermajorities may also be conceived as creating "shadow courts." An eight-vote supermajority in an eleven-member court can also be seen as the simple majority of a shadow fourteen-member court in which eight votes would be a majority. The elected branches have been granted a deference degree of three votes in the shadow court.

5.1.1.2 Supermajority Failure Decisions and Impasse Rules

Courts functioning under deferential supermajorities may achieve three different results after a vote. The court may reach a supermajority vote to strike down legislation, the court may reach a majority vote to uphold it, or a majority vote inferior to the supermajority requirement favoring the unconstitutionality of the statute. The first two scenarios satisfy the required decisional thresholds, while the third does not. If no impasse rule is designed or interpreted by the court, the dispute remains pending. That is rarely the case in deferential supermajorities.

In most countries, the case is resolved as if the statute had been found constitutional. An upholding impasse rule functions in the cases of Nebraska, North Dakota, the Czech Republic, the contemporary Peruvian Constitutional Court, and the intended Georgian model. Former supermajorities, such as Ohio, Czechoslovakia, and the Fujimorist supermajority, also held upholding impasse rules.

Within this model, even if the case is resolved as if the statute had been considered constitutional, there is a great variety pertaining to opinion writing. For example, in some constitutional courts, the blocking minority is assigned the ability to write the opinion on behalf of the court. This practice exists in Peru—contemporarily and in the former Fujimorist supermajority—and the Czech Republic.[6]

In the former Czechoslovak supermajority, a 4:3 supermajority failure decision did not transfer the ability to write a judgment on behalf of the court to the minority. Instead, the power was granted to the majority,[7] providing them an opportunity to advance their preference in the opinion despite the holding, such as in the *Vitorazsko and Valčicko* case.

In the case of the subnational supermajorities in the United States, the appealed decisions are affirmed, reversed, or remanded as if the statute had been declared constitutional. However, Chapter 3 accounted for nuanced

6 Beyond the selected jurisdictions, this seems to be the case in South Korea. For an example of the mechanics of opinion drafting in 4:5 decisions, *see* the Medical Service Act case (2010Hun-Ma275). The Constitutional Court of the Republic of Korea, Decisions of the Korean Constitutional Court (2010) 356 (2011).

7 The feature stems from the fact that the statute's unconstitutionality and the opinion's reasoning were submitted to a separate vote. *See* Tomáš Langášek, Ústavní Soud Československé Republiky a Jeho Osudy v Letech 1920-1948 85 (2011).

debates to determine the controlling opinion for a case[8] and the value of the doctrine set forth by the controlling minority.[9]

A second model would compel the court to issue a summary dismissal. In the Mexican case, failing to meet a supermajority does not result in a judgment upholding the statute. Instead, the court formally dismisses the case and reports through a summary decision that the votes are insufficient to invalidate the provision. The decision provides no reasoning on the provision's constitutionality; nor does the blocking minority provide an opinion of it.[10] There is no formal opinion from the court. The claim is rejected in terms similar to those applicable to a formal defect hindering the court's decisional ability.

Both options have advantages and shortcomings. On the one hand, the first model has the advantage of settling the constitutional dispute while ensuring that a degree of deference was provided to the legislation. On the other hand, it might cause unrest among politicians and civil society alike, especially when the legislation that is upheld is controversial, or the dispute is politically sensitive.

The atypical second model may have the disadvantage of failing to settle the dispute. The controversy may be dragged further into inferior courts or even come back to the constitutional/apex court. However, it does not force the court to issue a decision incompatible with the majority's opinion. Moreover, even though the matter is not settled, it opens a communication channel with the political branches.

5.1.2 Decisional Supermajorities

I call "decisional supermajorities" a neutral, qualified requirement for constitutional courts to decide.[11] Such a requirement may be imposed solely on

8 For example, a three-justice majority in North Dakota may not strike down a law but still control the final disposition of a case. Jed Handelsman Shugerman, *A Six-Three Rule: Reviving Consensus and Deference on the Supreme Court*, 37 GA. L. REV. 893, 955 (2003) (explaining that even if the four-fifths supermajority prevents striking down legislation, "the Court nevertheless does issue an opinion in which three members of the Court join").

9 North Dakota has had too few supermajority failures to assess its model definitively. In the early years, the court stated that: "[i]t becomes the duty of the Supreme Court to sustain the constitutionality of any legislative enactment of the state of North Dakota when two or more of the judges, who participate in the determination, hold the act to be constitutional." State ex rel. Sathre v. Bd. of Univ. & Sch. Lands of N. Dakota, 65 N.D. 687, 262 N.W. 60, 61 (1935). In its most recent supermajority failure (the *MKB Management Corp* case), the court held *per curiam* that a law "has not been declared unconstitutional under the federal constitution by a sufficient majority." MKB Mgmt. Corp. v. Burdick, 2014 N.D. 197, § 1, 855 N.W.2d 31. The language is different than in the *Sathre* case. In *Wrigley*, the Court referred to the *MKB* case by saying that "[t]his Court could not reach a sufficient majority to hold the underlying statute unconstitutional." Wrigley v. Romanick, 2023 N.D. 50, § 18, 988 N.W.2d 231, 239.

10 Outside of the selected jurisdictions, Chile's supermajority seemingly employs a similar model.

11 In other contexts, they have been referred to as symmetrical supermajorities or symmetrical special-majority rules. *See* Robert E. Goodin & Christian List, *Special Majorities Rationalized*, 36 BRIT. J. POLIT. SCI. 213, 215 (2006).

constitutional adjudication cases or be a general requirement for the court in issuing any decision.

While deferential supermajorities often operate with majority thresholds, decisional supermajorities do not. By requiring a supermajority to render any decision, they make upholding a statute as challenging as overturning it or finding that the petitioner lacks legal standing to bring the claim to court.[12] Through symmetry of voting thresholds, decisional supermajorities should have a more pronounced impact on constitutional courts than deferential supermajorities.

Decisional supermajorities are the least prevalent category of supermajorities. From the selected jurisdictions, the examples are the Peruvian supermajority of the Tribunal of Constitutional Guarantees (1982–1990), the supermajority of the Constitutional Court of the Dominican Republic (2010 to date), and the nonfunctional Polish supermajority (2015). Beyond the scope of our study, Taiwan's (1958–2022) and Lebanon's (2010 to date) models are examples of past and present decisional supermajorities.[13]

5.1.2.1 Lack of Deferential Nature

Decisional supermajorities do not produce a degree of deference to legislation, as deferential supermajorities do. One could argue that decisional supermajorities are equally deferential. The statute remains formally valid if a court does not gather enough votes either to strike the statute down or to uphold it. If a statute has not been declared unconstitutional, it remains formally valid under the presumption of constitutionality.[14] However, not only does the assertion

12 In doing so, decisional supermajorities are neutral rules, insofar as they require the same number of votes to choose either alternative. Schwartzberg, *supra* note 2, at 122.

13 Article 12 of Law 250 (1993) provides that seven votes of the ten-member Lebanese Constitutional Council are required to resolve cases regarding the constitutionality of statutes. The drafting of the provision does not allow inferring whether this is a decisional or a deferential supermajority. Nonetheless, Lübbe-Wolf states that interviews with justices evidenced that the requirement functions symmetrically. Gertrude Lübbe-Wolff, *Some Institutional Features of the Constitutional Court of Korea in a Comparative Perspective: With a View to the Court's Integrative Function*, *in* The Constitutional Court of Korea as a Protector of Constitutionalism 13 (2021). Justice Mesarra seems to confirm that view, as he argues: "The qualified majority *in any decision* provides an excess of legitimacy and confidence" (emphasis added). Antoine Messarra, *Catching up With the Global and Arab Changes in Constitutional Justice*, *in* Extension des attributions du Conseil constitutionnel au Liban: Actes du séminaire organisé par le Conseil constitutionnel et Fondation Konrad Adenauer 32, 29 (2016).

14 This seems to be the argument of Caviedes. Caviedes concedes that, in theory, supermajority rules may be neutral in some situations. However, Caviedes claims that "statutes are presumed constitutional unless declared unconstitutional." Cristóbal Caviedes, *Is Majority Rule Justified in Constitutional Adjudication?*, 41 Oxf. J. Leg. Stud. 376, 1165 (2021).

not prove intra-procedural asymmetry, but it is hard to sustain as a general claim, and is contingent on a jurisdiction's specific features.

From a conceptual perspective, a decisional supermajority might lead to the inability of such a court to issue any decision, as occurs in the Dominican Republic. If a supermajority is not met, the court cannot decide; thus, the constitutional issue remains *sub judice* until the proper supermajority is met. In a formal sense, the supermajority does not favor any option within the procedure.[15] The court is unable to uphold the law, even if a simple majority deems it constitutionally valid.

To consider that a decisional supermajority favors the statute because, given the presumption of constitutionality, the statute is still 'alive' when resolving the case is a de facto claim, not a de jure assertion on the decision-making procedure. Understood as a de facto claim, the argument is disputable, as it makes significant assumptions on several features of a constitutional system that vary across jurisdictions.

Consider a diffuse system of constitutional review in which judges perform judicial review in ordinary cases. If a case reaches the apex court after the statute was declared unconstitutional in lower instances, a decisional supermajority will prolong the *status quo*, namely, the survival of a first-instance court ruling declaring the law unconstitutional. In Kelsenian systems, provided the constitutional court can suspend a statute through a national injunction during the judicial review procedure,[16] the court's inability to decide will prorogue the statute's suspension, preventing the law's enforcement. Such injunctions also exist in the American model of judicial review.

The fact that constitutional courts often do not deal with appellate jurisdiction and national injunctions do not exist in some systems is a characteristic subject to variation among jurisdictions and not a de jure feature stemming from the alleged nonneutrality of decisional supermajorities.[17]

5.1.2.2 Decisional Supermajorities and Impasse Rules

Courts functioning under deferential supermajorities may achieve four different results after a vote. Supermajorities may have formed either to uphold or to strike down legislation, or majorities inferior to the required threshold may also favor one of those outcomes. Deferential supermajorities favoring the statute have coherent reasoning to provide impasse rules that uphold the

15 Adrian Vermeule, Mechanisms of Democracy: Institutional Design Writ Small 88 (2007).

16 As is the case of Mexico—since RR 95/2018-CA—and Georgia, which employ both supermajority rules.

17 Goodin and List outline this feature, arguing that "symmetrical special-majorities" may produce certain de facto outcomes. Goodin and List, *supra* note 11, at 215. Perhaps Caviedes intended to refer to de facto outcomes, as I have proven that no outcome is favored de jure, and characteristics of the legal system may change the de facto outcome.

provision. Since decisional supermajorities are neutral, designing impasse rules that favor no outcome is complicated.[18]

Some decisional supermajorities lack impasse rules. Without impasse mechanisms, a supermajority failure leads to no resolution. The case remains pending, and the court's ability to decide is preserved. The court is tasked with deliberating and attempting to achieve a supermajority favoring any outcome.[19] In this model, supermajority failure decisions result in court delays rather than court outcomes.

The Dominican Republic employs a 9:4 decisional supermajority. If a supermajority cannot be met, the case remains under the court's docket, waiting for new compromises or further deliberation. Delays can occur in contentious cases. Several features of different courts may help deal with this unintended negative consequence.[20]

From the selected jurisdictions, the Dominican Republic and arguably the nonoperative Polish supermajority featured such a model, lacking impasse rules.

A second model of decisional supermajorities may include an impasse rule of formal dismissal. In this model, supermajority failures lead to a formal rejection, communicating that no supermajority has been achieved and precluding the possibility of a further decision.

The 1979 Peruvian *Tribunal de Garantías Constitucionales* had interpreted its two-thirds supermajority as decisional. The court held that six votes were required, regardless of the preferred outcome. Both striking down and upholding legislation required a supermajority. When the threshold failed to be met, the court issued a summary statement (*pronunciamiento*) instead of retaining the case for further deliberation. *Pronunciamientos* briefly declared

18 Goodin and List consider that symmetrical special-majority rules entail that "no option is chosen" if neither option achieves the desired supermajority. *Id.* As the chapter shows, the impasse rules may determine whether a resolution on a case is either reached at the present or precluded indefinitely.

19 A system employing majority rule may also reach a situation where achieving a majority seems problematic, in the case of non-binary ties in odd courts or ordinary ties in even courts, absent impasse rules. *See* Chapter 2.

20 For example, the Dominican Republic has a staggered system for new court appointments. A third of the court is renewed every three years; thus, new supermajorities may be formed. On many occasions, the arrival of new magistrates meant cases could achieve the required supermajorities. A second factor is institutional and political pressure. As time passes and a case remains undecided, political pressure rises. Public opinion and relevant institutional actors perceive the court as not fulfilling its duty. Magistrates begin looking for narrow common ground to resolve cases. Institutional allegiance enhances the pressure to deliberate. Magistrate Acosta agrees with how such factors aid in resolving stalled cases but warns: "Even if partial renovations and social pressure aid in solving stalled cases, it still does not prevent cases being solved outside of the foreseen deadlines and sometimes after several years." Hermógenes Acosta de los Santos, *Interview with a Former Magistrate of the Dominican Constitutional Court* (unpublished, 2023).

that the supermajority failed to be met to make any decision[21] and attached the opinions of the magistrates defending their votes. The Peruvian TGC is the only example of this system from the jurisdictions analyzed. Some jurisdictions beyond our study, such as Lebanon, seem to follow this model.[22]

5.1.3 Mixed Models

Theoretically, it is possible to conceive supermajorities with institutional designs prioritizing aims beyond deference or consensus. Such systems are rarer than deferential or decisional supermajorities, but Chapters 3 and 4 mention a few examples.

Ohio's supermajority, arguably the first such rule in constitutional adjudication, was a mixed system. While intended to provide deference to the elected branches, it only required a supermajority when a Court of Appeals had found a statute constitutional. Reversing the decision required a supermajority, while a simple majority could affirm it.[23] However, if the Court of Appeals had found a statute unconstitutional, a simple majority sufficed to reverse or uphold the decision. The rule neither deferred to statutes nor to the Court of Appeals, which was true in all cases.[24]

Other supermajorities may have been born out of legitimacy concerns while distributing jurisdiction in judicial bodies. Within our selected jurisdictions,[25] the self-imposed Polish supermajority in five-member panels and the Peruvian supermajority while working in chambers are examples of the above.

21 César Landa, *Del Tribunal de Garantías al Tribunal Constitucional: El Caso Peruano*, 2 Pensamiento Constitucional 73, 80 (1995). *See also* Judgment 005-96-I/TC of the Constitutional Court. The court described the TGC supermajority stating "for the past legislation [that of the Tribunal of Constitutional Guarantees] if the legal threshold was not met to strike down a law, simply there was no decision."

22 Article 37 of Law 243 (*Règlement intérieur du Conseil Constitutionnel*) of the Constitutional Council of Lebanon provides the reporting procedure for when the court is unable to reach a decision. The regulation requires the court to issue "minutes" (*Procès-verbal*). For further explanation *see* I Conseil Constitutionnel, Recueil des Décisions du Conseil Constitutionnel 1994-2016: Décisions Relatives à la Constitutionnalité des Lois 331–33 (2017).

23 Robert L. Hausser, *Limiting the Voting Power of the Supreme Court: Procedure in the States*, 5 Ohio St. U. L.J. 54, 60 (1939); Shugerman, *supra* note 8, at 957.

24 A supermajority ensuring deference to the Court of Appeals would have required a qualified vote to overturn a decision, regardless of the previous outcome.

25 Beyond the selected jurisdictions, South Carolina's supermajority may be an example. Unanimity is required to resolve a constitutional challenge. As explained by Shugerman: "If the Justices cannot resolve a constitutional question unanimously, all of the circuit judges join the justices to create a superconstitutional court to decide the case by a simple majority." Shugerman, *supra* note 8, at 954. South Carolina's requirement seems to be mainly on Condorcetian accuracy grounds. The rule does not defer, as it promotes no outcome, nor does it protect the competence of a body. Adding Justices appears to be attempting to ensure a "correct" decision on constitutional questions. The supermajority is not followed in practice. Caminker, *supra* note 1, at 93.

In the case of Poland, a self-imposed agreement dictated that the unconstitutionality of a statute could be decided in a panel only if a 4:1 supermajority was reached. Otherwise, the case was labeled as complex and submitted to the resolution of the court *en banc*.[26] A three-member chamber may resolve individual complaints in the Peruvian Constitutional Court, but three votes must be reached, apparently, unanimity. If unanimity fails, the chambers may summon individual magistrates until three votes are gathered favoring any position.[27]

The Polish system attempts to allow effective subdivisions of the court to resolve constitutional challenges while avoiding that unstable bare majorities speak on behalf of the court. The rule preserves the authority of the court *en banc* while ensuring that decisions regarding the unconstitutionality of statutes enjoy broad legitimacy. Peru's model has a similar orientation, except the apparent unanimity requirement is applied regardless of the outcome. If unanimity fails to be met, the court's chamber automatically grows with "magistrados dirimentes," thus searching for subsequent 3:1 or 3:2 majorities.

5.2 The Legal Source of Supermajority Rules

Legal scholarship has paid little attention to the legal source through which a supermajority is introduced. As elsewhere argued,[28] the legal source impacts whether the rule will be subject to judicial review, although it plays a much broader role than determining the possibility of courts to analyze its constitutionality. The legal source is a strong indicator of consensus and legitimacy among the political branches and may play a further part in determining the rules' flexibility should the threshold be set too high. It might also affect how the court perceives the rule and approaches it.

Three primary legal sources exist: the Constitution, an ordinary statute, and a self-imposed rule. Constitutional and statutory supermajorities seem far more popular than self-imposed supermajorities. Conversely, statutory and constitutional supermajorities are balanced in the selected jurisdictions. I will now briefly discuss some of their characteristics and implications.

26 Piotr Tuleja, *Interview with a Former Judge of the Polish Constitutional Tribunal* (unpublished, 2023). Mirosław Granat, *Interview with a Former Judge of the Polish Constitutional Tribunal* (unpublished, 2023).

27 *See* Article 5 of the Organic Law of the Constitutional Court and Article 11-A of the internal rules of the Constitutional Court (*Reglamento Normativo del Tribunal Constitucional*). For an explanation of the mechanism, *see* Chapter 4.

28 Mauro Arturo Rivera León, *Judicial Review of Supermajority Rules Governing Courts' Own Decision-Making: A Comparative Analysis*, Glob. Con. 1, 4–5 (2023).

5.2.1 Constitutional Supermajorities

Supermajorities may be established in a constitution, either in the original text or introduced via a constitutional amendment. All constitutional supermajorities from the selected jurisdictions were introduced through amendment: Ohio, Nebraska, North Dakota, Mexico, and arguably the Dominican Republic.[29]

Introducing a supermajority in the Constitution has several advantages. In the first place, constitution-making procedures and constitutional amendments often result from broad debate and participatory discussions, gathering widespread attention. A constitutional supermajority may ensure the rule enjoys broad popular support and is at least formally subjected to an informed debate, which conveys higher democratic legitimacy.

In Ohio and Nebraska,[30] the constitutional conventions held comprehensive discussions. Supermajority rules received inclusive support, ensuring that the proposals were nonpartisan. Furthermore, the amendments were voted on by the electorate. A similar situation occurred in North Dakota. Despite being initially proposed by the Nonpartisan League in HB 44, the supermajority was eventually sponsored by a nonleague senator[31] and attained considerable electoral support.[32]

In the Dominican Republic, the process through which the supermajority was established in 2010 is widely recognized as one of the most participatory and democratic constitution-making experiences of that country.[33] In 1994, the constitutional reception of the supermajority in Mexico came when an amendment granted the court expansive powers, a pivotal transformation. Even if the *Partido de la Revolución Institucional* still dominated Congress, the amendments drew support from the opposition,[34] as they understood they formed part of a series of structural changes meant to pave the way for the country to operate in a future democratic transition.

A second advantage is stability. Constitutional supermajorities embed the rule within an enduring framework, guaranteeing it is harder for subsequent

29 Traditionally, Dominican Republic scholars call each amendment a new Constitution. Amendments are voted on separately, but the full revised text is discussed and approved, formally promulgating a new constitution after every revision. Leiv Marsteintredet, *Change and Continuity in Dominican Constitutions: The 2010 Reform Compared*, *in* New Constitutionalism in Latin America 223, 223 (Almut Schilling-Vacaflor & Detlef Nolte eds., 2016).

30 *See* Chapter 3. In Nebraska, the rule was subsequently reassessed by the Constitutional Revision Commission created by LB 244 and openly discussed in Congress.

31 Herbert L. Meschke & Ted Smith, *The North Dakota Supreme Court: A Century of Advances*, 76 North Dakota L. Rev. 217, 248 (2000).

32 *See* Chapter 3.1.2.

33 Marsteintredet, *supra* note 29, at 224.

34 José María Serna, The Constitution of Mexico: A Contextual Analysis 124 (2013).

legislatures to alter it.[35] Since constitutional amendments often require legislative supermajorities, a further guarantee exists that unstable congressional majorities will not modify the rule hastily or in a partisan manner.

However, constitutional supermajorities have shortcomings. Constitutionalizing voting protocols may generate rigidity and inflexibility. Decision-making rules of constitutional courts may tend to get entrenched under rigid constitutional amendment procedures, even if they prove defective. Subsequent elected officers will be reluctant to place themselves under checks their predecessors have not had. Inflexibility also implies that if the threshold is initially set too high, the rule may not be adjusted as desired if it produces unintended consequences in court.

Moreover, the rigidity associated with constitutional amendments can give rise to problems. Constitution-making procedures are inherently bounded. Delegates and representatives may possess only a limited understanding of the functioning of proceedings in the court in the case of an amendment, and they may even be unable to predict the dynamics that a future court will develop. As a result, these procedures often provide limited time for analysis, making it impossible to foresee all possible scenarios. The Mexican and Dominican supermajorities serve as two examples of unforeseen outcomes.

In 2010, the Dominican Republic implemented a supermajority requirement to achieve consensus and enhance legitimacy—specifically, this rule aimed to prevent controversial decisions from being made by bare majorities, as explained in Chapter 4. However, the constitutional court was initially designed to handle a limited number of select and significant cases, namely only normative abstract review, preventive review of international treaties, and competence conflicts. Nonetheless, the Constitution allowed delegating further tasks to the court through ordinary legislation. In 2011, secondary legislation granted the court the power to review individual complaint judgments as a second instance. Consequently, the court's workload significantly increased. Former Justice Acosta argues that the 2010 constitutional amendment did not anticipate this expansion.[36] The lion's share of the constitutional court's current workload pertains to the expanded jurisdiction to review judgments of lower courts, habeas corpus, habeas data, and Amparo, among others. The original jurisdiction of the court, for which the supermajority was conceived, constitutes less than one-third of the court's cases.[37] The 2010 policymakers intended the decisional supermajority to be employed in resolving a few cases,

35 Arguably, constitutions should have an ideal balance of rigidity and flexibility, allowing for change when it is called for but ensuring it comes with great consensus. *See* Richard Albert, Constitutional Amendments: Making, Breaking, and Changing Constitutions 98 (2019).

36 Acosta de los Santos, *supra* note 20.

37 *See Estadísticas de la Carga Procesal: Trimeste enero, febrero y marzo del 2023*, Dirección de Planificación y Desarrollo, Tribunal Constitucional de República Dominicana, Santo Domingo (comparing statistics from the court ranging from 2015 to 2023).

affording ample time for deliberation and compromise. Instead, the rule currently functions in a different framework.

The Mexican supermajority is a second example of unintended consequences. The 1994 supermajority had caution at its core. A PRI-dominated Congress wanted to create a robust and independent body, but was wary about granting the court too much power, which could disrupt institutional arrangements. The constitutional amendment opted for requiring a supermajority for abstract normative control and the so-called constitutional controversies, in which the court would play the role of an arbiter in federalist conflicts. Municipalities, states, and the federal government were granted legal standing to sue upon infringement of their powers. The overcautious amendment provided that, while the supermajority was required to declare the unconstitutionality of any law in federalist conflicts, such invalidity would be limited to inter partes effect if a lower level brings the challenge—*i.e.*, municipality v. state, municipality v. federal government or state v. federal government. The rule has proved more problematic than the supermajority itself, increased the workload of the court overwhelmed by hundreds of similar challenges,[38] and caused confusion regarding votes required to declare nonnormative decrees unconstitutional.[39] The 1994 constitutional amendment was a comprehensive process and had a reasonably participatory discussion, but could not foresee how the supermajority would interact with all other features of the legal system, mainly as many of those were also just being introduced.

5.2.2 Statutory Supermajorities

A second possibility is introducing a supermajority through ordinary legislation, such as an ordinary law, an organic law, or any other act not constitutional in nature. I deem this possibility a "statutory supermajority." From the selected jurisdictions, Czechoslovakia, the Czech Republic, the three Peruvian supermajorities (1982, 1995, 2002), Poland, and Georgia exemplify statutory supermajorities.[40]

38 For example, all municipalities must sue if a federal law infringes their jurisdiction. Otherwise, since the effects are inter partes, the statute would potentially be considered unconstitutional only for the suing municipalities, while valid and applicable in the rest, producing a similar problem as Ohio's double threshold. *See* Susana Berruecos García Travesí & Laurence Whitehead, *Constitutional Controversies in the Subnational Democratization of Mexico, 1994–2021*, 12 Lat. Am. Policy 405, 411 (2021).

39 *See* CC 217/2021, decided in 2023. The court devoted two full sessions to discuss whether a simple majority sufficed to strike down an executive order given the inter partes effects in constitutional controversies previously described. I have argued that the inter partes rule induces confusion and hinders the court. Mauro Arturo Rivera León, *Los Retos de la Defensa del Federalismo Mexicano Estándares Deferenciales y Asimetrías Procesales en Conflictos Normativos*, *in* Concurso Nacional de Ensayo sobre Federalismo 18 (2023).

40 Taiwan is an example of a past statutory supermajority. In 2022, the court's legislation was amended, lowering the threshold. Some scholars welcomed the change. Kuo Ming-Suo &

Statutory supermajorities provide the advantage of flexibility. In most countries, ordinary legislation is significantly more accessible to amend than the Constitution. Thus, statutory supermajorities allow the legislature to promote specific legitimate policy aims. Furthermore, a statutory rule may be quickly revised. If a supermajority forms part of a coherent model of constitutional adjudication, the legislature may decide to implement a determined configuration through a statute, which is revisable and amendable, providing room to adjust. Even though identifying an optimal degree for the supermajority is problematic,[41] adjusting the deference degree is not only a theoretical advantage; it has occurred in practice.

The 6:1 Peruvian supermajority was part of a plan by Fujimori to circumvent the system of checks and balances. During the legislative debates, the opposition advocated for a 5:2 supermajority.[42] After Fujimori's demise, a plural Congress amended the supermajority to lower the threshold to the desired five votes, better calibrating deference.[43] Had Fujimori managed to instate a constitutional and not a statutory supermajority, Congress may have been unable to caliber the deference level to a desired degree.

However, statutory supermajorities may also entail dangers. A statutory supermajority might be established when not all actors participate in its configuration. As the required consensus to amend legislation is significantly lower, legislatures may employ supermajorities rashly and impulsively, paving the way for partisan manipulation, jurisdiction curbing, or retaliating against undesired court positions. Furthermore, subsequent congressional majorities may modify the voting protocol, creating instability in the rule.

Notably, from the statutory supermajorities analyzed,[44] some were imposed as retaliation on courts or as obstruction mechanisms: Peru in 1995, Poland in 2015, and Georgia in 2016. Considering that the vast majority of cases in which supermajorities are employed to attack courts feature statutory

---

Chen Hui-Wen, *Constitutional Review 3.0 in Taiwan: A Very Short Introduction of Taiwan's New Constitutional Court*, I·CONNECT: BLOG OF THE INT'L J. CONST. L. (Jul. 1, 2022), https://bit.ly/3oxXmmE. However, other scholars argued that "the simple majority threshold can easily make the Court more ideological, if not partisan. Before 2022, the supermajority threshold ensured that the TCC would be bipartisan by forcing justices with opposite viewpoints to negotiate and compromise with each other if they wanted to hammer out any constitutional solutions." Chien-Chih Lin, *The Pros and Cons of Taiwan's Constitutional Court Procedure Act*, 2 USALI PERSPECTIVES 1, 2 (2022). Previously, Lin had argued that Taiwan's supermajority played a role in how Taiwan's Constitutional Court aligns with public opinion. Chien-Chih Lin, *Majoritarian Judicial Review: The Case of Taiwan*, 9 NAT'L TAIWAN U. L. REV. 103, 134 (2014).

41 Shugerman, *supra* note 8, at 105.

42 *See* the Parliamentary Debates, 13th Session, Wednesday, Oct. 5, 1994, 963–67.

43 An expression favored by Jacob E. Gersen & Adrian Vermeule, *Chevron as a Voting Rule*, 116 YALE L.J. 676, 701 (2007).

44 Beyond the jurisdictions analyzed, Taiwan in 1958 is an example of a supermajority employed to retaliate against a court. *See* subsection 3.4.

supermajorities, it seems that statutory supermajorities are a preferred vehicle of autocrats and illiberal regimes for constraining courts, as they require much less consensus and time. Away from reflectors and the spotlight traditionally associated with constitution-making, supermajorities might be discreetly introduced to tame courts.

5.2.3 Court Self-Imposed Supermajorities

The last source considered is a self-imposed supermajority. Shultz defines self-regulatory rules as "regular practices that reflect an agreement among the justices about how they should and do behave when exercising judicial practices."[45] Courts often introduce and follow rules concerning their decision-making procedure, such as opinion assignment, deliberation, and voting rules.

In the United States, some scholars even noted early on that the Supreme Court adopted nonmajority rules, allowing votes below a court majority to reach affirmative outcomes granting certiorari.[46] More recently, Justice Alito revealed that the court requires a six-vote supermajority for summary reversals, which Justice Breyer subsequently confirmed as a "custom."[47] Hence, even courts functioning within majority rule might find supermajorities useful for achieving certain aims.

Constitutional courts may choose to function under a supermajority by formally establishing such arrangement in their internal rules or adopting it through an informal voting protocol.[48] The idea of a court introducing a supermajority rule to strike down legislation is not new. As long ago as 1937, Mason had already deemed an internal supermajority possible.[49] In contemporary scholarship, Shugerman considered internal rules ideal for his envisaged supermajority model.[50] Gersen and Vermeule also turned to court self-adopted

45 Lisa Schultz Bressman, *The Rise and Fall of the Self-Regulatory Court*, 101 Texas L. Rev. 1, 11 (2022).

46 Richard Revesz & Pamela Karlan, *Nonmajority Rules and the Supreme Court*, 136 U. Pa. L. Rev. 1067, 1068 (1988).

47 Joan Biskupic, *The Secret Supreme Court: Late Nights, Courtesy Votes and the Unwritten 6-Vote Rule*, CNN Politics, Oct. 17, 2021, https://edition.cnn.com/2021/10/17/politics/supreme-court-conference-rules-breyer/index.html (last visited Feb. 2, 2023).

48 *See* Lee Epstein & Jack Knight, The Choices Justices Make 118 (1997) (identifying unwritten rules in the Supreme Court as informal institutions). Informal institutions are "socially shared rules, usually unwritten, that are created, communicated, and enforced outside of officially sanctioned channels." Gretchen Helmke & Steven Levitsky, *Informal Institutions and Comparative Politics: A Research Agenda*, 2 Perspectives on Politics 725, 727 (2004).

49 Apheus Thomas Mason, *Politics and the Supreme Court: President Roosevelt's Proposal*, 85 U. Pa. L. Rev. 659, 675 (1937).

50 Shugerman, *supra* note 8, at 951.

rules as the best option to introduce supermajority rules to guarantee deference under the Chevron doctrine.[51]

Peru and Poland provide two examples, although self-imposed supermajorities have been scarce in the jurisdictions selected. From 2004 to 2015, the Peruvian Constitutional Court had an informal rule requiring a five-vote supermajority to issue interpretative judgments and declare a precedent as binding. The internal noncodified practice continued until 2015, when a new majority at the court changed the custom by codifying a simple majority as a decisional threshold in the court's internal regulations.[52] Subsequently, Congress reinstated the supermajority for precedent purposes as an amendment to the court's legislation, where it sits now as a formal statutory rule. Interestingly, changing the internal practice led Congress as an external actor to reinstate the rule through a statute. In another instance of arguably self-adopted supermajorities, in the *Sangüesa* case,[53] the court aggressively interpreted supermajority impasse rules to cover a hypothesis not initially dealt with in the requirement.[54]I

Poland is another example. The Polish Constitutional Tribunal introduced a self-imposed supermajority for decisions concerning the constitutionality of statutes in five-member panels. A 4:1 supermajority was required by custom to invalidate legislation. Any lower majority would result in deferring the case for consideration of the tribunal *en banc*, functioning under majority rule.[55] Judges of the Polish Constitutional Tribunal felt that bare majorities would not signal the required legitimacy to invalidate legislation when the tribunal was not solving cases *en banc*. The rule had exceptions. In some instances, judgments on the unconstitutionality of statutes were issued by 3:2 bare majorities if an agreement arose in the panel that the case would not raise controversy.[56]

Self-imposed rules have the distinct advantage of flexibility[57] and may be perceived as a judicial self-restraint model of deference or consensus-seeking mechanism without congressional imposition. It might also save a debate on

51 Chevron U.S.A., Inc. v. Natural Resources Defense Council, Inc., 68 U.S. 837 (1984). The Chevron doctrine set forth a legal test enforcing deference to an Agency's interpretation of a statute provided it is not unreasonable. While Gersen and Vermeuele did not analyze supermajorities in constitutional adjudication, they considered whether a supermajority voting rule would better ensure such deference. They concluded that the best option was an internal rule, which they labeled "judicial supply."

52 *Resolución administrativa* No 138-2015-P/TC, issued on Oct. 7, 2015.

53 *See* Judgment 04664-2007-PA/TC.

54 Upon an absence, the court reached a 3:3 tie on a *recurso de agravio constitucional*, not requiring a supermajority. The court expansively interpreted Article 5 of the Organic Law as applicable to the case and dismissed the plaintiff's claim. Subsequently, the court abandoned such an interpretation and introduced an impasse rule in the court's internal regulations establishing a casting vote.

55 Tuleja, *supra* note 26.

56 Granat, *supra* note 26.

57 Shugerman, *supra* note 8, at 954.

the constitutionality of introducing supermajorities via statute when consensus for a constitutional amendment is far from present.[58]

However, such internal rules are not without problems. Scholars have envisaged compelling reasons for judges to comply with informal rules, such as an expectation that other judges will behave accordingly[59] or informal sanctions.[60] Nevertheless, an internal voting agreement might prove challenging to enforce if other participants break it.[61]

Few jurisdictions have adopted self-imposed supermajorities. Several reasons may account for it. By modifying a voting protocol, judges should agree beforehand to change the court's known dynamic. I have argued elsewhere that strategic accounting of judges may explain why courts might scrutinize more rigorously statutory supermajority rules introduced by Congress in some cases.[62] Perhaps some of the reasons are also applicable as to why judges choose not to modify a simple majority voting protocol. Justices might feel that supermajorities would diminish the value of individual votes in maximizing their policy preference[63] or might be fearful of shifting the balance of power[64] among judges depending on their preferred outcome on a case, as supermajority rules would create new deliberation and decisional dynamics.

Furthermore, such rules may be opaque and lack transparency.[65] Similarly to the case of the United States, where nonmajoritarian rules such as deferential vote-switching, namely the "courtesy fifth,"[66] are often unknown to

58 A self-imposed rule draws on the advantages perceived by Dahl in different contexts: Dahl deemed that the advantages of majority and supermajority rules could be combined if the members "could decide in advance, by majority rule, that in certain cases a supermajority rule would be required." Robert Alan Dahl, Democracy and Its Critics 154 (1989). Although it is unlikely that Dahl had in mind judicial supermajorities, this seems to be the case in self-imposed supermajorities.

59 Epstein and Knight, *supra* note 48, at 116.

60 *Id.* at 117; Helmke & Levitsky, *supra* note 48, at 733; Schultz Bressman, *supra* note 45, at 12–13.

61 *See* Scott Stephenson, *Constitutional Conventions and the Judiciary*, 41 Oxf. J. Leg. Stud. 750, 764 (2021) (arguing similarly that constitutional conventions "exist in a constant state of fragility").

62 Rivera León, *supra* note 28, at 10.

63 Lee Epstein & Jack Knight, *Reconsidering Judicial Preferences*, 16 Annu. Rev. Polit. Sci. 11, 19 (2013). In this work, Epstein and Knight reassessed their initial pure attitudinal model established in Epstein and Knight, *supra* note 48. Policy preference is considered by Epstein and Knight still to be a substantial factor in leading to judicial votes, although they currently consider other complementary factors.

64 Mason had already considered an internal rule hard to adopt in 1937 "because of the well-known political maxim that power is seldom relinquished voluntarily." Mason, *supra* note 49, at 675.

65 Biden's Presidential Commission shared a similar opinion concerning certain informal practices within the United States Supreme Court. *See* Presidential Commission on the Supreme Court of the United States, *Final Report*, 288 206–208 (2021), https://www.whitehouse.gov/pcscotus/ (last visited May 25, 2022).

66 *Id.* at 214–15.

the general public or political branches, in Poland, the 4:1 supermajority in panels was mainly known to judges and court clerks. Not having provoked any academic commentary, Justice Tuleja deems that it might well be that only internal workers were aware of it.[67]

Opacity prevents a better understanding of the court and might even take away one of the supermajority's main advantages: the awareness of the political branches of having been reviewed through a deferential standard.

5.2.4 Judicial Review of Supermajority Rules

The legal source of the supermajority seems to directly impact the possibility of assessing the constitutionality of supermajority rules through judicial review. In my previous work,[68] I have argued that the legal source of a supermajority seems to be, along with the chronology of its introduction, an essential factor in predicting the possible outcome of judicial review.

Although three distinct sources of supermajority rules have been analyzed, self-imposed supermajorities need not go through judicial review. Courts may change their internal rule or abandon the practice if they consider it inadequate. Nonetheless, constitutional and statutory supermajorities are imposed on courts. Several actors might be incentivized to challenge such rules, or the court may consider reviewing the rule's constitutionality as a previous step in resolving a case.[69]

Constitutional supermajorities have more substantial insulation from judicial review. By forming part of the Constitution, declaring their invalidity is possible only through declaring the Constitution itself unconstitutional. Such a possibility exists as some countries have explicit eternity clauses[70] or have adopted judicially created unamendability doctrines.[71] Nonetheless, even if the theoretical possibility exists, its undertaking is challenging. It would require adopting express unamendability clauses on judicial decision-making or interpreting a majority principle as inherent to judicial review within a constitution's basic structure or minimum core. No constitutional supermajority has been subjected to judicial review from the selected jurisdictions.

67 Tuleja, *supra* note 26.

68 Rivera León, *supra* note 28.

69 As suggested by a minority of magistrates of the Peruvian Constitutional Court in 005-96-I/TC, and as considered by scholars such as Sagües. Nestor Sagües, *Los Poderes Implícitos e Inherentes Del Tribunal Constitucional Del Perú y El Quórum Para Sus Votaciones*, 3 *in* La Constitución de 1993: Análisis y Comentarios, 111 (Francisco Fernández ed., 1996).

70 Eternity clauses are constitutional provisions "insulating essential state characteristics or core democratic guarantees" within the framework of constitutional design. Silvia Suteu, Eternity Clauses in Democratic Constitutionalism 19 (2021).

71 Such as the unconstitutional constitutional amendment doctrine. For a contemporary reference, *see* Yaniv Roznai, Unconstitutional Constitutional Amendments: The Limits of Amendment Powers (2017).

Statutory supermajorities, enacted through ordinary law, may be easier to subject to judicial review. All supermajorities from the selected jurisdictions that underwent judicial review were introduced via ordinary legislation: Peru, Poland, Georgia, and arguably, Ohio.[72] Twice such rules were deemed unconstitutional, while twice they were upheld.

In the second place, I have elsewhere stated that the chronology in which supermajority rules are introduced impacts their acceptance by courts.[73] If introduced within the court's creation—as in the Czech Republic—or pivotal moments of redefinition of the court's jurisdiction, often along with new powers, as in Mexico, courts could be more prompt to accept the rules. Nonetheless, if supermajorities were introduced in ordinary moments after the court was created, such as Ohio or the weaponized Polish and Georgian supermajorities, courts could be more reluctant to agree with the power shift that emerges along with them.[74]

Table 5.1 presents a condensed view of judicial review experiences in the selected jurisdictions. As the table portrays, no constitutional supermajority from the selected jurisdictions has been found unconstitutional or even subjected to judicial review. All supermajorities struck down by courts were statutory rules resulting from ordinary moments *ex post* the court's creation.

Table 5.1 Judicial review of supermajority rules in the selected jurisdictions

Jurisdiction	*Year*	*Legal source*	*Moment*	*Outcome*	*Constitution regulates majority*
U.S. (Ohio)	1930	Statutory	Ordinary	Constitutional	No
Peru	1996	Statutory	Court's creation	Constitutional	No
Poland	2016	Statutory	Ordinary	Unconstitutional	Yes
Georgia	2016	Statutory	Ordinary	Unconstitutional	No

72 The Ohio case warrants comment. Even though Ohio adopted supermajority rules through a constitutional amendment, Ohio is a subnational entity in the United States. Federal law overrides state law. As such, while analyzing Ohio's supermajority, the Federal Supreme Court confronted the state Constitution with the Federal Constitution, unconstrained by the contested provision. Although a conceptual distinction exists, for the purposes of this subsection, the nature of subnational constitutions in the United States allows the Federal Supreme Court to scrutinize state constitutional supermajorities in a manner akin to that of ordinary legislation.

73 Rivera León, *supra* note 28, at 6–11.

74 Regarding ordinary moments, I deemed that "Courts facing such changes in ordinary moments feel constrained. They do have a reference point to look back to when simple majorities reigned. Qualified majorities at non-pivotal times do not come with new powers (as in the case of Mexico). Therefore, courts cannot evaluate such rules as a compromise towards new arrangements. Supermajorities introduced in such times will face not only scrutiny but mistrust from courts." *Id.* at 8.

The following subsection provides an overview of the four episodes of judicial review of supermajority rules[75] in the jurisdictions analyzed.[76]

5.2.4.1 Ohio (1930)

The United States Supreme Court analyzed Ohio's supermajority in *Ohio v. Akron Park District*.[77] Ohio's Supreme Court was unable to strike down the Park District Act in *State, ex rel. v. Park District*.[78] The Park District Act delegated legislative power to nonelective commissioners and the probate court. Among the delegated powers were the acquisition of lands and the creation of parks and other reservations, including the ability to levy limited taxes. The Supreme Court characterized the state court's decision that failed to meet the supermajority requirement as "a result of a divided court."

The plaintiffs insisted on the unconstitutionality of the Park District Act. They also challenged the constitutionality of the supermajority rule, arguing it infringed the Fourteenth Amendment by denying due process of law and

75 I have previously analyzed the cases of Ohio, Peru, and Poland. *See id.* at 13–24.

76 South Korea (1971) is an interesting case beyond the jurisdictions analyzed above. Judicial review of supermajorities comes from Park Chung-hee's authoritarian government. During the Third Republic, from 1962 to 1972, judicial review faculties were granted to the Supreme Court. In 1967, the State Damages Redress Act was issued, establishing a limitation for military personnel to claim damages when injured by illegal acts of government officials during official duty. Joon Seok Hong, *Signaling the Turn: The Supermajority Requirement and Judicial Power on the Constitutional Court of Korea*, 67 AM J. COMP. L. 177, 181 (2019). Fearful of potential judicial review of controversial legislation, in 1970, the National Assembly modified the Court Organization Act, raising the majority to strike down legislation from a simple majority to a two-thirds supermajority. The Supreme Court declared both provisions unconstitutional (Supreme Court [S. Ct.], 70Da1010, June 22, 1971). The Court considered that Article 26 of the 1962 Constitution, an entire revision of the provision initially enacted in 1948, provided a right to receive compensation damages by unlawful acts of public officials, and that the limitation provided by law violated the essential content of the right. Nonetheless, the decision attained a simple majority: nine out of sixteen justices. The Court subsequently considered the constitutionality of the amendment to the Court's Organization Act of 1970 (Law 2222). The Court noted that the Constitution conferred the Supreme Court the power to decide "with finality" the matter of a law's constitutionality. In doing so, the Constitution did not impose limitations on the quorum or majority. The Court concluded that the majority and consensus requirements could not be modulated by law. The decision infuriated the military regime. Justices signing the majority opinion were forced out of Court. GRAHAM HASSALL & CHERYL SAUNDERS, ASIA-PACIFIC CONSTITUTIONAL SYSTEMS 171 (2002). One year later, the Yishin Constitution would be instated, depriving the Supreme Court of judicial review by transferring the power to the Constitutional Committee, also under a supermajority. Youngjoon Kwon, *Korea: Bridging the Gap between Korean Substance and Western Form*, *in* LAW AND LEGAL INSTITUTIONS OF ASIA 151, 170 (E. Ann Black & Gary F. Bell eds., 2011). For a translation of selected paragraphs from the decision, *see* Dae-Kyu Yoon, *Judicial Review in the Korean Political Context*, 17 KOREAN J. COMP. L. 133, 166 (1989).

77 281 U.S. 74 (1930).

78 120 Ohio St. 464 (Ohio 1929). *See* commentary on the case in Carl L. Meier, *Power of the Ohio Supreme Court to Declare Laws Unconstitutional*, 5 U. CIN. L. REV. 293 (1931).

equal protection, and claimed it violated the republican form of government. The Supreme Court argued that the plaintiff's arguments on the unconstitutionality of the delegation did not pose a federal question. Nonetheless, the Supreme Court analyzed the constitutionality of the supermajority, upholding it unanimously, with Chief Justice Hughes delivering the opinion of the Court.

The Court considered that the questions arising under the republican form of government were political, not judicial, and their consideration belonged to Congress and not the Court, citing a long line of precedents. The Supreme Court was unimpressed by the plaintiffs' claims on the due process clause, as it concluded that the right to appeal was not essential to the due process itself, noting that the plaintiffs had been able to contest all claims in the first instance.

Regarding the equal protection argument, the Supreme Court noted that Ohio's highest court had commented on the conflicts arising from the double threshold. Nonetheless, "it is not for this court to intervene to protect the citizens of the State from the consequences of its policy, if the State has not disregarded the requirements of the Federal Constitution." The decision remarked on the states' broad discretion in establishing jurisdiction and court systems. Noting that the Federal Constitution did not require an appeals method that would yield all litigants the same decisions regarding the questions raised, the court affirmed the judgment.

Some scholars questioned the decision. Hauser deemed that the court could have ruled differently in cases where Ohio's Supreme Court exercised original jurisdiction—impacting the ability to contest constitutional claims fully.[79] Meier deemed a supermajority incompatible with the Court's appellate jurisdiction.[80] The U.S. Supreme Court never again analyzed Ohio's supermajority,[81] nor any other to date.

5.2.4.2 Peru (1996)

After Fujimorists installed a near-unanimous 6:1 supermajority in the Organic Law of the Constitutional Court, several members of Congress filed an action of unconstitutionality, claiming that the supermajority established an unreasonable limitation on judicial review. The Constitutional Court of Peru resolved the challenge in Judgment 005-96-I/TC, and upheld the legislation by a 4:3 vote.

79 Hausser, *supra* note 23, at 73.

80 Meier, *supra* note 78, at 310.

81 Jonathan L. Entin, *Judicial Supermajorities and the Validity of Statutes: How Mapp Became a Fourth Amendment Landmark Instead of a First Amendment Footnote*, 50 Case Wes. L. Rev. 441, 460 (2002).

Among other arguments, the petitioners claimed that no court in the world required such a supermajority. They argued that the rule limited judicial review unreasonably, infringing the democratic principle while turning the court into a validation machine rather than an institution placing checks on the elected branches. Moreover, the applicants claimed the court could disregard the supermajority and resolve the case through a simple majority.

Perhaps considering that Fujimori loyalists García Marcelo and Acosta Sánchez would be adamant about relinquishing their authority to block unconstitutionality decisions, the petitioners intended to persuade the remaining magistrates that they could form a decision-making majority.[82]

A majority formed by Nugent, Acosta, García Marcelo, and Díaz Valverde upheld the supermajority. The result spared the court from debating the validity of a decision issued through the impasse mechanism, as feared by the parliamentary minority. The court's decisions considered that the Constitution did not set a specific majority threshold; nor was there an inherent majority rule for collegiate bodies. The judgment deemed that a supermajority was "a logical consequence" of the presumption of constitutionality.

Finally, the decision argued that the logic of majority/minority could not be applied to courts. The opinion noted that, irrespective of how many votes a failed proposal obtained, the opposing votes against the final judgment "cannot and should not be understood as a vote from the majority against the minority . . . but that of a magistrate or a group of magistrates against that of the court." Regardless of the vote, the court, and not court minorities, upholds legislation.

Magistrates Aguirre Roca, Rey Terry, and Revoredo de Mur filed a dissenting opinion. The minority deemed that the voting threshold forbade the court from exercising judicial review. The minority opinion claimed that the Thayerian presumption only reverted the burden of proof of the statute's unconstitutionality but that it should not be turned into a voting rule. They also deemed that a nonneutral supermajority of this nature, favoring the statute, did not exist in comparative law.[83] Aguirre, Rey, and Revoredo further claimed that the main problem of the provision being challenged was not the supermajority threshold but the bias exhibited by the asymmetrical

82 The majority and minority factions of the court held different conclusions on the matter. The majority position leaned toward adhering to the organic law, while the minority faction argued it had the authority to decide the case through an ordinary majority threshold. Professors Sagües and Segado continued the debate in scholarly analysis. *See* Sagües, *supra* note 69; Francisco Fernández Segado, *El Control Normativo de la Constitucionalidad en el Perú: Crónica de un Fracaso Anunciado*, Rev. Esp. Derecho Const. 11 (1999). *See also* Rivera León, *supra* note 28.

83 The claim was false. By 1996, several examples of deferential supermajorities existed or had existed. These included, inter alia, Ohio (repealed in 1968), Czechoslovakia (1920–1938), Nebraska, North Dakota, and Mexico, among others.

requirement, favoring the party being sued. The argument implied that a decisional supermajority would have been constitutional.[84]

Chapter 4 showed that the decision cleared the path for Fujimori's bid for reelection through Law 26657. Law 26657 led to internal confrontations in the split court, attempting to hinder the reelection by bypassing the supermajority rule, ultimately leading to the impeachment of several magistrates. Peru's contemporary 5:2 supermajority rule has never been subjected to judicial review.

5.2.4.3 Poland (2016)

The clash between *Prawo i Sprawiedliwość* (PiS) and *Platforma Obywatelska* (PO), analyzed in Chapter 4, culminated with a PiS-controlled Sejm imposing several constraints on the Constitutional Tribunal in 2015. The tribunal was placed under a supermajority for *en banc* decisions and a qualified quorum. After the amendments to the law on the Constitutional Tribunal, several petitioners challenged the constitutionality of the amendments.[85]

The Venice Commission had previously hinted at the unconstitutionality of the rule. The government argued that the supermajority was similar to the one functioning in the Czech Republic. The Commission replied that, contrary to the Czech Republic, Article 190.5 of the Polish Constitution provided for a "majority" as a decision-making threshold, and although the word "simple" was absent, the unanimous opinion of scholars[86] held it was to be understood as such.[87]

The Constitutional Tribunal struck down the amendments in K 47/2015 in March 2016. The tribunal noted in a methodological section that it was called to decide on provisions that simultaneously regulated its decision-making procedure.[88] The contested articles stipulated, inter alia, an aggravated quorum and a supermajority for the tribunal. The tribunal understood the situation to be a dilemma. On the one hand, the provisions constituted valid law. Not being declared unconstitutional, they were covered by the Thayerian

84 Nonetheless, the opinion also stated that for the supermajority to be constitutional, it would require a "complementary system," such as in the Supreme Court, to achieve the votes "regardless of the outcome." The vote refers to the *Magistrado dirimente* figure. *See* Chapter 4.

85 Namely, the first President of the Supreme Court, two parliamentary minorities entitled to challenge, the Polish Ombudsman, and the National Council of the Judiciary.

86 Banaszak had previously held a different opinion. He noted that "the Constitution does not define which majority of votes is required for a decision." Bogusław Banaszak, Konstytucja Rzeczypospolitej Polskiej: Komentarz 951 (2 ed. 2012).

87 Venice Commission, *Opinion No. 833/2015 On Amendments to the Act of 25 June 2015 on the Constitutional Tribunal (CDL-AD(2016)001*, 25 14 (2016).

88 According to Radziewicz, this was the first occasion in which the phenomena occurred in Poland. Piotr Radziewicz, *Refusal of the Polish Constitutional Tribunal to Apply the Act Stipulating the Constitutional Review Procedure*, XXVIII Rev. Comp. L. 27, 25 (2017).

presumption of constitutionality. Nonetheless, one the other hand the tribunal deemed it improper to review the challenged provisions based on those provisions themselves,[89] considering that if they were found unconstitutional, they would undermine the judgment.[90]

Faced with what the tribunal saw as a lack of decision-making guidelines, the judgment opted for a direct application of the Constitution.[91] The tribunal considered the word "majority," provided as a threshold by Article 190.5 of the Constitution, to be understood as a simple majority. As pointed out in a previous analysis,[92] the tribunal could have concluded the challenge on the methodological section for practical purposes. If the tribunal interpreted that the Constitution intended to refer to a "simple majority" by the term "majority," all departure from simple majority rule was unconstitutional.[93]

The tribunal proceeded to analyze the constitutionality of the supermajority, claiming it increased the risk of paralysis, departed from similar regulations on majority decisions, deviated from the drafters' declared aim of providing an efficient decision-making framework,[94] and violated rules of the legislative procedure. The supermajority was not the only provision invalidated. The tribunal invalidated the statute in its entirety.[95]

The Polish Prime Minister refused to publish the ruling and claimed that the case had been decided in breach of the provisions regulating decision-making. The supermajority saga concluded after PiS acquired a majority of the tribunal. The PiS-dominated Sejm issued a new law returning to a simple majority, presumably to allow the tribunal to perform its new role as the regime's enabler.[96]

89 Piotr Tuleja, *The Polish Constitutional Tribunal, in* THE MAX PLANCK HANDBOOKS IN EUROPEAN PUBLIC L. 619, 663 (Armin Bogdandy, Peter M. Huber & Christoph Grabenwarter eds., 2020).

90 Nonetheless, as was later pointed out, the argument works both ways: "If the court refrains from applying the challenged provisions and rules that they are constitutional, wouldn't the same paradox arise?" Rivera León, *supra* note 28, at 22. Could it not be argued that, had the tribunal found the qualified quorum to be constitutional, such a decision would have been invalid? The judgment would have been rendered by a tribunal lacking a constitutionally valid quorum.

91 Some scholars suggested that a possible way to avoid the paradox would be to stipulate that laws concerning the decision-making of the Constitutional Tribunal are to undergo constitutional review prior to their entry into force. Marcin Wiącek, *Constitutional Crisis in Poland 2015–2016 in the Light of the Rule of Law Principle*, 298 *in* DEFENDING CHECKS AND BALANCES IN EU MEMBER STATES 15, 29 (Armin von Bogdandy et al. eds., 2021).

92 Rivera León, *supra* note 28, at 23.

93 *Id.* at 22.

94 Tuleja, *supra* note 89, at 663.

95 Sadurski points out that such invalidation *in toto* of a statute was uncharacteristic of the last thirty years of the tribunal's precedents. WOJCIECH SADURSKI, POLAND'S CONSTITUTIONAL BREAKDOWN 71 (2019).

96 *Id.* at 75.

5.2.4.4 Georgia (2016)

Precisely as was the case in Poland, the Georgian Constitutional Court had to face a law that restricted its powers on several fronts. The 2016 amendments sponsored by Georgian Dream-Democratic Georgia introduced significant constraints. The new regulations required a quorum of seven out of nine justices, a 6:3 supermajority to strike down legislation, and transferred the ability to suspend laws to the court *en banc*, ensuring that the granting of suspensions would face considerable obstacles.[97] Upon a challenge by a parliamentary minority and several citizens, the court analyzed the provisions in N3/5/768,769,790,792.

The government knew the Venice Commission's opinion about Poland's supermajority and had done its homework. The explanatory note to the drafts remarked that the Georgian Constitution did not regulate the majority or quorum, as it did in Poland's case. Thus, the Georgian case was closer to the Czech example.[98]

The applicants claimed that the supermajority would significantly delay the procedures and undermine the right to prompt and timely justice. Referring to the previous opinion of the Venice Commission on the matter,[99] the applicants noted[100] that aggravated quorums and supermajorities could hinder the effectiveness of judicial review. They also argued that the absence of justices would negatively interact with the supermajority in the Georgian legal system.[101] In turn, Parliament claimed the provision was aimed at providing greater legitimacy to court decisions in assessing the constitutionality of statutes.

The court struck down the supermajority. The decision acknowledged that quorum and majorities were not constitutionally prescribed.[102] However, even if legislation may regulate majority requirements, such regulation must be issued "in accordance with the requirements of the Constitution."[103] The

97 For a brief commentary on the constitutional court's criteria on the suspension amendments, *see* Anna Kuchukhidze, *Review of Judicial Practice of the Constitutional Court of Georgia in the View of Suspension of Disputed Norm*, Constitutional L. Rev. 98, 106 (2021).

98 *See* the explanatory note attached to Venice Commission, *Preliminary Opinion 849/2016 on the Amendments to the Organic Law on the Constitutional Court and to the Law on Constitutional Legal Proceedings*, 10 (2016).

99 *Id.*

100 *Id.* at I para. 32.

101 *Id.* at I para. 33.

102 Alexander Graser et al., *Proportionality and Human Rights in German, Armenian and Georgian Constitutional Adjudication*, 116 Comp. Leg. Stud. 93 (2017).

103 Para. 109. The court claimed the legislature had ample leeway to regulate court majorities, as long as it did not paralyze the court. Simultaneously, holding a 6:3 supermajority unconstitutional, the lowest possible supermajority in the Georgian nine-member court, the decision implicitly stated that a simple majority was constitutionally required.

court noted that the absence of justices could paralyze the court due to the institutional design of the rule.[104]

In the second place, the court embarked on a Condorcetian defense of simple majorities.[105] The decision stated that "the probability of each member of the constitutional court making the right decision is higher than the wrong one."[106] The court went on to argue that claims supported by simple majorities were more likely to be correct, and by allowing a minority to block a declaration of unconstitutionality, "the probability of making the wrong decision will be higher."[107]

Nonetheless, the court itself recognized that some issues could merit a supermajority. The increasing likelihood of error could be balanced vis-à-vis the need for greater legitimacy in specific cases. In matters of greater importance, "it is permissible for the legislature to deviate from the general rule of deciding by the majority of attendees and establish a higher majority requirement."

Even if the court acknowledged that some instances would justify supermajority requirements, it concluded that the contested threshold was so expansively drafted that it constituted an unjustified barrier to judicial review. Although the supermajority was invalidated, the court was willing to concede that a narrower supermajority expressly focused on what the court deemed "systemic constitutional issues" would be constitutional.

5.3 Supermajorities Beyond Theory: A Peek Behind Policymakers' Reasons

The contemporary debate on supermajorities has been centered mostly around their deferential value (*i.e.*, granting an institutionalized form of deference to the elected branches supplementary or substitutive to the presumption of

104 *Id.* at para. 104. The court subsequently remarked that absences would increase the supermajority. Having a seven-member quorum, the court noted that it could even be forced to rule by a 6:1 supermajority (para. 119).

105 Broadly considered, Condorcet posited that a simple majority enhances the possibility for a group to arrive at a correct decision on a binary choice, provided each voter has more than 50 percent possibility of voting in favor of making the correct decision. Thus, increasing the group size raises the odds of favoring a correct outcome. Nonetheless, several circumstances pose a challenge to the theorem's applicability to judicial decision-making, inter alia, deliberation, information cascades, non-binary outcomes such as partial invalidation, and insincere voting. Furthermore, applying the theorem entails presupposing that there is a *correct* answer in constitutional adjudication. For an argument against the theorem's application, *see* David M. Estlund, Democratic Authority: A Philosophical Framework 225 (2 ed. 2008). But *see also* Waldron's contrary view. Waldron, *supra* note 3, at 1715. Schwartzberg does not discard deliberation within the theorem's framework. Schwartzberg, *supra* note 2, at 119.

106 *Id.* at II para. 112.

107 *Id.* at II para. 114.

constitutionality),[108] their consensus-building capabilities (which may foster deliberation),[109] and arguably a superior Condorcetian accuracy in constitutional adjudication.[110] Scholars contend that such rules will provide specific advantages. However, policymakers have supported supermajorities for several reasons, regardless of the institutional design they adopted.

Based on the analysis of the selected jurisdictions, including legislative discussions, preparatory works, and analysis of the political context in which such rules were established, the book contends that supermajorities are generally introduced for four distinctive reasons: deference, caution, attack, and consensus.[111]

5.3.1 Cautious Supermajorities

The first reason to establish supermajorities is caution. I define caution as an attitude of policymakers reflecting uncertainty toward new power balances after introducing strong judicial review figures. Policymakers might be induced to approach a court's institutional design prudently in uncertain contexts. When introducing constitutional courts or new strong judicial review institutions, politicians may have concerns that empowering an unelected body may undermine the democratic process and have an unintended disruptive effect. Czechoslovakia (1920), Peru (1982) and Mexico (1994) offer clear examples of the phenomenon.

The first constitutional court in the world, located in Czechoslovakia, opted for a 5:2 supermajority. In 1920, concentrated constitutional review was barely emerging as part of a relevant debate. Only the Austrian Constitution had envisaged a similar body, while the American judicial review had a completely different design than the one defended by Weyr and Hoetzel. Faced with the dilemma of regulating an unprecedented ability to invalidate laws with *erga omnes* effect, the entire design of the constitutional court was driven by caution.[112] It was so evident that institutional safeguards had to be adopted

108 Stewart T. Herrick, James J. Higgins & Nancy R. Tarlow, *Five-Four Decisions of the United States Supreme Court: Resurrection of the Extraordinary Majority*, 7 SUFFOLK U. L. REV. 807, 834–35 (1973); Caminker, *supra* note 1, at 91–101; Pablo Castillo-Ortiz, *The Dilemmas of Constitutional Courts and the Case for a New Design of Kelsenian Institutions*, 39 LAW AND PHILOSOPHY 617, 639 (2020); Cristóbal Caviedes, *A Core Case for Supermajority Rules in Constitutional Adjudication*, 20 INT'L J. CONST. L. 1162, 1182 (2022).

109 Caviedes, *supra* note 108, at 1177–80.

110 *Id.* at 1175–77.

111 Other reasons might have existed but played a minor role, such as Condorcetian accuracy and respect for precedent, inter alia. Although rationales were often interconnected, the chapter attempts to discern and emphasize the prevailing rationale for their implementation in the respective jurisdictions.

112 Cruz Villalón also concluded that caution and moderation account for Czechoslovakia's design of its Constitutional Court. PEDRO CRUZ VILLALÓN, LA FORMACIÓN DEL SISTEMA EUROPEO DE CONTROL DE CONSTITUCIONALIDAD (1918-1939) 289 (1987).

that the legislative report claimed there was little need to justify requiring a supermajority.[113]

In Peru, establishing a Tribunal of Constitutional Guarantees in 1979, the Constitution and legislation meant to ensure that the powers of the newly created TGC would not result in an imbalance with the elected branches. Legal standing was reduced, the court could not strike down legislation directly,[114] and decisions required a supermajority to be taken. Legislators were inexperienced with judicial review. Congressmen remembered the 1963 diffuse review system, which could hardly be described as functional.

In Mexico, judicial review had existed since 1847,[115] but the legal system was accustomed to refrain from applying a statute rather than general invalidation of laws. In 1994, when granting the Supreme Court unprecedented ability to invalidate laws with an *erga omnes* effect, the supermajority was a way of tempering its new powers through what was seen as careful design by the ruling party.

Czechoslovakia (1920), Peru (1982), and Mexico (1994) provide examples of cautionary design,[116] which can be inferred not only through the political and legal context but also from the additional safeguards such jurisdictions imposed on institutions that were legitimately intended to be functional.

5.3.2 Deference as a Core Goal

A second reason to impose supermajorities is to guarantee deference, a primary theoretical argument in the scholarship. The elected branches may try to ensure that the courts grant enough weight to their constitutional and statutory interpretation. Supermajorities may ensue from struggles where the elected branches feel courts overstep their boundaries and impose their policy views, or out of concern, they might do so.

113 Report of the Constitutional Committee to the Bill on the Act on the Constitutional Court, Prague, Feb. 24, 1920. "[i]t is such an important matter that it was recommended to require a supermajority for it."

114 Instead, the court's decision triggered an obligation for Congress to issue a law repealing the statute. *See* Article 301 of the 1979 Constitution for the Peruvian Republic.

115 Mauro Arturo Rivera León, *An Introduction to "Amparo" Theory: A Complex Mexican Constitutional Control Mechanism*, 12 KP 190, 192 (2020).

116 Beyond the scope of our study, perhaps South Korea constitutes an example of cautionary design. Upon South Korea's exit from the authoritarian period, which began with Park Chung-hee taking power, the 1987 Constitutional Court, already a part of the return to democracy, was seen with skepticism. This sentiment is discussed by Hong, *supra* note 76, at 183. Although other bodies were entitled to judicial review, their functioning was illusory. In the last 15 years previous to 1987, the Constitution Committee had not reviewed a single statute. Dae-Kyu Yoon, Law and Political Authority in South Korea 166 (1991). The prevailing context persuaded policymakers to establish a rule moderating the potential of a strong constitutional court to influence the political process, mainly since politicians were uncertain about the possible effects of such a body.

Ohio, arguably the first jurisdiction in the world to employ such a rule, established a strong supermajority to make its Supreme Court return to an acceptable level of deference.[117] In Ohio's 1912 Constitutional Convention, several delegates referred to the many cases in which the Supreme Court invalidated protective laws and favored big corporations without a clear constitutional basis for doing so.[118] In the discussions, delegates such as Anderson claimed that laws were being invalidated despite the House of Representatives, the Executive's lawyers, and the attorney general having also considered the statutes' constitutionality.[119] The court was striking down reasonable legislation, seemingly imposing its economic model on the grounds of policy preference, and so the legislature reacted.

A desire to ensure deference arises not only as a reaction to previous court decisions but may be established preventively as a matter of policy. Several jurisdictions employed supermajorities despite their courts having shown reasonable deference: North Dakota, Nebraska, or Peru.

As of 1919/1920, the state Supreme Courts of North Dakota and Nebraska had not been particularly aggressive in exercising judicial review.[120] However, the national context offered a stark contrast. In the United States, progressive legislation clashed with the Lochner era. The activist Lochner Court's lack of deference concerned delegates. Delegates felt that nothing in their institutional design prevented state Supreme Courts from following the Lochner example, just as Ohio's Supreme Court was doing.

Delegate Votava argued during Nebraska's Constitutional Convention that most arguments on the overreaching of courts could be addressed to the United States Supreme Court but not to Nebraska's, which had shown regular signs of restraint.[121] Votava concluded, "The court has not abused the power in the past, and what reason have we to believe it will abuse it in the future?"[122] Notwithstanding, delegates felt that institutionalizing deference through a supermajority was a safeguard against the type of potential overreach the U.S. Supreme Court showed.[123]

Something similar occurred in Peru. The opposition to Fujimori initially favored instating a 5:2 supermajority. The opposition was a minoritarian

117 Ohio's case proves policymakers may wrongly decide on institutional designs that fail to prioritize the outcomes they wish to promote. Seeking deference—best granted by an ordinary deferential supermajority—delegates approved a mixed system that only partially deferred to legislation, probably due to a lack of further legislative and electoral support (*see* Chapter 3).

118 For a reconstruction of the debate, *see* Chapter 3.

119 Ohio's 1912 Constitutional Convention. Fifty-Second Day (Legislative Day of Apr. 2), 1091.

120 *See* Chapter 3.

121 Journal of the Nebraska Constitutional Convention (1921), 1140–41 (Clyde H. Barnard ed., 1921).

122 *Id.* at 1141.

123 *See* Fauquet's reply. *Id.* at 1144–46.

group when the legislation was discussed. They had little incentive to raise the threshold, presumably diminishing the court's ability to invalidate legislation. It would even have been natural to push for a simple majority to increase the possibilities of their constitutional challenges being successful. The supermajority was, for them, a coherent model of institutionalized deference. Fujimori's 6:1 supermajority had proven to be nothing more than an attempt to paralyze the Court. After Fujimori's demise, Congress amended the supermajority. Legislators knew what the role of a constitutional court was supposed to be. Peru had a constitutional court in the Tribunal of Constitutional Guarantees (1982–1990) and struggled with attacks on an independent constitutional court during Fujimori's authoritarian regime (1995–2000). Congress valued the role of the court but considered that deferential thresholds were coherent and did not constitute a significant obstacle to placing checks on the legislature.

5.3.3 Consensus within the Court

In third place, supermajorities may be established to guarantee consensus. Decisional supermajorities are more prone to contribute to this aim. By placing high decisional requirements, politicians ensure that court decisions are perceived as having broad legitimacy, enhancing the court's authority. Furthermore, supermajority requirements strive to promote deliberative outcomes that encourage judges to deliberate and compromise rather than try to impose individualistic approaches to the court's decisions.

The Constitutional Court of the Dominican Republic is the best example of such an approach. As an expert advisor to the constitutional drafting procedure of 2010 conveyed,[124] the main reason to set up a supermajority was to promote consensus within the court and make all decisions appear as enjoying broad legitimacy. The expert drafter's Commission was familiar with a series of 5:4 decisions in the United States[125] that undermined the legitimacy of the court.[126] All decisions in the Constitutional Court of the Dominican Republic require a 9:4 supermajority. As a result, most decisions are unanimous, and the court is rarely perceived as split, although this has occurred in some cases, as discussed in Chapter 4.

124 Eduardo Jorge Prats, *Interview with a Former Member of the Presidential Constitutional Commission for the 2010 Constitutional Amendment* (unpublished, 2022).

125 *See* Shugerman, *supra* note 8, at 906–09.

126 Jorge Prats, *supra* note 124.

5.3.4 Supermajorities as Weapons

Finally, a fourth reason to employ supermajorities is to attack or tame an adverse court based on political calculus. Dixon and Landau have identified supermajorities as part of the court-curbing repertory.[127]

Supermajorities may be theoretically valid models but can also be powerful weapons if configured correctly against adverse courts,[128] particularly when combined with court-packing. The virtue of supermajorities may be turned into systemic weakness under certain conditions. Supermajorities may be used to limit the court's ability to function, prevent the effective exercise of judicial review, or be employed to protect the ruling party's interests.

The Peruvian Fujimorist and the transitory Polish and Georgian supermajorities are examples of a weaponized usage against courts.[129]

Determining when supermajorities are illiberal impositions on courts rather than coherent models requires knowledge of the conceptual background, the dynamics of the executive and legislative branches, and the supermajority's interaction with other institutional and political events, particularly with the court's composition.

Two similar supermajorities shed light on this issue: Ohio (1912–1968) and the Fujimorist supermajority in Peru (1995–2004). Both rules required a 6:1 supermajority. Nonetheless, Ohio's supermajority was established legitimately, intending to guarantee deference. In contrast, the Peruvian supermajority was a political calculus to obstruct the court. Peck and Chirinos defended the same proposal for different aims. Both democrats and autocrats may see a valuable tool in supermajorities.

In Ohio, even though the 85.7 percent degree of consensus may be deemed high, it was a measure of the desired degree of deference delegates deem that courts should grant political branches, particularly in considering economic legislation and workers' rights. In contrast, political calculus could not be more evident than it was in Peru. The government had conceded to draft a new Constitution to mitigate the sting of dictatorship caused by Fujimori's

127 Rosalind Dixon & David Landau, Abusive Constitutional Borrowing: Legal Globalization and the Subversion of Liberal Democracy 92 (2021).

128 Caviedes, *supra* note 14, at 1171.

129 Beyond the jurisdictions selected, Taiwan is a good example of the former. Taiwan's Council of Grand Justices—a body performing judicial review—issued Interpretation 76 of 1957, placing the Control Yuan and the National Assembly at a similar level to the Legislative Yuan. The Legislative Yuan retaliated. Until then, the Council of Grand Justices had been able to self-regulate its quorum and majority. One year later, the Legislative Yuan issued the Law Governing the Adjudication of the Grand Justice's Council as an open reprisal. The new regulations imposed a three-fourths quorum and a three-fourths supermajority. Jerry McBeath, *Democratization and Taiwan's Constitutional Court*, 11 Am. J. Chin. Stud. 51, 56 (2004); Tzu-Ti Lin, Ming-Sung Kuo & Hui-Wen Chen, *Seventy Years On: The Taiwan Constitutional Court and Judicial Activism in a Changing Constitutional Landscape*, 48 Hong Kong L.J. 995, 1013 (2018).

coup d'etat. During the Constitution's drafting, it had tried determinedly to part ways with a constitutional court, having fresh memories of an independent Tribunal of Constitutional Guarantees obstructing several Fujimorist policies. Fujimori failed to prevent the court from appearing in the draft under unsurmountable pressure. Through Chirinos, the government had then tried to impose a unanimity requirement. Failing to do so, the government successfully forced a 6:1 supermajority while placing two obscenely loyal magistrates in the court.[130] Magistrates Acosta and García Marcelo ensured that Fujimori's calculation paid off. They behaved openly as partisans, defending Fujimori's interests. García Marcelo even stole the court's internal documents[131] to ensure Fujimori's reelection would be unperturbed by the constitutional court. A 6:1 supermajority resulted from a defendable deference threshold in Ohio, while the same threshold resulted from basic partisan appointment mathematics in Peru.

Poland is the best-known recent example of a weaponized supermajority. The 2015 amendment to the Act on the Constitutional Tribunal featured the introduction of a two-thirds supermajority and a 13 out of 15 quorum. The supermajority, per se, was not particularly elevated.[132] Nonetheless, the Polish case resulted from an attack on the tribunal with deliberate political calculus, perceivable as in the Fujimorist supermajority.

The 2015 Polish constitutional crisis saw a confrontation between the parties PO and PiS, with both parties resorting to illegal attempts to control the appointment of five judges.[133] The Polish Constitutional Tribunal ruled materially[134] that PO had validly appointed three judges and illegally appointed two. PiS refused to recognize PO-appointed judges and contended that the Sejm had validly voided the previous appointments and elected five judges of its own. As a result, PiS claimed the tribunal had fifteen judges, while the Constitutional Tribunal, in turn, claimed it had merely twelve.[135] Knowledge of this situation is critical to understanding the ensuing calculations.

130 It seems that the Fujimorist supermajority accounts for an example of a threshold set through bargaining. *See* SCHWARTZBERG, *supra* note 2, at 150.

131 Constitutional Court v. Peru, Judgment of Jan. 31, 2001, (Merits, Reparations, and Costs), 15.

132 Considering other analyzed jurisdictions, it is clearly on the lower side of the comparative spectrum. The Polish 66 percent falls under North Dakota's 80 percent and Mexico's 72.7 percent, while barely passing the Czech Republic's 60 percent supermajority. Perhaps Castillo-Ortiz noticed this fact when he stated that "the disempowerment of the Polish Constitutional Court cannot be blamed only on this aspect [a too high threshold] but rather on its coupling with the PiS-controlled appointment of new judges and the composition of the Court." Castillo-Ortiz, *supra* note 108, at 650.

133 In the case of PO, through the premature appointment of two Judges, and in the case of PiS, by illegally voiding the election of those validly appointed. *See* Chapter 4.

134 Tuleja, *supra* note 89, at 661.

135 The Polish Constitutional Tribunal refused to allow the three illegally PiS-appointed judges to carry out official duties and continued functioning with twelve judges. *Id.*

The amendments passed on the Act on the Constitutional Tribunal raised quorum and majorities in a precise fashion. The 13-judge quorum requirement was a clear warning: either the tribunal would recognize the illegitimately appointed judges, or there would be no quorum and, consequently, no tribunal.[136] Even if the tribunal were to acquiesce, the two-thirds decisional supermajority ensured that PiS-appointed judges could block any undesired decision. There was little doubt that the bill intended to paralyze the tribunal.[137]

Additional regulations destined to constrain the court often provide further evidence of the weaponizing intention of the rule. In the cases of Poland and Georgia, the supermajority did not come alone. Both countries featured increased quorums and even rules on solving cases sequentially.[138] In the case of Peru, the rule came with further obstruction in issuing the court's legislation, delays in the appointments of magistrates, and partisan appointments once the supermajority requirement was secured.

Supermajorities may be used as weapons of attack for three purposes: retaliation, obstruction, and control. A supermajority may be instated as retaliation, a response of displeased political branches to independent behavior rendering adverse decisions.[139] A supermajority may attempt to obstruct the court by diminishing the court's capacity to perform judicial review and place checks on the elected branches. Finally, the qualified threshold may intend to control a court, *i.e.*, exerting influence, ensuring that the decisions align with the government's ideology and interests.

While retaliation and obstruction go hand in hand, obstruction and control may not. To obstruct a court does not necessarily mean to control or dominate it. Controlling a constitutional court can be useful to autocrats. It allows them to employ the court to legitimize the regime, provide a façade for credible democratic commitments, and delegate controversial decisions to them.[140]

A good example of control occurred in the 1995 Fujimorist supermajority. The rule was designed to compel the court to issue a decision to uphold the statute under challenge if the supermajority was not met. Deferential

136 Considering only the validly appointed judges, the tribunal could not decide cases because of the lack of quorum. Sadurski, *supra* note 95, at 73.

137 Bojan Bugarič & Tom Ginsburg, *The Assault on Postcommunist Courts*, 27 J. Democracy 69, 73 (2016).

138 That was the case in Poland. Sadurski, *supra* note 95, at 72.

139 Arguably, this would be Taiwan's case. *See* comments *supra*.

140 Tamir Moustafa, *Law and Courts in Authoritarian Regimes*, 10 Annu. Rev. L. Soc. Sci. 281 (2014); Tamir Moustafa & Tom Ginsburg, *Introduction: The Functions of Courts in Authoritarian Politics*, *in* Rule by Law: The Politics of Courts in Authoritarian Regimes 1, 5–10 (Tom Ginsburg & Tamir Moustafa eds., 2008); Michal Kovalčík, *The Instrumental Abuse of Constitutional Courts: How Populists Can Use Constitutional Courts against the Opposition*, 26 The Int'l J. Hum. Rts. 1160, 1169 (2022). Similarly, Nora Webb Williams & Margaret Hanson, *Captured Courts and Legitimized Autocrats: Transforming Kazakhstan's Constitutional Court*, 47 L. Soc. Inq. 1201, 203–04 (2022).

supermajorities may have a clear control motif. The supermajority turned the court into an ally of the regime, even though Fujimori only controlled two of the seven magistrates. The two loyal magistrates were able to issue decisions affirming the constitutionality of key governmental policies. The Truth and Reconciliation Commission, created during Paniagua's transitional government returning to democracy, argued that the 6:1 supermajority, combined with two magistrates unconditionally allied with the government, turned the court into a "machine of constitutionalizing any governmental action."[141]

In turn, the transitory Polish supermajority exemplifies why obstruction and domination may be separate features. In 2015, the PiS supermajority requirement managed to obstruct the court but not control it. The tribunal was not a threat, but neither was it an ally. The 2015 Polish supermajority was decisional, not deferential with upholding impasse rules. Thus, even if the PiS minority judges, coupled with the quorum requirement, could theoretically prevent any governmental legislation from being struck down, the ruling party could not employ the tribunal for further purposes, such as legitimacy-building or attacking legislation issued by the former ruling party.[142] Because of this, once PiS managed to capture the tribunal, the supermajority was no longer needed and "would have constituted a hindrance to the tribunal in playing its new role . . . the government's enabler."[143] The supermajority would have prevented PiS from using the tribunal to legitimize doubtful legislation and challenge older laws that the party ideologically abhorred, such as the abortion law.[144] A minority of independent judges could have blocked the decision.

While this subsection does not suggest that supermajority rules are primarily illiberal institutions, it acknowledges the possibility of their factious usage, as with other institutions and policies.[145]

141 Informe Final, 438 188 (2003).

142 Nonetheless, opting for a decisional supermajority had advantages for the ruling party. Under a deferential supermajority, a majority of the Court might have sought to bypass the requirement through majority decisions, as had occurred in Ohio (*Patten v. Aluminum Castings Co.*) or in Peru, where magistrates attempted to prevent Fujimori's reelection by declaring a statute "inapplicable" albeit not "unconstitutional," circumventing the requirement. In the Peruvian context, interpretative judgments had also been discussed as bypassing mechanisms, allowing the court to construe statutes narrowly or seemingly introduce normative elements when unable to reach a supermajority.

143 Sadurski, *supra* note 95, at 75.

144 Aleksandra Kustra-Rogatka, *The Hypocrisy of Authoritarian Populism in Poland: Between the Facade Rhetoric of Political Constitutionalism and the Actual Abuse of Apex Courts*, 19 European Const. L. Rev. 25, 37–39 (2023).

145 Caviedes, *supra* note 108, at 1185–86.

6 How Do Supermajorities Impact Constitutional Courts? Consensus Requirements and Paralysis Assessment

6.1 How Do We Calculate Supermajorities? Full Court and Quorum Models

Scholars have deemed that supermajority rules impact courts. Higher consensus requirements may lead to different outcomes, the inability of a court to decide, or a diminished capacity for acting as a check on the elected branches. It has been said that in some instances, a supermajority may give rise to court paralysis.[1]

As stated in Chapter 2, all majority rules have two components. In the first place, the threshold is the set number of votes, fractions, or percentages required. Secondly, the multiplicand represents the group over which such a threshold should be calculated.[2] Thresholds tend to be more visible than multiplicands,[3] but they are both equally relevant in assessing the burden a rule may pose.

The multiplicand choice usually pertains to whether the voting protocol requires a supermajority of the full court—through fixed thresholds—or of a set quorum. The first system treats absences and abstentions as votes against the proposal,[4] producing different consequences in decisional and deferential supermajorities.[5] Judges not present or recused are counted as either voting against the court's decision or voting to preserve the statute.[6]

In practice, the supermajority is recalibrated if we consider the decisional group smaller. In a nine-member constitutional court, attaining a six-vote supermajority is harder when seven members, not nine, are present. In turn,

1 *See* a theoretical discussion of the arguments in section 4.

2 Adrian Vermeule, *Absolute Majority Rules*, 37 Br. J. Polit. Sci. 643, 644 (2007).

3 *Id.* at 657.

4 Keith L. Dougherty & Julian Edward, *The Properties of Simple Vs. Absolute Majority Rule: Cases Where Absences and Abstentions Are Important*, 22 J. Theor. Polit. 85 (2010).

5 As I will argue, absences always favor the statute in deferential supermajorities. In decisional supermajorities, absences may favor or disfavor the statute. *See* Chapter 5.

6 The fixed number of votes equals an absolute multiplicand. The negative vote effect occurs since absences reduce "the pool from which the requisite fixed number of votes can be drawn." Adrian Vermeule, Mechanisms of Democracy: Institutional Design Writ Small 119 (2007).

DOI: 10.4324/9781003458272-9

the second system reconfigures the group over which the majority is calculated, and even though threshold distortions may occur out of the contingent fractional calculation, it attempts to preserve the supermajority set. The chapter will now address both systems.

6.1.1 The Numerical Model: Mobile Supermajority Thresholds

Supermajorities employing the numerical model establish a set number of votes, regardless of the members present. Numerical models find a justification in Condorcet's work. Condorcet's probability of correctness depended on the majority's absolute size, not the majority's proportion regarding the electorate.[7] The argument seems to favor fixed majority thresholds.[8] Some scholars have claimed that absolute margin rules are the appropriate types of supermajority rules.[9]

Direct vote requirements generally preclude relative multiplicands. Eight votes are required in the Mexican Supreme Court to invalidate a provision, regardless of whether a justice is absent due to sickness, recused, or if new appointments are pending. For the Court to rule that a statute is unconstitutional, it must summon eight votes.

The numerical model is by far the most common in our selected jurisdictions. Ohio (1912–1968), North Dakota, Nebraska, Czechoslovakia (1920–1938), the Czech Republic, Mexico, the Dominican Republic, all Peruvian supermajorities, and Georgia are examples of such a model.

The numerical model attempts to give certainty to the rule and impedes any group smaller than a supermajority of the court from speaking on behalf of it on matters regulated by the threshold.[10] In majority models, given quorum regulations, court minorities may decide cases provided absences occur.[11]

In the numerical model, treating absences/abstentions as votes against the proposal, when they occurr, increases the consensus degree, generating a

7 Jean-Antoine-Nicolas de Caritat Condorcet, Iain McLean & Fiona Hewitt, Condorcet: Foundations of Social Choice and Political Theory 37 (1994).

8 Nonetheless, it still presumes an equal value for juror competence. *See* Jan-Willem Romeijn & David Atkinson, *Learning Juror Competence: A Generalized Condorcet Jury Theorem*, 10 Polit. Philos. Econ. 237 (2011). For our purposes, fixed juror competencies imply presuming constitutional court judges are equally capable of resolving constitutional questions.

9 Christian List, *On the Significance of the Absolute Margin*, 55 Br. J. Philos. Sci. 521, 540 (2004).

10 Let us turn back to the example of the Mexican Supreme Court, requiring an eight-vote supermajority (72.7 percent). If a relative multiplicand were in place, the Court would be allowed to seek 72.7 percent of the justices voting and present, provided a quorum is met. Since the quorum is set at eight justices, 5.8 justices would be allowed to strike down a law under certain circumstances.

11 Jonathan Nash, *The Majority That Wasn't: Stare Decisis, Majority Rule, and the Mischief of Quorum Requirements*, 58 Emory L.J. 831, 859–60 (2009).

mobile threshold.[12] Since the vote requirement remains stable, but the pool of judges from which those votes are calculated decreases, the decisional threshold de facto rises. Theoretically, a supermajority may create a significant obstacle to a court's functioning[13] or even turn to unanimity if a sufficient number of absences occurs.

In deferential supermajorities, absences favor the statute. In decisional supermajorities, absences complicate arriving at any decision. The Mexican and Czech examples—for deferential supermajorities—and the Dominican Republic—for decisional supermajorities—will illustrate these characteristics.

In 2019, Mexican Justice Medina Mora resigned amidst accusations of corruption and rumors of presidential pressure.[14] It was an unprecedented event. No justice had resigned since the contemporary Supreme Court began functioning in 1994. President López Obrador, often depicted as a populist,[15] received an unexpected additional nomination to attempt to make the Court more favorable to his unorthodox policies. The resignation created a midterm absence. Ten justices, not eleven, sat on the bench, but the same eight votes were required to invalidate legislation. Justice Medina Mora's empty chair remained in the deliberation room, a powerful symbol. Justice Medina Mora was known to be ideologically distant from the President, often casting his vote against the policies of the *Movimiento de Regeneración Nacional*—MORENA, the ruling party. In turn, his empty chair was amicable to all laws enacted by the majoritarian party. Medina Mora's chair and Justice Esquivel, a justice widely regarded as favoring MORENA's policies in a partisan way, did not behave very differently for practical purposes.

As I have argued before, since absences support a statute, in those jurisdictions where the political branches are vested with the power to nominate and confirm justices, a theoretical incentive may exist to withhold nominations if the political branches consider that a case will be vigorously contested.[16] Empty chairs do not vote to invalidate legislation; appointed justices

12 Designing a numerical model with mobile thresholds to adapt to absences is theoretically possible. Senator Sansores in Mexico sponsored a proposal for a supermajority rule requiring a fixed number of votes, varying depending on the number of justices hearing a case. *See* Chapter 4.

13 The Lebanese Constitutional Council combines a 7:3 supermajority with an eight-member quorum. Upon three absences, the court is unable to decide even if it could theoretically still gather a unanimous vote. Conseil Constitutionnel du Liban (Réponses au Questionnaire), Assoc. Cours Const. Francoph. Bull. 325, 336–37 (2019).

14 Rebecka Villanueva Ulfgard, *Separation of Powers in Distress: AMLO's Charismatic Populism and Mexico's Return to Hyper-Presidentialism*, 6 Populism 55, 66 (2023).

15 Rebecka Villanueva Ulfgard, *López Obrador's Hyper-Presidentialism: Populism and Autocratic Legalism Defying the Supreme Court and the National Electoral Institute*, Int'l J. Hum. Rts. 1 (2023).

16 Mauro Arturo Rivera León, *Control and Paralysis? A Context-Sensitive Analysis of Objections to Supermajorities in Constitutional Adjudication*, Int. J. Const. L. (2023), doi.org/10.1093/icon/moad074.

do. President López Obrador learned this lesson the hard way. Having four appointments during his term, many believed he would choose partisan candidates. In an 8:3 supermajority, four votes suffice to preserve any statute. Two of López Obrador's appointments proved to be reliably partisan: Justices Esquivel and Ortiz Ahlf. In contrast, Justices González Alcántara and Ríos behaved independently, often becoming the seventh and eighth votes required to strike down key policies of the majority, such as the Federal Remuneration Law or the "Plan B," a controversial set of electoral amendments. From a partisan point of view, had the President foreseen the independent behavior of those two nominees, he might have considered refraining from making any appointments.

The Czech Republic, our second example, vividly portrays the mobile threshold problem. In 2004, the fifteen-member Czech Constitutional Court had been decimated through absence. Appointments were complicated, and the Senate had rejected several candidates.[17] Only eleven justices sat on the bench. In practice, the nine out of fifteen supermajority (60 percent) was raised to a little above 81 percent. Ordinarily, the court could strike down a law even if six justices dissented. In 2004, three dissenters would have blocked any invalidation. The plenum felt forced to stay the procedures and announced it would not hold sessions until a justice was appointed.[18] The justices felt that the absences were significantly distorting the decisional procedures.

Under propitious circumstances, political branches may realize their ability to deactivate the court or increase the deference level by refraining from appointing justices. The nomination withholding mechanism has not been detected in any of the analyzed jurisdictions, but arguably, it occurred elsewhere.[19]

17 David Kosař & Ladislav Vyhnánek, *The Constitutional Court of Czechia*, *in* The Max Planck Handbooks in European Public Law: Volume III: Constitutional Adjudication: Institutions 119, 132 (Armin von Bogdandy, Peter M. Huber & Christoph Grabenwarter eds., 2020).

18 *Id.* at 156.

19 South Korea's Constitutional Court must confirm an impeachment by a two-thirds supermajority. During Park Geun-hye's impeachment in 2016, two justices were about to finish their terms. There was a possibility that a seven-member court would have to confirm the impeachment by six votes, and "there were concerns that Park Geun-hye's lawyers were attempting to delay the court proceedings . . . to make it more difficult for the court to get the necessary six votes to confirm impeachment." Joon Seok Hong, *Signaling the Turn: The Supermajority Requirement and Judicial Power on the Constitutional Court of Korea*, 67 Am. J. Comp. L. 177, 202 (2019). Fearing it would be forced to decide a case requiring six votes with only seven members, the court "expedited the proceedings and issued the decision three days before it would be left with seven members." Chaihark Hahm, *Constitutional Court of Korea: Guardian of the Constitution or Mouthpiece of the Government?*, *in* Constitutional Courts in Asia: A Comparative Perspective 141, 162 (Albert H. Y. Chen & Andrew Harding eds., 2018). The delaying tactics did not go unnoticed by many political commentators. The Strait Times wrote, "Critics say Park's lawyers have been stalling the process, filibustering and calling up irrelevant witnesses . . . The court's chief justice retired last week, leaving an empty red-

In turn, in decisional supermajorities, neutral by nature, every absence equals a vote against the majoritarian view, irrespective of its particular form. Absences make deciding more challenging, which does not necessarily favor the statute.[20] The Tribunal of Constitutional Guarantees in Peru (1982–1990) was the best example of a decisional supermajority haunted by the issue.

Peru's TGC seemed destined for misfortune. Not only was it bound to a tragic death in the 1990 Fujimorist *coup d'état*, but absences dreadfully hindered its short life. The political branches caused appointment delays,[21] and the magistrates were struck by illness or died.[22] The nine-member body did not once sit in full bench in any of the cases involving the constitutionality of a statute.[23] The six-vote decisional supermajority proved too much for a court often sitting with six or seven justices. In one-third of its cases, it was unable to decide at all.

6.1.2 The Fractional Model: Playing with Decimals

A second model establishes supermajority thresholds via fraction or percentage requirements, often accompanied by relative multiplicands.[24] A statute may require a "two-thirds majority" instead of "six votes." Such systems aim at allowing the court to adapt to absences by setting a majority that presumably does not increase through a de facto threshold distortion.

Fractional models require a simple mathematical conversion to determine a concrete number of votes. In its standard version with relative denominators, the fractional model presents the advantage of adaptability. The supermajority may be less mobile in certain situations. Recusals and short or long-term absences may impact the court less meaningfully.

---

backed chair at the end of the bench, and another judge will step down at the end of her term in little over a month. By law six votes - a two-thirds majority of the full nine-member bench - are needed to uphold the impeachment, however many judges are sitting. That effectively means that from March 14, Park will need the backing of only two justices to return to the presidential Blue House - and most have conservative political allegiances." *Emptying South Korea Court Offers Park Geun Hye a Lifeline*, The Straits Times, Sept. 2, 2017, https://www.straitstimes.com/asia/east-asia/emptying-south-korea-court-offers-park-geun-hye-a-lifeline (last visited Feb. 24, 2023).

20 For a full development of this argument, *see* Chapter 5.1.2.1.

21 César Landa, *Del Tribunal de Garantías al Tribunal Constitucional: El Caso Peruano*, 2 Pensam. Const. 73, 84 (1995).

22 Yuri Tornero, *Estudio Liminar*, *in* Jurisprudencia Relevante del Tribunal de Garantías Constitucionales: Procesos de inconstitucionalidad 13, 39–40 (Constitutional Court of Peru ed., 2018).

23 I have reconstructed court membership in all cases based on the official compilation of the court's decisions. Tornero, *supra* note 22, at 55, 445.

24 It would be possible to design a fractional model with absolute multiplicands. For example, suppose there was a nine-member court. It would be possible to require "six votes" or "two-thirds of the court's members." The drafting would then be a simple matter of style, with no difference from the numerical model.

To illustrate, let us take a model similar to the 2015 transitory Polish supermajority. The rule required a two-thirds majority for the court *en banc*. In the fifteen-member court, the conversion implied ten votes. If such a court dropped to twelve members[25] due to appointment delays, eight judges would constitute the required supermajority.

Fractional models may have, in turn, two inconveniences. Often, fraction requirements tend not to produce integer numbers, which would either raise doubts about the required votes or diminish their efficacy in preventing the supermajority from increasing with absences. Let us turn back to the previous example. An absence would translate the two-thirds requirements into 9.33 votes in such a fifteen-member court. Presumably, decimals should be rounded up to the following higher integer number. Voting rules are minimum requirements. If a two-thirds threshold is required, nine votes would not satisfy the condition, as it would entail a 64.2 percent majority. The difference, infinitesimal as it is, implies the threshold has not been met. Upon one absence, the Polish supermajority would have required the same votes. Only upon two absences would the rule grant flexibility, becoming an 8.66 voting requirement, producing effectively a nine-vote supermajority. The adaptability of the system is contingent on court size.[26]

Secondly, depending on concrete configurations, supermajorities with relative multiplicands could allow for evading the supermajority requirement,[27] a phenomenon also known in legislative bodies[28] that may result in passing to minorities the body's decisional ability contingent on absences.[29] Some have argued against absolute multiplicands, claiming that in legislative bodies,

25 The example is merely illustrative and could not have occurred in Poland. The Law on the Constitutional Tribunal raised the quorum to 13 out of 15 judges. Piotr Tuleja, *The Polish Constitutional Tribunal*, *in* THE MAX PLANCK HANDBOOKS IN EUROPEAN PUBLIC LAW 619, 662 (Armin von Bogdandy, Peter M. Huber & Christoph Grabenwarter eds., 2020). Since only twelve judges were sitting on the tribunal, it was unable even to convene if the requirement was applied. WOJCIECH SADURSKI, POLAND'S CONSTITUTIONAL BREAKDOWN 73 (2019).

26 Take two frequent court compositions in supermajorities: a seven-member court—formerly Ohio and Czechoslovakia, and currently Nebraska and Peru—and a nine-member court—such as the Peruvian TGC or South Korea's Constitutional Court. In a seven-member court with a five sevenths supermajority, the rule would imply that the same five votes (4.28) are required upon one absence, and four if two members are absent (3.57). In a nine-member court with the classical two-thirds supermajority, with one absence, six votes would be required (5.33); with two absences, five (4.66); and with three absences, four votes.

27 *See supra* note 10.

28 Bentham coined the term "danger of surprise" to label "every proposition the success of which has resulted from absence, and which would have been rejected in the full assembly." JEREMY BENTHAM, POLITICAL TACTICS 58 (Michael James, Cyprian Blamires & Catherine Pease-Watkin eds., 1999).

29 Furthermore, Condorcet also preferred absolute margin rules rather than percentages or proportions. MELISSA SCHWARTZBERG, COUNTING THE MANY: THE ORIGINS AND LIMITS OF SUPERMAJORITY RULE 74 (2013).

majorities should bear the costs for abstentionism.[30] The same argument does not apply in judicial bodies, where recusals are legally mandated and the remaining absences fortuitous, including deaths, appointment delays, among others.

Fractional requirements also may have further unintended consequences. In constitutional courts with mixed selection, fluctuations in court composition and nonfixed voting rules allow certain actors to influence the court's propensity to strike down legislation to a higher degree than intended.[31] Furthermore, if supermajorities are chosen on epistemic accounts, proportions may be counterproductive vis-à-vis absolute margin rules.[32]

The parliamentary procedure of the democratic 1982 Peruvian supermajority featured a debate on the issue. The Constitutional Commission of the Chamber of Deputies modified an initial proposal of requiring a two-thirds supermajority instead of the six-vote requirement, which ultimately prevailed. The Commission deemed that "to avoid that, given licenses or recusals, such majority [supermajority] would be arbitrarily reduced, the Commission has established both the quorum and the required majority taking into account the members of the court, and not percentages or parts of it."[33]

Fractional models are rare guests in supermajorities. The only model employing such a requirement from the jurisdictions analyzed was Poland. Even then, the high thirteen-member quorum significantly diminished its potential for providing flexibility, as its illiberal intent did not mean to produce a functional court. In the United States, some supermajority proposals have considered requiring percentages,[34] although none has been approved.

30 *Id.* at 187.

31 Lydia Brashear Tiede, Judicial Vetoes: Decision-Making on Mixed Selection Constitutional Courts 235 (2022). This was the case of the Czechoslovak Constitutional Court and the Peruvian TGC. Landa, *supra* note 21, at 99. Beyond our selected jurisdictions, the constitutional courts of Chile and South Korea have mixed selection, and function under supermajority rule.

32 List, *supra* note 9, at 535.

33 *See* Dictamen de la Comisión de Constitución en los Proyectos de Ley Referente a la Ley Orgánica del Tribunal de Garantías Constitucionales, Chamber of Deputies, Proy. Sen-Just. 10 y Proy. No. 669, 1ra Legislatura ordinaria de 1981, para. 4.

34 Caminker provides an exhaustive list of all supermajority proposals to the Supreme Court presented to Congress until 2003. As he notes, "the denominator sometimes refers to the total number of justices actually participating in the decision, and other times refers to the total number of justices on the Court even if one or more is not participating." *See* Evan H. Caminker, *Thayerian Deference to Congress and Supreme Court Supermajority Rules: Lessons from the Past*, 78 Indiana L.J. 73, 117–22 (2003).

6.1.3 Countering the Mobile Threshold Problem: Formal Rules and Informal Practices

Absences may lead to a de facto distortion of the consensus degree. Several jurisdictions have established replacement mechanisms destined to temper the problem. Others had previously established them and became beneficial once supermajorities were introduced. Furthermore, constitutional courts often employ several informal practices related to agenda-setting and docket control to tackle the issue. We will briefly examine those solutions.

6.1.3.1 Formal Rules

Some jurisdictions have instated formal rules to guarantee that a full court will sit when deciding cases under supermajority requirements. Two main mechanisms have been set up in the analyzed jurisdictions: substitute/surrogate judges and term prorogation with holdover judges. The historical supermajorities are excellent examples of both mechanisms.

Ohio was forced to engineer a replacement system after the 1912 supermajority produced absence-related problems. From 1912 to 1944, Ohio functioned with no replacement mechanism.[35] In *McBride v. White Motor Co*,[36] *Pennsylvania Railroad Company v. Pottery Company*,[37] and *State v. Chester*,[38] absences severely hindered the court. In a 6:1 supermajority, two absences effectively impeded judicial review.[39] The variations in the supermajority led scholars to suggest addressing the dilemma of absences openly.[40] Ohio's Judicial Council proposed an amendment to allow calling Court of Appeals judges to sit on the court.[41] The amendment was approved in 1944, shortly before the rule's repeal in 1968.

35 During the debates, delegates had seemingly agreed to require a supermajority of the judges sitting on the bench, but the formulation disappeared in the final draft. Ohio's 1912 Constitutional Convention. Fiftieth Day (Legislative Day of Apr. 2), 1029.

36 106 Ohio St. 366, 138 N.E.45 (1922). The decision was merely a couple of paragraphs: "Three of the members of this court as at present constituted, for personal reasons, declined to participate in the consideration or decision of this case . . . here being an insufficient number of judges concurring to reverse the judgment of the court of appeals same is hereby affirmed."

37 122 Ohio St. 503, 174 N.E.2 (1930).

38 42 N.E.2d 993 (Ohio 1942).

39 Jonathan L. Entin, *Judicial Supermajorities and the Validity of Statutes: How Mapp Became a Fourth Amendment Landmark Instead of a First Amendment Footnote*, 50 Case West. L. Rev. 441, 461 (2002).

40 William A. Eggers, *Influence of the Non-Participating Judge*, 5 U. Cin. L. Rev. 375, 378 (1931).

41 Entin, *supra* note 39, at 461.

North Dakota[42] and Nebraska were unaffected by absences. Both states allowed calling inferior judges or retired justices to sit on the Supreme Court, guaranteeing a full bench.[43]

The Czechoslovak Constitutional Court established substitute judges combined with a self-adopted holdover system. Substitutes could only replace the member they had been appointed to substitute. The predominant opinion at the time was that such a measure guaranteed the representation of the appointing body.[44] The system served as a remedy for temporary absences but not for the lack of new appointments. When the first judge's term expired in 1931 and no new appointments were made, the Court seemed destined to disappear. The original judges agreed to remain in office until new ones were elected, instating a de facto term extension system.[45] The government recognized the practice as legitimate.[46] The mechanism had only a moderate effect since several circumstances[47] diminished the number of judges sitting on the bench, and soon, the court was unable to convene.

Contemporary supermajorities have occasionally set term extensions to counter the problem of absences. Peru and the Dominican Republic employ holdover judges to avoid long-term absences resulting from appointment delays. In Peru, appointment delays[48] have been known to grant an extension of up to almost three years to former magistrates, while in the Dominican Republic, the prorogation system is combined with a fast-track substitute mechanism.[49]

42 In the case of North Dakota, a holdover system exists. Article V, Section 7 of the North Dakota Constitution provides that justices "shall hold office until their successors are duly qualified."

43 Such mechanisms did not merit comment for ROBERT D. MIEWALD & PETER JOSEPH LONGO, THE NEBRASKA STATE CONSTITUTION 105–107 (2011); JAMES E. LEAHY, THE NORTH DAKOTA STATE CONSTITUTION 125 (2011).

44 TOMÁŠ LANGÁŠEK, ÚSTAVNÍ SOUD ČESKOSLOVENSKÉ REPUBLIKY A JEHO OSUDY V LETECH 1920-1948 32 (2011).

45 JANA OSTERKAMP, VERFASSUNGSGERICHTSBARKEIT IN DER TSCHECHOSLOWAKEI (1920-1939): VERFASSUNGSIDEE, DEMOKRATIEVERSTÄNDNIS, NATIONALITÄTENPROBLEM 87 (2009).

46 The government was prompt to accept such an interpretation. After being informed of the decision, it continued punctually paying judges their remuneration. LANGÁŠEK, *supra* note 44, at 125.

47 For example, the retirement of Judges Konstantin Petrovič Mačík and Václav Vlasák. For a further analysis of all circumstances that rendered the court unable to convene, *see id.* at 125–27.

48 Lydia Brashear Tiede & Aldo Fernando Ponce, *Evaluating Theories of Decision-Making on the Peruvian Constitutional Tribunal*, 6 J. POLIT. LAT. AM. 139, 144 (2014).

49 Article 21 of the Act of the Constitutional Court provides that magistrates will remain on the bench until new magistrates have been appointed. In turn, Article 22 establishes that vacancies shall be covered within a maximum of two months by a substitute magistrate (*Juez Reemplazante*) who will finish the term of the magistrate he/she is tasked to replace. The "Juez Reemplazante" is even regulated by Article 187 of the Constitution.

While surrogate judges ensure a full court as proven by Ohio (1944–1968), North Dakota, and Nebraska,[50] holdover judges only aid in case of appointment delays of judges whose term has expired but leave the court vulnerable to other short-term or long-term absences, as proven by the Peruvian contemporary case.

All mechanisms come with some disadvantages. For example, one could argue that substitution mechanisms may distort the court's doctrine, and holdover judges allow a fair share of political maneuvering and may even discourage political consensus from producing timely appointments. In the case of surrogates, the appointment decision and surrogate eligibility may impact the case's outcome, and thus, the possibility of strategic behavior in some instances may not be wholly discarded.

Other formal means exist. In the case of the Nebraska Supreme Court, the notice required by § 2-109 (E) of Nebraska Court Rules of Appellate Practice for constitutional challenges is a further mechanism implemented by the court to ensure a full bench.

6.1.3.2 Informal Practices

Aside from formal mechanisms, constitutional courts often have some freedom in agenda-setting and docket control. Courts may possess discretion in case selection. Even under mandatory jurisdiction, courts may decide when to discuss and resolve cases.[51] Through agenda-setting, courts can, up to a certain extent, adapt to absences either by avoiding deciding certain cases that presumably would require a full court or informally postponing deliberation of a case. Instances of the latter as a response to absences are common in courts functioning with majority rule. As a recent example, upon Justice Scalia's death, the Republican-controlled Senate refused to consider Obama's nomination of Judge Garlan, leaving President Trump to fill the vacancy,[52] which lasted for over a year. The U.S. Supreme Court deferred consideration of several cases until a new justice was appointed.[53]

50 In Czechoslovakia, since every judge had a specific substitute, several extraordinary circumstances allowed both the judges and substitutes to be absent, leading to the court's temporary disappearance from 1931 to 1937. *See* Chapter 3.2.2.

51 Courts may employ "timing control" to issue decisions in more favorable times or circumstances. Diego Werneck Arguelhes & Ivar A. Hartmann, *Timing Control without Docket Control: How Individual Justices Shape the Brazilian Supreme Court's Agenda*, 5 J. L. Courts 105 (2017).

52 Peter J. Eckerstrom, *The Garland Nomination, the Senate's Duty, and the Surprising Lessons of Constitutional Text*, 21 Univ. Pa. J. Const. L. 22 (2018).

53 David Orentlicher, *Judicial Consensus: Why the Supreme Court Should Decide Its Cases Unanimously*, 54 Conn. L. Rev. 303, 333 (2022).

Postponing deliberation seems to be a standard practice in the Mexican and Czech supermajorities.[54] In the Mexican case, several justices have indicated the existence of an informal agreement in which, if one vote is missing to reach the supermajority, the voting is postponed if a justice is temporarily absent.[55]

Agenda-setting is effective mostly in countering short-term absences but ineffective in handling recusals or long-term absences. Even though a court may postpone a case for an extended period, this may have certain institutional costs. The case remains undecided, and the court is unable to perform its natural function in judicial review. Such a situation occurred in the Czech Republic when, in 2004, decimated by the lack of appointments, the Constitutional Court decided to stay all proceedings until further appointments were made to relieve a severe problem of absences.[56]

Not all courts have made use of agenda-setting possibilities. In Peru's TGC, magistrates often voted on contentious cases even upon absences. As early as 1986, some scholars noted that the court failed to employ its agenda-setting abilities to delay voting, waiting for a full court.[57] The lack of adjustments resulted in decisions that presumably would have changed upon a full court membership.

Finally, some courts have developed other supplementary arrangements. As explained in Chapter 4, after the Covid-19 pandemic, the Mexican Supreme Court kept allowing individual justices on leave to participate through video conference calls. In several cases, such as CC 44/2021 and AI 171/2022, a justice joined the Court through Zoom, while other justices participated *in situ*.

6.2 Justifying a Supermajority Threshold: An Empirical and Theoretical Debate

Supermajorities are often considered with undue uniformity. Threshold choice may presumably change the supermajority's impact. Every multimember court

54 Beyond our selected jurisdictions, the South Korean Constitutional Court has also employed agenda-setting to avoid problems caused by absences to the supermajority requirement. *See* Hong, *supra* note 19, at 201.

55 Inter alia, while discussing AI 36/2014 on September 23, 2014, Justice Pérez Dayán referred to "our agreement regarding that if we have seven votes, we need to wait until the eighth one." While discussing AI 88/2016 on August 20, 2019, the Chief Justice proclaimed after having reached a majority one vote short of achieving the supermajority requirement: "We will have to suspend the vote and wait until Justice Pardo returns to see if he supports the unconstitutionality."

56 Kosař and Vyhnánek, *supra* note 17, at 156.

57 Aníbal Quiroga, *El Tribunal de Garantías Constitucionales: Ante El Dilema de Ser o No Ser*, Themis Rev. Derecho 40, 44 (1986).

above five members[58] has two or more thresholds to choose from, exceeding majority rule.

In a seven-member court—such as in former Czechoslovakia or contemporary Nebraska and Peru—there are three options to establish a higher consensus threshold: 5:2, 6:1, and 7:0. The larger the court, the more options it has available. With its fifteen members, the Constitutional Court of the Czech Republic has up to six configurations of supermajority rules, plus unanimity. Which supermajority to choose? And why?

While analyzing threshold choice in legislative bodies, Schwartzberg considered that a lack of justification led supermajorities to be selected upon bargaining or picking.[59] In our case, most jurisdictions seem to have arrived at thresholds via the latter.

In Czechoslovakia, the legislature deemed it was evident that the importance of striking down normative acts merited a supermajority. The preparatory works reveal that unanimity was the originally desired requirement but fearing possible partisan behavior from the judge appointed by Carpathian Ruthenia,[60] lawmakers opted for a 5:2 supermajority. No explanation was given as to why a 5:2 and not a 6:1 supermajority was chosen. Almost eighty years later, in the Czech Republic, the 9:6 supermajority was justified as being "not so small that a change in the court's opinion does not require a substantial majority of judges, but not so big to block the development of the constitutional court's case law."[61] However, there was no explanation of why precisely nine votes generated such a desired outcome while a ten-vote supermajority was unable to do so.

In Mexico, the legislative commissions reduced President Zedillo's initial proposal of a nine-vote supermajority to an eight-vote rule. Neither the reports nor legislative discussions justified the chosen threshold. It remains unclear why President Zedillo deemed a 9:2 supermajority ideal, why the

58 In a two-member court, unanimity is the only possible majority decision. In a three-member court, unanimity is available (3:0), with 2:1 being the minimum majority. Finally, in a four-member court, only 3:1 produces a majority decision.

59 SCHWARTZBERG, *supra* note 29, at 150.

60 Langášek explained that many feared that the judge from Carpathian Ruthenia would make it impossible to strike down legislation from that region. LANGÁŠEK, *supra* note 44, at 32.

61 *See* the explanatory memorandum (*Důvodová zpráva*) to law 182/1993, https://bit.ly/43vieNz (last accessed Jun. 9, 2023). Furthermore, as Chapter 4 clarifies, that explanation was deemed to justify the supermajority to overturn precedent and to put the President of the Republic to trial, not to strike down legislation. Thus, even that mild justification was not initially conceived to justify a deferential degree.

Senate believed an 8:3 was superior to it,[62] or why the Chamber of Deputies agreed with that threshold laconically described as "adequate."[63]

The 1995 authoritarian supermajority in Peru was a product of a Fujimorist bargain and precise political calculation (see Chapter 5.3.4). The subsequently implemented 5:2 supermajority in 2002 seemed to return to estimates. There were no reasons justifying that such a threshold produced a more suitable deference level than majority rule or even why the existing 6:1 supermajority could not function effectively with unbiased magistrates, released from Fujimori's politically motivated appointments.

The supermajorities of Ohio,[64] the Dominican Republic, and the Peruvian 1982 supermajority share a similar experience. Even concerning the multiple proposals for introducing supermajorities in the United States, Caminker noted virtual silence concerning threshold justification.[65]

Most jurisdictions introduced supermajorities without addressing the reasons for threshold choice. While in some cases, debates, preparatory works, and political context allow inferring why supermajorities were adopted, the consensus degree embraced remains a mystery, probably a product of simple estimations.

6.2.1 Threshold Arbitrariness? Scholarly Discussion of Threshold Justification

Justifying the selected supermajority threshold presents conceptual challenges. It has been pointed out that supermajority rules in legislative bodies tend to select thresholds arbitrarily, contrary to simple majorities or unanimity, whose thresholds have clearer philosophical justifications.[66] The argument also seems to hold some weight when applied to supermajority rules in constitutional adjudication. Not only policymakers but also scholars analyzing supermajority rules have passed over the matter.[67]

62 *See* the Legislative Opinion of the Joint Constitutional and Legislative Studies Commission, Mexican Senate, Dec. 16, 1994: "With the same intention, we have reflected, within this joint commission, to reduce from 9 to 8 the voting quorum so decisions of the Supreme Court … may have general effects."

63 *See* the Legislative Opinion of the Joint Government and Constitutional Studies Commission, Mexican Chamber of Deputies, Dec. 20, 1994.

64 Ohio's unanimity proposal had a philosophical clear mistake justification. The final 6:1 threshold did not, as it seems to have been the product of a bargain to temper the proposal. *See* Ohio's 1912 Constitutional Convention, Fifty-First Day (Legislative Day of Apr. 2), 1064–65.

65 Caminker, *supra* note 34, at 101.

66 Melissa Schwartzberg, *The Arbitrariness of Supermajority Rules*, 49 Soc. Sci. Inf. 61 (2010).

67 For example, Caviedes recognizes the existence of a wide array of supermajority possibilities. Even though he argues that preventing false negatives may be dealt with "by calibrating supermajority rules downwards," he takes no position on the ideal threshold or how to determine it. Cristóbal Caviedes, *A Core Case for Supermajority Rules in Constitutional Adjudication*, 20 Int. J. Const. L. 1162, 1185 (2022). Castillo-Ortiz simply notes that the threshold should not be "too high." Pablo Castillo-Ortiz, *The Dilemmas of Constitutional Courts and the Case for a New Design of Kelsenian Institutions*, 39 L. Philos. 617, 640 (2020). Roznai proposes

Caminker is skeptical of the critique's applicability to judicial supermajorities. He notes that the arbitrariness critique applies to many other rules set in the Constitution[68] and, for that matter, to many legal rules—we might add. Why is the minimum age to vote 18, not 17 and 10 months? Or why is the maximum serving time for a determined felony six years instead of 5 years, 11 months, and twenty-nine days? Why amend the Constitution through a two-thirds and not a 69 percent majority? Many legal values are set as approximate estimates of the goal to achieve.

In turn, Gersen and Vermeule, proposing a supermajority to guarantee deference to statutory interpretation by administrative agencies, considered that supermajorities allow calibrating a court's deference by increasing or decreasing the threshold.[69] Even though they do not offer a concrete justification for a threshold, they argue that different voting percentages can be categorized into different deferential standards from which to choose.[70] Their work suggests that, while assessing thresholds *a priori* is imprecise, empiric experience allows calibrating to find an ideal supermajority for a given court.[71]

6.2.2 Searching for Objective Thresholds

Even though the arbitrariness objection may seem substantial, several approaches might be explored in search of objective threshold choice under relevant underlying reasons. It would be possible to conceive of a supermajority primarily aimed at ending bare majority decisions, supplemented with minimal deference. Shugerman's proposal of a 6:3 supermajority for the United States Supreme Court relied heavily on the 5:4 ideological distribution at the time, producing controversial bare majority decisions overturning acts of Congress.[72] The goal of preventing bare majorities from striking down

---

a two-thirds supermajority as a general model without tackling the threshold's justification. Yaniv Roznai, *Introduction: Constitutional Courts in a 100-Years Perspective and a Proposal for a Hybrid Model of Judicial Review*, 14 ICL J. 355, 366 (2021). Sitaraman and Epps offer some explanation in their proposal of supermajority rules for the U.S. Supreme Court. Their understanding of the threshold proposed passes directly by the current court composition. Daniel Epps & Ganesh Sitaraman, *How to Save the Supreme Court*, 129 YALE L.J. 148, 184 (2019).

68 Caminker, *supra* note 34, at 102.

69 Jacob E. Gersen & Adrian Vermeule, *Chevron as a Voting Rule*, 116 YALE L.J. 676, 702 (2007).

70 *Id.* at 701–702.

71 Some scholars have argued that the evaluation of supermajority threshold requirements is context-dependent. Matt Qvortrup & Leah Trueblood, *The Case for Supermajority Requirements in Referendums*, 21 INT. J. CONST. L. 187, 203 (2023).

72 Jed Handelsman Shugerman, *A Six-Three Rule: Reviving Consensus and Deference on the Supreme Court*, 37 GA. L. REV. 893, 906 (2003).

legislation provides a specific number of votes for any multimember court: the majority plus one.[73]

In systems in which supermajorities were introduced to a preexisting constitutional framework, one could also make a case for employing the threshold established for constitutional amendments. While the amendment threshold remains mathematically unjustified,[74] the supermajority would not set an arbitrary threshold. The rule would employ a preexisting threshold symbolizing consensus in a different framework. The practice may reinforce constitutional values, underscoring that invalidating statutes is a constitutional decision.[75] One could even hypothesize further arguments justifying the employment of the amendment's threshold for the supermajority, such as the function of constitutional interpretation as constitutional change[76] or constructing a doctrine that employs seemingly arbitrary parameters as internal structures to create coherent thresholds.[77]

Finally, the threshold may be supplemented by considering other features of a constitutional system. Suppose a jurisdiction has staggered terms for justices. In that case, a supermajority can be set not allowing the blocking minority to be constituted by the possible ordinary number of appointments

73 A supermajority, solely to preclude bare majorities, would lead to a 5:2 rule in a seven-member court; in a nine-member court, to a 6:3 supermajority; in an eleven-member court, it would lead to a 7:4 supermajority; in a fifteen-member court, it would lead to a nine-vote supermajority.

74 Schwartzberg, *supra* note 66, at 66.

75 Some countries employ a similar threshold for courts to invalidate laws as for legislative bodies to approve constitutional amendments. In the Czech Republic, a three-fifths vote is required to amend the Constitution (60 percent), precisely the threshold for the Czech Constitutional Court to overturn an act of Parliament. The Peruvian Constitution requires an absolute majority in two successive legislatures plus a referendum. For Congress to rescind the referendum, requires a two-thirds supermajority, translating into the current five-vote supermajority (4.66). Constitutional revision assemblies require a two-thirds supermajority in the Dominican Republic, which would again preserve the current nine-vote supermajority (8.66 votes). For Mexico, the requirements translate to a 7.33 supermajority. Depending on the rounding, the rule would translate to seven or eight-vote requirements, consistent with the current version of the rule. Beyond our selected jurisdictions, South Korea's Constitution requires the same supermajority for amending the Constitution as for the court to strike down legislation (two-thirds).

76 For an argument on how constitutional interpretation gives rise to a new understanding of the constitutional text that generates new rules, *see* Zachary Elkins, Tom Ginsburg & James Melton, The Endurance of National Constitutions 29 (2009).

77 Take, for instance, the doctrine of proportionality in criminal law. Through ordinals and cardinals, criminal law doctrine has employed a preexisting sanction to create a scale to evaluate the coherence of penalties. Andrew von Hirsch, *Proportionality in the Philosophy of Punishment*, 16 Crime Justice 55, 77–85 (1992). Thus, one could claim that even though the initially qualified consensus set forth by the Constitution may be arbitrary, it is still possible to use it as a reference to create a coherent margin of consensus requirements for other purposes.

political branches are likely to sanction during one term in office to discourage partisan strategic calculations.[78]

6.3 Court Paralysis in Practice: The Start of an Empiric Discussion

From John Marshall[79] to Fujimori's opponents,[80] from early[81] to contemporary scholars,[82] and even among international advisory bodies,[83] it has been frequently argued that supermajorities carry substantial risks of court paralysis. The objection is as old as supermajority rules themselves.

A higher threshold might hinder the court's ability to perform judicial review or disable it altogether. This claim has been labeled the *paralysis argument*.[84] Formulating a definition of the paralysis argument presents multiple challenges. Although the concept seems intuitive, it lacks a measurable indicator in supermajorities. What exactly is paralysis?

In decisional supermajorities, court paralysis theoretically should be easier to identify. A too-high threshold would disable the court from deciding. If a court is unable to issue any decision within a year, it certainly should be

78 As early as 1973, scholars considered the influence of the executive branch in appointing justices as a factor to consider in supermajority rules. Stewart T. Herrick, James J. Higgins & Nancy R. Tarlow, *Five-Four Decisions of the United States Supreme Court: Resurrection of the Extraordinary Majority*, 7 Suffolk Univ. L. Rev. 807, 836–37 (1973).

79 John Marshall, letter of Dec. 22, 1823 to Henry Clay. A digitalized copy is available at the Gilder Lehrman Institute of American History, gilderlehrman.org/collection/glc00141 (last accessed Jun. 9, 2023).

80 Peruvian Congress, *see* Parliamentary Debates, 13th Session, Wednesday, Oct. 5, 1994, 974.

81 *See* Carl L. Meier, *Power of the Ohio Supreme Court to Declare Laws Unconstitutional*, 5 U. Cin. Rev. 293, 300 (1931) (arguing that achieving the supermajority is "extremely difficult").

82 Shugerman, *supra* note 72, at 985 (arguing that "An overly burdensome degree of consensus effectively would be a checkmate against the essential power [of judicial review]"). Castillo-Ortiz, *supra* note 67 (claiming that too high a threshold may paralyze the court). Roznai, *supra* note 67, at 371 (noting that "the higher the consensus requirement, the more paralyzed the court may be and the more difficult it will be to declare legislation as unconstitutional"). Ryan D. Doerfler & Samuel Moyn, *Democratizing the Supreme Court*, 109 Calif. L. Rev. 1703, 1773 (2021) (arguing that a supermajority rule would disempower the Supreme Court in contestable constitutional cases by requiring a higher threshold of consensus).

83 The Venice Commission warned that supermajorities carry the risk of paralyzing the courts while addressing the proposals in the Polish and Georgian cases. *See* Venice Commission, *Opinion No. 833/2015 on Amendments to the Act of 25 June 2015 on the Constitutional Tribunal (CDL-AD(2016)001*, 25 (2016); Venice Commission, *Preliminary Opinion 849/2016 on the Amendments to the Organic Law on the Constitutional Court and to the Law on Constitutional Legal Proceedings*, 10 (2016). In turn, Biden's advisory Commission on Amendments to the United States Supreme Court differed: "No matter how the requirement is designed, a supermajority voting requirement is likely to affect only a limited number of cases as a practical matter." Presidential Commission on the Supreme Court of the United States, *Final Report*, 288 176 (2021), https://www.whitehouse.gov/pcscotus/ (last visited May 25, 2022).

84 Rivera León, *supra* note 16.

considered "paralyzed" by any standard. Rarely does paralysis come in such a crystal clear presentation. How many cases suffice to proclaim paralysis?

The problem is equally persistent in deferential supermajorities. Since deferential supermajorities often comprise default rules that either uphold the law or dismiss a case, the supermajority does not "paralyze" the court in the sense that decisional supermajorities do. Nonetheless, a too-high threshold could presumably lead to the court rendering decisions too often by impasse rules.

Defining "court paralysis" by setting a concrete percentage of supermajority failure decisions is nearly impossible. Every constitutional system has different features, which in turn produce unconstitutionality rate variations. Just as there is no "ideal" unconstitutionality rate a constitutional court should achieve, there is no ideal supermajority failure decision rate.

Acknowledging the aforementioned concerns, this study defines court paralysis as a state where supermajority rules directly or indirectly lead the court to be substantively unable to perform its primary function in judicial review effectively.

Paralysis is not to be singly understood as a binary state but has a broader spectrum of nuanced degrees that must be contextually assessed vis-à-vis court workload, political factors, functions, and quality of the constitutional challenges, inter alia. Even if such degrees are indeterminate, it is expected that paralysis should produce plainly perceptible and quantifiable impacts, either by the court's inability to issue judgments or by the preponderance of decisions issued in accordance with impasse rules. In this way, court paralysis is characterized by functional stagnation and high rates of decisional discrepancy between the court's majority and its decisions.

Testing the paralysis argument requires both qualitative and quantitative analysis to verify if the imposed supermajorities significantly affect the court's ability to reach the required consensus, isolating their impact from other elements of institutional design.[85]

Furthermore, engaging in an actual comparative exercise to assess whether courts functioning under supermajority rules behave similarly to those under simple majority rules is complex. Comparison of what would presumably be ideal indicators, such as unconstitutionality percentages, is particularly hard given the significant variations in institutional design that invariably impact court outcomes and unconstitutionality rates.[86]

85 *Id.*
86 Tiede and Ponce, *supra* note 48, at 156.

6.3.1 *Threshold Impact: A First Overview*

Rousseau deemed that "various uneven divisions" existed between majority rule and unanimity.[87] Supermajorities are not monolithic but vary greatly depending on thresholds and other elements of institutional design. Gersen and Vermeule posited that diverse thresholds produce different degrees of deference.[88] This section offers a threshold typology. Subsequently, employing qualitative black-letter methodology, I will overview if certain types of thresholds are associated with jurisdictions that are considered to possess functional institutions of judicial review. In the second place, I will then endeavor to provide a more nuanced statistical analysis of the rule's impact in the selected jurisdictions.

6.3.1.1 A Threshold Typology

Supermajorities are rules exceeding the ordinary majority threshold. From our analyzed examples, different jurisdictions chose options ranging from 60 percent to 85.7 percent. Based on the comparative analysis, there are generally three levels of consensus/deference: moderate, strong, and unanimity-like.

I deem moderate thresholds a supermajority below 70 percent of the court. Such thresholds oscillate typically between 60–69.99 percent. In our selected jurisdictions, moderate thresholds usually call for merely an additional vote beyond a simple majority, with the Dominican Republic being the exception.

The category was drafted considering that most constitutional courts provide majority thresholds inferior to 60 percent[89] but would exceed that threshold (remaining mostly inferior to 70 percent) upon introducing a supermajority rule that merely precludes bare majorities, demanding an additional vote.[90]

87 Jean-Jacques Rousseau, Rousseau: The Social Contract and Other Later Political Writings 125 (Victor Gourevitch ed., 2 ed. 2018).

88 Gersen and Vermeule, *supra* note 69, at 702.

89 Let us exemplify with ordinary configurations from our selected jurisdictions: seven-member court (57.1 percent), nine-member court (55.5 percent), eleven-member court (54.5 percent), and fifteen-member court (53.3 percent). The only exception is a five-member court, whose reduced number renders a 60 percent ordinary majority threshold. The categories may be generalizable to jurisdictions outside our sample. Considering eighteen post-communist constitutional courts, Ginsburg's data accounts for nine-member and fifteen-member courts to appear most frequently. Courts under seven or over fifteen justices are rare. Tom Ginsburg, *Economic Analysis and the Design of Constitutional Courts*, 3 Theor. Inq. L. 49, 75–76 (2002). Brashear provides a list of seventy-nine constitutional courts under mixed selection. A nine-member court is by far, the most popular configuration. Configurations under seven judges and above fifteen judges are scarce. *Cf.* Tiede, *supra* note 31, at 239–54. The data allows us to reasonably assume that configurations up to fifteen-member courts would cover a significant amount of jurisdictions.

90 The first possible supermajority in a nine-member court is 66 percent; in an eleven-member court, 63 percent; in a thirteen-member court, 61 percent; and in a fifteen-member court,

Within this model, the lowest supermajority is that of the Czech Republic (60 percent), followed by TGC Peru, as well as the Polish and Georgian supermajorities that were never applied—all above at 66.6 percent. The strongest moderate supermajority is the decisional model of the Constitutional Court of the Dominican Republic, lying at the border of the metric (69.2 percent).

A second set of supermajorities employ what the typology deems a strong deference/consensus threshold, lying within the range of 70 percent to 80 percent, not inclusive. In devising this category, I selected the naturally segmented inferior borderline, while the upper limit was drawn to map those jurisdictions still permitting the existence of a dismissible minority proportional to court size. Within this model, the former Czechoslovakia, Nebraska, and the contemporary Peruvian supermajority established 71.4 percent, while Mexico represents 72.7 percent.

Finally, a last set of jurisdictions employs a unanimity-like threshold. Unanimity-like thresholds equal or exceed 80 percent of the court, surpassing the previous category borderline, but remain under unanimity requirements. These are the cases of North Dakota (with an 80 percent supermajority), Ohio, and the Peruvian Fujimorist supermajority (at 85.7 percent). In all these models, a single dissent is the limit after which the threshold is not met. Contingent to court size, such a characteristic would disappear in odd courts equaling or surpassing eleven members.[91]

In many jurisdictions, practical shortcomings of a unanimity-like threshold may closely resemble those posed by the unanimity rule,[92] particularly when coping with even a few partisan or not pluralistic appointments.

An objection could be drawn that the proposed typology lacks conceptual grounds to distinguish edge cases, especially in boundary areas where categories hinge on minimal percentage differences. Nonetheless, an attempt to produce an objective typology has been offered with substantial justification for each category's inferior and upper borderline. The typology relies on established academic practices employing standardized parameters for a systematic analysis.

---

60 percent. Seven or five-member courts are an exception, as their small membership distorts percentages, although a seven-member court ranges closely, at 71.4 percent.

91 In a nine-member court, an 80 percent threshold would result in 7.2 votes, which would be rounded up to eight votes. Thus, two dissents would prevent invalidating legislation.

92 Namely, problems generated by a single erroneous or self-interested member. SCHWARTZBERG, *supra* note 29, at 105. Schwartzberg's claim could be translated to judicial settings in factors such as partisanship, peculiar judicial philosophies, among others.

6.3.1.2 Qualitative Overview

Previous to an statistical analysis to assess the impact of supermajorities, a qualitative analysis may help provide a first overview of the matter in the selected jurisdictions and contextualize the subsequent results.[93]

I have classified the examined supermajorities according to their perceived functionality:[94] highly, moderately, marginally or minimally functional, and nonfunctional. I omitted the transitory supermajorities of Poland and Georgia in the assessment as they were never consistently applied.[95]

The attained classification is based on scholarship consensus on the rule's impact on the court's primary ability to perform judicial review, not on its statistical occurrence. For example, since there is a prevailing consensus in Ohio's case (see Chapter 3), I classify it as marginally functional despite that, numerically, the rule did not affect the outcome of many cases. Conversely, I classified Czechoslovakia as highly functional, even though features external to the supermajority limited the role of the constitutional court.[96] As statistically shown in the following subsection, the supermajority barely hindered the court.

93 The classification is based on the scholarly assessment of the respective jurisdictions described in Chapters 3 and 4. Since court functionality is a perceived matter of degree, I have deemed a court to be highly functional when it has consistently delivered decisions within the supermajority threshold, attaining minimal or no hindering in its judicial review capabilities aside from sporadic instances. Moderately functional courts can generally function within the threshold but face occasional challenges that still pose no considerable threat to judicial review. Marginally functional courts are those struggling to achieve the supermajority threshold, experiencing consistent difficulties in rendering decisions ungoverned by impasse rules. Minimally functional courts are those in which the threshold substantially hinders the court's function. Finally, I deem nonfunctional those courts directly or indirectly incapacitated by the supermajority rule in their judicial review functions.

94 The classification pertains singly to procedures/cases in which the supermajority is applicable. In some jurisdictions, a supermajority applies to all cases before a court, as in the Dominican Republic or Czechoslovakia. In other jurisdictions, the rule is required in specific procedures—as in Mexico or Chile—or in specific cases—such as in Nebraska, North Dakota, and formerly Ohio, in which the rule was only applicable when the court considered the constitutionality of statutes. It would be imprecise to consider cases under majority rule as part of a court's supermajority workload to assess the impact of the supermajority threshold.

95 The Constitutional Courts of Poland and Georgia declared supermajority rules unconstitutional and did not apply them. While these episodes are valuable in understanding the motives and intentions of introducing supermajorities, their examples lack any implications regarding the empirical impact of supermajority rules on courts.

96 Kosař and Vyhnánek, *supra* note 17, at 123–24.

The results are condensed in Table 6.1, allowing a broad comparison of threshold levels[97] and perceived qualitative functionality of judicial review institutions with other factors of institutional design, including court size.[98]

Table 6.1 Supermajorities and Threshold Strength

Jurisdiction	*Threshold level %*	*De facto mobile*	*Classification*	*Court size*	*Relevant experience*	*Functionality level*
Peru Fujimorist	85.7	Yes	Near-unanimity	Medium	Yes	NF
Ohio	85.7	Yes	Near-unanimity	Medium	Yes	Mar. F
North Dakota	80	No	Near-unanimity	Small	Yes	HF
Mexico	72.7	Yes	Strong	Large	Yes	MF
Czechoslovakia	71.4	Yes	Strong	Medium	Yes	HF
Nebraska	71.4	No	Strong	Medium	Yes	HF
Peru contemporary	71.4	Yes	Strong	Medium	Yes	MF
Dominican Republic	69.2	Yes	Moderate	Large	Yes	HF
Peru TGC	66.6	Yes	Moderate	Medium	Yes	Mar. F
Poland	66.6	No	Moderate	Large	No	-
Georgia	66.6	Yes	Moderate	Medium	No	-
Czech Republic	60	Yes	Moderate	Large	Yes	HF

Two of the three unanimity-like supermajorities have equaled or neared nonfunctionality: Ohio[99] and the Fujimorist Peruvian supermajority.[100] Only North Dakota has produced a highly functional court able to place checks on the legislative branch.

97 Regardless of requirement mechanics, I provide supermajority thresholds calculated as percentages over the full court to allow cross-comparison. I classify as de facto mobile supermajorities those lacking an effective replacement system or relative multiplicands (*i.e.*, jurisdictions where absences can increase the supermajority threshold). By relevant experience, I understand whether the rules were applied by courts, thereby providing material for assessing their impact.

98 In smaller courts, deliberation and bargaining may be more accessible, but each vote carries greater weight than in medium and larger courts. Peculiarities attributed to a single justice may have an disproportionate impact that would not occur in larger courts in cases usually deemed noncontroversial. I deem as small a court with up to five members, as medium a court with up to ten members, and as large a court with more than ten members. Ginsburg's previous study indicates that constitutional courts (set up under the 1989–2002 period) have an 11.25 mean of justices, while Supreme Courts with constitutional review powers have a mean of 8.25. Ginsburg, *supra* note 89, at 64. Since a five-member court is the smallest court configuration employing supermajority rules and the largest court in our sample possesses fifteen justices (Czechia and Poland), I have divided the court size into thirds using the smallest court membership as a reference pattern, which would match Ginsburg's margins. My category is not deemed to be a generalized assessment of the constitutional courts' size worldwide.

99 Entin, *supra* note 39, at 466–68; Shugerman, *supra* note 72, at 956–60.

100 Eduardo Dargent, *Determinants of Judicial Independence: Lessons from Three 'Cases' of Constitutional Courts in Peru (1982–2007)*, 41 J. LAT. AM. STUD. 251, 268–71 (2009). In the case of the Fujimorist supermajority, the rule—and its evasion attempt in preventing Fujimori's reelection—arguably resulted in a massive court crisis, leading to the impeachment of three Magistrates and broader court paralysis.

Several factors could account for some of these failures. At least in the case of Ohio, other causes unrelated to the supermajority influenced its lack of success,[101] although a similar argument could inversely be made for the only unanimity-like functional supermajority.[102] The above does not preclude concrete formulations of unanimity-like supermajorities, such as North Dakota, from being perceived as functional under specific contexts.

The cases of strong and moderate supermajorities vary drastically vis-à-vis unanimity-like supermajorities. Strong consensus/deference supermajorities have existed in four moderately functional and highly functional courts: Mexico, the Dominican Republic, Czechoslovakia, Nebraska, and the contemporary Peruvian model. Moderate supermajorities have only one example of a failed system—the Peruvian TGC marginally functional supermajority.[103]

Again, even in Peru's TGC case, the supermajority was severely increased by the constant absences of magistrates through deaths, appointment delays, and sick leaves. If we examine the situation de facto, the threshold would be higher. However, similar examples exist in jurisdictions classified as functional, such as the former Czechoslovakia[104] and the Czech Republic.[105]

6.3.2 Nuanced Court Paralysis

Having explored institutional design elements and provided a qualitative dimension, our inquiry turns to empirical statistical evidence to complement the assessment.[106]

Table 6.2 reflects the statistical impact of supermajority rules in courts. The Table provides supermajority failure decision rates—the proportion of decisions in which the supermajority prevented striking down legislation as confronted with the total decisions issued under supermajority requirements. The sample

101 In Ohio, a relevant factor was the sabotage of the rule by the Supreme Court and the fact that delegates opted for a supermajority possessing different thresholds depending on the decision issued by the Court of Appeals.

102 North Dakota has fewer than a million inhabitants. One could claim that the North Dakota Supreme Court resolves fewer cases under supermajority rule than constitutional or Supreme Courts. Furthermore, being a subnational supermajority, it is possible to argue that federal courts can still guarantee rights or perform an alternative review even if the supermajority would be too high, provided a federal question arises.

103 Landa, *supra* note 21, at 81–83.

104 In almost half of its cases, Czechoslovakia had a de facto threshold of roughly 80 percent.

105 The intricate political procedure for the Senate to confirm justices nominated by the President has generated constant absences within the court. In 2004, the court even had to issue a stay in constitutional procedures requiring a supermajority since the court was functioning with only eleven justices. The court declared it would only session again once a twelfth justice was appointed. The 2004 episode is the most extreme example, but other appointment delays have varied the supermajority. Thus, even if normatively the Czech threshold is moderate, in practice, it has often behaved as a strong one and, for a few months, has resembled a unanimity-like threshold.

106 Rivera León, *supra* note 16.

Table 6.2 Supermajorities in the selected jurisdiction: Institutional Design and Impact on Courts

Jurisdiction	*Votes required*	*Threshold level %*	*Supermajority type*	*De facto mobile*	*Classification*	*Court size type*	*Relevant experience*	*SFD Rate %*	*Period*	*Sample Size*	*Functionality level*
Peru Fujimorist	6/7	85.7	Def.	Yes	Near-unanimity	Medium	Yes	17.6	(1996-1998)	17	NF
Ohio	6/7	85.7	Def.	Yes	Near-unanimity	Medium	Yes	5.2	(1920-1936)	189	Mar. F
North Dakota	4/5	80	Def.	No	Near-unanimity	Small	Yes	2.77	(1992-2022)	144	HF
Mexico	8/11	72.7	Def.	Yes	Strong	Large	Yes	10.1	(1995-2022)	1357	MF
Czechoslovakia	5/7	71.4	Def.	Yes	Strong	Medium	Yes	2.1	(1920-1938)	47	HF
Nebraska	5/7	71.4	Def.	No	Strong	Medium	Yes	0.77	(1992-2022)	260	HF
Peru contemporary	5/7	71.4	Def.	Yes	Strong	Medium	Yes	6.1	(2004-2023)	489	MF
Dominican Republic-P	9/13	69.2	Dec.	Yes	Moderate	Large	Yes	< 7.97	(2013-2022)	7662	MF
Peru TGC	6/9	66.6	Dec.	Yes	Moderate	Medium	Yes	33.3	(1982-1992)	15	Mar. F
Poland	10/15	66.6	Dec.	No	Moderate	Large	No	-	-	-	-
Georgia	6/9	66.6	Def.	Yes	Moderate	Medium	No	-	-	-	-
Czech Republic-P	9/15	60	Def.	Yes	Moderate	Large	Yes	1.9–5.44	(1993-2015)	367	HF

* *"P" represents "Proxy"*

size and the period from which such data is calculated, as well as the supermajority type are also presented. The table additionally provides the qualitative assessment of the supermajority's functionality as offered by the previous subsection.

6.3.2.1 Overview of the Impact of Supermajority Rules in Decisional and Deferential Supermajorities

Thresholds impact decisional and deferential supermajorities differently.[107] *Ceteris paribus*, decisional supermajorities theoretically should impact the court more significantly. Decisional supermajorities employ the same threshold to strike down legislation and uphold it. Since it is reasonable to assume courts statistically would uphold legislation in a significant number of cases, deferential supermajorities often function under majority rule. In contrast, decisional supermajorities require summoning a qualified majority in all cases.

Data is elusive in decisional supermajorities. Decisional supermajorities appear less frequently than deferential ones. From the analyzed jurisdictions, only the Peruvian TGC, the Dominican Constitutional Court, and Poland's 2015 transitory supermajority qualify as such. Poland's, having never been applied, cannot be used to assess the potential impact of decisional supermajorities. Furthermore, given that the traditional consequence of not achieving the required majority is that the case remains undecided,[108] decisional supermajorities present critical challenges in assessing the rule's impact on a court. In many cases, it would be complicated to determine whether the supermajority was applied.

As portrayed by Table 6.1, the available information is inconclusive. There are strong signs that the Dominican decisional supermajority has functioned well with with a proxy SFD rate of under 7.97 percent[109] operating with a

107 In the following analysis, I will use the abbreviation SFD to refer to "supermajority failure decisions." An SFD rate is the proportion of SFD within the total cases the court resolves under supermajority requirements.

108 Alternatively, as Krishnamurthi says: "no judgment will be reached." Guha Krishnamurthi, *For Judicial Majoritarianism*, 22 U. Pa. J. Const. L. 1201, 1233 (2019). *See also* Robert E. Goodin & Christian List, *Special Majorities Rationalized*, 36 Br. J. Polit. Sci. 213, 215 (2006).

109 The book turned to proxy analysis through the court's docket. The court does not detail average or individual case length statistics, thus, the calculations employed yearly clearance reports. Proxy calculations assumed cases resolved outside the yearly term to be delayed due to the lack of supermajority consensus. The assumption, used to illustrate a possible maximum limit, is untrue. The court may take over a year to decide due to case complexity, Judge-Rapporteur's delay, avoidance, or court strategic behavior such as timing control. While the proxy is unreliable in determining an accurate rate of supermajority failure decisions, it provides a likely absolute maximum rate of SFD, although prone to overrepresentation for the aforementioned factors. If we consider the existence of a margin of error, the rate might be much lower. Other institutions in the Dominican Republic have recently reported inferior clearance rates working under majority rule. In its last 2023 statistical report, the Supreme Court reported the following clearance rate for its subdivisions: First Chamber (65.15 percent), Second Chamber (144.42 percent), Third Chamber 69.22 percent, Joint Chambers (54.14 percent), Plenary (68.94 percent). The Supreme Court had an average

69.2 percent consensus threshold. Furthermore, SFD rates in the Dominican Republic portray theoretical instances of delay in yearly clearance rates. Cases potentially affected by SFDs may still be solved within reasonable periods. However, one may impeach the reliability of proxy analysis absent concrete information on internal court protocols and procedure lengths. Conversely, the Peruvian TGC sample is not representative, but its 33 percent SFD rate appears to convey that a significant hindrance to the court's functionality occurred. Finally, the Polish case was never operative, but its configuration makes it reasonable to assume that the rule would have significantly hindered the court had it been regularly applied, at least in the context in which it was introduced, with a high quorum requirement amidst court-packing.

Further analysis would be required on other decisional supermajorities to produce more accurate data. The task will be challenging as decisional supermajorities do not tend to allow gathering the accurate insights the Peruvian TGC's peculiar interpretation granted us, and docket proxy analysis calls for careful consideration.

Conversely, deferential supermajorities statistically exhibited low SFD rates, except for the Fujimorist supermajority with a near-unanimity 85.7 percent threshold. Other deferential supermajorities seem to have low rates of supermajority failure decisions, most closely approximating 5 percent with marginal variations. North Dakota (2.77 percent), Czechoslovakia (2.1 percent), and Nebraska (.77 percent) are jurisdictions in which the rule has a barely perceptible impact. Contemporary Peru (6.1 percent) and the proxy model for the Czech Republic (ranging from 1.9 percent–5.44 percent) also exhibit restrained signs of impact on the court.

Mexico is the deferential model possessing a higher SFD, with a 10.1 percent rate. Nonetheless, as previous analysis suggested, the rate overrepresents the rule's impact. Provision-based analysis with qualitative assessment has concluded that the supermajority had significantly impacted a case in Mexico in less than 6 percent of the cases the Court resolved in abstract review.[110] If we were to consider constitutional controversies that the methodology advocated to exclude, the rate would be even lower.[111]

Ohio is a puzzle. Although scholars portrayed Ohio's supermajority (1912–1968) as disproportionately impacting the court, the story is different

clearance of 75.86 percent. *See Informe Estadístico 2023 Labor Secretarial,* Poder Judicial de la República Dominicana, Santo Domingo, 2023, p. 13.

110 Rivera León, *supra* note 16.

111 As argued before, constitutional controversies have significant peculiarities that diminish the data's reliability in portraying the supermajority rule's impact on the court. For example, take a previously made comprehensive dataset of all constitutional controversies on federalism conflicts (690 decisions within the period from January 1, 1995 to June 21, 2022). Only on sixteen occasions (2.3 percent) has the supermajority saved any provision. If we analyze the impact per provision, those supermajority failure decisions protected 0.024 percent of the challenged provisions in all Federalism conflicts. Mauro Arturo Rivera León, *Los Retos de La Defensa Del Federalismo Mexicano Estándares Deferenciales y Asimetrías Procesales En Conflictos Normativos, in* Concurso Nacional de Ensayo sobre Federalismo 18, 35–37 (2023).

statistically. Data show the rule impacted seventeen cases[112] in fifty-six years. Fite and Rubinstein provided data for the 1912–1936 period, accounting for an SFD rate of 5.29 percent.[113] Only seven supermajority failure decisions were issued in the remaining thirty-two years of the rule's functioning, making drastic rate changes unlikely, considering SFDs are finite and the improbability of drastic docket reductions.[114] The highly critical evaluation of the rule can be attributed to the court's contentious attitude and unique double threshold, which impeded uniformity across the state. Perhaps the lack of uniformity, a quintessential function of an apex court, resulted in such a critical assessment despite its rare occurrence.

6.3.2.2 General Implications

Within the sample of analyzed jurisdictions, scholarship has somehow critically evaluated higher thresholds. As shown, in some jurisdictions with higher thresholds, high SFD rates appeared, aligned with the functionality assessment of such jurisdictions in the literature. This fact is also present in other countries employing supermajorities beyond our selected jurisdictions. For the six-three supermajority in South Korea, Hong provided data[115] from which an SFD rate of 7.13 percent can be calculated. The near-unanimous Chilean Constitutional Court, requiring an 80 percent supermajority, has a high 28.5 percent SFD rate. In both countries, the threshold and SFD rates would be expected, taking into account their qualitative assessment in the literature.[116]

112 Entin, *supra* note 39, at 452–66. Shugerman, *supra* note 72, at 957.

113 Katherine B. Fite & Louis Baruch Rubinstein, *Curbing the Supreme Court: State Experiences and Federal Proposals*, 35 MICH. L. REV. 762, 774 (1937).

114 As a simple illustration, employing Fite's and Rubinstein's period as a proxy for the sample size, the court would have resolved 252 challenges to legislation in the remaining period. Thus, the second period would have a 2.7 percent SFD. The sample size estimations may be too conservative. Scholars detected an increased trend of state constitutional litigation from 1940 onwards, resulting in more constitutional cases being heard in State Supreme Courts. Robert A. Kagan & Gregory Elinson, *Constitutional Litigation in the United States*, *in* CONSTITUTIONAL COURTS IN COMPARISON: THE U.S. SUPREME COURT AND THE GERMAN FEDERAL CONSTITUTIONAL COURT 25, 29 (Ralf Rogowski & Thomas Gawron eds., 2016).

115 Hong, *supra* note 19, at 188.

116 South Korea is a highly functional jurisdiction. Chile is marginally functional in procedures requiring a supermajority. For South Korea, I rely mainly on Hong, *supra* note 19; Hahm, *supra* note 19. For Chile, I based the classification on TIEDE, *supra* note 31. I also relied on the report by the expert group on amending the constitutional court and the compiled dataset described in the Appendix. In Chile, the claim refers solely to the procedures in which a supermajority is required, constituting a small size of the court's docket. *Id.* at 93. Most of the constitutional court's jurisdiction pertains to individual complaints (*requerimiento de inaplicabilidad)* that may lead to inter partes effects. Only *erga omnes* effects demand a supermajority. The analysis does not posit that Chile's Constitutional Court is not functional. The 2019 Expert Group on amending the Constitutional Court concluded that "Declarations of unconstitutionality are necessary . . . The absence of unconstitutionality declarations breaks the model of judicial review. We deem the cause of this problem to be the high quorum required for the unconstitutionality (4/5, that is, eight votes)." Grupo de Estudio de Reforma al Tribunal Constitucional, *Informe Final*, 23 (2019).

As a threshold increases, the mathematical likelihood of attaining it decreases. In supermajorities, one might logically assume that consensus problems posed on courts by supermajorities should increase proportionally to threshold increment. That is not the case.

No significant correlation seems to appear between threshold strength and SFD rates, based on the data obtained from the analyzed jurisdictions. When the data[117] was subjected to elements of formal statistical analysis in the form of linear regression, the results portray the lack of relationship between threshold strength and supermajority failure decision occurrence. The value of R-squared (0.0084)[118] indicates a lack of correlation.[119]

Figure 6.1 illustrates the argument. The fact that the trendline fitted to the available datapoints is almost flat indicates that the two variables—supermajority threshold strength and SFD rate—are broadly independent from one another.

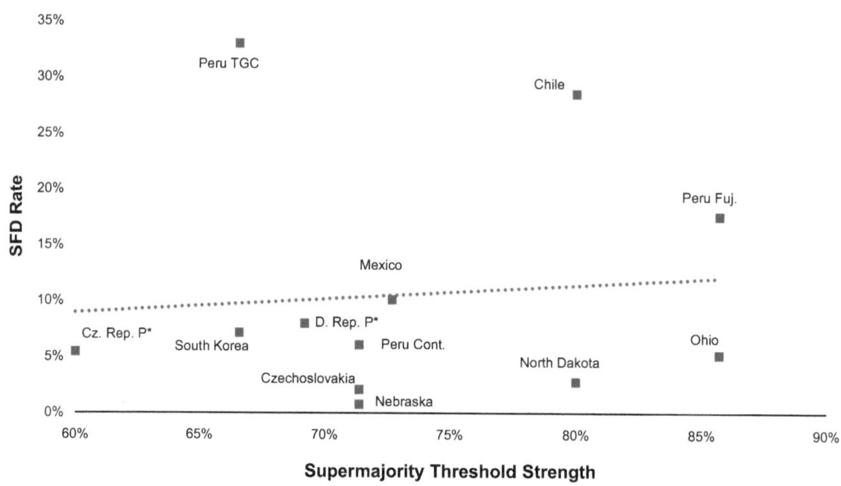

Figure 6.1 SFD Rate and Threshold Strength

117 To improve the representativeness of the results, Figure 6.1 considered the jurisdictions of Chile and South Korea, for which data is available on supermajority failure decisions. *See* the Appendix.

118 R-squared shows the proportion of the variation of the dependent variable attributable to the relationship. y= 0.1209x + 0.0169, or, in other words, how well the data supports the hypothesis of the existence of a presumed relationship. Thus, $R^2 = 0.0084$ suggests a weak or nonexistent relationship between the variables examined.

119 The validity of the model is limited due to the small sample (an inherent characteristic given the limited countries employing supermajority rules) and lack of formal model diagnostics. The analysis remains a preliminary exploration, which requires further studies. Additional limitations need to be acknowledged, such as a limited sample size for some jurisdictions and time period variability, inter alia.

In a nutshell, increasing or decreasing supermajority thresholds seems not to result automatically in significant SFD variations. The outliers, differing from most other data points, may be due to inherent features of these jurisdictions. The evidence suggests that simplistic claims attributing court paralysis solely to higher thresholds are unsupported by empirical analysis.

The results of many jurisdictions also suggest that, often, supermajority requirements do not substantially hinder courts. In many cases, supermajority rules merely shift a fraction of decisions from the courts to the elected branches, in the case of deferential supermajorities, or require additional effort, deliberation, and compromise to reach consensus in the case of decisional supermajorities.

Given that the threshold strength appears to exert minimal influence on SFD rates, the results might contradict a claim that ex ante, without nuanced considerations on other factors of institutional design, supermajorities lead to court paralysis.[120]

The absence of a strong direct relationship between threshold strength and SFD rates does not mean that the threshold strength is entirely unimportant but that it needs to be assessed in its interplay with many other factors that affect the functionality of courts under supermajority rules. Nuanced qualitative analysis is required to understand the rule's statistical impact. Political influence, historical evolution, and the broader interplay of institutional design features of a court affect the rule's functioning.

Institutional design of courts and informal practices. There is an immense interplay of institutional design features within a court. The higher a court's workload, the less time for deliberation and consideration of cases. Access to courts, remedies, features pertaining to justices' appointments and terms of office, discretionary jurisdiction, formal and informal internal court procedures, frequency of absences, and decision-drafting techniques, among other aspects, may substantively affect the rule's functioning. Chapters 3 and 4 provided several examples of how those factors produced substantively different outcomes in the rule's functioning, even in jurisdictions with similarly drafted supermajorities.

Collegiality tradition. The collegial tradition of a jurisdiction may impact the rule. A rooted history of dissenting opinions, court clashes, or personalization of figures, such as the cult status of justices, may negatively impact the rule. Collegial courts or jurisdictions without a dissent tradition operate in more favorable environments.

120 While the risk may not be substantial, court paralysis is indeed a possibility. Peru's TGC had strikingly high rates of supermajority failure decisions. Even if the data can be challenged as nonrepresentative, it still shows that the paralysis argument can prove true with unusually elevated normative or de facto thresholds in interplay with other elements of institutional design. The Peruvian TGC, despite a 66.6 percent requirement, had a de facto 79.68 percent supermajority, given the dynamics of absences, and functioned in a noncollegial court.

Influence of the political context. Courts in politically polarized environments may likely be affected by the rule to a higher degree than courts in neutral contexts. The Mexican supermajority in 2018–2022, under President López Obrador, has functioned in a court subjected to attacks from the political branches using confrontational rhetoric, threats of court-curbing, court-packing, and budget cuts. The political opposition has brought hundreds of challenges to the court. The Supreme Court functions with three justices that some depict as openly loyal to the regime. The polarization makes it likely that justices divide not only in legal opinions but also in considerations regarding strategic avoidance and deference in attempting to circumvent further escalation of the confrontation.

Another example of political influence is the cases of Nebraska and North Dakota. Both states have a long, strong Republican Party tradition. It is perhaps to be expected that democratic one-party dominance may tend to align the ideology and interpretation methods of the justices, producing more collegial courts if no mixed selection exists. In North Dakota, justices are elected in a nonpartisan election, while in Nebraska, justices, although appointed by the governor, are subject to a retention vote. The dynamic is expected to influence the court, tempering strong ideological disagreements, which might foster collegiality.

Limitations. This study acknowledges several limitations. Lacking an objective percentage that serves as a paralysis measurement, the definitive assessment of the impact of a supermajority requires a case-by-case analysis combined with, rather than determined by, SFD rate measurements. Furthermore, any analysis must be accompanied by a qualitative assessment of the impact on the court, mainly when providing more nuanced perspectives, such as counting the outcome of individual provisions and a qualitative assessment of the rule's impact on every case.

In the second term, the analysis in this chapter does not entirely refute nuanced versions of the paralysis argument. A refined version of the argument could be that the interplay of specific institutional design features, not present under majority rule, increases the likelihood of supermajority rules affecting the court's functioning significantly. This claim requires further research.

Furthermore, a statistical survey of instances in which supermajority rules protected legislation does not account for the full impact of such rules on courts. Judges may feel ex-ante constrained and dissuaded from proposing or voting on statutes' unconstitutionality when calculating that such a position will not meet the qualified threshold. The political branches may also tailor legislation differently, trusting supermajorities to supplement them with the deference it would not be granted under majority rule. Thus, while helpful, SFD rates cannot provide a comprehensive assessment of all possible impacts on courts generated by supermajority rules not reflected in instances of voting.

7 Conclusions

7.1 Main Findings

Constitutional courts have fascinated scholars from their inception. Nonetheless, their voting protocols, which determine the outcome of cases after deliberation, have been largely ignored. Although majority voting is the most common decision-making threshold, several jurisdictions employ supermajority rules.

Constitutional adjudication substantially impacts social and political life. Constitutional courts decide on contentious social topics such as abortion rights or religious freedoms, and determine key political issues such as reelection and state sovereignty. Whether they do so through majority or supermajority rules seems to be a meaningful difference. In many of the countries that have adopted supermajority rules, policymakers have sought to rebalance the constitutional court's position vis-à-vis the elected branches, establishing deferential or consensus mechanisms that shift decisions on disputed cases.

The functioning of such rules has been a pending area of research. This book has attempted to help fill that gap through a comparative analysis of supermajority rules in eight jurisdictions through twelve different models. The study has sought to gain more nuanced insights into the function of supermajority rules and the formal and informal mechanisms surrounding them. The following subsections briefly review the book's findings on the institutional design of supermajority rules and how they impact court functioning.

7.1.1 Institutional Design

The literature often presents supermajority rules as monolithic. This book makes a strong counterargument to that point of view. Institutional design on supermajority rules varies greatly. Deferential supermajorities attempt to supply deference via double threshold mechanisms, while decisional supermajorities create symmetrical requirements forcing consensus. Although some have deemed that symmetrical supermajorities privilege the status quo equally, the book has shown such assertion to be a de facto claim contingent on the specific institutional design, which varies across jurisdictions. The different impasse

DOI: 10.4324/9781003458272-10

rules dealing with supermajority failure decisions provided by deferential and decisional supermajorities range from the law being upheld to formal dismissal of a case without opinion; rules may even be absent, leaving the case pending. The precedential status of those decisions remains under debate.

The legal source of supermajority rules also constitutes a critical choice in conveying institutional design. Constitutional supermajorities, a priori those representing more substantial political consensus, considerably insulate supermajorities from judicial review, although the theoretical possibility exists in the case of eternity clauses or judicial unamendability doctrines. In turn, statutory supermajorities are more flexible but may be declared unconstitutional through judicial review. All analyzed episodes of judicial review of supermajority rules occurred under statutory supermajorities.

The book has also shown that self-imposed supermajority rules are not merely theoretical. As part of a self-restraint conception, courts in some jurisdictions adopted different formulations of such rules in various aspects of constitutional adjudication, such as issuing interpretative judgments, creating precedents, or striking down legislation.

While institutional design determines the values supermajority rules attempt to foster, policymakers have had their own set of aims in establishing them. Although the book has argued that deference and consensus are the most common objectives privileged by different versions of supermajority rules, the reason such rules are employed by policymakers goes far beyond them. Apart from deference and consensus, several jurisdictions introduced supermajority rules as a cautionary mechanism, wary of substantial shifts in power when granting courts broader attributions. Other jurisdictions have been known to weaponize supermajority rules to attempt to obstruct and control a court. While not inherently illiberal, supermajority rules may erode democracy when purposely employed to undermine a court's ability to place checks on the elected branches, particularly combined with court-packing measures.

7.1.2 Impact on Courts

Supermajority rules have been said to impact courts but with little empirical analysis of how they have done so. As with institutional design, scholars have overgeneralized an aspect requiring a nuanced approach. The variations in such rules create differences too significant to make general claims. The supermajority's multiplicand, the specific threshold adopted, and even court size represent significant variables.

Systems calculating supermajority thresholds over the entire court's membership tend to use numerical models, while fractional models are usually reserved for systems establishing supermajority rules over set quorums. The first is the most common model and has broader theoretical support in the supermajority literature, but the second is also possible. Numerical requirements often produce mobile thresholds by computing absences as negative votes against a given proposal, impacting decisional and deferential supermajorities.

Some jurisdictions have adopted formal rules to prevent the problem, such as substitute or surrogate judges and term prorogation. In most jurisdictions, constitutional courts seem to have used their agenda-setting capabilities as informal instruments to address the mobility threshold problem, among other mechanisms.

Supermajority thresholds have been particularly neglected in the literature. Most jurisdictions have failed to provide comprehensive reasoning in adopting a set threshold beyond estimations. The literature's critique of arbitrariness, predicated on other supermajority thresholds, seems to apply to such rules in constitutional adjudication. Nonetheless, the book has provided several possibilities to seek coherent thresholds.

The combination of institutional design features, multiplicands, majority thresholds, and court size is a basis for exploring court impact and court paralysis. When can a court be deemed paralyzed by a supermajority? When is the supermajority's impact too high on a court? Establishing an objective measurement for those questions is challenging enough in itself. Paralysis assessments require contextual analysis of specific jurisdictions.

The book has identified three threshold levels based on the comparative analysis: moderate, strong, and near-unanimity. Scholars in several jurisdictions have been critical of higher thresholds. Nonetheless, no significant correlation between threshold strength and the rate of supermajority failure decisions was detected.

Threshold strength does not directly account for higher court paralysis. The above indicates that the impact of supermajority rules is not determined by simplistic explanations of increased requirements, but by the interplay of a complex set of factors. Higher thresholds may prove functional—North Dakota—and milder ones dysfunctional—Peru TGC.

There is evidence to suggest that supermajorities do not paralyze courts. Many jurisdictions have a supermajority failure decision rate approximating to 5 percent, with marginal variations. The counterexamples and other limitations highlighted in the study advise reading the results carefully.

7.2 Broader Implications

As admitted in earlier chapters, several limitations accompany this analysis. The number of jurisdictions may be considered under-representative. The available data may be deemed limited except for specific models. Some jurisdictions, such as the Czech Republic and the Dominican Republic, by design, are unable to provide specific information, forcing us to resort to proxy analysis.

Moreover, calculating supermajority failure decisions entails the same problems as cross-comparing unconstitutionality rates in different jurisdictions. Variations of institutional features such as legal standing, discretionary jurisdiction, federalism, the strength of political actors, and too many others will inevitably produce differentiating circumstances that necessitate carefully interpreting the data when comparing across jurisdictions. In supermajority requirements, the resultant effect is produced by the combination of characteristics and rules of a constitutional system, rather than solely by the arbitrary selection of a threshold.

Nonetheless, I believe the analysis does offer possible broader implications in assessing other supermajority rules, *ceteris paribus*. The features of the institutional design examined will tend to function similarly, and the framework for court impact might be replicated. Even if a definitive assessment is not possible, a compelling case has been made that a general causal claim of court paralysis is inaccurate. Generally, constitutional courts may prove functional under supermajority rules, particularly in deferential configurations, where more data suggests their viability.

7.3 Future Research

This study has focused on the empirical functioning of supermajority rules in a selected sample of jurisdictions. Through it, an attempt has been made to provide a typology of their institutional design and an overview of their impact. Further research is needed pertaining to other jurisdictions. Supermajorities established in various contexts offer valuable lessons and insights worth exploring. Chile, India, Taiwan, Lebanon, Costa Rica, El Salvador, the Philippines, and other past and present supermajorities remain unexplored.

Even within the selected jurisdictions, further statistical analysis is required to produce specific datasets that better outline the impact of supermajority rules in courts, and perhaps provide detailed information such as the disposition of the case regarding other normative provisions whose invalidation was not obstructed by the supermajority rule. Nuanced attempts at contextualized comparison of unconstitutionality rates between supermajorities and majority models are a future challenge.

A more systematic study of internal voting networks, strategic behavior, vote bargaining, and non-evident evasion practices in supermajorities represents an upcoming area for exploration. Chapters 3 and 4 revealed that courts employ a set of practices and informal institutions to address supermajority rules. Although some instances of open evasion exist, techniques such as constitutional conforming interpretation or narrow reading of statutes are unexplored. Such research would also have implications for informal institutions surrounding majority voting protocols and, more broadly, general judicial decision-making. Furthermore, while many scholars claim that supermajority rules are better suited than majority rule to foster deliberative courts, the literature lacks empirical evidence to support the claim. Testing such a hypothesis could potentially allow nuanced verification of supermajorities' impact on models through a comparison of jurisdictions both with and without court public deliberations.

The philosophical discussion surrounding supermajority rules is ongoing. While much additional work is required to better understand their functioning, this book has attempted to provide a first foray into a necessarily global conversation of comparative law.

Appendix

DATA SOURCES/COLLECTION METHODS

1. Decisional Supermajorities

Peru TGC. Data was obtained from the court's official publication of judgments.[1] I considered the entire functioning of the court (from November 19, 1982 to April 5, 1992). The coding was performed manually. The court failed to muster a supermajority in five instances.

The Dominican Republic. The institutional design of the Constitutional Court of the Dominican Republic does not offer the possibility of accurately determining supermajority failure decisions (SFDs). Deliberations are not public, nor do decisions recall the number of times a case has been listed for discussion. Deliberation protocols are not disclosed. Even though occasionally the public has learned about specific instances of SFD impasses through information leaking by law clerks and justices themselves, that is also rare. The book turned to proxy analysis through the court's docket. As the court does not provide a detailed average of individual case length statistics, the calculations employed annual clearance reports. The annual clearance as a proxy overemphasizes SFD rates (see Chapter 6) but may allow for providing maximum estimations. The study employed the 2012–2022 annual clearance rate provided by official sources.[2]

Calculations did not consider 2012, as it would distort the rate through anomalies. Considering the first year of the court in the calculations is problematic. The court was initially even precluded from issuing decisions. The different court procedures require court formalities, brief filing, respondent briefs, inter alia, which even de jure made it impossible for the court to render judgments for several months in many cases. After such an initial situation and once the learning curve and institutional dynamics had settled, a dramatic rise occurred in the following periods due to procedural optimization, showing a stable trend. By eliminating the first-year anomaly, the annual clearance

1 JURISPRUDENCIA RELEVANTE DEL TRIBUNAL DE GARANTÍAS CONSTITUCIONALES (Constitutional Court of Peru ed., 2018).

2 *See* Estadística de la Carga Procesal, Dirección de Planeación y Desarrollo "Justicia Constitucional Ciudadana," Dominican Constitutional Court, Santo Domingo, April, 2023.

Table 8.1 Case balance at the Dominican Constitutional Court

Year	*Cases received*	*Judgments issued*	*Rate %**
2012	799	104	13.01
2013	551	290	52.6
2014	853	407	47.7
2015	798	626	78.4
2016	900	724	80.4
2017	657	835	127
2018	642	973	151.5
2019	740	636	85.9
2020	497	566	113.9
2021	468	527	112.6
2022	757	532	70.2

* Since undecided cases in a judicial term may be decided in a future one, the percentage of cases resolved in certain years may exceed those filed.

amounts to 92.03 percent, giving a maximum of 7.97 percent of supermajority failure decisions.

2. Deferential Supermajorities

Ohio, North Dakota, and Nebraska. For Ohio (1912–1936) and North Dakota (1919–1936), the analysis relies on the data provided by Fite and Rubinstein.[3] For Nebraska, Madgett provided data for the period from 1921 to 1968.[4]

North Dakota's and Nebraska's data for the contemporary period (1992–2022) was obtained as follows. Westlaw database was employed for conducting searches accounting for cases pertaining to the constitutionality of a statute/municipality ordinance in the period from January 1, 1992 to December 31, 2022. The inquiry compared results from a general search under the following search language (UNCONSTITUTIONAL /p STATUT! PROVISION! INVALID /p STATUT! PROVISION! VOID /p STATUT! PROVISION! OVERTURN /p STATUT! PROVISION!)[5] against all cases appearing in Westlaw Keys 92 (Constitutional Law) for the said period, under subkeys 92V (Construction and operation of Constitutional Provisions), 92V(F) (Constitutionality of statutory provisions), and 92Key655 (in general). The coding was done manually. Only cases in which the constitutionality of a

3 Katherine B. Fite & Louis Baruch Rubinstein, *Curbing the Supreme Court: State Experiences and Federal Proposals*, 35 Mich. L. Rev. 762 (1937).

4 Paul W. Madgett, *The Five-Judge Rule in Nebraska*, 2 Creighton L. Rev. 329, 338 (1968).

5 The methodology is similar to Langer's. Laura Langer, Judicial Review in State Supreme Courts: A Comparative Study 135–36 (2002).

legislative enactment was raised or analyzed by the court are considered.[6] In North Dakota, four instances of SFD occurred in the period, while in Nebraska, for the said period, two instances of SFD were accounted for.

Czechoslovakia. Calculations are based on Langášek's data (1920–1938) concerning court procedures, quorums, and votes.[7] Langášek provides data only for the proceedings that were deemed to be part of the court's jurisdiction. His data does not include instances in which the court rejected a plea, considering the petitioner lacked legal standing or other formal defects. Langášek's data considers cases filed to the court, even if they were unresolved due to the circumstances ensuing from the Nazi aggression. Taking Langášek's data, the study made a limited dataset comprising the forty-seven cases in which the court issued a decision. The coding was done manually. Only one instance of SFD was detected.

Peru (Fijimorist). The period considered is from the court's installation in June 1996 to May 21, 1998, when Congress passed Law 26954, establishing a transitory unanimity requirement in the *intermezzo* after the impeachment of three magistrates (see Chapter 4). The period is 719 days (1.969 years), and calculations were provided on a two-year round-up. The analysis omits the irregular period from May 1998 to the enactment of the new supermajority in 2004.[8] Calculations were based on data provided by Montoya *et al.*[9] The study considered decision 0003-1996-AI/TC to be an instance of the application of the supermajority.[10] Three instances of SFD occurred.

6 A case was counted as involving the constitutionality of a statute (*i.e.*, ordinances and statutes to which the rule applies) even if the court refused to address the challenge on procedural grounds such as mootness, ripeness, lack of standing, etc. Broader constitutional cases were excluded. For example, cases involving the constitutionality of administrative and court regulations, policies, administrative decisions, and all non-legislative enactment challenges were not considered.

7 Tomáš Langášek, Ústavní Soud Československé Republiky a Jeho Osudy v Letech 1920-1948 230–7 (2011).

8 From 1998 to roughly 2000, the court functioned under a transitory unanimity requirement imposed by Law 26954. In 2000, the impeached magistrates were reinstated following Fujimori's demise and the Inter-American Court's decision in *Tribunal Constitucional v. Peru*. The former supermajority was applicable. The presence of loyal Fujimorist magistrates produced an exceptionally delicate situation. Politicians did not believe the court to be an impartial body and were discouraged from challenging legislation. The court was not deemed to function regularly until those magistrates were replaced in 2002. Luis López Zamora, *Constitutional Court of Peru*, *in* The Max Planck Encyclopedia of Public International Law, 11, para. 29 (Rüdiger Wolfrum, Frauke Lachenmann & Ana Harvey eds., 2021).

9 Víctorhugo Montoya, Evelyn Chilo & Carlos Quispe, El Proceso de Inconstitucionalidad en la Jurisprudencia (1996-2014) 123–223 (2015) (providing a detailed table containing all decisions the constitutional court issued from 1994 to 2014, published and unpublished).

10 As described in Chapter 4, in Judgment 0003-1996-AI/TC, a minority of three magistrates issued a "decision" absent quorum and majority requirements to circumvent the supermajority, attempting to prevent Fujimori's reelection. The decision portrays a precise instance of both evasion and a statute preserved on account of the rule, given that said magistrates were impeached and the decision was not executed.

Peru (Contemporary). The calculations were performed from the database of the Peruvian Constitutional Court comprising 489 judgments on the abstract unconstitutionality of statutes from 2004 to January 1, 2023.[11] The court's database accounts for decisions filed with a 2006 and up registry—the oldest decision being 0030-2005-PI/TC.[12] Montoya *et al.* previously compiled a dataset covering the period from 1996 to 2014, enabling bridging this dataset with the court's database, accounting for the missing period.[13] All decisions were manually classified. Thirty instances of SFD were detected.

The Czech Republic. The Czech Republic does not allow a precise account of supermajority failure decisions. Decisions do not disclose the concrete vote behind them. While scholars can occasionally second-guess the voting, this is due mainly to dissenting or concurring opinions, which are not mandatory. Theoretically, the supermajority may be applied without being so stated.[14] Even if a list of cases in which the supermajority was definitively applied is relatively simple to gather, it is impossible to confidently state that those are the only cases in which the court applied the rule. Other cases might not be traceable, and through impasse rules, there is no impact on the court's docket.

I employed estimations provided by law clerks, high court officials, and justices to provide a proxy analysis. According to several interviews, the rule has been applied fewer than twenty times in the court's history.[15] That is

11 The study analyzes the decisions issued in the so-called *proceso de inconstitucionalidad*, abbreviated by the court's nomenclature as "AI" and subsequently "PI," after the new Code of Constitutional Procedures was issued. Other court procedures not strictly pertaining to the constitutionality of statutes may require statutory or self-imposed supermajorities, such as issuing binding precedents, interpretative judgments, or solving conflicts of competencies among bodies, as per Article 112 of the Constitutional Procedural Code. Since those are supermajorities inconsistent with the book's scope on the unconstitutionality of statutes, they are not considered in the sample.

12 *See* the court's database at Jurisprudencia.sedetc.gob.pe.

13 Montoya, Chilo, and Quispe, *supra* note 10, at 137–64.

14 Both justices and former law clerks confirmed the possibility of judgments not explicitly recognizing the rule's application during deliberations. Jiří Zemánek, *Interview with a Justice of the Czech Constitutional Court* (unpublished, 2022). Tomáš Langášek, *Interview with Administrative Supreme Court Judge and Former General Secretary of the Czech Constitutional Court* (unpublished, 2022). In the literature, *see* Jan Filip, Pavel Holländer & Vojtěch Šimíček, Zákon o Ústavním Soudu 66 (2 ed. 2007).

15 Justice Zemánek considered that the rule would have been applied between 10 and 20 times by February 22, 2022. He based his estimation on the rule's practice during his term at the Court. Zemánek, *supra* note 15. In turn, Tomáš Langášek, former General Secretary of the Constitutional Court, estimated that the supermajority may have played a role in ten cases at most by the same date. However, he deemed it essential to stress that "the supermajority clause comes openly into play only when a judge-rapporteur presents the plenary with a derogatory ruling that does not acquire the majority of nine. In many cases, it is applied tacitly." After conveying that there are several ways in which the supermajority may impact a case, depending on whether or not the original draft proposed upholding or striking down the legislation, Langášek concluded that in his estimates, "one cannot always be sure whether all have been considered and counted." Langášek, *supra* note 15.

consistent with the slightly smaller number of publicly acknowledged SFDs. For the sample size, I employed data provided by Šipulová[16] for *en banc* proceedings up to 2015.[17]

As explained before, not all decisions are acknowledged, which would account for the divergences between the listed judgments and the data estimates provided by law clerks and justices. If we take such data on the upper limits of the estimations (twenty decisions by February 22, 2022) and suppose all occurred by 2015,[18] the SFD rate would be 5.44 percent. The book acknowledges that reasonable objections may be raised against the usage of such proxy data.

Mexico. All calculations are based on a previously analyzed dataset, comprising all actions of unconstitutionality and general declarations of unconstitutionality in the period from January 1, 1995 to April 27, 2022.[19]

South Korea. All calculations are based on data provided by Hong.[20] Hong's dataset comprises the period from September 15, 1988 to March 31, 2017,[21] considering cases pertaining to the constitutionality of statutes, impeachment, dissolution of political parties, competence disputes, and constitutional complaints.[22] Hong provided sixty-two cases in which a majority of judges favoring the unconstitutionality of legislation lost to minority votes.[23] Such a definition excludes conflict of competences, individual complaints, impeachments, etc. Thus, the calculations were done solely vis-à-vis the workload provided for the constitutionality of statutes.[24]

16 Katarína Šipulová, *The Czech Constitutional Court: Far Away from Political Influence*, *in* CONSTITUTIONAL POLITICS AND THE JUDICIARY 32, 36 (Kálmán Pócza, ed., 2018).

17 By 2015, at least seven supermajority failure decisions had been expressly acknowledged by the Court or were inferable via vote count (Pl. ÚS 9/07, Pl. ÚS 12/94, Pl. ÚS 16/2000, Pl. ÚS 3/96, Pl. ÚS 36/93, Pl. ÚS 17/97, Pl. ÚS 14/02). Thus, the rule had at least a 1.9 percent rate of occurrence.

18 To provide an example that deliberately portraits the maximum SFD rate, the calculation makes an assumption that is not valid. By 2015, at least the self-acknowledged SFD Pl. ÚS 2/20 and Pl. ÚS 11/17 had not occurred.

19 Mauro Arturo Rivera León, *Control and Paralysis? A Context-Sensitive Analysis of Objections to Supermajorities in Constitutional Adjudication*, INT'L J. CONST. L. 1 (2023).

20 Joon Seok Hong, *Signaling the Turn: The Supermajority Requirement and Judicial Power on the Constitutional Court of Korea*, 67 AM. J. COMP. L. 177 (2019).

21 *Id.* at 188.

22 The data provided by Hong comprises procedures requiring a supermajority but not necessarily pertaining to the constitutionality of statutes, such as impeachment or upholding individual complaints unrelated to the constitutionality of laws. As an exception, Hong included competence disputes resolved through a majority vote. *See* Hong's explanation. *Id.*

23 *Id.* at 194.

24 A small precision. Hong's information on the Court's workload is up to March 31, 2017. However, his account of supermajority failure decisions is up to December 31, 2016. *Id.* To avoid the discrepancy, the calculations were made based on the official Court workload for the period covered by Hong for SFD decisions. Incidentally, the number of decisions for cases pertaining to the constitutionality of statutes is identical; thus, the divergence is insignificant. *See* the Constitutional Court's statistics, https://english.ccourt.go.kr/site/eng/jurisdiction/caseLoadStatic.do.

Chile. Calculations are made based on a simplified dataset elaborated from the court's official database of judgments.[25] The study considered all procedures regarding *the erga omnes* unconstitutionality of a provision from February 1, 2006 to May 26, 2022. In all, fourteen judgments were considered, and four instances of SFD were detected.[26]

25 Available at https://tcchile.cl/busqueda/busqueda.php.

26 The count substantially matches that of Tiede. Tiede counts fifteen decisions. The divergence is due to Rol 558-06 and Rol 590-06. Although jointly resolved, they appear as individual results in the court's database. As they were jointly resolved (*see* "Vistos" of Rol 558), Chilean scholars treat them as a single decision, and so do the present calculations. *See* an example of the citing practices regarding joint decisions in Enrique Navarro, El Control de Constitucionalidad de las Leyes en Chile (1811-2011) 130 (2011).

Bibliography

Abebe, Adem Kassie. "Taming Regressive Constitutional Amendments: The African Court as a Continental (Super) Constitutional Court." *International Journal of Constitutional Law* 17, no. 1 (May 6, 2019): 89–117. https://doi.org/10.1093/icon/moz006.

Acosta, Hermógenes. "El Impacto de la Vigencia y Funcionamiento del Tribunal Constitucional Dominicano en la Protección de Los Derechos Fundamentales." *Revista de la Sala Constitucional*, no. 1 (2019): 36–80.

———. "El Proceso de Amparo en el Nuevo Modelo de Justicia Constitucional Dominicano." In *Treinta Años de Jurisdicción Constitucional en el Perú*, edited by Eto, Gerardo, 145–94. Lima: Centro de Estudios Constitucionales, 2014.

Addison E., Sheldon. "The Nebraska Constitutional Convention, 1919-1920." *The American Political Science Review* 15, no. 3 (1921): 391–400.

Adler, František. *Die Grundgedanken Der Tschechoslowakischen Verfassungsurkunde in Der Entwicklungsgeschichte Des Verfassungsrechts*. Berlin: Hermann Sack, 1927.

———. *Grundriß Des Tschechoslowakischen Verfassungsrechtes*. Reichenberg: Verlag von Gebrüder Stiepel, 1930.

Aguirre Roca, Manuel. "El Tribunal de Garantías Constitucionales Ante la Crítica." *Derecho PUCP*, no. 42 (December 1, 1988): 187–92. https://doi.org/10.18800/derechopucp.198801.008.

———. "La Razón Principal del Fracaso del TGC." *Themis: Revista de Derecho*, no. 20 (1991): 7–12.

Albert, Richard. *Constitutional Amendments: Making, Breaking, and Changing Constitutions*. New York: Oxford University Press, 2019.

Amar, Akhil Reed. *America's Unwritten Constitution: The Precedents and Principles We Live By*. New York: Basic Books, 2012.

Aprasidze, David. "Consolidation in Georgia: Democracy or Power?" *Yearbook on the Organization for Security and Co-Operation in Europe (OSCE)* 2015 (2016): 107–15.

Arguelhes, Diego Werneck, and Ivar A. Hartmann. "Timing Control without Docket Control: How Individual Justices Shape the Brazilian Supreme Court's Agenda." *Journal of Law and Courts* 5, no. 1 (2017): 105–40. https://doi.org/10.1086/690195.

Astudillo, César, and José Estrada. *Nombramiento de Ministros de la Suprema Corte de Justicia de la Nación en el contexto de los modelos de designación en el derecho comparado*. Mexico City: Porrúa, 2019.

Aumann, F. R. "The Course of Judicial Review in the State of Ohio." *American Political Science Review* 25, no. 2 (May 1931): 367–76. https://doi.org/10.2307/1947665.

Avaliani, Tamar. "Annual Report: State of Human Rights in Georgia." Tsibilis: Human Rights Center, 2017.

Banaszak, Bogusław. *Konstytucja Rzeczypospolitej Polskiej: Komentarz.* 2nd ed. Warsaw: C.H. Beck, 2012.

Barry, Brian M. *How Judges Judge: Empirical Insights into Judicial Decision-Making.* Abingdon: Informa Law from Routledge, 2021.

Beçak, Rubens, and Jairo Lima. "When 5x4 Is Not a Winning Majority: Judicial Decision-Making on Unconstitutional Constitutional Amendments." In *Violent Conflicts, Crisis, State of Emergency, Peacebuilding: Constitutional Problems, Amendments and Interpretation*, edited by Oesten Baller, 161–79. Berlin: Berliner Wissenschafts-Verlag, 2019. https://doi.org/10.35998/9783830541264.

Benák, Jaroslav. "Historický Vývoj Ústavního Soudnictví a Přístupu Jednotlivce k Ústavnímu Soudu." *Časopis pro Právní Vědu a Praxi* 26, no. 3 (2018): 397–417.

Benítez-R., Vicente F. "Petrificando la Rama Judicial en Colombia: Autointerés Judicial y Control de Constitucionalidad Inapropiado de Reformas Constitucionales a la Justicia." *International Journal of Constitutional Law* 20, no. 4 (December 15, 2022): 1618–46. https://doi.org/10.1093/icon/moac067.

Bentham, Jeremy. *Political Tactics.* Edited by Michael James, Cyprian Blamires, and Catherine Pease-Watkin. The Collected Works of Jeremy Bentham. Oxford: New York: Clarendon Press; Oxford University Press, 1999.

Berruecos García Travesí, Susana, and Laurence Whitehead. "Constitutional Controversies in the Subnational Democratization of Mexico, 1994–2021." *Latin American Policy* 12, no. 2 (November 2021): 405–23. https://doi.org/10.1111/lamp.12229.

Bertel, Maria. "El Test de Proporcionalidad en la Jurisprudencia del Tribunal Constitucional Peruano." *International Journal of Constitutional Law* 15, no. 2 (April 2017): 541–45. https://doi.org/10.1093/icon/mox025.

Biagi, Francesco. *European Constitutional Courts and Transitions to Democracy.* Cambridge University Press, 2019. https://doi.org/10.1017/9781108776783.

Bickel, Alexander M. *The Least Dangerous Branch.* New Haven: Yale University Press, 1962. https://doi.org/10.12987/9780300173338.

Bifulco, Raffaele, and Davide Paris. "The Italian Constitutional Court." In *The Max Planck Handbooks in European Public Law: Volume III: Constitutional Adjudication. Institutions*, 447–504. Oxford University Press, 2020.

Biskupic, Joan. *Nine Black Robes: Inside the Supreme Court's Drive to the Right and Its Historic Consequences.* New York: William Morrow, 2023.

Biskupic, Joan. "The Secret Supreme Court: Late Nights, Courtesy Votes and the Unwritten 6-Vote Rule." *CNN Politics*, October 17, 2021. https://edition.cnn.com/2021/10/17/politics/supreme-court-conference-rules-breyer/index.html.

Borah, William. "Five to Four Decisions as Menace to Respect for Supreme Court." *The New York Times*, February 18, 1923.

Bosworth, Matthew H. *Courts as Catalysts: State Supreme Courts and Public School Finance Equity.* Albany: State University of New York Press, 2001.

Brage, Joaquín. *La acción abstracta de inconstitucionalidad.* Mexico City: IIJ-UNAM, 2005.

———. “La acción peruana de inconstitucionalidad.” In *El Derecho Procesal Constitucional Peruano*, edited by José Palomino, 2nd ed., 2:801–38. Universidad Inca Garcilaso de la Vega, 2015.

Bremner, Robert H. “The Civic Revival in Ohio.” *American Journal of Economics and Sociology* 8, no. 1 (1948): 61–68. https://doi.org/10.1111/j.1536-7150.1948.tb00731.x.

Brewer-Carías, Allan R. *Constitutional Courts as Positive Legislators: A Comparative Law Study*. Cambridge University Press, 2011. https://doi.org/10.1017/CBO9780511994760.

Bricker, John W. “Shall the Powers of the Supreme Court Be Abridged?” *Proceedings of the Academy of Political Science* 16, no. 4 (1936): 40–57. https://doi.org/10.2307/1172758.

Brown, Vincent, ed. “Legislative Journal of the State of Nebraska. Volume I. Eighty-Second Legislature First Session.” Nebraska Legislature, 1971.

Bruce, Andrew Alexander. *Non-Partisan League*. New York: Macmillan, 1921.

Bugarič, Bojan, and Tom Ginsburg. “The Assault on Postcommunist Courts.” *Journal of Democracy* 27, no. 3 (2016): 69–82. https://doi.org/10.1353/jod.2016.0047.

Bustamante, Thomas. “The Ongoing Search for Legitimacy: Can a ‘Pragmatic yet Principled’ Deliberative Model Justify the Authority of Constitutional Courts?” *The Modern Law Review* 78, no. 2 (March 2015): 372–93. https://doi.org/10.1111/1468-2230.12120.

Calabresi, Steven Gow. *The History and Growth of Judicial Review, Volume 2: The G-20 Civil Law Countries*. Vol. 2. 2 vols. Oxford University Press, 2021.

Caminker, Evan H. “Playing with Voting Protocols on the Supreme Court [Unpublished Draft],” 2002.

———. “Thayerian Deference to Congress and Supreme Court Supermajority Rules: Lessons from the Past.” *Indiana Law Journal* 78, no. 1 (2003): 73–122.

Carpizo, Jorge. “Propuestas de modificaciones constitucionales en el marco de la denominada reforma del Estado.” In *El proceso constituyente mexicano*, edited by Diego Valadés and Miguel Carbonell, 183–226. Mexico City: IIJ-UNAM, 2007.

———. “Reformas constitucionales al Poder Judicial Federal y a la jurisdicción constitucional.” *Boletín Mexicano de Derecho Comparado* 1995, no. 83 (1995): 807–42.

Caruso, Corrado. “Majority.” In *Max Planck Encyclopedia of Comparative Constitutional Law*. Oxford University Press, 2022.

Castillo-Ortiz, Pablo. “The Dilemmas of Constitutional Courts and the Case for a New Design of Kelsenian Institutions.” *Law and Philosophy* 39, no. 6 (December 2020): 617–55. https://doi.org/10.1007/s10982-020-09378-3.

———. “The Illiberal Abuse of Constitutional Courts in Europe.” *European Constitutional Law Review* 15, no. 1 (March 2019): 48–72. https://doi.org/10.1017/S1574019619000026.

Caviedes, Cristóbal. “A Core Case for Supermajority Rules in Constitutional Adjudication.” *International Journal of Constitutional Law* 20, no. 3 (2022): 1162–87. https://doi.org/10.1093/icon/moac072.

———. “Is Majority Rule Justified in Constitutional Adjudication?” *Oxford Journal of Legal Studies* 41, no. 2 (July 22, 2021): 376–406. https://doi.org/10.1093/ojls/gqaa055.

Cerna, Christina M. “Judgment TC/0168/13 (Const. Ct. Dom. Rep.) & Statement of the Inter-American Commission on Human Rights on Judgment TC/0168/13.”

International Legal Materials 53, no. 4 (August 2014): 662–726. https://doi.org/10.5305/intelegamate.53.4.0662.
Chemerinsky, Erwin. "Assessing Chief Justice William Rehnquist." *University of Pennsylvania Law Review* 154, no. 6 (2006): 1331–34.
Choudhry, Sujit. "The Lochner Era and Comparative Constitutionalism." *International Journal of Constitutional Law* 2, no. 1 (January 1, 2004): 1–55. https://doi.org/10.1093/icon/2.1.1.
Clyde H. Barnard, ed. *Journal of the Nebraska Constitutional Convention (1921).* Lincoln: The Kline Pub. Co., 1921.
Cohen, David. "A Tale of Two Vote Switches." *Texas Law Review Online* 100, no. 39 (2021): 39–59.
———. "The Precedent-Based Voting Paradox." *Boston University Law Review* 90, no. 1 (2010): 183–251.
Cohen, Mathilde. "Ex Ante Versus Ex Post Deliberations: Two Models of Judicial Deliberations in Courts of Last Resort." *American Journal of Comparative Law* 62, no. 4 (December 22, 2014): 951–1008. https://doi.org/10.5131/AJCL.2014.0028.
Comisión de la Verdad y Reconciliación. *Informe Final.* Lima: Peru, 2003.
Conaghan, Catherine M. *Fujimori's Peru: Deception in the Public Sphere.* Cambridge: University of Pittsburgh Press, 2005.
Condorcet, Jean-Antoine-Nicolas de Caritat, Iain McLean, and Fiona Hewitt. *Condorcet: Foundations of Social Choice and Political Theory.* Aldershot-Brookfield: Edward Elgar Publishing, 1994.
Congreso Constituyente Democrático. *Debate Constitucional. Pleno: 1993.* Lima: Congreso de la República, 1998.
Conseil Constitutionnel. *Recueil des Décisions du Conseil Constitutionnel 1994-2016: Décisions Relatives à la Constitutionnalité des Lois.* Vol. I. Beyreuth: République Libanaise Conseil Constitutionnel, 2017.
"Conseil Constitutionnel du Liban (Réponses au Questionnaire)." Association des Cours Constitutionnelles Francophones Bulletin, no. 13 (2019): 325–39.
Constitutional Court of Peru, ed. *Jurisprudencia Relevante del Tribunal de Garantías Constitucionales.* Lima: Tribunal Constitucional del Perú, 2018.
Constitutional Court of the Dominican Republic. "Questionnaire of the Seminary (Dominican Republic)." Cartagena: Iberoamerican Conference on Constitutional Justice, November 20, 2019.
Contesse, Jorge. "Resisting the Inter-American Human Rights System." *Yale Journal of International Law* 44, no. 2 (2019): 179–237.
Cooter, Robert D., and Michael D. Gilbert. *Public Law and Economics.* New York: Oxford University Press, 2022. https://doi.org/10.1093/oso/9780197655870.003.0004.
Corte, Nieves and Juan Moreno. "Artículo 90." In *Comentarios a la Ley Orgánica 2/1979, de 3 de octubre, del Tribunal Constitucional*, edited by Juan José González Rivas and Andrés Javier Gutiérrez Gil, 1019–23. Madrid: Fundación Wolters Kluwer; Boletín Oficial del Estado Tribunal Constitucional, 2020.
Cossío Díaz, José Ramón. "Artículo 105." In *Constitución Política Mexicana Comentada.* Mexico City: IIJ-UNAM, 1995.
Cruz Villalón, Pedro. "Dos Modos de Regulación del Control de Constitucionalidad: Checoslovaquia (1920-1938) y España (1931-1936)." *Revista Española de Derecho Constitucional*, no. 5 (1982): 115–46.

———. *La Formación del Sistema Europeo de Control de Constitucionalidad (1918-1939)*. Madrid: Centro de Estudios Constitucionales, 1987.

Cushman, Barry. "Court-Packing in Context." *Journal of Supreme Court History* 48, no. 3 (2023): 174–214.

da Silva, Virgilio. "Deciding without Deliberating." *International Journal of Constitutional Law* 11, no. 3 (July 1, 2013): 557–84. https://doi.org/10.1093/icon/mot019.

———. "Big Brother Is Watching the Court." *Verfassung Und Recht in Übersee / Law and Politics in Africa, Asia and Latin America* 51, no. 4 (2018): 437–55.

Dahl, Robert Alan. *Democracy and Its Critics*. New Haven: Yale University Press, 1989.

Dargent, Eduardo. "Determinants of judicial independence: Lessons from three 'Cases' of constitutional courts in Peru (1982–2007)." *Journal of Latin American Studies* 41, no. 2 (2009): 251–78.

Davidson, Ron. "The Mechanics of Judicial Vote Switching." *Suffolk University Law Review* 38, no. 1 (2004): 17–72.

Debates in the Massachusetts Constitutional Convention *1917-1918*. Boston: Wright & Potter Printing Co., State Printers, 1919.

Delaney, Erin F. "Analyzing Avoidance: Judicial Strategy in Comparative Perspective." *Duke Law Journal* 66, no. 1 (2016): 1–67.

Dinan, John J. *The American State Constitutional Tradition*. Lawrence: University Press of Kansas, 2006.

Dixon, Rosalind, and Samuel Issacharoff. "Living to Fight Another Day: Judicial Deferral in Defense of Democracy." *Wisconsin Law Review* 2016, no. 6 (2016): 683–731.

Dixon, Rosalind, and David Landau. *Abusive Constitutional Borrowing: Legal Globalization and the Subversion of Liberal Democracy*. Oxford University Press, 2021.

Doerfler, Ryan D., and Samuel Moyn. "Democratizing the Supreme Court." *California Law Review* 109, no. 5 (2021): 1703–72. https://doi.org/10.15779/Z38TX3571X.

Domingo, Pilar. "Judicial independence: the politics of the Supreme Court in Mexico." *Journal of Latin American Studies* 32, no. 3 (2000): 705–35.

Doubek, Pavel. "Sterilization of Transgender People: A Worrying Judgement of the Czech Constitutional Court." *ECHR Blog* (blog), n.d. https://www.echrblog.com/2022/04/sterilization-of-transgender-people.html.

Dougherty, Keith L., and Julian Edward. "The Properties of Simple Vs. Absolute Majority Rule: Cases Where Absences and Abstentions Are Important." *Journal of Theoretical Politics* 22, no. 1 (January 2010): 85–122. https://doi.org/10.1177/0951629809347557.

Duncan, Dwight. "A Modest Proposal on Supreme Court Unanimity to Constitutionally Invalidate Laws." *Brigham Young University Journal of Public Law* 33, no. 1 (2018): 1–14.

Durnová, Anna P., and Eva M. Hejzlarová. "Navigating the Role of Emotions in Expertise: Public Framing of Expertise in the Czech Public Controversy on Birth Care." *Policy Sciences*, no. 56 (2023): 549–71. https://doi.org/10.1007/s11077-022-09471-5.

Dussauge-Laguna, Mauricio I. "'Doublespeak Populism' and Public Administration: The Case of Mexico." In *Democratic Backsliding and Public Administration*, edited by Michael W. Bauer, B. Guy Peters, Jon Pierre, Kutsal Yesilkagit, and Stefan

Becker, 178–99. Cambridge, United Kingdom ; New York: Cambridge University Press, 2021. https://doi.org/10.1017/9781009023504.009.

———. "The Promises and Perils of Populism for Democratic Policymaking: The Case of Mexico." *Policy Sciences* 55, no. 4 (December 2022): 777–803. https://doi.org/10.1007/s11077-022-09469-z.

Eckerstrom, Peter J. "The Garland Nomination, the Senate's Duty, and the Surprising Lessons of Constitutional Text." *University of Pennsylvania Journal of Constitutional Law* 21, no. 1 (2018): 22–72.

Eggers, William A. "Influence of the Non-Participating Judge." *University of Cincinnati Law Review* 5, no. 4 (1931): 375–84.

Elkins, Zachary, Tom Ginsburg, and James Melton. *The Endurance of National Constitutions.* New York: Cambridge University Press, 2009. https://doi.org/10.1017/CBO9780511817595.

Entin, Jonathan L. "Judicial Supermajorities and the Validity of Statutes: How Mapp Became a Fourth Amendment Landmark Instead of a First Amendment Footnote." *Case Western Law Review* 50, no. 2 (2002): 441–70.

Epps, Daniel, and Ganesh Sitaraman. "How to Save the Supreme Court." *The Yale Law Journal* 129, no. 1 (2019): 148–207. https://doi.org/10.2139/ssrn.3288958.

Epstein, Lee, James L. Gibson, and Michael L. Nelson. "Public Response to Proposals to Reform the Supreme Court (Report Prepared for the New York Times)," 2020. https://epstein.usc.edu/courtreformsurvey.

Epstein, Lee, and Jack Knight. "Reconsidering Judicial Preferences." *Annual Review of Political Science* 16, no. 1 (May 11, 2013): 11–31. https://doi.org/10.1146/annurev-polisci-032211-214229.

———. *The Choices Justices Make.* Washington: CQ Press, 1997.

Ernst, Wolfgang. "The Fine-Mechanisms of Judicial Majoritarianism." In *Collective Judging in Comparative Perspective: Counting Votes and Weighing Opinions*, edited by Birke Häcker and Wolfgang Ernst. Intersentia, 2020. https://doi.org/10.1017/9781839700804.

Estlund, David M. *Democratic Authority: A Philosophical Framework.* 2nd ed. Princeton, NJ: Princeton University Press, 2008.

Fedeli, Silvia. "Simple Majority." In *Encyclopedia of Law and Economics*, edited by Alain Marciano and Battista Ramello, Giovanni, 1918–22. New York: Springer, 2019.

Ferejohn, John, and Pasquale Pasquino. "Constitutional Courts as Deliberative Institutions: Towards an Institutional Theory of Constitutional Justice." In *Constitutional Justice, East and West. Democratic Legitimacy and Constitutional Courts in Post-Communist Europe in a Comparative Perspective*, edited by Wojciech Sadurski, 21–36. The Hague; London; New York: Springer, 2002.

Fernández Segado, Francisco. "El Control Normativo de la Constitucionalidad en el Perú: Crónica de un Fracaso Anunciado." *Revista Española de Derecho Constitucional*, no. 56 (1999): 11–42.

Ferrer Mac-Gregor, Eduardo, and Rubén Sánchez. *Efectos y contenidos de las sentencias en acción de inconstitucionalidad.* Mexico City: IIJ-UNAM, 2009.

Ferreres Comella, Víctor. *Constitutional Courts and Democratic Values: A European Perspective.* Yale University Press, 2009. https://doi.org/10.12987/yale/9780300148671.001.0001.

Figueroa, Giovanni. "La presunción de constitucionalidad de la ley como criterio jurisprudencial: Especial análisis del caso mexicano." In *Constitucionalismo: Dos siglos de su nacimiento en América Latina*, edited by César Astudillo and Jorge Carpizo, 237–65. Mexico City: IIJ-UNAM, 2013.

Filip, Jan. "Procedure of Preventive Review of the Lisbon Treaty in the Czech Republic." *Časopis pro Právní Vědu a Praxi* 16, no. 3 (2008): 206–2014.

Filip, Jan, Pavel Holländer, and Vojtěch Šimíček. *Zákon o Ústavním Soudu*. 2nd ed. Prague: C.H. Beck, 2007.

Finkel, Jodi. "Judicial Reform as Insurance Policy: Mexico in the 1990s." *Latin American Politics and Society* 47, no. 1 (2005): 87–113. https://doi.org/10.1111/j.1548-2456.2005.tb00302.x.

Fino, Susan P. *The Role of State Supreme Courts in the New Judicial Federalism*. New York: Greenwood Press, 1987.

Fite, Katherine B., and Louis Baruch Rubinstein. "Curbing the Supreme Court - State Experiences and Federal Proposals." *Michigan Law Review* 35, no. 5 (1937): 762–87.

Fix-Zamudio, Héctor. *Introducción al Estudio de la Defensa de la Constitución en el Ordenamiento Mexicano*. Mexico City: IIJ-UNAM, 1998.

Freedom House. "Georgia, 2018." Freedom House, 2018. https://freedomhouse.org/country/georgia/nations-transit/2018.

García Belaunde, Domingo. "Apéndice: Instituto International de Derecho Público." In *El Control del Poder*, edited by Domingo García Belaunde and Peter Häberle, 2:899–906. Lima: Universidad Inca Garcilaso de la Vega, 2012.

———. *El Derecho Procesal Constitucional en Perspectiva*. 2nd ed. Lima: Idemsa, 2009.

García Cobián, Erika. "Límites del Control Parlamentario Frente a Las Decisiones de la Jurisdicción Constitucional: Reflexiones a Propósito de la Acusación Constitucional Contra Magistrados del Tribunal Constitucional Por El Caso El Frontón." In *Libro Homenaje del Área de Derecho Constitucional Por Los 100 Años de la Facultad de Derecho de la Pontificia Universidad Católica del Perú*, 15–34. Lima: Pontificia Universidad Católica del Perú, 2019.

Gardbaum, Stephen. "What the World Can Teach Us About Supreme Court Reform." *UCLA Law Review Discourse* 70, no. 1 (2023): 184–202.

Gersen, Jacob E., and Adrian Vermeule. "Chevron as a Voting Rule." *The Yale Law Journal* 116, no. 4 (2007): 676–731.

Gianella Malca, Camila, and Ursula Baertl Espinoza. "Peru." In *The Oxford Handbook of Constitutional Law in Latin America*, edited by Conrado Hübner Mendes, Roberto Gargarella, and Sebastián Guidi, 239–55. Oxford University Press, 2022. https://doi.org/10.1093/oxfordhb/9780198786900.013.12.

Ginsburg, Tom. "Economic Analysis and the Design of Constitutional Courts." *Theoretical Inquiries in Law* 3, no. 1 (January 7, 2002): 49–85. https://doi.org/10.2202/1565-3404.1042.

———. "International Courts and Democratic Backsliding." *Berkeley Journal of International Law* 37, no. 2 (2019): 265–88.

———. *Judicial Review in New Democracies: Constitutional Courts in Asian Cases*. Cambridge, New York: Cambridge University Press, 2003.

Glasser, Michael. "Letting the Supermajority Rule: Nonunanimous Jury Verdicts in Criminal Trials." *Florida State University Law Review* 24, no. 3 (1997): 659–78.

Gómez, Carlos. "La Ley Federal de Revocación de Mandato y la mayoría calificada en la Suprema Corte de Justicia Mexicana." *Hechos y Derechos*, no. 67 (February 21,

2022). https://revistas.juridicas.unam.mx/index.php/hechos-y-derechos/article/view/16705/17299.

González Mantilla, Gorki. "La Reforma de la Justicia en el Perú: Entre la Constitución y las Demandas de la Realidad." *Parlamento y Constitución* 2004, no. 8 (2004): 239–60.

Goodin, Robert E., and Christian List. "Special Majorities Rationalized." *British Journal of Political Science* 36, no. 2 (April 2006): 213–41. https://doi.org/10.1017/S0007123406000135.

Graser, Alexander, et al. "Proportionality and Human Rights in German, Armenian and Georgian Constitutional Adjudication." H. Tsibilis: Deutsche Gesellschaft für Internationale Zusammenarbeit, 2017.

Grupo de Estudio de Reforma al Tribunal Constitucional. "Informe Final," 2019.

Hahm, Chaihark. "Constitutional Court of Korea: Guardian of the Constitution or Mouthpiece of the Government?" In *Constitutional Courts in Asia: A Comparative Perspective*, edited by Albert H. Y. Chen and Andrew Harding, 141–67. Cambridge: Cambridge University Press, 2018. https://doi.org/10.1017/9781108163903.

Hakansson-Nieto, Carlos. "Los Principios de Interpretación y Precedentes Vinculantes en la Jurisprudencia del Tribunal Constitucional Peruano." *Díkaion* 23, no. 18 (2009): 57–77.

Hartnett, Edward A. "Ties in the Supreme Court of the United States." *William and Mary Law Review* 44, no. 2 (2002): 643–78.

———. "A Matter of Judgment, Not a Matter of Opinion." *New York University Law Review* 74, no. 1 (1999): 123–60.

Hassall, Graham, and Cheryl Saunders. *Asia-Pacific Constitutional Systems.* Cambridge: Cambridge University Press, 2002. https://doi.org/10.1017/CBO9780511549960.

Hausser, Robert L. "Limiting the Voting Power of the Supreme Court: Procedure in the States." *Ohio State University Law Journal* 5, no. 1 (1939): 54–87.

Heckelman, Jac C. "A Note on Majority Rule and Neutrality with an Application to State Votes at the Constitutional Convention of 1787." *Public Choice* 167, no. 3–4 (June 2016): 245–55. https://doi.org/10.1007/s11127-016-0339-2.

Helmke, Gretchen and Steven Levitsky. "Informal Institutions and Comparative Politics: A Research Agenda." *Perspectives on Politics* 2, no. 4 (2004): 725–40.

Herrera García, Alfonso. "¿4 es más que 7? Por qué debe eliminarse la mayoría calificada en acciones de inconstitucionalidad." *Nexos: El juego de la Suprema Corte* (blog), February 10, 2022. https://bit.ly/3Gqe4wz.

———. "Algunas Propuestas de Reforma a la Controversia Constitucional en el Contexto de la Función de Jurisdicción Constitucional en México." In *Derecho Procesal: Estudios en Homenaje a Don Jorge Fernández Ruiz*, edited by David Cienfuegos and Miguel López Olvera, 273–99. Mexico City: IIJ-UNAM, 2005.

———. "Jurisprudencia Constitucional de la Suprema Corte de Justicia de México en el 2020." *Anuario Iberoamericano de Justicia Constitucional* 25, no. 2 (December 29, 2021): 607–20. https://doi.org/10.18042/cepc/aijc.25.21.

Herrick, Stewart T., James J. Higgins, and Nancy R. Tarlow. "Five-Four Decisions of the United States Supreme Court: Resurrection of the Extraordinary Majority." *Suffolk University Law Review* 7, no. 4 (1973): 807–916.

Hewitt, James W. *Slipping Backward: A History of the Nebraska Supreme Court.* Lincoln: University of Nebraska Press, 2007. https://doi.org/10.2307/j.ctt1djmgx7.

Hirschl, Ran. “The Judicialization of Mega-Politics and the Rise of Political Courts.” *Annual Review of Political Science* 11 (2008): 93–118.

Hoetzel, Jiří. “Ke Sporu o Meze Moci Nařizovací.” *Právník* LXII (1923): 390–92.

———. “Ku Vzniku Ústavní Listiny.” *Právník* LXVII (1928): 558–63.

Holmøyvik, Eirik, and Anne Sanders. “A Stress Test for Europe’s Judiciaries.” Edited by Ernst Hirsch Ballin, Gerhard van der Schyff, and Maarten Stremler. *European Yearbook of Constitutional Law 2019*, European Yearbook of Constitutional Law, 1 (2020): 289–312. https://doi.org/10.1007/978-94-6265-359-7_12.

Hong, Joon Seok. “Signaling the Turn: The Supermajority Requirement and Judicial Power on the Constitutional Court of Korea.” *The American Journal of Comparative Law* 67, no. 1 (June 17, 2019): 177–217. https://doi.org/10.1093/ajcl/avz008.

Hornkohl, Lena, et al. “Judicial Deliberation: A Comparative Analysis of the Decision-Making Processes in the Highest Civil Courts, Constitutional Courts and International Courts.” *Max Planck Institute Luxembourg for Procedural Law Research Paper Series*, no. 2022 (2) (2022). https://doi.org/10.2139/ssrn.4078587.

Hübner Mendes, Conrado. *Constitutional Courts and Deliberative Democracy*. Oxford University Press, 2013. https://doi.org/10.1093/acprof:oso/9780199670451.001.0001.

Huerta Guerrero, Luis. “El Proceso de Inconstitucionalidad en el Perú.” In *El Derecho Procesal Constitucional Peruano*, edited by José Palomino, 2nd ed., II:839–84. Lima: Instituto Iberoamericano de Derecho Constitucional, 2015.

Huneeus, Alexandra, and René Urueña. “Treaty Exit and Latin America’s Constitutional Courts.” *AJIL Unbound* 111 (2017): 456–60. https://doi.org/10.1017/aju.2017.101.

Jellinek, Georg. *Ein Verfassungsgerichstshof Für Österreich*. Vienna: Alfred Hölder k.k. Hof- und Universitäts-Buchhändler in Wien, 1885.

Jirásek, Jiří. “From Monarchy to the Independent Czechoslovakia.” In *Legal Studies on Central Europe*, edited by Lóránt Csink and László Trócsányi, 57–71. Central European Academic Publishing, 2022. https://doi.org/10.54171/2022.lcslt.ccice_4.

Jorge Prats, Eduardo. *Derecho Constitucional*. 3rd ed. Vol. I. II vols. Santo Domingo: Editora Jusnovum, 2015.

Jorge Prats, Eduardo, Luis Sousa Duvergé, and Roberto Medina Reyes. “Informe Sobre El Anteproyecto de Ley Que Declara la Necesidad de Reforma Constitucional.” Santo Domingo: Jorge Prats- Abogados & Consultores, January 3, 2022.

Kagan, Robert A., and Gregory Elinson. “Constitutional Litigation in the United States.” In *Constitutional Courts in Comparison: The U.S. Supreme Court and the German Federal Constitutional Court*, edited by Ralf Rogowski and Thomas Gawron, 25–61. New York: Berghahn Books, 2016.

Kaiser, Roman. *Das Mehrheitsprinzip in der Judikative*. Tübingen: Mohr Siebeck, 2020. https://doi.org/10.1628/978-3-16-159408-3.

Kapiszewski, Diana, Gordon Silverstein, and Robert A. Kagan, eds. *Consequential Courts: Judicial Roles in Global Perspective*. Comparative Constitutional Law and Policy. Cambridge; New York: Cambridge University Press, 2013.

Katia Miguelina Jiménez. Acento Dominicano, July 7, 2021. https://bit.ly/3JE46LJ.

———. D’Agenda. Television, September 26, 2021. https://bit.ly/3JD41I0.

Kauffman, Adam W. "You Can't Take My Land: Is Thompson v. Heineman, 289 Neb. 798, 857 N.W.2d 731 (2015), Transformative Law or a Political Anomaly." *Nebraska Law Review* 95, no. 2 (2016): 548–73.

Kaufman, Risa, Rebecca Brown, Catalina Martínez Coral, Jihan Jacob, Martin Onyango, and Katrine Thomasen. "Global Impacts of Dobbs v. Jackson Women's Health Organization and Abortion Regression in the United States." *Sexual and Reproductive Health Matters* 30, no. 1 (December 31, 2022): 2135574. https://doi.org/10.1080/26410397.2022.2135574.

Kelsen, Hans. "La Garantie Juridictionnelle de la Constitution." *Revue de Droit Public* 45 (1928): 185–257.

Knoll, Vilém, and Tomáš Pezl. "Continuity and Discontinuity of Czechoslovak Interwar Law. Basic Introduction of the Topic with an Example of Criminal Law." *Krakowskie Studia z Historii Państwa i Prawa* 15, no. 2 (June 30, 2022): 179–201. https://doi.org/10.4467/20844131KS.22.013.15716.

Komárek, Jan. "Czech Constitutional Court Playing with Matches: The Czech Constitutional Court Declares a Judgment of the Court of Justice of the EU *Ultra Vires* ltra Viresitutional Court Playing with Match*Slovak Pensions XVII.*" *European Constitutional Law Review* 8, no. 2 (June 2012): 323–37. https://doi.org/10.1017/S1574019612000193.

Kopeček, Lubomír, and Jan Petrov. "From Parliament to Courtroom: Judicial Review of Legislation as a Political Tool in the Czech Republic." *East European Politics and Societies: And Cultures* 30, no. 1 (February 2016): 120–46. https://doi.org/10.1177/0888325414561784.

Kornhauser, Lewis and Lawrence Sager. "The One and the Many: Adjudication in Collegial Courts." *California Law Review* 81, no. 1 (1993): 1–60.

Kosař, David, and Katarína Šipulová. "Comparative Court-Packing." *International Journal of Constitutional Law* 21, no. 1 (May 30, 2023): 80–126. https://doi.org/10.1093/icon/moad012.

Kosař, David, and Ladislav Vyhnánek. "The Constitutional Court of Czechia." In *The Max Planck Handbooks in European Public Law: Volume III: Constitutional Adjudication: Institutions*, edited by Armin von Bogdandy, Peter M. Huber, and Christoph Grabenwarter, 119–81. Oxford University Press, 2020. https://doi.org/10.1093/oso/9780198726418.001.0001.

———. "The Evolution and Gestalt of the Czech Constitution." In *The Max Planck Handbooks in European Public Law*, edited by Armin von Bogdandy, Peter M. Huber, and Christoph Grabenwarter, 56–108. Oxford University PressOxford, 2023. https://doi.org/10.1093/oso/9780192846693.003.0002.

Kovalčík, Michal. "The Instrumental Abuse of Constitutional Courts: How Populists Can Use Constitutional Courts against the Opposition." *The International Journal of Human Rights* 26, no. 7 (August 9, 2022): 1160–80. https://doi.org/10.1080/13642987.2022.2108017.

Krejčí, Jaroslav. *Delegace zákonodárné moci v moderní demokracii*. Prague: J. Kosátka knihkupectví, 1924.

Krishnamurthi, Guha. "For Judicial Majoritarianism." *University of Pennsylvania Journal of Constitutional Law* 22, no. 5 (2019): 1201–70.

Kuchukhidze, Anna. "Review of Judicial Practice of the Constitutional Court of Georgia in the View of Suspension of Disputed Norm." *Constitutional Law Review*, no. 15 (2021): 98–114.

Kühn, Zdeněk. "The Constitutional Court of the Czech Republic." In *Comparative Constitutional Reasoning*, edited by András Jakab, Arthur Dyevre, and Giulio Itzcovich, 199–236. Cambridge University Press, 2017. https://doi.org/10.1017/9781316084281.008.

———. "The Czech Republic: From a Euro-Friendly Approach of the Constitutional Court to Proclaiming a Court of Justice Judgment Ultra Vires." In *National Constitutions in European and Global Governance: Democracy, Rights, the Rule of Law*, edited by Anneli Albi and Samo Bardutzky, 795–833. The Hague: T.M.C. Asser Press, 2019. https://doi.org/10.1007/978-94-6265-273-6_17.

Kühn, Zdeněk, and Jan Kysela. "Nomination of Constitutional Justices in Post-Communist Countries: Trial, Error, Conflict in the Czech Republic." *European Constitutional Law Review* 2, no. 2 (June 2006): 183–208. https://doi.org/10.1017/S1574019606001830.

Kumm, Mattias. "Constitutional Courts and Legislatures: Institutional Terms of Engagement." *Católica Law Review* I, no. 1 (2017): 55–66.

Kunz, Raffaela. "Judging International Judgments Anew? The Human Rights Courts before Domestic Courts." *European Journal of International Law* 30, no. 4 (December 31, 2019): 1129–63. https://doi.org/10.1093/ejil/chz063.

Kuo, Ming-Suo, and Hui-Wen Chen. "Constitutional Review 3.0 in Taiwan: A Very Short Introduction of Taiwan's New Constitutional Court." *I·CONnect: Blog of the International Journal of Constitutional Law* (blog), July 1, 2022. https://bit.ly/3oxXmmE.

Kustra-Rogatka, Aleksandra. "The Hypocrisy of Authoritarian Populism in Poland: Between the Facade Rhetoric of Political Constitutionalism and the Actual Abuse of Apex Courts." *European Constitutional Law Review* 19, no. 1 (March 2023): 25–58. https://doi.org/10.1017/S1574019622000499.

Kwon, Youngjoon. "Korea: Bridging the Gap between Korean Substance and Western Form." In *Law and Legal Institutions of Asia*, edited by E. Ann Black and Gary F. Bell, 151–84. Cambridge: Cambridge University Press, 2011. https://doi.org/10.1017/CBO9780511921131.006.

Kysela, Jan, and Jakub Stádník. "Kam Ústavní Soud Nechodí (a Nejen o Tom)." *Pravnik*, no. 11 (2021): 899–918.

Lampe, Joanna. "Congressional Control over the Supreme Court." Congressional Research Service, 2023.

Landa, César. "Del Tribunal de Garantías al Tribunal Constitucional: El Caso Peruano." *Pensamiento Constitucional* 2, no. 3 (1995): 73–114.

———. *Derecho Procesal Constitucional.* Lima: Pontificia Universidad Católica del Perú, 2018.

———. "La Jurisdicción Constitucional en el Perú: Parte I." *Revista Do Curso de Direito* IV, no. 7 (2014): 27–61.

———. *Tribunal Constitucional y Estado Democrático.* Lima: Fondo Editorial de la Pontificia Universidad Católica del Perú, 1999.

Landa, Dimitri, and Jeffrey Lax. "Disagreements on Collegial Courts: A Case-Space Approach." *Disagreements on Collegial Courts: A Case-Space Approach* 10, no. 2 (2008): 305–30.

Landfried, Christine, ed. *Judicial Power: How Constitutional Courts Affect Political Transformations.* Cambridge, UK; New York: Cambridge University Press, 2018.

Langášek, Tomáš. *Ústavní Soud Československé Republiky a Jeho Osudy v Letech 1920-1948.* Pilsen: Vydavatelství a nakladatelství Aleš Čeněk, 2011.

Langdale, Larry L. "Constitutional Law the Sterilization of the Mentally Deficient a Reasonable Exercise of the Police Power." *Nebraska Law Review* 47, no. 4 (1968): 784–96.

Langer, Laura. *Judicial Review in State Supreme Courts: A Comparative Study*. SUNY Series in American Constitutionalism. Albany: State University of New York Press, 2002.

Lansing, Michael J. *Insurgent Democracy: The Nonpartisan League in North American Politics*. Chicago and London: The University of Chicago Press, 2015.

Lasser, Mitchel De S.-O.-l'E. *Judicial Deliberations: A Comparative Analysis of Transparency and Legitimacy*. Oxford University Press, 2009. https://doi.org/10.1093/acprof:oso/9780199575169.001.0001.

Leahy, James E. *The North Dakota State Constitution*. The Oxford Commentaries on the State Constitutions of the United States. New York: Oxford University Press, 2011.

Leib, Ethan. "Supermajoritarianism and the American Criminal Jury." *Hastings Constitutional Law Quarterly* 33, no. 2 & 3 (2006): 141–96.

Leiman, Joan. "The Rule of Four." *Columbia Law Review* 5, no. 7 (1957): 975–92.

Levmore, Saul. "Fractured Majorities and Their Reasons." *Penn State Law Review* 127, no. 2 (2023): 331–44.

Lima, Jairo. "Decisão por Supermaioria nas Cortes Constitucionais: o caso das emendas constitucionais inconstitucionais." *Revista Estudos Institucionais* 6, no. 3 (December 30, 2020): 1310–31. https://doi.org/10.21783/rei.v6i3.509.

Lin, Chien-Chih. "Majoritarian Judicial Review: The Case of Taiwan." *National Taiwan University Law Review* 9, no. 1 (2014): 103–59.

———. "The Pros and Cons of Taiwan's Constitutional Court Procedure Act." *USALI Perspectives* 2, no. 17 (2022): 1–4.

Lin, Tzu-Ti, Ming-Sung Kuo, and Hui-Wen Chen. "Seventy Years On: The Taiwan Constitutional Court and Judicial Activism in a Changing Constitutional Landscape." *Hong Kong LJ* 48, no. 3 (2018): 995–1028.

List, Christian. "On the Significance of the Absolute Margin." *The British Journal for the Philosophy of Science* 55, no. 3 (2004): 521–44.

Lockard, Annique M. "Abortion and Birth Control: Constitutional Law: Constitutionality of North Dakota's Legislative Ban on Abortions before Viability." *North Dakota Law Review* 90, no. 1 (2014): 212–26.

López Zamora, Luis. "Constitutional Court of Peru." In *The Max Planck Encyclopedia of Public International Law*, edited by Rüdiger Wolfrum, Frauke Lachenmann, and Ana Harvey, Vol. 11. Oxford University Press, 2021.

Lübbe-Wolff, Gertrude. "Integrating or Polarising? How to Promote Integrative Decision-Making in Constitutional Courts." In *Constitutional Review in the Middle East and North Africa*, edited by Anja Schoeller-Schletter, 189–208. Nomos Verlagsgesellschaft mbH & Co. KG, 2021. https://doi.org/10.5771/9783748912019-189.

———. "Some Institutional Features of the Constitutional Court of Korea in a Comparative Perspective – With a View to the Court's Integrative Function." In *The Constitutional Court of Korea as a Protector of Constitutionalism*, 13–35. Seoul: The Constitutional Court of the Republic of Corea, 2021.

Mączyński, Andrzej and Jan Podkowik. "Art. 190." In *Konstytucja Rzeczypospolitej Polskiej*, edited by Marek Safjan and Leszek Bosek, 2:1125–1316. Warsaw: C.H. Beck, 2016.

Maddox, W. Rolland. "Minority Control of Court Decisions in Ohio." *American Political Science Review* 24, no. 3 (August 1930): 638–48. https://doi.org/10.2307/1946931.

Madgett, Paul W. "The Five-Judge Rule in Nebraska." *Creighton Law Review* 2, no. 2 (1968): 329–53.

Madrazo, Alejandro, and Estefanía Vela. "The Mexican Supreme Court's (Sexual) Revolution." *Texas Law Review* 89, no. 7 (2010): 1863–93.

Magaloni, Ana. "Ocho Votos." *Reforma*, March 26, 2022. https://bit.ly/3lJrhXH.

Malíř, Jan, and Jana Ondřejková. "Law-Making Activity of the Czech Constitutional Court." In *Judicial Law-Making in European Constitutional Courts*, edited by Monika Florczak-Wątor, 111–27. London: Routledge, 2020.

Marsteintredet, Leiv. "Change and Continuity in Dominican Constitutions: The 2010 Reform Compared." In *New Constitutionalism in Latin America*, edited by Almut Schilling-Vacaflor and Detlef Nolte, 223–42. Abingdon: Routledge, 2016. https://doi.org/10.4324/9781315597904.

Marsteintredet, Leiv, Eduardo Jorge Prats, and Emmanuel Cedeño-Brea. "Dominican Republic." In 2019 *Global Review of Constitutional Law*, edited by Richard Albert, David Landau, Pietro Faraguna, and Simon Drugda, 97–101. Boston: I•CONnect and the Clough Center for the Study of Constitutional Democracy at Boston College, 2020.

Mason, Apheus Thomas. "Politics and the Supreme Court: President Roosevelt's Proposal." *University of Pennsylvania Law Review* 85, no. 7 (1937): 659–77.

Matochová, Soňa. "The Role of Constitutional Courts, Particularly of the Constitutional Court of the Czech Republic, While Introducing Human Rights." In *From Eastern Partnership to the Association: A Legal and Political Analysis*, edited by Naděžda Šišková, 206–36. Cambridge Scholars Publishing, 2014.

May, Kenneth O. "A Set of Independent Necessary and Sufficient Conditions for Simple Majority Decision." *Econometrica: Journal of the Econometric Society* 20, no. 4 (1952): 680–84.

McBeath, Jerry. "Democratization and Taiwan's Constitutional Court." *American Journal of Chinese Studies* 11, no. 1 (2004): 51–71.

Meier, Carl L. "Power of the Ohio Supreme Court to Declare Laws Unconstitutional." *U. Cin. L. Rev.* 5, no. 3 (1931): 293–310.

Mejia, Nicia C. "Dominican Apartheid: Inside the Flawed Migration System of the Dominican Republic." *Harv. Latino L. Rev.*, no. 18 (2015): 201–30.

Meschke, Herbert L., and Ted Smith. "The North Dakota Supreme Court: A Century of Advances." *North Dakota Law Review* 76, no. 2 (2000): 217–310.

Messarra, Antoine. "Catching up With the Global and Arab Changes in Constitutional Justice." In *Extension Des Attributions Du Conseil Constitutionnel Au Liban: Actes Du Séminaire Organisé Par Le Conseil Constitutionnel et Fondation Konrad Adenauer*, 32. Beyrouth: Conseil Constitutionnel, 2016.

Miewald, Robert D., and Peter Joseph Longo. *The Nebraska State Constitution*. Oxford: Oxford University Press, 2011.

Miguel Tejada, Adriano, ed. *Discursos del Presidente del Tribunal Constitucional: Milton Ray Guevara*. Santo Domingo Oeste, República Dominicana: Constitutional Court of the Dominican Republic, 2018.

Milligan, William W., and James E. Pohlman. "The 1968 Modern Courts Amendment to the Ohio Constitution." *Ohio St. LJ* 29, no. 4 (1968): 811–48.

Montoya, Víctorhugo, Evelyn Chilo, and Carlos Quispe. *El Proceso de Inconstitucionalidad en la Jurisprudencia (1996-2014)*. Lima: Centro de Estudios Constitucionales, 2015.
Morales Saravia, Francisco. *El Tribunal Constitucional del Perú: Organización y Funcionamiento. Estado de la Cuestión y Propuestas de Mejora*. Lima: Academia de la Magistratura, 2014.
Morlan, Robert L. *Political Prairie Fire: The Nonpartisan League, 1915-1922*. Minneapolis: University of Minnesota Press, 1955.
Moustafa, Tamir. "Law and Courts in Authoritarian Regimes." *Annual Review of Law and Social Science* 10, no. 1 (November 3, 2014): 281–99. https://doi.org/10.1146/annurev-lawsocsci-110413-030532.
Moustafa, Tamir, and Tom Ginsburg. "Introduction: The Functions of Courts in Authoritarian Politics." In *Rule by Law: The Politics of Courts in Authoritarian Regimes*, edited by Tom Ginsburg and Tamir Moustafa, 1–22. Cambridge: Cambridge University Press, 2008. https://doi.org/10.1017/CBO9780511814822.
Nakashidze, Malkhaz. "Georgia." In 2016 *Global Review of Constitutional Law*, edited by Richard Albert, David Landau, Pietro Faraguna, and Simon Drugda, 102–7. Boston: I•CONnect and the Clough Center for the Study of Constitutional Democracy at Boston College, 2018.
Nash, Jonathan. "A Context/Sensitive Voting Protocol Paradigm for Multimember Courts." *Stanford Law Review* 56, no. 1 (2003): 75–160.
———. "The Majority That Wasn't: Stare Decisis, Majority Rule, and the Mischief of Quorum Requirements." *Emory Law Journal* 58, no. 4 (2009): 831–88.
Naugle, Ronald C. *History of Nebraska*. 4th ed. Lincoln and London: University of Nebraska Press, 2014.
Navarro, Enrique. *El Control de Constitucionalidad de Las Leyes En Chile (1811-2011)*. Santiago: Tribunal Constitucional, 2011.
Nebraska Constitutional Revision Commission. "Report of the Nebraska Constitutional Revision Commission: Submitted to the People, the Governor, and the Legislature of the State of Nebraska." Lincoln: Nebraska Constitutional Revision Commission, 1970.
Nebraska Legislature. "Minutes of the Constitutional Revision Committee: Public Hearing on LB 301, 302, 304 and 305." Unpublished, April 2, 1971.
———. "Minutes of the Nebraska Constitutional Revision Commission." Unpublished, 1970.
Niembro Ortega, Roberto. "Seeing the Whole Picture of the Debate in the Mexican Supreme Court: A Response to 'When Judges Threaten Constitutional Governance: Evidence from Mexico.'" *Int'l J. Const. L.* Blog (blog), 2022. http://www.iconnectblog.com/2022/06/seeing-the-whole-picture-of-the-debate-in-the-mexican-supreme-court-a-response-to-when-judges-threaten-constitutional-governance-evidence-from-mexico/.
North Dakota Law Review Associate Editors. "North Dakota Supreme Court Review." *North Dakota Law Review* 88, no. 2 (2012): 516–40.
———. "North Dakota Supreme Court Review." *North Dakota Law Review* 90, no. 3 (2014): 637–94.
O'Connor, Maureen. "The Ohio Modern Courts Amendment: 45 Years of Progress." *Albany Law Review* 76, no. 4 (2012): 1963–76.
Olaiz-González, Jaime. "Mexican Supreme Court at Crossroads: Three Acts of Constitutional Politics." *ICL Journal* 14, no. 4 (February 23, 2021): 447–71. https://doi.org/10.1515/icl-2020-0022.

Orentlicher, David. "Judicial Consensus: Why the Supreme Court Should Decide Its Cases Unanimously." *Connecticut Law Review* 54, no. 2 (2022): 303–44.

Osorio Gonsen, Frida. "Seeking a Balance of Power through a Neutral Third Party Mechanism." *Mexican Studies/Estudios Mexicanos* 33, no. 1 (February 1, 2017): 125–52. https://doi.org/10.1525/mex.2017.33.1.125.

Orzoff, Andrea. *The Battle for the Castle*. Oxford University Press, 2009. https://doi.org/10.1093/acprof:oso/9780195367812.001.0001.

Osterkamp, Jana. *Verfassungsgerichtsbarkeit in der Tschechoslowakei (1920-1939): Verfassungsidee, Demokratieverständnis, Nationalitätenproblem*. Studien zur Europäischen Rechtsgeschichte, Band 243. Frankfurt am Main: V. Klostermann, 2009.

———. "Verfassungshüter ohne politischen Rückhalt. Das tschechoslowakische Verfassungsgericht nach 1920 im Vergleich mit Österreich." *Beiträge zur Rechtsgeschichte Österreichs*, no. 2 (2011): 275–90. https://doi.org/10.1553/BRGOE2011-2s275.

Palazzo, Nausica. "Law-Making Power of the Constitutional Court of Italy." In *Judicial Law-Making in European Constitutional Courts*, edited by Monika Florczak-Wątor, 46–70. London: Routledge, 2020.

Parashu, Dimitrios. "Die Entwicklung Der Verfassungsgerichtsbarkeit in Tschechien Und Der Slowakei." *OER Osteuropa Recht* 57, no. 1 (2011): 47–59.

Parness, Jeffrey A., and Christopher C. Manthey. "Public Process and Ohio Supreme Court Rulemaking." *Cleveland State Law Review* 28, no. 2 (1979): 249–81.

Pedelski, Theodore B. "A Constitution Implements Popular Democracy." In *The Constitutionalism of American States*, edited by George E. Connors, and Cristopher W. Hammons, 549–64. Columbia: University of Missouri Press, 2008.

"Peruvian Senate. 2a Sesión- Martes, 4 de Agosto de 1981." Lima, April 8, 1981.

Ploszka, Adam. "It Never Rains but It Pours. The Polish Constitutional Tribunal Declares the European Convention on Human Rights Unconstitutional." *Hague Journal on the Rule of Law* 15, no. 1 (April 2023): 51–74. https://doi.org/10.1007/s40803-022-00174-w.

Post, David, and Steven C. Salop. "Issues and Outcomes, Guidance, and Indeterminacy: A Reply to Professors John Rogers and Others." *Vanderbilt Law Review* 49, no. 4 (1996): 1069–86.

———. "Rowing Against the Tidewater: A Theory of Voting by Multijudge Panels." *The Georgetown Law Journal* 80, no. 3 (1991): 743–74.

Pou Giménez, Francisca. "Changing the Channel: Broadcasting Deliberations in the Mexican Supreme Court." In *Justices and Journalists*, edited by Richard Davis and David Taras, 209–34. Cambridge: Cambridge University Press, 2017. https://doi.org/10.1017/9781316672228.011.

Pou Giménez, Francisca, and Andrea Pozas-Loyo. "The Paradox of Mexico's Constitutional Hyper-Reformism: Enabling Peaceful Transition While Blocking Democratic Consolidation." In *Constitutional Change and Transformation in Latin America*, edited by Richard Albert, Carlos Bernal, and Juliano Zaiden Benvindo, 221–42. Hart Publishing, 2019. https://doi.org/10.5040/9781509923533.

Pozas-Loyo, Andrea. "Assessing Constitutional Efficacy: Lessons from Mexico's Hegemonic Party Era." In *Morality, Governance, and Social Institutions*, edited by Thomas Christiano, Ingrid Creppell, and Jack Knight, 233–58. Cham: Springer International Publishing, 2018. https://doi.org/10.1007/978-3-319-61070-2_9.

Pozas-Loyo, Andrea, Camilo Saavedra Herrera, and Francisca Pou Giménez. "When More Leads to More: Constitutional Amendments and Interpretation in Mexico 1917-2020." *Law & Social Inquiry*, September 2, 2022, 1–32. https://doi.org/10.1017/lsi.2022.35.

Presidential Commission on the Supreme Court of the United States. "Final Report." Washington, December 2021. https://www.whitehouse.gov/pcscotus/.

Procházková, Andrea. "How to Form the Czech Constitutional Court?" *Verfassungsblog: On Matters Constitutional*, August 31, 2023. https://doi.org/10.17176/20230831-182922-0.

———. "Ústavní Soud ČR Mezi Právem a Politikou." *Právník* 161, no. 11/2022 (2022): 1084–97.

Quiroga, Aníbal. "El Tribunal de Garantías Constitucionales: Ante El Dilema de Ser o No Ser." *Themis: Revista de Derecho*, no. 4 (1986): 40–44.

Qvortrup, Matt, and Leah Trueblood. "The Case for Supermajority Requirements in Referendums." *International Journal of Constitutional Law* 21, no. 1 (May 30, 2023): 187–204. https://doi.org/10.1093/icon/moad013.

Radziewicz, Piotr. "Refusal of the Polish Constitutional Tribunal to Apply the Act Stipulating the Constitutional Review Procedure." *Review of Comparative Law* XXVIII (2017): 27–40.

Rawls, John. *Political Liberalism*. The John Dewey Essays in Philosophy, no. 4. New York: Columbia University Press, 1993.

Redmond, William. "Requirement in State Constitution of More than a Majority of the Supreme Court to Invalidate Legislation." *Nebraska Law Bulletin* 19, no. 1 (1940): 32–50.

Revesz, Richard, and Pamela Karlan. "Nonmajority Rules and the Supreme Court." *University of Pennsylvania Law Review* 136, no. 4 (1988): 1067–1133.

Riley, William Jay. "To Require That a Majority of the Supreme Court Determine the Outcome of Any Case Before It." *Nebraska Law Review* 50, no. 4 (1970): 622–41.

Ríos Figueroa, Julio. "Fragmentation of Power and the Emergence of an Effective Judiciary in Mexico, 1994–2002." *Latin American Politics and Society* 49, no. 1 (2007): 31–57. https://doi.org/10.1111/j.1548-2456.2007.tb00373.x.

Rivera León, Mauro Arturo. "An Introduction to 'Amparo' Theory: A Complex Mexican Constitutional Control Mechanism." *Krytyka Prawa* 12, no. 2 (March 15, 2020): 190–208. https://doi.org/10.7206/kp.2080-1084.389.

———. "Control and Paralysis? A Context-Sensitive Analysis of Objections to Supermajorities in Constitutional Adjudication." *International Journal of Constitutional Law*. (2023): 1–27. https://doi.org/10.1093/icon/moad074.

———. "Judicial Review of Supermajority Rules Governing Courts' Own Decision-Making: A Comparative Analysis." *Global Constitutionalism*, May 9, 2023, 1–25. https://doi.org/10.1017/S2045381723000047.

———. "¿La tumba de Otero? Naturaleza, funcionamiento y problemáticas de la declaratoria general de inconstitucionalidad en México." *Anuario Iberoamericano de Justicia Constitucional* 26, no. 1 (2022): 57–88.

———. *Las Partes en el Juicio de Amparo*. Mexico City: Tirant lo Blanch, 2023.

———. *Las puertas de la Corte: la legitimación en la controversia constitucional y acción de inconstitucionalidad en México*. Biblioteca Porrúa de Derecho Procesal Constitucional 118. Mexico City: Porrúa, 2016.

———. "Los Retos de la Defensa del Federalismo Mexicano Estándares Deferenciales y Asimetrías Procesales En Conflictos Normativos." In *Concurso Nacional de Ensayo Sobre Federalismo*, 18–64. Mexico City: Instituto Belisario Domínguez, 2023.

———. "Understanding Constitutional Amendments in Mexico: Perpetuum Mobile Constitution." *Mexican Law Review* 1, no. 18 (December 14, 2016): 3–27. https://doi.org/10.22201/iij.24485306e.2017.18.10774.

Rogers, John. "Issue Voting by Multimember Appellate Courts: A Response to Some Radical Proposals." *Vanderbilt Law Review* 49, no. 4 (1996): 997–1044.

Romeijn, Jan-Willem, and David Atkinson. "Learning Juror Competence: A Generalized Condorcet Jury Theorem." *Politics, Philosophy & Economics* 10, no. 3 (August 2011): 237–62. https://doi.org/10.1177/1470594X10372317.

Rousseau, Jean-Jacques. *Rousseau: The Social Contract and Other Later Political Writings*. Edited by Victor Gourevitch. 2nd ed. Cambridge University Press, 2018. https://doi.org/10.1017/9781316584606.

Roznai, Yaniv. "Introduction: Constitutional Courts in a 100-Years Perspective and a Proposal for a Hybrid Model of Judicial Review." *ICL Journal* 14, no. 4 (February 23, 2021): 355–77. https://doi.org/10.1515/icl-2020-0039.

———. *Unconstitutional Constitutional Amendments: The Limits of Amendment Powers*. Oxford, U.K: Oxford University Press, 2017.

Russell, Martin. "Georgia's Bumpy Road to Democracy. On Track for a European Future?" European Parliamentary Research Service, 2021.

Sabján, Nikolas. "Critical Legal Perspective on the Recent Czech Transgender Case: (Pl. ÚS 2/20)." *Bratislava Law Review* 6, no. 1 (June 30, 2022): 125–36. https://doi.org/10.46282/blr.2022.6.1.288.

Sadurski, Wojciech. "Judicial Review and Public Reason." In *Comparative Judicial Review*, edited by Erin F. Delaney and Rosalind Dixon. Edward Elgar Publishing, 2018. https://doi.org/10.4337/9781788110600.00026.

———. *Poland's Constitutional Breakdown*. Oxford Comparative Constitutionalism. Oxford: Oxford University Press, 2019.

———. *Rights before Courts: A Study of Constitutional Courts in Postcommunist States of Central and Eastern Europe*. Dordrecht, Netherlands: Springer, 2005.

Sagas, Ernesto, and Ediberto Roman. "Who Belongs: Citizenship and Statelessness in the Dominican Republic." *Geo. JL & Mod. Critical Race Persp.* 9, no. 1 (2017): 35–56.

Sagüés, Néstor Pedro. "Los Poderes Implícitos e Inherentes del Tribunal Constitucional del Perú y El Quórum Para Sus Votaciones." In *La Constitución de 1993. Análisis y Comentarios*, edited by Francisco Fernández, Vol. 3. Lima: Comisión Andina de Juristas/Konrad Adenauer Stiftung, 1996.

———. "Tras Las Huellas de Hans Kelsen. A Cien Años de la Primera Corte Constitucional y Ochenta de la Primera Sala Constitucional." *Parlamento y Constitución. Anuario*, no. 21 (2020): 179–204.

Salazar, Pedro. "Cuatro votos judiciales." *Hechos y Derechos*, no. 67 (February 4, 2022). https://revistas.juridicas.unam.mx/index.php/hechos-y-derechos/article/view/16642/17256.

Santaolalla, Fernando. "El Voto de Calidad del Presidente del Tribunal Constitucional." *Revista Española de Derecho Constitucional*, no. 85 (2009): 201–11.

Schapiro, Robert A. "Contingency and Universalism in State Separation of Powers Discourse." *Roger Williams University Law Review* 4, no. 1 (1998): 79–108.

Schelle, Karel, and Jiří Bílí. *Dějiny Českého Soudnictví*. Prague: Wolters Kluwer, 2018.

Schulte-Bockholt, Alfredo. *Corruption as Power*. Peter Lang CH, 2013. https://doi.org/10.3726/978-3-0351-0496-7.

Schultz Bressman, Lisa. "The Rise and Fall of the Self-Regulatory Court." *Texas Law Review* 101, no. 1 (2022): 1–87.

Schwartz, Edward and Warren Schwartz. "Decisionmaking by Juries under Unanimity and Supermajority Voting Rules." *Georgetown Law Journal* 80, no. 3 (1992): 775–808.

Schwartzberg, Melissa. *Counting the Many: The Origins and Limits of Supermajority Rule*. New York: Cambridge University Press, 2013. https://doi.org/10.1017/CBO9781139013970.

———. "The Arbitrariness of Supermajority Rules." *Social Science Information* 49, no. 1 (March 2010): 61–82. https://doi.org/10.1177/0539018409354474.

Šejvl, Michal. "Fundamental Rights in Czechoslovakia between 1920 and 1938: Their Doctrinal Theorizing and Judicial Application." *Krakowskie Studia z Historii Państwa i Prawa* 15, no. 3 (September 29, 2022): 413–32. https://doi.org/10.4467/20844131KS.22.028.16176.

Selden, Edward. "Judicial Veto and the Ohio Plan." *St. Louis Law Review* 9, no. 1 (1923): 60–66.

Serna, José María. "The Concept of Jurisprudencia in Mexican Law." *Mexican Law Review* I, no. 2 (2009): 131–45.

———. *The Constitution of Mexico: A Contextual Analysis*. Oxford: Hart Publishing, 2013.

Sethi, Amal. "Sub-Constitutionally Repairing the United States Supreme Court." *Common Law World Review* 52, no. 4 (2023): 128-49.

Shelton, Dinah, and Alexandra Huneeus. "In Re Direct Action of Unconstitutionality Initiated Against the Declaration of Acceptance of the Jurisdiction of the Inter-American Court of Human Rights." *American Journal of International Law* 109, no. 4 (October 2015): 866–72. https://doi.org/10.5305/amerjintelaw.109.4.0866.

Shipley, Kristymarie. "Stateless: Dominican-Born Grandchildren of Haitian Undocumented Immigrants in the Dominican Republic." *Transnational Law & Contemporary Problems* 24, no. 2 (2014): 459–87.

Shugerman, Jed Handelsman. "A Six-Three Rule: Reviving Consensus and Deference on the Supreme Court." *Georgia Law Review* 37, no. 3 (2003): 893–1018.

Šimíček, Vojtěch. "Poznámky k Proceduře Rozhodování Pléna Ústavního Soudu." *Časopis pro Právní Vědu a Praxi* 5, no. 3 (1997): 458–63.

Šipulová, Katarína. "The Czech Constitutional Court: Far Away from Political Influence." In *Constitutional Politics and the Judiciary*, edited by Kálmán Pócza, 32–60. London: Routledge, 2018.

Sládeček, Vladimír. "Ještě k Otázce Rozhodování Pléna Ústavního Soudu o Návrhu Na Zrušení Zákona." *Časopis pro Právní Vědu a Praxi* 6, no. 1 (1998): 99–104.

Slocum, Brian. "Rethinking the Canon of Constitutional Avoidance." *University of Pennsylvania Journal of Constitutional Law* 23, no. 3 (2021): 593–660.

Smekal, Hubert, Jaroslav Benák, and Ladislav Vyhnánek. "Through Selective Activism towards Greater Resilience: The Czech Constitutional Court's Interventions into High Politics in the Age of Populism." *The International Journal of Human Rights* 26, no. 7 (August 9, 2022): 1230–51. https://doi.org/10.1080/13642987.2021.2003337.

Spigno, Irene. "'Additive Judgments': A Way to Make the Invisible Content of the Italian Constitution Visible." In *The Invisible Constitution in Comparative Perspective*, edited by Rosalind Dixon and Adrienne Stone, 457–81. Cambridge; New York: Cambridge University Press, 2018. https://doi.org/10.1017/9781108277914.016.

Spigno, Irene, Mauro Arturo Rivera León, and Alfonso Herrera. "Mexico." In 2019 *Global Review of Constitutional Law*, edited by Richard Albert, David Landau, Pietro Faraguna, and Simon Drugda, 192–96. Boston: I•CONnect and the Clough Center for the Study of Constitutional Democracy at Boston College, 2020.

Stahr, Walter. *Salmon P. Chase: Lincoln's Vital Rival.* New York: Simon & Schuster, 2021.

Steinglass, Steven H. "Constitutional Revision: Ohio Style." *Ohio St. LJ* 77, no. 2 (2016): 281–354.

Steinglass, Steven H. and Gino J. Scarselli, *The Ohio State Constitution.* 2nd ed. Oxford University Press, New York, 2022.

Stene, Edwin O. "Is There Minority Control of Court Decisions in Ohio?" *University of Cincinnati Law Review* 9, no. 1 (1935): 23–40.

Stephenson, Scott. "Constitutional Conventions and the Judiciary." *Oxford Journal of Legal Studies* 41, no. 3 (September 25, 2021): 750–75. https://doi.org/10.1093/ojls/gqaa047.

Stokes, Michael L. "Judicial Restraint and the Presumption of Constitutionality." *University of Toledo Law Review* 35, no. 2 (2003): 347–76.

Stopler, Glia. "The Israeli Government's Proposed Judicial Reforms: An Attack on Israeli Democracy." *ConstitutionNet* (blog), February 16, 2023. https://constitutionnet.org/news/israeli-governments-proposed-judicial-reforms-attack-israeli-democracy.

Suk, Julie C. "A World Without Roe: The Constitutional Future of Unwanted Pregnancy." *William and Mary Law Review* 64, no. 2 (2022): 43–524. https://doi.org/10.2139/ssrn.4088869.

Suteu, Silvia. *Eternity Clauses in Democratic Constitutionalism.* Oxford University Press, 2021. https://doi.org/10.1093/oso/9780198858867.001.0001.

Sweet, Alec Stone. "Constitutional Courts." In *The Oxford Handbook of Comparative Constitutional Law*, edited by Michel Rosenfeld and András Sajó, 817–29. Oxford: Oxford University Press, 2012.

Talcott, Stanley M. "Amending the Nebraska Constitution in the 1971 Legislature." *Nebraska Law Review* 50, no. 4 (1971): 676–91.

Tarr, Alan G. and Mary Cornelia Porter. *State Supreme Courts in State and Nation.* New Haven and London: Yale University Press, 1988.

Tauchen, Jaromír. "Ermächtigungsgesetzgebung in der Tschechoslowakei." *Beiträge zur Rechtsgeschichte Österreichs* 1 (2018): 428–40. https://doi.org/10.1553/BRGOE2018-2s428.

———. "The Supreme Courts in the Protectorate of Bohemia and Moravia." In *Supreme Courts Under Nazi Occupation*, edited by Venema, Derk, 227–50. Amsterdam: Amsterdam University Press, 2022.

———. "Tschechoslowakei/Tschechien." In *Konfliktlösung im 19. und 20. Jahrhundert*, edited by Peter Collin, 4:417–34. Handbuch zur Geschichte der Konfliktlösung in Europa. Berlin, Heidelberg: Springer, 2021. https://doi.org/10.1007/978-3-662-56076-1_31.

Terzian, Barbara A. "Ohio's Constitutions: An Historical Perspective." *Cleveland State Law Review* 51, no. 3 & 4 (2004): 357–94.

Thayer, James B. "The Origin and Scope of the American Doctrine of Constitutional Law." *Harvard Law Review* 7, no. 3 (October 25, 1893): 129. https://doi.org/10.2307/1322284.

The Constitutional Court of the Republic of Korea. *Decisions of the Korean Constitutional Court (2010)*. Seoul: The Constitutional Court of the Republic of Korea, 2011.

The Straits Times. "Emptying South Korea Court Offers Park Geun Hye a Lifeline." September 2, 2017, sec. Asia. https://www.straitstimes.com/asia/east-asia/emptying-south-korea-court-offers-park-geun-hye-a-lifeline.

Tiede, Lydia Brashear. *Judicial Vetoes: Decision-Making on Mixed Selection Constitutional Courts*. Cambridge University Press, 2022. https://doi.org/10.1017/9781009058254.

Tiede, Lydia Brashear, and Aldo Fernando Ponce. "Evaluating Theories of Decision-Making on the Peruvian Constitutional Tribunal." *Journal of Politics in Latin America* 6, no. 2 (2014): 139–64.

Tocqueville, Alexis de. *Democracy in America: Translated, Edited, and with an Introduction by Harvey C. Mansfield and Delba Winthrop*. Chicago: University of Chicago Press, 2000.

Tornero, Yuri. "Estudio Liminar." In *Jurisprudencia Relevante del Tribunal de Garantías Constitucionales. Procesos de Inconstitucionalidad*, edited by Constitutional Court of Peru, 13–49. Lima: Tribunal Constitucional del Perú, 2018.

Transparency International: Georgia. "The State of the Judicial System 2016-2020," October 10, 2020.

Tsereteli, Nino. "Backsliding into Judicial Oligarchy? The Cautionary Tale of Georgia's Failed Judicial Reforms, Informal Judicial Networks and Limited Access to Leadership Positions." *Review of Central and East European Law* 47, no. 2 (June 28, 2022): 167–201. https://doi.org/10.1163/15730352-bja10067.

Tuleja, Piotr. "The Polish Constitutional Tribunal." In *The Max Planck Handbooks in European Public Law*, edited by Armin von Bogdandy, Peter M. Huber, and Christoph Grabenwarter, 619–72. Oxford University Press, 2020. https://doi.org/10.1093/oso/9780198726418.003.0012.

Tuttle, R.M. (Official Stenographer). *Official Report of the Proceedings and Debates of the First Constitutional Convention of North Dakota (July 4th to August 17th, 1889)*. Bismarck: Tribune, State Printers and Binders, 1889.

Tuzet, Giovanni. "More Votes, More Irrationality." *The American Journal of Jurisprudence* 64, no. 1 (June 1, 2019): 61–78. https://doi.org/10.1093/ajj/auz005.

Utter, William T. "Judicial Review in Early Ohio." *The Mississippi Valley Historical Review* 14, no. 1 (June 1927): 3. https://doi.org/10.2307/1892041.

VandeWalle, Gerald W. "North Dakota Distinctives." *Albany Law Review* 76, no. 4 (2013 2012): 2019–26.

Velasco-Rivera, Mariana. "Constitutional Rigidity: The Mexican Experiment." *International Journal of Constitutional Law* 19, no. 3 (2021): 1043–61. https://doi.org/10.1093/icon/moab087.

———. "When Judges Threaten Constitutional Governance: Evidence from Mexico." *Int'l J. Const. L.* Blog (blog), 2022. http://www.iconnectblog.com/2022/06/when-judges-threaten-constitutional-governance-evidence-from-mexico/.

Venice Commission. "Opinion No. 833/2015 On Amendments to the Act of 25 June 2015 on the Constitutional Tribunal (CDL-AD(2016)001." Venice: Venice Commission, November 3, 2016.

———. "Opinion No. 932/2018 On Separate Opinions on Constitutional Courts." Venice: Venice Commission, November 3, 2016.

———. "Preliminary Opinion 849/2016 on the Amendments to the Organic Law on the Constitutional Court and to the Law on Constitutional Legal Proceedings." Strasbourg: Venice Commission, May 27, 2016.

Vermeule, Adrian. "Absolute Majority Rules." *British Journal of Political Science* 37, no. 4 (October 2007): 643–58. https://doi.org/10.1017/S000712340700035X.

———. *Mechanisms of Democracy: Institutional Design Writ Small.* Oxford-New York: Oxford University Press, 2007.

———. "The Force of Majority Rule." In *Majority Decisions*, edited by Stéphanie Novak and Jon Elster, 132–58. Cambridge University Press, 2014. https://doi.org /10.1017/CBO9781107286160.007.

Vikarská, Zuzana. "Evasive, Insensitive, Ignorant, and Political." *Verfassungsblog: On Matters Constitutional* (blog). Fachinformationsdienst für internationale und interdisziplinäre Rechtsforschung, April 6, 2022. https://intr2dok.vifa-recht.de/ receive/mir_mods_00012411.

Villanueva Ulfgard, Rebecka. "López Obrador's Hyper-Presidentialism: Populism and Autocratic Legalism Defying the Supreme Court and the National Electoral Institute." *The International Journal of Human Rights*, May 2, 2023, 1–25. https://doi.org/10.1080/13642987.2023.2207464.

———. "Separation of Powers in Distress: AMLO's Charismatic Populism and Mexico's Return to Hyper-Presidentialism." *Populism* 6, no. 1 (February 6, 2023): 55–79. https://doi.org/10.1163/25888072-bja10043.

Villanueva Ulfgard, Rebecka, and César Villanueva. "The Power to Transform? Mexico's 'Fourth Transformation' under President Andrés Manuel López Obrador." *Globalizations* 17, no. 6 (August 17, 2020): 1027–42. https://doi.org /10.1080/14747731.2020.1718846.

Vogel, Robert. "Justice Robinson and the Supreme Court of North Dakota." *North Dakota Law Review* 58, no. 1 (1982): 83–96.

von Danwitz, Thomas. "Qualifizierte Mehrheiten Für Normverwerfende Entscheidungen Des BVerfG? Thesen Zur Gewährleistung Des Judicial Self-Restraint." *JuristenZeitung* 51, no. 10 (1996): 481–89.

von Hirsch, Andrew. "Proportionality in the Philosophy of Punishment." *Crime and Justice* 16 (January 1992): 55–98. https://doi.org/10.1086/449204.

Wagnerová, Eliška. "§ 13." In *Zákon o Ústavním Soudu s Komentářem*, edited by Wagnerová, Eliška, et al., 56–65. Prague: Wolter Kluwers, 2007.

Waldron, Jeremy. "Five to Four: Why Do Bare Majorities Rule on Courts." *The Yale Law Journal* 123, no. 6 (2014): 1692–1730. https://dx.doi.org/10.2139/ssrn .2195768.

———. *Law and Disagreement.* Oxford: New York: Clarendon Press laOxford University Press, 1999.

———. "The Core of the Case against Judicial Review." *The Yale Law Journal* 115, no. 6 (2006): 1346–1407.

Walinski, Richard S., and Mark D. Jr. Wagoner. "Ohio's Modern Courts Amendment Must Be Amended: Why and How." *Clev. St. L. Rev.* 66, no. 1 (2017): 69–122.

Walker, James L. "The Ohio Constitution: Normatively and Empirically Distinctive." In *The Constitutionalism of American States*, edited by George E. Connors, and Christopher Hammons, 447–59. Missouri: University of Missouri Press, 2008.

Warner, Hoyt Landon. *Progressivism in Ohio* 1897-1917. 1964: Ohio State University Press, 1964.

———. "Ohio's Constitutional Convention of 1912." *Ohio State Archaeological and Historical Quarterly* 61, no. 1 (1952): 11–31.

Watkins, Albert. *Illustrated History of Nebraska: A History of Nebraska*. Edited by Morton, Julius Sterlin, Watkins, Albert, and Miller, George. Vol. 3. 3 vols. Lincoln: Western Pub. and Engraving Co, 2005.

Way, Lucan Ahmad. "Georgia, Moldova, and Ukraine: Democratic Moments in the Former Soviet Union." In *Democracy in Hard Places*, edited by Scott Mainwaring and Tarek Masoud, 1st ed., 128–59. New York: Oxford University Press, 2022. https://doi.org/10.1093/oso/9780197598757.003.0005.

Webb Williams, Nora, and Margaret Hanson. "Captured Courts and Legitimized Autocrats: Transforming Kazakhstan's Constitutional Court." *Law & Social Inquiry* 47, no. 4 (November 2022): 1201–33. https://doi.org/10.1017/lsi.2021.85.

Weiler, Joseph. "Israel: Cry, the Beloved Country." *Int'l J. Const. L.* Blog (blog), December 28, 2022. http://www.iconnectblog.com/2023/01/red-lines-for-israels-constitutional-reforms/.

Weinrib, Laura M. "From Left to Rights: Civil Liberties Lawyering Between the World Wars." *Law, Culture and the Humanities* 15, no. 3 (October 2019): 622–55. https://doi.org/10.1177/1743872116641871.

Weyr, František. *Das Verfassungsrecht Der Tschechoislowakischen Republik*. Wien: Franz Deuticke, 1920.

Wheeler, Everett P. "The New Constitution of Ohio- Power of Courts to Review Acts of the Legislatures." *Central Law Journal* 75 (1912): 437–42.

Wiącek, Marcin. "Constitutional Crisis in Poland 2015–2016 in the Light of the Rule of Law Principle." In *Defending Checks and Balances in EU Member States*, edited by Armin von Bogdandy, et al., 298:15–33. Beiträge Zum Ausländischen Öffentlichen Recht Und Völkerrecht. Berlin; Heidelberg: Springer, 2021. https://doi.org/10.1007/978-3-662-62317-6_2.

Wieser, Bernd. "Prag Und Wien." *Austrian Law Journal*, no. 3 (2022): 39–45. https://doi.org/10.25364/01.9:2022.3.5.

Winter, A.B. "Constitutional Revision in Nebraska: A Brief History and Commentary." *Nebraska Law Review* 40, no. 4 (1961): 580–95.

Wishnatsky, Martin. "Taming the Supreme Court." *Liberty University Law Review* 6, no. 3 (2012): 597–674.

W.L.O. "Constitutional Amendments, Self-Executing and Otherwise, Providing for the Initiative and Referendum." *Michigan Law Review* 15, no. 4 (1917): 334–38.

Wunder, John R., and Mark R. Scherer. *Echo of Its Time*: The History of the Federal District Court of Nebraska, *1867-1933*. Lincoln: University Press of Nebraska, 2019. https://doi.org/10.2307/j.ctvbtzmhp.

Yingling, Patrick. "Judicial Conventions: An Examination of the US Supreme Court's Rule of Four." *Dublin University Law Journal* 38, no. 2 (2015): 477–88.

Yoon, Dae-Kyu. "Judicial Review in the Korean Political Context." *Korean Journal of Comparative Law* 17 (1989): 133–78.

———. *Law and Political Authority in South Korea*. Seul: Westview Press and Kyungnam University Press, 1991.

Zamora, Stephen, and José Ramón Cossío. "Mexican Constitutionalism after Presidencialismo." *International Journal of Constitutional Law* 4, no. 2 (April 1, 2006): 411–37. https://doi.org/10.1093/icon/mol011.

Zdobinský, Stanislav. *Československá Ústava: Komentář*. Prague: Panorama, 1988.

Zedelashvili, David. "2017 Constitutional Reform in Georgia: Another Misguided Quest or Genuine Opportunity?" *ConstitutionNet* (blog), January 31, 2017. https://constitutionnet.org/news/2017-constitutional-reform-georgia-another-misguided-quest-or-genuine-opportunity.

Zellmer, Sandra, and Kathleen Miller. "The Fallacy of Judicial Supermajority Clauses in State Constitutions." *University of Toledo Law Review* 47, no. 1 (2015): 73–88.

Index

References to tables are in **bold**.

Kolibri 360 GmbH
Ferdinand-Jühlke-Straße 7
99095 Erfurt, Deutschland
produktsicherheit@kolibri360.de